THE CATHOLIC LAITY IN ELIZABETHAN ENGLAND
1558–1603

THE CATHOLIC LAITY IN ELIZABETHAN ENGLAND
1558–1603

WILLIAM RALEIGH TRIMBLE

THE BELKNAP PRESS OF
HARVARD UNIVERSITY PRESS
Cambridge, Massachusetts
1964

282.42
T735c

COPYRIGHT © 1964 BY THE PRESIDENT AND FELLOWS OF HARVARD COLLEGE
ALL RIGHTS RESERVED

PUBLISHED IN GREAT BRITAIN BY OXFORD UNIVERSITY PRESS, LONDON

LIBRARY OF CONGRESS CATALOG CARD NUMBER 63–20773

PRINTED IN THE UNITED STATES OF AMERICA

To my father, William
To my mother, Catherine
To my sister, Carolyn

PREFACE

This study was begun some years ago as a doctoral dissertation at Harvard University with a different emphasis and structure. Further research during the intervening years has caused me to alter it substantially, limiting my subject principally to the Elizabethan Catholic laity.

In completing this work I owe to many a debt of gratitude: to Professor W. K. Jordan of Harvard University for his kindly interest in my work from its inception as a dissertation under his direction to its final completion in its present form; to the American Philosophical Society for a generous grant which permitted a year's research in English archives; to the libraries of Harvard University, and of Loyola University of Chicago, the Newberry Library of Chicago, and the Public Library of Portland, Oregon; and to Paul S. Lietz, chairman of the Department of History, Loyola University, Chicago, and to the authorities of that institution for concessions in order to prepare this study for publication.

My debt of obligation to persons and institutions in England is very great: to the Marquess of Salisbury for permission to use the archives at Hatfield House, Herts., and to Miss Clare Talbot, the librarian, for her helpfulness; to the British Museum, London, the Institute for Historical Research at the University of London, and the Bodleian Library, Oxford; to the Historical Manuscripts Commission for permission to quote from the third volume of the *Report on Manuscripts in Various Collections;* to the Stationery Office for permission to quote from the *Acts of the Privy Council of England;* and to the Public Record Office, London, for the use of the State Papers of Elizabeth I and James I. Unpublished Crown-copyright material in the Public Record Office, London, has been reproduced by permission of the Controller of H. M. Stationery Office.

I wish also to express my appreciation both for help and hospitality to Monsignor Philip Hughes (now of the University of Notre Dame) and to the Jesuit Fathers of Farm Street, London. Certain members of my family have been of very great assistance, especially my aunt, Annie C.

PREFACE

Rogers of Oakland, California, and my brother-in-law and sister, Howard Van Nice and Carolyn Trimble Van Nice, of Portland, Oregon. Without the unsparing assistance of my sister this book could not have been finished.

W. R. T.

Portland, Oregon
Chicago, Illinois
May 1963

CONTENTS

	INTRODUCTION	1
I	THE DORMANT YEARS OF CATHOLICISM, 1559–1573	9
	1. CHAOS OF DISESTABLISHMENT, 1559–1563	9
	2. YEARS OF INERTNESS, 1564–1568	24
	3. THE FUTILITY OF ACTION, 1569–1573	49
II	THE ATTEMPTED REVIVIFICATION OF CATHOLICISM, 1574–1583	68
	1. INITIAL OFFICIAL REACTION, 1574–1577	68
	2. THE PROCEDURES OF OFFICIAL POLICY, 1577–1580	88
	3. CATHOLICISM CONTAINED, 1581–1583	107
III	THE DECLINE OF CATHOLICISM, 1584–1603	122
	1. MOUNTING TENSIONS, 1584–1587	122
	2. THE CRISIS, 1588	134
	3. THE REACTION AFTER THE ARMADA, 1589–1594	139
	4. THE ELIZABETHAN CATHOLIC POLICY UNCHANGED, 1595–1599	155
	5. THE ULTIMATE MEASURE OF DISESTABLISHMENT, 1600–1603	164
IV	THE SOCIAL AND ECONOMIC STATUS OF THE ELIZABETHAN CATHOLICS	177
	1. THE ASSESSMENT OF CATHOLIC WEALTH IN THE 1580'S	178
	2. THE ADMINISTRATION OF DISTRAINT OF PROPERTY	242
	3. THE LEVY OF HORSES OF 1598	248
V	THE END OF THE REIGN	253
	CONCLUSION	264
	APPENDICES:	
	A. SUMMARY OF THE MASTER SHEET OF THE OFFERS OF COMPOSITION, 1586–1587: S.P.12/189/54, 55 (May 1586)	269
	B. A LIST OF 128 RECUSANTS IN 22 COUNTIES (studied in Chapter IV)	271
	BIBLIOGRAPHY	275
	INDEX	283

THE CATHOLIC LAITY IN ELIZABETHAN ENGLAND
1558–1603

ABBREVIATIONS

A.P.C.	*Acts of the Privy Council*
B.M.	British Museum
Cal. S.P. Dom.	*Calendar of State Papers, Domestic*
Cal. S.P. Span.	*Calendar of Letters and State Papers, Relating to English Affairs . . . Simancas*
C.P.	Cecil Papers, Hatfield House
C.R.S., *Misc.*	Catholic Record Society, *Miscellanea*
H.M.C., *Var. Coll.*	Historical Manuscripts Commission, *Report on Manuscripts in Various Collections,* vol. III: *The Papers of Sir Thomas Tresham*
S.P.12	State Papers, Domestic, Elizabeth
S.P.14	State Papers, Domestic, James I
S.P.15	State Papers, Domestic, Additional, Elizabeth and James I

In citations from the Cecil Papers the order is:
  (1) the volume; (2) the folio page.
In citations from the State Papers Domestic the order is:
  (1) the reign; (2) the volume; (3) the folio page. In a footnote where there are numerous citations from these papers, the reign and volume are given only once.

INTRODUCTION

THE Protestant Reformation introduced into Europe a new problem with which it was not prepared to deal — the existence of a plurality of religious creeds within the framework of existing society.[1] During the Middle Ages dissent from Catholicism usually had concerned only individuals or small groups; rarely, except in the case of the thirteenth-century Albigensians in southern France and of the fifteenth-century Hussites in Bohemia, had a large population within a defined area embraced some other belief than the traditional papal church. By long acceptance the norm of law, both canon and civil, sanctioned only intolerance of the heretic, and the main currents of philosophic thought supported this viewpoint. During the sixteenth century, however, the formulation of new creeds had been too rapid and too extensive for the civil arm, whether Catholic or Protestant, to stamp them out successfully; and it became necessary to think out afresh the attitude of government toward dissidence and toward the dissenters.

The final decision whether the old religion was to be retained or rejected lay with the civil authorities: this was as true of France, Spain, the Italian states, the Spanish Netherlands, and the parts of Germany and Switzerland, which remained Catholic, as of the other parts of Germany and Switzerland, the United Provinces, Scandinavia, England and Scotland, which became Protestant. Only when a dissenting religion had effective political and military leadership, as in the case of the Huguenots in France, the Calvinists in the Low Countries, and the German Lutherans before the Peace of Augsburg of 1555, was a new church able suc-

[1] The principal studies of the development of religious toleration up to and through the age of Elizabeth I, are W. K. Jordan, *The Development of Religious Toleration in England,* vol. I (London, 1932), and Joseph Lecler, *Histoire de la tolérance au siècle de la réforme,* 2 vols. (Paris, 1955).

cessfully to defy the decision of the legal authority and maintain its existence intact. To what extent, then, did the dissenters cling to their conscientious beliefs in opposition to the state? How did the state treat this opposition?

These two questions contain the basic legal and sociological problems facing sixteenth-century governments. In the various German principalities after the Peace of Augsburg, those refusing conformity to the religion prescribed by the prince, whether Catholic or Lutheran, were to emigrate from their residence to a principality accepting their beliefs. In France the various proposals of Catherine de' Medici made during the religious wars and the later Edict of Nantes recognized the Huguenots as a separate legal entity, with certain rights as such; this was also the basis of the legal toleration which prevailed in Poland during the second half of the sixteenth century. In Austria the Lutheran nobles as a class, with their dependents, received a degree of toleration under the Emperor Maximilian II, which was restricted, but not abolished, under his successor, Rudolph II. The idea, however, of integrating religious dissenters into the framework of society on a footing of civil and religious equality with the dominant church, so that creed became a matter of private conscience, was not yet recognized; the medieval theory of "one faith, one law, one king" prevailed, and dissent was tolerated for expedient reasons, not as a matter of right. Increasingly during the latter half of the sixteenth century the opinion prevailed that freedom of conscience (since the exercise of conscience was an interior act) belonged of right to a man and was beyond the jurisdiction of the state; but liberty of cult — the right to worship according to a certain ritual publicly or privately — remained within the bounds of state control, since it concerned external acts and affected both civil obedience and the recognized prerogative of the civil government to prescribe public worship.

The quandary facing sixteenth-century statesmen came from the pressures exerted by the dominant religious group, clergy and laity, on the one side, demanding suppression of dissent and preservation of the legally established church, and on the other side, the possibility of civil disturbances if wide-scale suppression of nonconformity were undertaken. The added danger existed of interference from the outside on the part of states sympathetic to the religious group suffering repression. And a humanitarian dislike of forcing suffering upon human beings for reasons of conscience inclined some sixteenth-century statesmen to rethink the whole question of the presence of a plurality of religions within society.

The answer was long in coming, but by the time Elizabeth I ascended the throne of England in 1558 Protestantism was well into its second generation of existence, Catholicism was in the first dynamic stages of the Counter Reformation, and the rulers of Europe were becoming increasingly aware that it was next to impossible to wipe out of existence a whole sect, even if quite small. Therefore, a legalized or at least a tacit acceptance of the extralegal sects had to be incorporated into the over-all state policy governing spiritual and civil relations, even though that policy did not completely discard the use of inducements or pressures to dispose the dissenters toward conformity.

The English government had to face this problem a number of times during the forty-four years of Queen Elizabeth's reign. On the one side the traditional Catholic faith still existed; on the other side, various Protestant groups were developing, which differed in their thinking from the Established Church. The purpose of this study is to inquire how the Elizabethan Catholics, holding to that church which long had been the sole recognized religious belief in England, adjusted themselves to a regime which prescribed a different church and used certain types of pressures to incline them toward conformity. This causes a number of questions. Where did the traditional church retain membership within England? How strong among the laity who adhered did belief in the Catholic creed seem to be? To what extent did this group retain its integrity or tend to dissolve?

We do not at present know, and very possibly historians will never be able precisely to determine, how many of Elizabeth I's subjects were Catholic or Protestant when the religious change was inaugurated in 1559.[2] In some sections of the realm there is little or no evidence that the Roman Church in the early 1560's or later possessed a hold over any considerable number of the people; in other sections the evidence is abundant that a strong body of Catholics continued to make valiant efforts for many years to maintain their faith.

[2] Both the general population figure of England under Elizabeth I and the number of adherents of the various religious groupings can only be known by approximation. In regard to the latter there are so many variable factors and unknown quantities, such as exterior conformity and confusion of thought, that an absolute answer is impossible. Even a better approximate answer must depend upon more intensive research into the history of the various counties.

Why, after nearly a thousand years of existence in England, Catholicism apparently died out so quickly in some areas and not in others is beyond the scope of this study to investigate; but the evidence that will be developed in the various chapters shows that geographical location, the outlook of influential families, the attitude of the local authorities, the degree of supervision from London, the presence or absence of priests, Marian or Continental-trained,[3] within a county, the reading of apologetic, theological, and devotional books, and very probably in some sections something of a Catholic renaissance under Mary Tudor (which some evidence tends to indicate), explain much.

Certain commonplaces of the Reformation throw considerable light upon the ease with which England and parts of Continental Europe turned from Catholicism to Protestantism. The moribund condition of Catholicism in so many areas, evident in the poor quality of clergy and weakly instructed laity and the lagging condition of Catholic theological thought, provided the Reformers with an arsenal of ammunition. They pointed to existing abuses and preached constantly and widely that they intended to bring Christianity back to the more simplified structure and the more fluid beliefs of the early Fathers. The dynamism of this approach convinced many throughout Europe, and it was not countered by an equal dynamism on the part of the Catholics until the Counter Reformation got into full swing in the second half of the sixteenth century.

A very decisive factor, also, was the influence of the upper classes in a hierarchically organized society. The ingrained habits of obedience and respect of the lower classes for those above them, although occasionally and sometimes violently thrown off in the era of the Reformation, in many areas of Europe — and it was certainly true in parts of England — inclined acceptance of the decision of creed determined by the powerful, the wealthy, and the educated. The ease with which both clergy and laity in sixteenth-century England accommodated themselves to a series of religious changes indicates a lack of sound religious conviction and training and makes manifest the compelling force, on both the psychological and the legal plane, of obedience to the Crown. Certainly, the whole pattern of England's religious history from 1534 to 1559 tended

---

[3] It is difficult to arrive at even an approximate number of either the Marian or the later Continental-trained priests who performed sacerdotal functions during Elizabeth's reign.

to induce the upper classes, and through them the lower classes, to accept governmental decrees concerning religion. The fact that only a vocal minority opposed these under the last four Tudor monarchs bears this out.

After 1559 the English Catholics lacked guidance. Their spiritual leaders, the bishops, were in prison or under surveillance. The English nobility was few in numbers; only a few peers were openly declared Catholics; none had national stature or the ability to unite and direct his coreligionists in a party. And there was no member of the ruling dynasty able to protect them or to watch out for their interests. A royal family, in fact, was nonexistent. Elizabeth was the last of the Tudors; there were no princes of the blood; a few English noble families had, at the most, only distant claims to the throne; and the very problem of succession was confused and unsettled.

A comparison with contemporary France is relevant. The ruling dynasty, the Valois, was Catholic, but threatened with extinction. The chief princes of the blood, the Bourbons and the Condés, were Huguenots, actively leading and protecting their fellow Protestants, with the help of a strong and influential minority of the nobility converted to Calvinism. Such highly placed leadership was able to negotiate successfully for foreign aid against Catholic repression; and by marshaling the Protestant forces into a cohesive group, the chiefs of the Huguenots waged a civil war for over thirty years, and in the end effected a peace by compromise. On the contrary, in England the protection of Catholicism, due to lack of national leadership, became a local problem depending upon the attitude of the squires, the magistrates, and the gentry families. Their conformity inevitably reduced Catholicism to a condition of secrecy and of eventual near-extinction within a locality.

The most basic question facing the English Catholics was the degree of obedience that they could render to Elizabeth I. Their dilemma stemmed from the Acts of Supremacy and Uniformity enacted in 1559,[4] during the first year of the Queen's reign. The first of these, the Act of Supremacy, declared spiritual jurisdiction to be the prerogative solely of the Crown and forbade adherence to foreign ecclesiastical authority. An oath attesting this was prescribed for ecclesiastics and certain classes of laymen under penalty. The second, the Act of Uniformity, substituted a liturgy of Protestant orientation for the Catholic liturgy; and this, too,

[4] 1 Eliz. c. 1 and c. 2. These laws came into effect on June 24, 1559.

was to be enforced under penalty. In the eyes of the Elizabethan Catholic the Act of Supremacy forbade acceptance of papal primacy, a point of doctrine, and the Act of Uniformity required a form of worship differing from what he believed. Since few were required to swear to the Queen's spiritual supremacy, but all were obliged to worship in their parish churches according to the Book of Common Prayer, it was the second, not the first, of these laws, which caused the crisis of conscience for the remaining adherents of Rome. A committee of the Council of Trent, acting on a petition transmitted through the Portuguese ambassador at London at the request of some English Catholic laymen, condemned any degree of conformity. A committee of the Inquisition, presided over by Cardinal Ghislieri (the future Pope Pius V), gave the same ruling in answer to a petition sent by the Spanish ambassador to England also at the request of some Catholics within the realm. In subsequent years the enforcement of the Elizabethan religious laws was countered by repetitions of these prohibitory decrees by the Catholic authorities. In turn these conflicting pressures created problems for the English Catholics which at the immediate moment seemed beyond solution.[5]

The history of the Elizabethan Catholic laity contains little that is startling or dramatic. Within the realm there were a few colorful figures but no outstanding leader or writer or thinker. The Catholic gentry, the only sizable group of that religious belief possessing affluence, was a stable, property-owning unit, little desirous of changing its ways, anxious for a quiet life and peace of conscience, and important only on the local level. These Catholics, it must be remembered, were almost a generation removed from the complex religious life of pre-Reformation England, with its monasteries and convents, its shrines, pilgrimages, and, further back in the fourteenth century, its efflorescence of mysticism. Present conditions rendered impossible any of the magnificent spiritual life now flourishing in southern Europe and due eventually to move northward, with its mystics, its intense spiritual devotions, its schools and active, well-run religious orders. Instead, the Elizabethan Catholics experienced for the most part the more militant aspects of the Counter Reformation, which created so many vicissitudes for them.

---

[5] See Philip Hughes, *The Reformation in England,* III (London, 1954), 247–252, for a short but full treatment of the problem of Catholic attendance at the services of the Establishment.

INTRODUCTION

The English government, with all the strength and prestige of the civil state, had little difficulty in controlling the Catholics. It could apply pressures to induce conformity. The creed and ritual of the Establishment offered a positive substitute for those Catholics whose faith in time became attenuated. And the fervent nationalism of the Elizabethans, evidenced in the 1580's and 1590's, provided a strong motivation to all to follow the Queen's lead in religion. All through the forty-four years of Elizabeth's reign the steady progress of conformity will be noticeable; obviously, only the most convinced adherents of the ancient faith and those who, for some reason, remained unaffected by these last-mentioned inducements, formed that group termed "the recusants."

In the larger picture of the sixteenth century the acuteness of the dilemma of the English Catholics becomes clearer. They were caught in the conflict of two allegiances and of two sovereignties.

The medieval church, exercising ecclesiastical jurisdiction over western and central Europe and holding itself to be the guardian and preserver of Christian orthodoxy, considered dissent to spring from bad faith. For this reason, in the age of the Reformation and probably up to the end of the Thirty Years War, the Catholic authorities thought that Protestantism was only temporary and that the fractured unity of Christianity would at length be restored. To accomplish this, persuasion and even resort to civil force — following out the long-standing cooperation between the spiritual and the civil realms — was contemplated, a notable example being the Armada of 1588. An essential element of this policy was that the restoration of the Roman Church and therefore of traditional orthodoxy would be effected in areas where it had been disestablished if rulers or influential classes responsible for the alteration in religion were put down from power. Especially after the Council of Trent the success of the Counter Reformation in reclaiming individuals and in converting some defected areas was too great for the Catholic leaders to realize how deeply Protestantism had become impregnated in various other parts of Europe.

Opposing Catholicism were certain unitary states, products of the new state system, which had embraced one or another of the Protestant movements, thereafter refusing legal toleration to the older church within their borders. This decision was considered to be a valid exercise of sovereignty; it was so recognized in the changes of religion in England under

Henry VIII, Edward VI, Mary I, and Elizabeth I, and in Germany it became a fundamental law at Augsburg in 1555. The strong nationalism everywhere infusing sixteenth-century states strengthened this act of sovereignty, because it comprehended the official religion as an essential element bound up with loyalty to the ruler. Externally, some of these Protestant realms pursued a policy of foreign alliances, aimed at limiting Catholicism as a potential enemy or even at destroying it; as a positive end some of them actively promoted their creeds outside their borders as a counter orthodoxy to the older church.

Certain factors, however, hindered both Catholics and Protestants from following out their aims completely. The recurring pressures of internal problems, shifting foreign alliances (whenever state needs rendered this desirable), and defeats in war accounted considerably for the lessening of aggressiveness. And of equal weight was the waning interest of princes and of laymen, who hesitated to hazard public or individual welfare for religious reasons, which seemed only vaguely valuable to the state or possibly wasteful of its resources.

It was within this very complex pattern that the English Catholics, torn between two conflicting loyalties and comprehended in the conflicting claims of two sovereignties, attemped to work out an adjustment which would prove their civil loyalty and maintain the integrity of their religious belief.

We have severely limited the purpose of this study. It is to probe the condition of the Catholic laity in Elizabethan England. Only where necessary do we deal either with the Marian or the later, Continental-trained, priests. Nor do we examine the plots of the reign, except the Northern Rebellion (for reasons apparent in Chapter I), because these concern small groups rather than the main body, upon which we wish to focus our attention. We shall find that the government was fully cognizant who were the leading Catholics in various counties; its policy was largely directed toward controlling them; their names and condition will repeatedly become familiar. By 1603 Elizabethan Catholicism will have risen and fallen with them.

CHAPTER I

THE DORMANT YEARS OF CATHOLICISM
1559–1573

1. CHAOS OF DISESTABLISHMENT, 1559-1563

During the first years after the Acts of Supremacy and Uniformity went into effect in June of 1559, the official policy of Elizabeth I and her government was: (1) to determine the number of Catholic recusants; (2) to keep the more important and active Catholic ecclesiastics and laymen under surveillance or in prison; (3) to prevent manifestations of Catholic life. Much of this depended upon the installation of the new bishops, the chief agents in each diocese in establishing the Elizabethan settlement. To forestall any opposition the government early immobilized the leading laymen along with the more important clergy; the rest of the problem was shifted over to the new bishops. The Privy Council, busy with many problems, could thus more easily supervise the success of its religious policy in local areas without having to undertake actual administration from a distance.

In June of 1559 commissions were appointed to administer the Oath of Supremacy.[1] They busied themselves, as we know, with the clergy; only a few of the laity who legally had to subscribe were asked to make sub-

[1] A valuable contemporary list of the leading English Catholics, clerical and lay, is Nicholas Sander's undated report to Cardinal Morone (thought to be May 1561) in Catholic Record Society, I, *Miscellanea,* I (London, 1905), 1–23 (Latin text), 24–47 (English translation).

mission, as subsequent inquisitions show. A second ecclesiastical commission was appointed on July 30, 1562. It proved to be a sterner body; but the Council, the diocesan bishops, sheriffs, and other secular magistrates also proved throughout the reign to be its necessary adjuncts and frequently the most important instruments in the execution of the religious laws. Their duty — the integration of the Establishment into national life — was a process slow and exacting.

About 1561 or 1562 the ecclesiastical commission drew up a census, more or less national in scope, of important Catholics, prominent in the preceding reign and now known to be opposed to the Establishment.[2] This survey included Catholics who were at large but restricted to specified places, or against whom complaint had been made but who could not be found (being secretly hidden), or who had fled abroad, or who had been committed by the commission to prison. Altogether ninety-six persons were named, most of them ecclesiastics or lecturers and students at the universities. Certain of the clergy listed had a direct effect upon the maintenance of Catholicism in local areas. The deposed Suffragan Bishop of Hull, Robert Purseglove, and Anthony Salvyn, former prebendary of Durham, were both held in "estimation" in Yorkshire, where they were required to reside. Two former prebendaries of Exeter, John Blaxton and Walter Mugge, Philip Morgan of Oxford, John Arden, onetime prebendary of Worcester, and Friar Gregory, *alias* Gregory Bassett, "a common Masse-sayer," Ely, onetime Master of St. John's College, Oxford, and a priest, Haverden, were protected in Herefordshire by John Scudamore, a Mr. Pie, and William Luson, a prebendary of Hereford. Blaxton and Mugge were maintained so secretly that it was impossible to find them to summon them before the ecclesiastical commission. Henry Comberforde of Lichfield, long a very active Marian priest, was noted as "wilfull." Alban Langdale, another prominent Marian priest, was committed to the care of Lord Montague, one of the few Catholic peers. Lawrence Vawse (or Vaux), in the previous reign Warden of Manchester, and Richard Hart, a curate of Manchester, were suspected, despite their recognizances, to be behaving "very seditiously" and to

[2] S.P.15/11/45. Much of this document is reproduced in Hughes, *Reformation in England*, III, 422–427; it is given completely in *Calendar of State Papers, Domestic, . . . Elizabeth, 1601–1603*, M. A. E. Green, ed., VI (London, 1870), 521–525. The date is uncertain; "1561" is written in pencil on the original, and it certainly belongs to the earlier years of Elizabeth I's reign.

"secretlie lurk" in Lancashire, being maintained by leading persons of that county. Dr. Marshall, former Dean of Christchurch, Oxford, reportedly had been dealing suspiciously with the Earl of Cumberland and also with his brother-in-law, Metcalf, a resident of Yorkshire; and the former Dean of Durham, Dr. Robinson, was under suspicion of encouraging recusancy in Yorkshire. Murren, who had been chaplain to Bishop Bonner of London, now was behaving "very seditiouslye" in Staffordshire, Cheshire, and Lancashire and was responsible for a "seditious libel" circulated in Chester. Another priest, Robert Grey, similarly traveled around ministering, and had received considerable support from Sir Thomas Fitzherbert. The ecclesiastical commissioners continued:

We are enfourmyd that through thexample of Sir Thomas Fitzharbert, John Sacheverell and John Draycot, esquires, being by us commytted to pryson and remayning, and through the bearing and supporting of ther wyves, frendes, kynsfolkes, alies and servauntes, a greate part of the sheres of Stafford and Derbye are generally evill enclyned towardes religion, and forbear comyng to church and partycipating of the sacraments, using also very broade speches in alehowses and ellswhere . . .

In a directive sent to the bishops about this time they were enjoined to confer once a year with all the recusants and schismatics within their dioceses:[3] eventually occasional conferences became a settled practice, and one of the most effective in inducing conformity. So early a definition of policy as is this directive is also proof of the difficulties being faced and of the uncertainty on the part of the government that Catholics of conviction, whatever their number might be, had conformed quickly and conscientiously. Edmund Grindal, the Bishop of London, put his finger on the source of much of the trouble: the temporal law, he told Sir William Cecil, did not "meddle" with the Catholics and the ecclesiastical penalties were not sufficiently severe to curb them.[4]

During these first years of solidifying the Establishment, certain of the local ordinaries ran into real difficulties in executing their duties. The success of the religious change could not be measured and the extent of Catholicism could not be determined until a trustworthy and competent clergy were in possession of the parishes. This obviously became the first concern of the new bishops, and explains much of the paucity of efforts

[3] S.P.15/11/23 [?July 1561].   [4] S.P.12/16/49 (April 17, 1561).

to investigate into and uproot Catholicism. However, available evidence also tends to prove that recusancy — refusal to attend the state church — was not very widespread, indicating either indifference or a lack of recognized policy on the part of admitted Catholics in this regard.

The diocese of Winchester early proved a trouble spot. Refusal to conform exhibited itself among the leading clergy in June of 1559, at the very inauguration of the Establishment.[5] Robert Horn, the new bishop, again and again found refractoriness a problem in his first visitations: the clergy generally seemed conformable, but difficulties arose from absentee pastors, vacant pastorates, incompetent clerics, and some who had intentionally abandoned their cures.[6] In the ensuing months the bishop strove for uniformity in religion, but his efforts encountered obstacles due to opposition to the new tenets, to apathy on the part of the local magistrates, and to lack of an adequate ministry. Priests attached to the cathedral had not sincerely conformed and still taught the Catholic doctrines; they derived strength from prominent laymen, opponents of the new settlement in religion and nonreceivers of communion since the beginning of Elizabeth's reign, who set the example for the lower classes. Writing to Cecil, the bishop, dispirited by futility, threatened these members of the laity with the limits of his powers, prosecution.[7]

In an official visitation of the University of Oxford, which he was required to make, Bishop Horn found there sufficient evidence both of Catholicism and of an unwillingness to conform that he prudently conducted himself with a tolerant spirit, not pressing acceptance of the new religion too strongly for the time being.[8] And in another area of his jurisdiction, the two Channel islands of Jersey and Guernsey, recalcitrancy was nourished by proximity to France.[9] The legal question whether or not the laws of religion enacted by Parliament extended to Guernsey was decided by the Queen, who ordered their enforcement and named the

[5] S.P.12/4/72 (June 30, 1559). The Spanish ambassador reported opposition to the religious change in the diocese of Winchester, apparently by both clergy and laity, three days after it took legal effect (*Calendar of Letters and State Papers relating to English Affairs, . . . Simancas. Elizabeth,* M. A. S. Hume, ed., 4 vols. [London, 1892–1899], I, 79, June 27, 1559), and confirmed this a few days later (*ibid.,* 82, July 1, 1559).

[6] S.P.12/17/23 (June 8, 1561).

[7] S.P.12/19/36 (August 29, 1561), /21/7 (January 12, 1562).

[8] S.P.12/19/56 (September 26, 1561).

[9] S.P.15/9/53.1 (January 25, 1560), /13/25 (August 28, 1566); *Cal. S.P. Span.,* I, 561 (June 23, 1566).

THE DORMANT YEARS OF CATHOLICISM

Bishop of Winchester as ordinary in place of the Bishop of Coutances in Normandy.[10] Few people there, however, worshiped according to the prescribed rites, or they attended them only after previously hearing mass; the rural population insulted the new clergy and evinced a strong Catholic loyalty; a conforming Jersey-born priest, Pacquet, was imprisoned in Guernsey after he was found violating the Oath of Supremacy by celebrating the Catholic rites; and the other Guernsey priests were also under suspicion.[11]

The diocese of Chichester, embracing the county of Sussex, likewise proved to be a trouble spot from the beginning of Elizabeth's reign up until its end. The bishop, William Barlow, quickly recognized the source of the difficulty, answering the question why such obstinate recusancy was to be found among a people who had experienced four vital religious changes in twenty-five years: Thomas Stapleton, a known Catholic and still legally a prebendary of his cathedral, but actually an exile living currently at Louvain and thought to have attended the closing sessions of the Council of Trent, had been brought up "in Papistry" from his early years.[12]

Sometime during this early period a census was made of nonconformists within the county of Suffolk, a part of the diocese of Norwich, which serves as an excellent introduction to some of the names and some of the evidence of religious life to be met with repeatedly in the county that contained the most affluent Catholics within the realm.[13] One hundred

---

[10] S.P.15/11/53 (May 16, 1562), /13/25 (August 28, 1566), /76 (May 10, 1567), /77*(May 10, 1567), /77.1 (April 12, 1567); /14/37 (October 27, 1568); *Cal. S.P. Span.*, I, 561 (June 23, 1566).

[11] S.P.15/9/53.1 (January 25, 1560), /11/53 (May 16, 1562), /55 (December 15, 1562), /12/45 (February 26, 1565; document is dated "4 Cal. Martii, 1564"). The Spanish ambassador wrote to Philip II that the Protestant ministers sent over from England were making conversions in the once strongly Catholic islands and that the Bishop of Coutances was making strenuous new efforts to reconvert the people (*Cal. S.P. Span.*, I, 561, June 23, 1566).

[12] S.P.12/11/25 (n.d.). The document bears a notation that it is in the handwriting of Bishop Barlow of Chichester. Stapleton, it says, was reported to have attended the Council of Trent during the previous summer. This would date the document somewhere between 1562 and 1564, since the Council of Trent convened for the third series of sessions on January 18, 1562 and terminated its sittings on December 4, 1563.

[13] C.P.2/21, 22, 23. This is listed as "Persons Recusants, 1559." The date is obviously an error since the document mentions known Catholics who had not received communion for some years and had refrained from attending church for some periods of time. Certain internal evidence indicates an approximate dating:

and twenty-eight persons, most of them listed by name, were reported; this was supplemented by an indefinite number identified under different headings such as "family." A good many of the names are those of admitted Catholics, although their degree of nonconformity varied — some failed to come to church; some, it would seem probable, worshiped according to the prescribed rites but absented themselves from the sermon; others did not receive communion. Michael Hare and his wife were strongly recalcitrant; they had neither attended church nor received communion since he had been released from the Tower. William Hare and his wife likewise were nonconforming, and a Hare child had been christened under suspicious circumstances. The child of Henry Jerningham had been baptized by Lady Bedingfield's chaplain, a nonjuring priest. Lady Jerningham, less obstinate, had received communion in the Establishment, but now lived in fear of eternal damnation for it. Two separate members of the Temperlie family, Thomas and Mistress Temperlie and also her household, were recusants, as were also two Throckmortons and the Rookwood family; in a later entry a Mr. Rookwood was

---

John Almott had not received communion for about four to five years and Simon Potter not for two years; Sir Alan Chenery is recorded in prison lists for the early 1560's but not later, possibly indicating his death since there is no record of his conformity; a Michael Hare was in the Tower "for Papistrie" on June 14, 1572 (*Misc.*, I, 59, quoting from the B.M., Lansdowne MSS., vol. LXXIII, no. 16); a William Greene was imprisoned in the Marshalsea by order of the Bishop of London on June 15, 1571, and was still there in 1580 (S.P.12/140/40, July 1580). These facts indicate that the document dates from some years after 1559. We would place it sometime in the 1560's because of failure to discover evidence of the priest, Sir Alan Chenery, in the next decade and assuming that the William Greene imprisoned in 1571 was the man mentioned in this census and currently free. We do not know if Michael Hare was imprisoned in the Tower at any other time, complicating the dating. Under any circumstances this report belongs to the first generation of Catholics under Elizabeth's reign and is more than likely before 1575 and possibly in the 1560's. Some other evidences of the religious sentiments of Suffolk appear: William Bridgeman derided a married clergy; Robert Smithe, Robert Jetter, and Thomas Woodroffe were "depravers" and "enemies" of the Establishment. Thomas Blessenden, schoolmaster of a Mr. Butler and possibly also a priest, abstained from both church and communion, while Mounford Scott and John Donne did not receive communion. Not all included in the census were Catholics. Four refused to attend church because the minister wore a surplice, and some, at least, were simply indifferent toward religion. *Calendar of the Manuscripts of the Marquis of Salisbury . . . at Hatfield House*, 18 vols., H.M.C. (London, 1883–1940), I, 165, contains only a very abbreviated, seven-line notice of this valuable document, dated under 1559 (no. 589, "Recusants in Suffolk"). It is given *in extenso* in *Miscellanea: Recusant Records*, Clare Talbot, ed. C.R.S. LIII (n.p., 1961), 108–111.

listed as not receiving communion, while his wife did not come to church. Sir Thomas Cornwallis and his wife and Dame Alice Sulliard did not receive communion, while Evans Fludd, George Downs and his wife, Henry Drury and his wife, William Yaxley, Henry Everard, his wife and two servants, and Sir Henry Bedingfield and his wife refrained from both church and communion. Robert Jetter was already noted to be, what future years will bear out, an ardent opponent of the Establishment. Perhaps the most significant aspect of this report is the variations it exhibited in degrees of recusancy during this early period within a closed milieu of Catholics.

Throughout Elizabeth's reign and for many years thereafter, the diocese of Hereford stood out as a center of trouble: the constant reports to the government are simply a reiteration of the same story unchanged. Bishop Scory found what the ecclesiastical commissioners previously had discovered and reported [14] — that nonjuring Marian priests were openly functioning in the diocese, protected by prominent persons, including local magistrates. The same names are reported: the priests Mugge, Blaxton, Arden, Gregory, Ely, and Havard (or Haverden); and John Scudamore was again identified as one of their protectors, described as a man of predominating influence in the county. The bishop had punished some of the recusants, securing a degree of conformity; but his report that certain priests, refugees from other dioceses, were openly entertained and that they received protection from the local magistrates, was proof that whatever the degree of outward conformity, a strong Catholicism had not yet been uprooted, for "I assure your honour [Sir William Cecil] that among the worshipful of this shire, there be not many favourers of true religion." [15]

Four dioceses in the north also proved to be centers of recalcitrancy — Durham, Carlisle, Chester, and York.[16] In the first, Durham, the nonconformity of the clergy had early set the pattern for the laity, which in so backward a county proved difficult to overcome. Many of the justices of the peace adhered to the old religion; some members of the Council

---

[14] S.P.15/11/45 [?1561].

[15] S.P.12/19/24 (August 17, 1561). Bishop Scory also found that Catholic fasts and holydays were still being observed.

[16] The Spanish ambassador reported opposition in the north to the religious change as early as July 1, 1559, and subsequently (*Cal. S.P. Span.*, I, 82, July 1, 1559; 249, June 27, 1562; 251, July 4, 1562).

of the North, apparently residents of Durham, and a number of other officials, possibly Catholics, refused to swear their religious allegiance to the Queen and retained their positions, setting an example of obstinate recusancy for lesser people to imitate. The law was obviously not enforced, and the bishop and his authority were held in little respect. The strength of the Roman Church in this area and the part its clergy still played became plainly visible to the new bishop, James Pilkington, when a young priest summoned to take the Oath of the Queen's Supremacy, refused. He openly preached to the assembled men and women a denial of royal supremacy because jurisdiction in spiritual matters belonged only to the pope.[17]

In July 1561 when John Best made a visitation of his diocese of Carlisle, he found a willingness to conform among the common people and respectful treatment toward him on the part of the gentry. Lord Dacre, who was "something too mighty" in the county, similar to a "prince," and the Earl of Cumberland protected some of the nonjuring priests, and the Earl of Westmorland also influenced the inhabitants against the new religion. Due to the connivance of Dacre and of some other officials mass was still celebrated openly in places, indicating a situation that could only be altered by the authority and the power of the Council of the North. A cause of worry, the bishop felt, one needing to be looked into, was that some of the Catholics lived in hope of a change; they were, in fact, looking for it imminently, and the local magistrates in no way interfered.[18]

In the neighboring diocese of Chester, which in the years to come manifested so very strong a Catholic spirit, opposition to the statutes of religion was already sufficiently evident for the Queen to appoint an ecclesiastical commission to enforce the laws.[19]

---

[17] S.P.12/20/5 (October 13, 1561), /25 (November 14, 1561). The future Bishop of Winchester, then Dean of Durham, Robert Horne, complained early in 1560 of the lack of able Protestant clergy in the diocese of Durham (S.P.12/11/16, February 18, 1560).

[18] S.P.12/18/21 (July 19, 1561), /21/13 (January 14, 1562). One feels, reading the correspondence of Bishop Best, that he was an alarmist, who exaggerated the situation in the north, especially the Catholic hope for a foreign invasion. S.P.12/21/13.1 is apparently a document in French that the bishop sent to Sir William Cecil as evidence of propaganda circulated at that time within the diocese to arouse Catholic hopes of an alteration in religion. If our opinion is correct, we cannot see how this document, which concerns the current Huguenot difficulties in France and is not propagandistic, could be a cause of great dread.

[19] S.P.12/23/56 (July 20, 1562).

The metropolitan of the north, Thomas Young, Archbishop of York, came to realize within a year of his appointment that in the area under his jurisdiction, even in official circles, religious conformity was slack. He found it necessary to ask that the justices of the peace within his archdiocese be required to take the Oath of Supremacy; but his attempt at enforcement ran up against the opposition of these local magistrates, who submitted only after protesting that the oath was strange to them, alleging that they had not been required previously to swear to it.[20]

The tensions affecting England's relations with other states, especially those that were Catholic, rendered suspicious any contact between English Catholics and foreign ambassadors. Whenever Catholics heard mass at embassy chapels, they avoided fulfillment of the new laws governing religious worship; they also caused concern to the Council that any gathering under foreign auspices might be to plan opposition to the governing regime. Those Catholics who attended mass at the French embassy on the Feast of the Purification, 1560, were arrested and an unnamed official took note of those who came that day to worship at the Spanish embassy, although no one was apprehended.[21] However, some months later those attending Easter mass at the Spanish embassy were arrested.[22] Three years later, communication between that diplomatic residence and the outside was cut off from ten in the morning until one in the afternoon in order to prevent attendance at mass.[23] The government became very strict during 1563, refusing permission even to Catholics not of English birth, who did not reside at the Spanish embassy, to worship there, after arresting and imprisoning those who were present that year on the Feast of the Purification.[24]

The Spanish ambassador, a bishop, found from the very beginning of his legation at London that masses were being celebrated in various parts of the capital secretly.[25] Any such evidence of Catholic life became a cause of anxiety to the government once news spread abroad of the imminent convocation of the long-adjourned Council of Trent, and once

---

[20] S.P.12/21/27 (January 25, 1562).
[21] *Cal. S.P. Span.*, I, 126 (February 7, 1560).
[22] *Cal. S.P. Span.*, I, 156 (May 23, 1560).
[23] *Cal. S.P. Span.*, I, 290 (January 10, 1563).
[24] *Cal. S.P. Span.*, I, 295 (February 7, 1563), 301 (February 15, 1563), 304 (February 20, 1563).
[25] *Cal. S.P. Span.*, I, 122 (January 1560).

English Catholics learned that Queen Elizabeth was going to receive an invitation from Pope Pius IV to send representatives,[26] an invitation dispatched on two separate occasions.

At the time of the proposed visit of the second papal envoy, the Abbot Martinengo, certain leading Catholics were arrested for hearing mass upon the confession of a priest, John Coxe, alias Devon. He stated that another priest, Jolly, had performed the forbidden rites at the residence in Essex of Sir Thomas Wharton, a councillor of Elizabeth's predecessor, Mary Tudor, and that Dr. John Ramridge, the deposed Dean of Lichfield, had celebrated mass at the house at Borley in Essex of another councillor of that queen, Sir Edward Waldegrave. Devon, planning to go overseas to the Continent, had received money from two English Catholics, one of them Waldegrave, and had received a promise of further help from Sir Francis Englefield, also a onetime councillor of Mary Tudor, now living in exile for religion. Devon, on his part, admitted a promise to deliver certain small articles abroad.[27]

Such a confession, showing both religious connections outside the realm and the active practice of Catholicism within, was bound to arouse the higher officials. The Earl of Oxford seized the Wharton residence and committed the servants into custody. Wharton pleaded that he had offended the Queen in matters "onely towchinge the Masse." His admission of his fault resulted in a requirement to deposit a recognizance that he, his family, and his dependents would be forthcoming when summoned. Waldegrave's house was also searched, his letters being impounded and sent to the Council.[28] Wharton, Waldegrave, and other persons, known Catholics, who had had associations with them were variously questioned, presumably about the saying and hearing of mass and the reception of communion, any news which they had received concerning the dispatch of a papal legate to England, what information had come to them concerning a General Council and how they had obtained

[26] Cf. S.P.12/16/14 (n.d.), /41 (March 21, 1561), /66 (n.d. [?April ?1561]); S.P.15/11/7 (April 1561).

[27] S.P.12/16/49.1 (April 14, 1561), /49.2 (April 17, 1561), /50.2 (n.d. [?April ?1561]), /59 (April 22, 1561). These documents indicate that masses were being said in and around London. In London Devon (also known as Coxe) had associated with Thomas Langdon, formerly a monk at Westminster Abbey, who had stated to Devon his unequivocal adherence to the old faith. Ramridge was apparently visiting the Waldegrave family for some period of time.

[28] S.P.12/16/50 (April 19, 1561).

it, and what communications they had held with other English Catholics within the realm.[29] As a result those implicated were imprisoned during the spring and early summer of 1561.[30] On July 4 Wharton, having been brought to trial and convicted, petitioned the Queen to release him from his fine of one hundred marks (£66. 13s. 4d.) or to reduce it, as he could not pay it in full unless set free in order to obtain the money.[31] He was refused permission to leave the prison unless he first took the Oath of Supremacy and gave bond for good behavior; on July 16 he did both, agreeing to pay the unpaid fine within eight days, and was set at liberty.[32] Sir Edward Waldegrave, who had been more recalcitrant, consented on July 4 to pay his own and his wife's fines.[33] Others implicated in the case also made answer on that day to the judgments levied against them.[34] Lord Hastings of Loughborough, a transitory Catholic peer, in a statement to the Council regretted that his hearing of mass, which contravened the laws, constituted a failure of his duty to the Queen. On July 16 he took the Oath of Supremacy in order to effect his release.[35]

Others, too, near to and distant from the capital, came in for super-

[29] *Ibid.*; S.P.12/16/66 (n.d.), /18/19 (July 16, 1561); S.P.15/11/7 (April 1561). The last reference is a statement of the interrogatories to be asked of Lady Waldegrave and presumably of the others arrested at this time.

[30] Those implicated and others, numbering twenty-two, were recorded in April 1561 as being "prisoners for the mass"; four women and a serving man were reported at liberty in S.P.15/11/8 (April 1561). The prisoners are also listed in S.P.12/16/55 (April 20, 1561), and S.P.12/16/65 [?April 1561]. These documents are also in *Misc.*, I, 49–50. In May, Waldegrave, his wife, Dr. Ramridge, William Jolly, William Rice, and a physician, Dr. Freer, were still in the Tower, with certain of the leading Marian clergy (S.P.12/17/13, May 26, 1561). In June they and others, listed as "prisoners for mass," were in the commission of oyer at Brentwood, Essex (S.P.12/17/19, June 3, 1561). This list of prisoners is in *Misc.*, I, 51–52. *Calendar of State Papers, Domestic . . . of Edward VI, Mary, Elizabeth, 1547–1580*, Robert Lemon, ed., I (London, 1856), 176, erroneously lists this document as no. 18. On July 3 they and Sir Thomas Wharton were listed as imprisoned in the Tower, while other prisoners for religion, including some persons implicated in this case, were in the Marshalsea, the King's Bench, and the Fleet (S.P.12/18/1, July 1, 1561, /2, July 2, 1561, /3, July 3, 1561, /5, July 2 [?3 ?1561]). These lists of prisoners are in *Misc.*, I, 52–56.

[31] S.P.12/18/7 (July 4, 1561).
[32] S.P.12/18/19 (July 16, 1561).
[33] S.P.12/18/7 (July 4, 1561).
[34] *Ibid.*; S.P.12/12/13 [?April ?1560; date suggested by *Cal. S.P. Dom., 1547–1580*, 152]. This document seems most likely to be correctly dated about July 4, 1561.
[35] S.P.12/18/8 (July 5, 1561), /19 (July 16, 1561). The Spanish ambassador reported that Loughborough was questioned whether or not he favored Philip II of Spain to be Mary Tudor's successor (*Cal. S.P. Span.*, I, 207, June 3, 1561).

vision and prosecution for violation of the religious laws. In Wales, where many Catholic practices remained a part of the pattern of religious life long after the settlement of 1559, the report of a cross formed in the grain of a tree blown over in a storm on the estate of Sir Thomas Stradling in Glamorganshire led the Council to investigate and to imprison Sir Thomas.[36] In September 1562 he was still a prisoner, confined to the Tower in company with some of the leading Marian clergy.[37] Six students of Oxford University, who, being Catholics, had resisted the removal of the crucifix in their college chapel, were also currently imprisoned.[38] Thomas Somerset was recommitted to the Fleet, after refusing submission to the Council when accused of translating an oration of the Cardinal of Lorraine from the French and printing it without authorization.[39] Both Lady Hobblethorne of Essex and a priest, Nicholas Bush (or Busshe), were imprisoned, the former in the Fleet, the latter in the King's Bench, because Bush had celebrated mass and administered the sacraments according to Catholic rites to Lady Hobblethorne.[40] On September 8, 1562, the London residence of a cousin of the Queen, Lady Cary, was raided on information that a mass was to be celebrated there. All those arrested were eventually condemned to prison, after neither the priest, Havard, nor any of the laity present, would confess to their fault.[41]

By the end of the first three years following the change of 1559 Eliza-

---

[36] S.P.12/17/18 (n.d.; *Cal. S.P. Dom., 1547–1580*, 176, erroneously lists this document as no. 19), /19 (June 3, 1561), /20 (June 5, 1561), /18/3 (July 3, 1561); S.P.15/11/8 (April 1561).

[37] S.P.12/24/39.1 (September 5, 1562).

[38] *Cal. S.P. Span.*, I, 218 (November 15, 1561). In May 1560 the Spanish ambassador, Bishop Quadra, had reported the arrest of Oxford students and law students in London for religion (*ibid.*, 156, May 23, 1560).

[39] *Acts of the Privy Council of England*, John Roche Dasent, ed., n.s., 32 vols. (London, 1890–1907), VII, 108 (June 27, 1562).

[40] S.P.12/16/55 (April 20, 1561), /65 [?April ?1561], /17/19 (June 3, 1561), /18/1 (July 1, 1561), /5 [?July 2 (?3) ?1561], /7 (July 4, 1561); S.P.15/11/8 (April 1561). The priest, Nicholas Bush, who still possessed a benefice, declared himself "penitent" after judgment was given on June 3 (S.P.12/17/19, June 3, 1561); on July 4, however, he was convicted of saying mass and administering the sacraments to Lady Hobblethorne according to the Catholic rites S.P.12/18/7, July 4, 1561).

[41] C.P.154/32 (September 13, 1562); *Three Fifteenth-Century Chronicles,* James Gairdner, ed., Camden Society, n.s., XXVIII (Westminster, 1880), 121–122. Mass apparently was said customarily at Lady Cary's (the name is given variously as Cary and Carewe) at St. Dunstan's in the West in London, judging from the references given above and from S.P.12/16/49.2 (April 17, 1561), the answers of the priest, Coxe (or Devon), to questions of Bishop Grindal of London.

beth and her government had successfully faced and overcome the initial administrative difficulties of establishing the new Church of England. After 1562 the problem was much more to solidify their work, especially to repress remaining evidences of nonconformity. The new bench of bishops was empowered by various legal means to deal with local situations; the role of the Council became that of supporting them and of handling problems arising from any aspect of Catholicism that might affect the nation as a whole or England's international relations. The question of Catholicism had not yet been solved in the realm at large: certain dioceses or parts of dioceses contained unnumbered aggregations of Catholics, openly or secretly practicing their religion with the aid of a nonjuring clergy, and the connivance of a complaisant magistracy. The Queen and the Council recognized this situation for what it was — that of a disobedient but not a traitorous element not yet convinced of the rightfulness of the government's policy. There is no indication of the existence of a Catholic party — a union of all Catholics under recognized leadership, pursuing a defined policy. As far as the Catholics of London had any guidance during these first years of Elizabeth's reign, it was haphazardly provided by the Spanish ambassador, Alvaro de Quadra, Bishop of Aquila, but there is little evidence that he had much influence over the whole body of English Catholics either in spiritual or in political matters. However, his reports show that he considered a Catholic party to exist (an opinion also held by the preceding ambassador, Count de Feria) and to depend upon him for leadership, and that it expected him to act as its protector vis-à-vis the Elizabethan government.[42] He also was under the impression — and this had been true of Count de Feria — that the English Catholics were willing to accept outside aid, even military conquest by Spain or France, to reestablish their faith.[43] How many and how in-

---

[42] *Cal. S.P. Span.*, I, 34 (1559), 85 (July 12, 1559), 124 (February 3, 1560), 141 (March 28, 1560), 170–171 (July 25, 1560), 184 (February 23, 1561), 187 (March 25, 1561), 192–193 (April 12, 1561), 206 (June 3, 1561), 209 (June 30, 1561), 234 (April 2 [?3], 1562), 243 (June 6, 1562), 279 (January 10, 1563), 333 (June 15, 1563), 341 (June 26, 1563). At various times the Spanish ambassador reported that a pro-Spanish attitude on the part of the English Catholics wavered for various reasons, especially whenever the English Catholics felt their situation was hopeless because of Philip II's tolerant attitude toward Elizabeth I in the 1560's. Cf. *ibid.*, 77 (June 19, 1559), 85 (July 12, 1559), 170–171 (July 25, 1560), 226 (January 31, 1562), 234 (April 2 [?3], 1562).

[43] *Cal. S.P. Span.*, I, 34 (1559), 51 (April 11, 1559), 77 (June 19, 1559), 85 (July 12, 1559), 206 (June 3, 1561), 209 (June 30, 1561), 226 (January 31, 1562), 297 (February 7, 1563), 333 (June 15, 1563).

fluential his contacts with Catholics within the realm were cannot be determined. His reports mention communications at times with the deposed Archbishop of York, Nicholas Heath; Lord Paget; Henry Cole, the deposed Dean of St. Paul's; Abbot Feckenham; Viscount Montague; and Thomas Thirlby, the onetime Catholic Bishop of Ely.[44] On a few matters the ambassador was of definite help to the English Catholics. He acted as an agent for transmitting information to the Continent, such as knowledge of the English Catholics' scandal at the inquisitorial process against the incumbent Archbishop of Toledo and other Spanish clerics;[45] and he presented to Rome, at English request, the question whether or not Catholics could attend the services of the Establishment.[46] Bishop de Quadra was unwilling to give a definite answer on his own authority, and he hesitated to use faculties to deal with the English Catholics sent to him from Rome without permission of his king, Philip II.[47] He consented, however, to obtain consecrated oils from Belgium for use within England;[48] and he was helpful, as far as his means permitted, to those clergy and students who were in financial straits after they had been dispossessed of their livings for refusing to swear to the royal supremacy.[49]

It is hard to say just how much of England still remained Catholic by 1563 when new legislation dealing with the Roman Church was enacted. Notably the dioceses of Carlisle, Chester, Chichester, Coventry and Lichfield, Hereford, and Winchester indicated disobedience to the new laws on religion; evidence of masses elsewhere shows that Catholicism was not extinct, but also not a threat to the Establishment. No proof, however, other than some reports of the Spanish ambassador, evinced either a desire for, or an intention to plot for, a change in government. Catholic opposition, little as it ever was manifested, was directed against royal supremacy, the supremacy of a layman or a laywoman, in religion. For

---

[44] *Cal. S.P. Span.*, I, 93 (August 18, 1559), 108 (October 29, 1559), 124 (February 3, 1560), 135 (March 7, 1560), 162 (June 28, 1560), 184 (February 23, 1561), 192 (April 12, 1561), 200 (May 5, 1561), 206 (June 3, 1561), 209 (June 30, 1561), 243 (June 6, 1562), 267 (November 8, 1562), 297 (February 7, 1563), 341 (June 26, 1563).
[45] *Cal. S.P. Span.*, I, 108 (October 29, 1559).
[46] *Cal. S.P. Span.*, I, 258 (August 7, 1562), 267 (November 8, 1562).
[47] *Cal. S.P. Span.*, I, 267–268 (November 8, 1562).
[48] *Cal. S.P. Span.*, I, 235 (April 2 [?3], 1562).
[49] *Cal. S.P. Span.*, I, 132 (March 7, 1560).

one thing, the Catholics had no well-defined, active spiritual leadership. Perhaps the deposed Bishop of Peterborough, David Poole, not imprisoned but living in a private residence in Staffordshire, acted as a kind of Catholic ordinary for England, but the proofs are too scanty to give a clear picture.[50] Rome made no forthright effort to provide any kind of aid, religious or otherwise, during the midsixties, except for one or two minor attempts, not far-reaching in nature. There was no provision for training and ordaining priests or consecrating bishops, who might live in exile but secretly communicate with priests and laymen in England. The Catholics were faced with a spiritual starvation that made transition to the Establishment relatively easy, the more that contacts with the older church were attenuated. Impressive as details of Catholic existence might seem between 1559 and 1569 when spread over the pages of a book, they were relatively few, confined to certain areas or a few individuals. None of the stirring dynamism of the Counter Reformation on the Continent was imparted to the English Catholics, largely because the contacts between them and ecclesiastics and laymen abroad were few and very much a matter of chance.

In official eyes, however, Catholicism was not dormant. Four years after the legal change in religion the government believed that stronger laws were necessary to plug loopholes since the supporters of papal primacy had, so it was asserted, "grown to marvellous outrage and licentious boldness."[51] The new law of 1563[52] enacted that those upholding the primacy of the pope and refusing to swear to the Oath of Supremacy a year after conviction should incur, for the first offense, the penalties of praemunire, for the second, the status of being guilty of high treason, which was to entail the penalties attached to that crime. The scope of this oath was

---

[50] There are two references to the activities of Bishop Poole at this period, when the deposed prelate was living in Staffordshire at the residence of Brian Fowler. Priests conferred there with him ("A Collection of Original Letters from the Bishops to the Privy Council, 1564, etc.," Mary Bateson, ed., Camden Society, *The Camden Miscellany*, IX, n.s., LIII, Westminster, 1895, 40–41). Testimony that Bishop Poole acted as kind of a Catholic ordinary for England is contained in the confession of John Felton, an elderly priest, apparently ordained in the reign of Henry VIII (S.P.12/156/29.1, December 15, 1582): "And from thense went to one Mr. ffowlers house nere unto Stafford, where he founde Doctor Poole late Bishopp of Peeterborough, who reconcyled him to the Catholyke Churche agayne (meaning the Churche of Rome/) And being demaunded in what manner he reconcyled him, hee sayeth, by shryving him, absolving him and enioyning him pennaunce of fastinge . . ."

[51] 5 Eliz. c. 1 (preamble). [52] 5 Eliz. c. 1.

widened to include all members of the House of Commons, those admitted to holy orders or a university degree, schoolmasters and teachers, barristers, attorneys, and persons engaged in the execution of the law. Many more laymen were now subject to the terms of the Act of Supremacy.

2. YEARS OF INERTNESS, 1564–1568

Government policy, judged by its execution of the act of 1563, purposed to secure the conformity of key figures whose influence within a locality or within a professional or political body helped to maintain the old religion alive: otherwise it intended to discharge recusant officeholders from their official positions and to substitute persons conformable, who would cooperate in enforcing the religious laws. Beyond this its policy remained what it had been since 1559 — to segregate recognized leading Catholics, imprisoning them if they were legally proved to be nonconformists. The death penalty was not yet envisaged, no matter what the letter of the law read.

As a consequence, the Council circularized the bishops on October 17, 1564, asking (1) that they classify and forward to it the names of the justices of the peace in their dioceses who were favorable to, neutral toward, or hostile to the Established Church, and (2) that they recommend who should be ejected from the commission of peace and who should be appointed to it. The ordinaries were also to consult with leading men of their dioceses known to be favorable to the government and then to forward to Westminster suggestions of further means to suppress Catholicism, to promote the Establishment, and to remedy civil disorders.[53]

Since the justices of the peace represented the main element in the framework of Elizabethan local government, their attitude of mind was of direct concern to the Council. And their position locally, where they were members of that class economically and socially the most affluent, rendered their influence over those under their jurisdiction, especially

[53] Bateson, ed., "Letters from Bishops to Privy Council," Camden Society, LIII, iii. We have examined the original of this document at Hatfield House, but did not have the time to use it sufficiently for the purposes of this study. Further verification of the questions the bishops were to answer about the religious sentiments of the local magistracy and the answers sent in come, somewhat garbled, from the Spanish ambassador, who wrote (apparently referring to this survey of the justices of the peace) to his king that Protestants were to be distinguished by the letter "G" and other letters were to be used for the "moderates" and for the Catholics (*Cal. S.P. Span.*, I, 393, November 21, 1564).

those socially and culturally their inferiors, to be of the utmost importance. Several of the bishops, however, faced a dilemma: within their dioceses some of those who possessed ability to administer the law competently were not adherents of the Establishment, and the ordinaries could not recommend the displacement of such influential recusants when their civil loyalty was not in doubt and no equally suitable replacement was available.

The information gathered by this census, although of immediate value to the central government, was apparently intended to enable the Council by slow degrees to secure a Protestant magistracy. Local government could not be overturned at once, and in sections strongly Catholic it would have been imprudent to stir up local animosity. Further research is needed to learn how fully the Council made use of the data sent in; there is no evidence of widespread removals in the years immediately subsequent to the survey. However, in March and April, 1565, the Spanish ambassador reported that, after having been deferred temporarily, Catholic magistrates in some parts of England had been removed and replaced by Protestants.[54]

A census such as this, compiled by a number of persons using a differing terminology and emphasizing varying points, is difficult to analyze. Obviously, some of the bishops took their obligation more seriously than others, and turned in more detail and expressed themselves more clearly than others. Five of the twenty-six dioceses and archdioceses of England and Wales sent in no reports at all — Bangor, Bristol, Rochester, St. Asaph, and St. David's, although Bristol may have been included in the report of the Bishop of Bath and Wells and Rochester may have been included in Archbishop Parker's report for Canterbury.

The returns showed that a very large preponderance of the justices were favorable to the Establishment, although we cannot arrive at an exact figure because two of the bishops, those of Bath and Wells and of Gloucester, rendered an indeterminate "all," and the Bishop of London reported the same concerning the city of London. The Bishop of Norwich reported that all the justices of Norfolk were favorable, qualifying this with the statement that by "common fame" four of the justices were not, but that he had no certain knowledge of it. However, he had sufficient confidence in this judgment to recommend as unnecessary any in-

[54] *Cal. S.P. Span.,* I, 406 (March 12, 1565), 416 (April 7, 1565).

REPORT OF THE BISHOPS TO THE PRIVY COUNCIL CONCERNING THE JUSTICES OF THE PEACE, 1564

Diocese	Religious Outlook of Justices of Peace			
	Favorable	Unfavorable	Neutral	Undetermined
Bath and Wells.........	all			
Canterbury.............	42			
Carlisle................	8	12		
Chester................	28	50		
Chichester.............	10	15		
Coventry and Lichfield..	40	20	6	
Durham...............	11	2		34
Ely....................	32	7		
Exeter.................	1	5		
Gloucester.............	all			
Hereford...............	30	43	20	
Lincoln................	36	18	29	8
Llandaff...............				17
London................	54+	11	12	4
Norwich...............	indeterminate		8	
Oxford................				22
Peterborough..........	14	11	3	
Salisbury..............	16	2	11	
Winchester............	33	15	4	
Worcester.............	36	46	30	
York..................	47	36	2	
Totals: 21.............	438+	293	125	85

crease in the number of these magistrates. In regard to Suffolk he limited his report only to those who were inclining toward indifference, which further deprives us of an adequate picture of East Anglia. All the justices in the dioceses of Llandaff and Oxford must be put into the category "undetermined," because we lack more precise information. And in a number of reports the wording leaves a margin of doubt how we should characterize certain individuals. Our final conclusion is that 438 justices were favorable to the Establishment, but that the correct number is more, probably much more, than that. This is not only greater than either the unfavorable, 293, and the neutral, 125, but is larger than those two totals combined. It is a truism of the Reformation era that the laity accommodated themselves without much grumbling to whatever creed and ritual the government prescribed. In line with this fact it was but normal that the influential gentry, represented by the local magistracy, should have, in large part, conformed early to the Elizabethan Establishment.

In determining the categories "favorable," "unfavorable," and "neutral," we have had to generalize from the differing and sometimes confusing terminology of the bishops. Most of them, in composing their reports, relied upon the advice of civil and ecclesiastical authorities, who generally seem to have been responsible persons, although Archbishop Parker spurned such help as coming from interested and untrustworthy sources.[55] It is our judgment, based on scattered evidence, that the bishops considered those who worshiped according to law — attending the ritual of the Book of Common Prayer, receiving the sacraments according to that ordinal, hearing the sermons preached in one's parish church, and not dissenting from the spiritual supremacy of the Queen or from a hierarchically organized church — to be favorable. These, after all, constituted the criteria used throughout the Queen's reign to judge whether or not a person was loyal in religion. Since all evidence indicates that general recusancy — conviction for nonfulfillment of the laws governing public worship — was not widespread at this time, the bishops and their advisers most likely grouped as unfavorable those who were so by general reputation, or who openly made known their dissent in doctrine, or who publicized their refusal to worship according to the Book of Common Prayer. Those whom we have termed "neutral" form a group that it is difficult to define. Apparently they were known or suspected to be uncommitted in religious preference or to lack ardor of belief or practice. It would have been hard to determine them other than by common reputation or by a refusal to worship according to law. More than likely many of them were, in modern terminology, "fencesitters": the persons who kept in mind that the two preceding Tudor monarchs had lived briefly, but within that short time had enacted very fundamental religious legislation and had penalized disagreement. They were waiting to see how Elizabeth and her church would fare before making a decision which might put them in jeopardy in case of another religious change.

Each of these categories gives us a picture of Elizabethan Catholicism, since the traditional church hardly more than five years before had been the sole legal religion of the realm, and its hold upon Englishmen can

[55] Bateson, ed., "Letters from Bishops to Privy Council," Camden Society, LIII, 81.

in good part be measured by the attitude of mind of the influential classes which dominated the local communities.

The diocese of London and the dioceses neighboring it, Norwich, Winchester, Salisbury, and Lincoln, which contained together the largest concentration of population and wealth within the realm, had also a greater aggregation of justices favorable to the Establishment than is to be found separately in either of the categories, "unfavorable" or "neutral." Farther away, Bath and Wells, Canterbury, Coventry and Lichfield, Ely, Gloucester, Peterborough, and York also had a majority of "favorable." The category, "unfavorable," was larger than either of the other two separately in the dioceses of Carlisle, Chester, Chichester, Hereford, and Worcester. But the question arises, how many of the justices listed as being unfavorable were Catholics and how many belonged to the Protestant nonconformists? We have no definitive answer, but the bulk of this category are to be found in those areas where Catholicism persisted longest and in greatest strength during the Elizabethan era. But this does not rule out the presence of nonconforming Protestant justices there, because subsequent evidence will show a growing Protestantism in the jurisdictions of the Bishops of Chester and Hereford, which probably had the largest aggregations of ardent Catholics within the realm.

Of interest to us, too, are the areas where we find more than a most minute fraction of the justices to be neutral — in the dioceses of Hereford, Lincoln, London, Salisbury, and Worcester. We must conclude that if the Establishment had not been too successful in winning the adherence of some, the traditional church had also not retained their allegiance. In the years to come what undermined Catholicism was the gradual slipping away of its members of all classes, persons whose religious beliefs gradually were sapped by doubts and uncertainties. The neutrals of 1564 are among the first indications of this trend.

When we break down the dioceses into their component counties we see even more clearly the distribution of religious sentiment of the influential classes. Bath and Wells, contained in the county of Somerset, and Canterbury, restricted to a part of Kent, reported only favorable justices, the former "all," the latter forty-two. Carlisle, composed of Cumberland and Westmorland, reported twenty justices: in the former county there were six unfavorable justices to five favorable; in the latter the difference was slightly greater, six unfavorable to three favorable. The diocese of

Chester, reporting seventy-eight justices, presents an uneven complexion. The county of Chester numbered seventeen favorable and seventeen unfavorable; Lancashire, more strongly Catholic, had six favorable and eighteen unfavorable; the Archdeaconry of Richmond, made up of sections of four counties, had five favorable and fifteen unfavorable, although possibly some of the latter should have been classified under neutral. Chichester, embraced within Sussex, reported twenty-five justices, ten favorable and fifteen unfavorable, which, considering the considerable nonconformity within that county, probably reflects the correct distribution of religious sentiment. Coventry and Lichfield reported sixty-six justices. Two counties, Derby and Shropshire, and the fraction of Warwick all had a preponderance of favorable justices, nine, sixteen, and eight respectively, with only a small number of unfavorable, three, four, and three. Stafford, however, had ten unfavorable and seven favorable. In the 1570's, when the government began its intensive drive against recusancy, Stafford was the first county whose Catholic gentry was called in for questioning, which makes us feel that very probably the unfavorable justices were all Catholics and that they represented the dominant religious sentiment of the county. Within the diocese of Durham, reporting forty-seven justices, the county of Durham had one justice who was unfavorable, but twenty whose preference cannot be determined; Northumberland had eleven favorable, one unfavorable and fourteen whose views are not known and must be placed in the category, "undetermined." Within the bounds of Ely, reporting thirty-nine justices, the county of Cambridge and the Isle of Ely each had sixteen favorable justices; Cambridge had seven unfavorable, and the Isle none. In view of the influence of the University of Cambridge and its strongly Protestant composition, these figures indicate the weak hold of the historic church in eastern England and the strong trend toward Protestantism there early in Elizabeth's reign.

Exeter reported only six justices: Cornwall had four unfavorable; Devon had one unfavorable and one favorable. Obviously these numbers are too small to reflect accurately the religious complexion of these counties. In Gloucester, composed of the county of Gloucester, all the justices were favorable. The diocese of Hereford reported ninety-three justices: the county of Hereford had fifteen favorable, twenty-seven unfavorable, and seventeen neutral; the city of Monmouth had six favorable and four unfavorable; the section of Radnor within the diocese had six unfavorable; the section of Shropshire had seven favorable, five unfavorable and three neutral; and the section of Worcester had two favorable and one unfavorable. The large diocese of Lincoln reported ninety-one justices. In Bedford six were favorable, and three each were unfavorable and neutral; in Bucks no justice was favorable, but three were unfavorable, six were neutral, and eight were undetermined; in Herts. (only part of which was under the Bishop of Lincoln) five were favorable and four unfavorable; in Hunts two were favorable, one was unfavorable and four were neutral; in Leicester ten were favorable, two were unfavorable and four were neutral; in Lincoln thirteen were favorable, five were unfavorable and twelve were neutral. In Llandaff the returns for both Glamorgan and Monmouth give no information by which we can judge the outlook of the magistracy.

The diocese of London reported eighty-one justices. The pattern is strongly in favor of the Establishment: Essex had twenty-one favorable, five unfavorable, five neutral, and three others whose sincerity was doubted by Bishop Grindal; in Herts. nine were favorable, four were unfavorable and two were neutral; all of the justices in London were favorable; in Middlesex twenty-four were favorable, two were unfavorable, five were neutral and the bishop did not know the religious sentiment of one. But the number of unfavorable and neutral in an area so closely under the scrutiny of the Privy Council shows how tolerantly the central government had been dealing with dissent, no matter what was the letter of the law. Norfolk, part of the diocese of Norwich, had no justices other than favorable, although four possibly were doubtful; Suffolk, the other county in that diocese, reported only eight justices inclining toward indifference. Obviously we have only an incomplete picture of Norwich. The diocese of Oxford, although other evidence shows a considerable Catholicism there throughout the reign, cannot be appraised because of lack of data. Peterborough reported twenty-eight justices: Northampton had thirteen favorable, eight unfavorable and two neutral justices, demonstrating that the Protestant influence radiating out of East Anglia and of the University of Cambridge overrode the prestige of such Catholic families as the Vauxes of Harrowden, perhaps the only sincerely Catholic family in the peerage. Tiny Rutland reported one favorable justice, three unfavorable and one neutral. Salisbury reported twenty-nine justices: Berkshire and Wiltshire, the two counties forming the diocese, each had eight favorable justices; the former had two unfavorable and two neutral; the latter had none unfavorable but nine neutral. Winchester reported fifty-two justices: in Hampshire twenty-five were favorable and fifteen unfavorable; in Surrey eight were favorable and four were neutral. Worcester reported one hundred and twelve justices: Warwick, where a strong Catholicism was to be found as late as the 1590's, had eight favorable justices, twenty-one unfavorable and twelve neutral; Worcester had twenty-eight favorable, twenty-five unfavorable and eighteen neutral. The archdiocese of York reported eighty-five justices: Nottingham had seven favorable and seven unfavorable and two neutral; Yorkshire, under the supervision of the Council of the North, had forty favorable and twenty-nine unfavorable. These latter obviously were retained because their local importance ruled out any other course.

Most of the bishops recommended future replacements in the commission of peace within their dioceses, but on a large scale only in Chester (thirty-three), Coventry and Lichfield (nineteen), Hereford (twenty-one), Lincoln (forty-two), Worcester (twenty-one) and the archdiocese of York (seventeen for Yorkshire). Bishop Bentham of Coventry and Lichfield recommended that among the thirteen who should retain their magistracies in Staffordshire six known to be unfavorable should be included, among them a Catholic of almost national reputation, Brian Fowler, with whom the deposed Bishop Poole of Peterborough lived; and among the ten incumbents recommended for retention in Derbyshire Godfrey Fuljambe, irregularly a Catholic, was listed.[56] In the diocese of Chester, where throughout the reign a considerable aggregation of firm Catholics was to be found, a manifest effort was made to recommend persons favorable in religion.[57] This, perhaps, set a precedent, since later in the reign in Catholic Lancashire we will find conformism, at least exteriorly, to be spreading within the ranks of the commission of peace. In one part of the Bishop of Durham's jurisdiction, that under the civil administration of the Earl of Bedford, no incumbent was fit for reappointment to the commission of peace and no suitable replacements could be found, although it is not clear whether the earl's criteria were religion, competency, or both.[58] Because of zeal or necessity the Bishops

---

[56] Bateson, ed., "Letters from Bishops to Privy Council," Camden Society, LIII, 42–43.
[57] Ibid., 73–80.
[58] Ibid., 65.

of Chester, Chichester, Hereford, and Lincoln also reported about the religious outlook of a small number of other officials, but the data are hardly sufficient to give us a clear picture of the religious preferences of officeholders other than the justices of the peace.

Other evidences of the religious preferences of sections of the realm are to be found in the details of the bishops' reports. Bishop Barlow of Chichester suspected the secret practice of Catholicism, but found that it was very difficult to get information because of a network of Catholic sympathizers.[59] The city of Winchester, according to Bishop Robert Horne of that diocese, set the example for religious disobedience within his jurisdiction, since almost all those in public authority were sympathetic to the old religion. Among the fifteen justices of Hampshire listed as unfavorable were such persons of high prominence and influence as Lord Saint John, Lord Chidiock Paulet, and William Paulet.[60] Bishop Jewel of Salisbury, the noted controversialist, reported that in Berkshire the eminent Catholic barrister, undoubtedly the foremost Catholic of cultural attainments of that day, Edmund Plowden, was "supposed a hinderer" in matters of religion and that John Yate had never communicated since the beginning of Elizabeth's reign, thereby incurring excommunication.[61]

From the southwest of England, Bishop Alley of Exeter reported among the influential of his diocese two persons of major importance in the current history of Cornish Catholicism, Sir John Arundell of Lanherne and Francis Tregian.[62] Bishop Cheyney of Gloucester stated that all officials, including the justices of the peace, had always been most willing to enforce the law and to cooperate with him. He also referred to, but did not elaborate about, some religious disorders in his diocese, which rendered no exact information about Catholic obedience.[63]

Bishop Sandys of Worcester, writing with the evidence of unrepressed Catholicism about him, suggested the displacement of all public authorities unwilling to take the Oath of Supremacy. Each new appointee should

---

[59] *Ibid.,* 9–11. Among the recusants reported by the bishop were William Shelley of Michelgrove, William Dautrey, Richard Lewkenour, Thomas Lewkenour, William Stapleton, Arthur Gunter, Sir Edward Gage of Ferle, James Gage, William Culpepper, Henry Poole.
[60] *Ibid.,* 54–56.
[61] *Ibid.,* 38–39.
[62] *Ibid.,* 69–70.
[63] *Ibid.,* 52–53.

swear publicly to the supremacy, and each one should prove his adherence to the Establishment quarterly by receiving communion and hearing a sermon. Significant for an understanding of the condition of his see were two suggestions: (1) justices of the assizes and justices of the peace should inquire into religious conditions, punishing transgressors; and (2) fugitive Catholic priests, maintained openly by the gentry "and had in greate estimacion with the people" in keeping Catholicism alive, should be imprisoned and offered the oath.[64]

Bishop Scory of Hereford reiterated his previous complaints, and some of the same names reappear, John Scudamore of Kenchurch, Richard Seborne of Sutton, Thomas Havard of Hereford. The last, Havard, who sat upon the municipal council, of which not one member was favorable to the Establishment, was singled out for castigation because of his earnest support of Catholicism; it was noted that his family evinced the same strong feelings. The perennial disobedience in religion in Herefordshire stemmed from the fugitive priests — Blaxton, Mugge, Arden, Ely, and Friar Gregory were again named, who were devoted to the traditional faith, and who received maintenance from certain laymen and clergy — again with familiar names, among them William Luson, a canon of Hereford cathedral, Thomas Havard, and John Scudamore of Kenchurch. The canons of the cathedral, exempt from episcopal jurisdiction, were singled out as especially wedded to Catholicism and negligent of their religious duties. Various persons who seldom or never came to church and did not communicate were suspected of having masses in their houses, where opposition to the state religion waxed. The example reverberated in its influence on the lower classes; amendment could be achieved only by vigorous action of the Council supporting the policy of the bishop, with the aid of such justices as were obedient in religion.[65]

In the diocese of Coventry and Lichfield Bishop Bentham found that his Midland see contained much evidence of recalcitrance. The activities of the dispossessed Bishop of Peterborough, David Poole, who lived with Brian Fowler near Stafford, were an important cause of this, since priests

---

[64] *Ibid.*, 1–3, 5–8. The bishop listed among the "adversaries of true religion," Sir Thomas Baskerville, Sir John Bourne, Michael Ligon, John Middlemore of King's Norton, William Heath, Robert Blount, Thomas Lewkener, Sir Robert Throckmorton, and John Somerfield.

[65] *Ibid.*, 11–23. The report is very full with names and facts which prove that Hereford was one of the strongholds of Catholicism during the Elizabethan era.

conferred there with him, while a pro-Catholic "knot" of laymen also fostered recusancy. The extent of such intractability necessitated an ecclesiastical commission to deal, among other things, with those who moved outside the incumbent bishop's jurisdiction when threatened with proceedings. The chief source of trouble, Bentham felt, lay in the refusal of public officers to assist him.[66]

Due to the apparent negligence of Bishop Downman of Chester, the Archbishop of York, Thomas Young, sent in a report for that northwestern diocese, which fairly reflects its subsequent history as an area of considerable Catholic strength.[67] In the neighboring see of Carlisle the bishop, John Best, found that his task of securing conformity was hindered by the incumbent sheriff of Westmorland, as well as by his predecessors, who permitted Catholicism to be discussed openly and even to be preached in out-of-the-way places. The extent of this violation of the laws was further abetted by certain of the lower officials. No matter how the justices of the assizes appeared toward religion in court, even the lower classes knew that privately they opposed the established religion. The influence of the upper classes was quite decisive: tenants feared to evince Protestant sympathies for fear of losing their farmholds. Further, those on the commission of peace in Cumberland who were unfavorable in religion formed an important group: Lord Dacre, as well as his wife, both known to be Catholics; the *custos rotulorum*, Sir Thomas Dacre of Lannercost; and within the confines of the city of Carlisle two (one of whom was now deceased) and these two were of doubtful soundness in their spiritual loyalty.[68]

In another northern diocese, Durham, two causes kept the old religion alive, according to Bishop James Pilkington — the activity of refugee Scottish priests, and the considerable number of natives of the area living, unlicensed, at Louvain, who unsettled the population by sending

[66] *Ibid.*, 40–46. Among the persons disaffected in religion mentioned by the bishop were Henry Vernon of Hilton, Humphrey Wells, Ralph Adderley, Brian Fowler, Sir George Vernon of Nether Haddon ("a great Jester at Religion"), Sir Robert Throckmorton, Thomas Throckmorton, and Michael Purefey.

[67] Bateson, ed., "Letters from Bishops to Privy Council," Camden Society, LIII, 73–80.

[68] *Ibid.*, 48–51. Among others mentioned as being unfavorable in religion were Richard Salkeld, William, Oliver, and John Myddleton, Sir Thomas Wharton of Wharton.

in books and letters; and the latter, in return, sent them financial aid.[69] Equally pressing and more varied problems faced Bishop Bullingham of Lincoln: the keys to the situation were defect of clear authority, laxity of enforcement of the law, nonconformist magistrates, and want of exact knowledge of the names and conditions of individual recusants. The presence within Bullingham's jurisdiction of such affluent Catholics as Robert Dymocke and Sir Robert Tyrwhitt, both justices of the peace, and Sir William Dormer, Sir Robert Peckham, and George Peckham, explained the bishop's clearly voiced need for further dealings both with Catholics currently in prison and those "straglinge abrode," and remedying the retention of Roman practices in the cathedral and collegiate churches and the openness of Catholic worship and belief.[70]

In the diocese of Peterborough Bishop Scambler found almost the same picture. Catholic ecclesiastics, those at liberty and apparently those under restraint, were keeping the old religion alive, secretly or openly. Much good, the ordinary felt, could be accomplished by presenting these non-juring clergy with the alternatives of conforming or of suffering some form of restraint. Catholics boldly attacked the religious settlement and were a source of trouble; the over-all way to deal with them was through an ecclesiastical commission which the diocese of Peterborough at present lacked, and the removal of certain officials known as pro-Catholic. As elsewhere, nonconforming schoolmasters were maintained by gentlemen unsympathetic to the change in religion and they influenced the locality in which they lived: schoolmasters, it was recommended, should be examined and licensed by the local ordinary.[71]

The bishops' reports gave the government, half a decade after the religious change had taken place, fairly detailed data concerning what were the dispositions of the people in the various parts of the realm. We can measure the unhurried and fairly tolerant official policy throughout the rest of the decade, up to the rebellion of 1569, by the criterion that the Queen and her Council knew quite accurately the lagging strength and the lagging intensity of the older religion. Obviously, the Roman Church was not dead, but without sustenance from outside the realm or

---

[69] *Ibid.*, 66–67. The bishop mentioned as Catholics Sir Robert Ellercar and John Swynborne.
[70] *Ibid.*, 26–33.
[71] *Ibid.*, 34–35.

a revitalized dynamism within, it would as a matter of course have disappeared. Whatever resistance to the new order it showed in 1564 came from the older generation, the adults of Mary's reign and at the time of Elizabeth's accession, and from the nonjuring Catholic clergy, small in number, of the 1550's.

Certain factors militated against any large-scale resuscitation of Catholicism in a Protestant England. On the eve of the Reformation the urban areas in England (as in much of Continental Europe which became Protestant) evinced a spirit of anticlericalism; it was but one step to anti-Catholicism. Dr. Nicholas Sander in a report to Cardinal Morone in 1561 affirmed that the leading cities within the realm had seceded from the traditional church; that the urban classes were Protestant; that the strength of Catholicism lay outside the important urban centers.[72] This removed from Catholic ranks the dynamic new mercantile element, which was rising to wealth and influence. When the missionaries came in the 1570's and later they found their chief support among the rural landed gentry, a more static group, and it is to them that they made their appeal.

The greatest blow to Catholicism was the lack of any plan to supply missionary priests during the 1560's. A generation of men and women then reached maturity, a generation that had been deprived of even the most elemental contacts with Catholic doctrine and Catholic spiritual life. We can better picture the situation if we look at the religious vacuum prevailing in those parts of contemporary France plagued by absentee bishops and priests, a condition which proved a ready-made nursery for the Reformers. What rescued the remnant of the once great medieval church from near obliteration in Elizabeth's reign was the unnumbered group of Continental-trained priests, Englishmen by birth, who returned to their homeland in the 1570's and later and who worked zealously, though with only a modicum of success, to repair the chaos which so early resulted from disestablishment.

Between 1564 and 1569 the government of Elizabeth I was never oblivious to the Catholic problem, but it never felt sore-pressed to take prolonged and harsh measures. Its policy was to meet difficulties as they arose; certainly, the official mind was not one of persecution, but rather

[72] *Misc.*, I, 45.

of constraint. It kept watch over London, over the cases of some individuals, chiefly persons of some importance, over the importation of books, so effective a means in the age of the Reformation in hardening belief, and over significant evidences of Catholicism within counties known to have aggregations of adherents of the older church.

In and around London the Privy Council ordered raids to be made wherever it learned that masses were being celebrated; a check was customarily required of all persons present and of letters and books found in the environment. An example of this watchfulness took place in March 1568 when the lords of the Council wrote to Bishop Grindal of London that masses were being said in the capital and money was being collected there for fugitives abroad. The sheriff of Middlesex was directed to make domiciliary visits and search for Catholic objects, especially for articles needed for mass and for Catholic books and letters.[73] A further verification that the Catholic rites were being performed in the capital is to be found in the papers of the Spanish embassy to England. Don Guzman de Silva, the ambassador, reported in April 1565 that a considerable number of priests still secretly solemnized mass in the capital and that many Catholic laymen and laywomen went to confession and received communion according to the Catholic rites.[74] In December 1567 some English who had heard mass at the Spanish embassy were questioned by the government and a few were imprisoned when they refused to swear to the oath *ex officio*.[75] As a consequence the ambassador agreed to exclude Englishmen from his chapel in the future.[76] The following April the Portuguese ambassador was warned to close his embassy to all others than his immediate household; any others worshiping there would be punished.[77] His failure to comply led to a raid on his house, the next October 25, in order to arrest eight English subjects participating there in the Catholic service.[78]

---

[73] S.P.12/46/44 (March 1, 1568). For other evidence indicating raids of masses and listings of the persons worshiping and of letters and books, see *Cal. S.P. Span.*, II, 22 (April 10, 1568), 135 (March 12, 1569).

[74] *Cal. S.P. Span.*, I, 418 (April 14, 1565).

[75] *Cal. S.P. Span.*, I, 686–687 (December 1, 1567), 687 (December 6, 1567), 689–690 (December 21, 1567), 690 (December 29, 1567).

[76] *Cal. S.P. Span.*, I, 686 (December 1, 1567).

[77] *Cal. S.P. Span.*, II, 26 (April 24, 1568).

[78] S.P.12/48/26 (October 25, 1568), /26.1 (October 24, 1568); *Cal. S.P. Span.*, II, 80 (October 25, 1568).

Philip II of Spain considered himself to be the protector of the English Catholics,[79] and he considered asking Queen Elizabeth, as the Emperor Ferdinand already had,[80] for a church for the Catholics in each town,[81] but failed to press the point.[82] The Spanish ambassador to England in the mid-1560's, Don Guzman de Silva, constantly reminded his sovereign of his role as protector and assured him, on the basis of information, the exactness of which is doubtful without further substantiating data, that the Catholics looked to him as their deliverer.[83] It is difficult to determine whom among the English the Spanish ambassadors of the middle and late years of the sixties consulted, and who were their friends. Their dispatches mention that for one reason or another they had relations with the Earl of Northumberland,[84] with the brother-in-law of Viscount Montague,[85] and with the imprisoned Bishop Bonner.[86] But the suspicion which this arouses against these diplomats must be balanced against the fact that in October 1564 the current envoy advised the Catholics of the realm to speak respectfully of Queen Elizabeth and to be obedient to her as their lawful superior in matters other than conscience.[87]

Individuals for various reasons attracted the concern of the Council, which dealt with their cases instead of leaving them to lesser authorities. A Dr. Babington, who had resided with the Lord Darcy since his return from Louvain, was remanded in April 1564 to the custody of the Archbishop of York.[88] George Etheridge, a physician of Thame in Oxfordshire, known to be a prominent Catholic recusant and highly objectionable to the Council for his activities in behalf of the old faith, was or-

[79] *Cal. S.P. Span.*, I, 352-353 (January 15 [?19], 1564).
[80] S.P.15/28/58.5 (November 24, 1563).
[81] *Cal. S.P. Span.*, I, 353 (January 15 [?19], 1564).
[82] *Cal. S.P. Span.*, I, 384 (October 7, 1564), 392 (November 13, 1564).
[83] *Cal. S.P. Span.*, I, 369 (July 22, 1564), 378 (September 4, 1564), 413 (March 31, 1565), 516 (January 28, 1566).
[84] *Cal. S.P. Span.*, I, 565 (July 6, 1566). The ambassador was Don Guzman de Silva; his contact with the Earl of Northumberland was apparently political, the latter pledging his attachment both to the King of Spain and to the Queen of the Scots.
[85] *Cal. S.P. Span.*, II, 83 (November 6, 1568). The ambassador was Don Guerau de Spes. The contact with the brother-in-law of Viscount Montague was apparently of a political nature, but that is not clear from the context.
[86] *Cal. S.P. Span.*, I, 389 (October 14, 1564). The ambassador was Don Guzman de Silva; he apparently had offered to help the imprisoned Bishop Bonner, to whom acceptance of the Oath of Supremacy had been proposed at this time.
[87] *Ibid.*
[88] *A.P.C.*, VII, 142 (April 22, 1564).

dered to be arrested and committed to the charge of the ecclesiastical commission.[89] Likewise, fear that the deposed Archbishop of York, Nicholas Heath, might be influencing the laity whenever he went abroad, led to a conciliar order that he be questioned and, if necessary, lightly tortured to secure full answers.[90] When Lady Waldegrave attempted to send two daughters to Flanders, the Council, which had dealt with her about religion two years before, arrested the young ladies and their companions and demanded an explanation from their mother.[91] Of greater importance to the Council due to his social prestige, past services, and family connections was the hitherto partial recusancy of Sir Thomas Cornwallis, a privy councillor under Mary Tudor. In 1567 when the government questioned him about his beliefs, he consented to confer with Gabriel Goodman, Dean of Westminster, whose arguments eventually persuaded him to conform temporarily.[92] The case of Sir Thomas is significant because it shows the struggle of conscience a Catholic endured under the pressure to conform. Cornwallis weighed the question of the Queen's and the pope's authority, with the fear always present that the decision affected his eternal salvation. When he decided to conform, the nervous strain momentarily affected his health.[93]

Enforcement of the laws governing religion became stricter during 1568, although 1567 had been noted by the Spanish ambassador as a year of relative peace for Catholics.[94] The names of Catholic sympathizers had come to light with the seizure of Wilson, a priest, engaged in collecting funds for the English scholars at Louvain. His account book contained incomplete information concerning his activities, but under threats of torture he revealed more definite information, leading to proceedings against some of the subscribers, including the barrister, William Roper, and Sir Henry Copley.[95] Wilson was released shortly afterward;[96] government policy at this time generally was to keep recusants in prison only for short periods. Roper, a man of prominence in his profession,

---

[89] *A.P.C.*, VII, 168 (November 23, 1564).   [90] *A.P.C.*, VII, 222 (June 22, 1565).
[91] *A.P.C.*, VII, 242 (August 16, 1565), 247 (August 19, 1565).
[92] S.P.12/43/9, 10 (June 21, 1567), /10.1 (n.d.). The Queen and the Cornwallis family had long been on terms of close personal friendship and their loyalty to her was never doubted.
[93] S.P.12/43/9 (June 21, 1567).
[94] *Cal. S.P. Span.*, I, 672 (August 16, 1567).
[95] *A.P.C.*, II, 17 (March 27, 1568), 49–50 (July 3, 1568).
[96] *A.P.C.*, II, 58 (July 17, 1568).

submitted in July of 1568; his fault had been aggravated because of his help to the English at Louvain who had written against the Queen's religious supremacy.[97] Copley, a cousin of Elizabeth I and a convert from Protestantism, was fined and imprisoned briefly for his recusancy.[98] A number of others were also arrested at this time, among them three lawyers, one of them a man of some prominence, Dr. Windham.[99] Two women of social rank, Lady Brown and Lady Cary (or Carey), the latter of whom had been arrested before for religious reasons, were taken into custody for having masses celebrated in their houses.[100] Apparently, Lady Cary received a pardon from the Queen; Lady Brown had to find surety for her future behavior.[101]

The importation of Catholic books from abroad and their distribution within the realm remained an unsolved problem throughout Elizabeth's reign, despite repeated attempts to prevent such subversion of the laws. Raids on Catholic residences and examinations of individual Catholics showed the influence of these writings. They circulated fairly widely in certain areas, strengthening the beliefs of Catholics there.[102] The current debate in print between Bishop Jewel of Salisbury and a number of Catholic apologists overseas, John Harding foremost,[103] and the continuing publication overseas of Catholic apologetic and devotional books

---

[97] S.P.12/47/7 (July 8, 1568); *Cal. S.P. Span.*, II, 50 (July 3, 1568), 52 (July 10, 1568), 58 (July 17, 1568). Roper was married to Margaret, daughter of Sir Thomas More.

[98] *Cal. S.P. Span.*, II, 50 (July 3, 1568), 52 (July 10, 1568), 58 (July 17, 1568).

[99] *Cal. S.P. Span.*, II, 22 (April 10, 1568).

[100] *Cal. S.P. Span.*, II, 22 (April 10, 1568), 44 (June 26, 1568).

[101] *Cal. S.P. Span.*, II, 44 (June 26, 1568). The husband of Lady Brown was described as "a rich merchant."

[102] S.P.12/39/18 (January 24, 1566), /44/52 (November 28, 1567). It is clear from considerable evidence throughout Elizabeth's reign that these books circulated widely in the capital and in the areas where there was a concentration of Catholics. The Spanish ambassador attested to the effectiveness of Catholic books circulating in England (*Cal. S.P. Span.*, I, 390, October 14, 1564); Philip II on the basis of information sent him also attested to the success of books smuggled in from Louvain (*ibid.*, 432, June 6, 1565).

[103] The English Catholic theologian, John Harding, now resident at the University of Louvain, engaged in a long-drawn-out controversy with Bishop Jewel of Salisbury, which resulted in that prelate's famous *Apologia Ecclesiae Anglicanae* of 1562, which was translated into English by Ann, Lady Bacon, under the title, *An apologie or aunswer in defence of the Church of England*. Two of Harding's books which circulated in England at this time were *An Answere to Maister Iuelles Chalenge* (1564) and *A Confutation of a Booke Intituled An Apologie of the Church of England* (1565).

in English, helped to maintain Catholic morale. The Queen, early in 1566, alarmed about the effects of this smuggling, recommended that boats be searched for books and that the Bishop of London be appointed to censor them.[104] Almost two years later, the Lord Keeper denounced the ill-effects of such writings to the Privy Council and condemned the connivance of officials in tolerating their illegal importation.[105]

During the five years which elapsed between the survey of the justices of the peace and the outbreak of the Northern Rebellion only five areas of England gave considerable concern either to the Privy Council or to other ranks of authorities because of manifestations of Catholicism.

In April of 1565 Bishop Bentham of Coventry and Lichfield indicated the degree to which Catholicism remained alive in his diocese, when he drew up a list of injunctions to guide one of his prebendaries in making a diocesan visitation. Vestiges of Catholic practices still extant were to be abolished, among them Catholic prayers and prayerbooks, the use of beads, various burial practices, and the keeping of the onetime holydays. The rector or some other person in charge of the church was to take note of recusants and if one admonition to any of them was not heeded the guilty party was to incur the fine of 12d. levied by the Act of Uniformity. And, as in other places, indicative of the hidden religious sentiments of at least some among the clergy and the laity, was the command to destroy those vessels of Catholic worship secreted in places within the church, and so to alter the church buildings that they no longer retained evidences of former practices and beliefs.[106]

In October 1567 the Bishop of Bangor, Nicholas Robinson, sent in a report covering the shires of Caernarvon, Anglesey, and Merioneth. The people there were most loyal except in religion, due partly to an insufficiently trained and an insufficiently zealous clergy.[107] In regard to religion a pattern was described that recurred for years to come in subsequent reports showing the persistence of Catholic practices.

Recusancy in the diocese of Chichester continued unrepressed, probably

---

[104] S.P.12/39/18 (January 24, 1566).
[105] S.P.12/44/52 (November 28, 1567).
[106] S.P.12/36/41 (April 28, 1565).
[107] S.P.12/44/27 (October 7, 1567). Bishop Robinson was a native of Wales. He complained that the existing body of clergy did not know Welsh, and most of them lacked the ability to preach. Such Catholic practices remained as the use of rosaries, the practice of vigils and watches, the making of pilgrimages, the use of relics, and the burning of candles to the saints.

due to lax enforcement of the laws. In 1568, when the question arose of a successor to Bishop Barlow, an urgent consideration was the widespread existence of Catholicism throughout the diocese.[108] The following year, the see still being vacant, Archbishop Parker of Canterbury had a metropolitical visitation made by a deputy. In his very long report one fact became manifest — the Establishment encountered serious obstacles, due partly to opposition by confirmed Catholics, partly to such administrative abuses as absentee clergy, want of preachers and of effective preaching, and decayed church buildings. A list of prominent persons, influential by their status in society, who neither attended church nor received communion, was given. Six possessors of benefices, without surrendering them, had ceased to preach after the end of Mary Tudor's reign. Three nonjuring priests, Stephen Hopkins, Davy Michell, and Thomas Cotesmore, continued to perform the Catholic rites in Sussex and Hampshire; and a Fr. Moses, a former friar in Chichester, and various unlicensed schoolmasters were known to labor among the laity to keep Catholic practices alive. Lady Poole, Thomas Poole and other members of that family, Arthur Gunter and his family, Mr. Leedes of Steyning and his brother-in-law refrained from church services and communion, leaving the county each year until Easter was past, while Mr. Lewkner of Selsey and Mistress Bishop of Enfield did not receive communion at Easter, and others received in private chapels in their homes under circumstances causing suspicion that the prescribed legal rites were not used. Catholics within the diocese, among them the incumbent parson of Clapham, Sir Davy Spencer, gave aid to fugitives abroad, including the theologian, Thomas Stapleton; in return, Catholic books were sent over from the Continent and circulated in the county. Of these, Sander's *Rock of the Church,* all copies of which a royal proclamation had ordered to be delivered up to the bishop of each diocese, was probably the most widely read. Strong hope existed that Catholicism would return: articles needed for Catholic rites were still publicly displayed or hidden awaiting use and some Catholic religious practices, such as reciting the beads, were openly performed. All of the diocese of Chichester except Lewys and to some degree the city of Chichester evinced a lively Catholicism: Racton Parish and Battle were well-recognized centers. In the latter, for instance, the inhabitants would walk out of the church if

[108] S.P.12/47/40 (August 14, 1568).

the preacher attacked the pope. It seemed useless to look to the civil law, if the city of Chichester were representative of diocesan sentiment: there the aldermen, simultaneously being justices of the peace, were strongly suspected of favoring Catholicism.[109]

Different from the diocese of Chichester, the neighboring archdiocese of Canterbury showed much less evidence of Catholic recusancy in the metropolitical visitation of 1569. Some names possibly Catholic appear, and some statements would seem to refer to Catholics, but Kent and the peculiars of the archdiocese elsewhere seem early and thoroughly to have become Protestantized.[110]

Increasingly the government focused its attention on the two counties of York and Lancaster.[111] The former, being the seat of the Council of the North, was subjected to a constant degree of supervision; the latter, fairly distant from London and not easily accessible from York, could conduct its traditional way of life without too great interference. Each exhibited a pattern of Catholic beliefs and practices so traditionally integrated into county life that strong pressures were continuously applied to uproot them. It would appear, comparing the intensity of northern Catholicism in the 1560's with the lesser fervor of the 1530's and 1540's, that Yorkshire, and possibly also Lancashire, underwent a considerable strengthening of its long devotion to the Roman Church under Mary Tudor, which Elizabeth's rule could not altogether undo.

In the 1560's Archbishop Young of York attempted to secure conformity by imprisoning the leading lay recusants or by keeping them under surveillance within a prescribed area. Sir Thomas Metham, Sir William Babthorpe, Sir John Nevill, Sir William Mallerie, William Hussey, and Peter Vavasour were recorded in 1565 as very irreconcilable.[112] In August of that year Metham and his wife and Hussey were im-

---

[109] S.P.12/60/71 (1569). In the list of recusants were, among others, Viscount Montague, Lady Case, John Gage, James Gage, Lady Pole, Thomas Pole, Maria Pole, Arthur Gunter and wife, Anna Lyne (?Kyne), William Shelley, Richard Shelley, and a yeoman, Nicholas Bacon.

[110] S.P.12/60/71 (1569). Robert Gage, his wife and his sister are mentioned as recusants in the parish (and deanery) of Croydon, a peculiar of the archdiocese of Canterbury. Presumably, they were Catholics. We have had difficulty identifying other names.

[111] Reports of the Spanish ambassador, Don Guzman de Silva, reiterate the strong Catholicism of the north. See *Cal. S.P. Span.*, I, 478 (September 17, 1565), 670 (August 9, 1567).

[112] S.P.15/12/68.2 [?June 23, 1565].

prisoned; some other recusants were allowed to continue at liberty only under bond.[113] When the two Methams remained unyielding, they were kept in prison for some years. Sir Thomas inflexibly refused either to attend the ritual or sermons of the Establishment or to receive communion in it, nor would he read any book except one bearing the approval of the Catholic Church and he especially favored books published at the University of Louvain. He further refused to confer about religion with the clergy of the Establishment or to answer to the ecclesiastical commission, and contrary to the wishes of Elizabeth I he maintained two of his sons at Louvain.[114] The ecclesiastical commission had also limited two other leading Catholics, Dr. Carter and Dr. Siggeswike, to circumscribed areas.[115] Two physicians, Vavasour and Lee, were still at large and known to be influencing their neighbors: the former received such strong protection that he could not be found, although common knowledge held him to be a supporter of Catholic practices; the latter reputedly sustained Catholic morale by traveling from one Catholic house to another.[116]

The example of such people was telling, and the lack of vigorous prosecution spread abroad the opinion that the Catholics and their practices would be more or less tolerated.[117] In the eyes of the authorities much could be done if the justices of the peace were ordered to be more diligent in assisting the state clergy. These magistrates were directed in 1568 to give the fullest assistance to evangelizing efforts of the clergy of the Establishment, even to soliciting audiences for the preachers, and it was suggested that some of the gentry who adhered to the Establishment ought to confer with the nonconformists to attempt to secure their submission.[118] This was imperative because the laxity in enforcing conformity discouraged the Protestants of the north, and negligence in preaching the doctrines of the Establishment gravely hindered its successful spread among those people who continued to believe in the old religion.[119]

[113] S.P.15/12/79 (August 16, 1565).
[114] S.P.15/17/72 (February 16, 1570). The document is a letter addressed to Sir William Cecil by a "private person" whose name has been cut off.
[115] *Ibid.* [116] *Ibid.*
[117] S.P.15/12/68 (June 23, 1565).
[118] S.P.15/14/17 (July 11, 1568), /42.1 (November [9], 1568).
[119] S.P.15/12/68 (June 23, 1565), /14/42.1 (November [9], 1568).

Lancashire more than ever came into the direct orbit of government attention during the late 1560's. Hitherto, so distant and sparsely populated an area had been left to the care of Bishop Downman of Chester, with little supervision from London or York. The unexplainable laxity of this bishop and evidence that Catholicism flourished within the county aroused conciliar attention, both at Westminster and at York. It was found that the purpose of the ecclesiastical commission for Chester had been negated by the presence on it of practicing Catholics, whose removal was proposed.[120] Early in February 1568 the concern of the Queen, both because the religious laws were being flagrantly violated in Lancashire, and because various persons within the county were under pressure not to conform, led to a royal order commanding the Bishop of Chester and his fellow ecclesiastical commissioners to arrest those men of consequence who were violating the statutes dealing with religion.[121] Three weeks later the Queen enumerated six persons, four of them nonjuring Marian clergy — Vaux, the former Warden of Manchester; Murren, once chaplain to Bishop Bonner of London; Marshall, once Dean of Christchurch, Oxford; and Hargrave, former vicar of Blackbourne — and the future cardinal, William Allen, not yet in priestly orders; and "one Norreys, terming himself a Physician," all of whom had been maintained privately in Lancashire, where they influenced others to continue the practice of Catholicism. They were to be arrested, and those harboring them were to be punished.[122] The success of the Earl of Derby in apprehending Catholics was proof to the Queen that laxity in law enforcement by others accounted for the widespread religious difficulties in that county: the bishop, his jurisdiction long fortified by an ecclesiastical commission, possessed ample powers if he had wished to

---

[120] S.P.15/13/123 [?1567].

[121] S.P.12/46/20 (February 3, 1568). A written statement, unsigned but apparently by a Mr. Glaseour, probably about cases before the Court of Ecclesiastical Causes in Lancashire, reported an agreement by Catholics to boycott the Anglican services, including communion, and to worship only according to the Catholic rites (S.P.12/48/35 [n.d.]). This is confirmed by a report of an Edward Hurleston to the Earl of Pembroke that many gentlemen, perhaps numbering five hundred, had sworn not to receive communion as long as Elizabeth I lived (S.P.12/44/56, December 20, 1567). Each of the two writers agreed that the strength of Catholic feeling seemed to be leading to a possible civil disturbance. The validity of these statements is doubtful, however, since Lancashire did not join in the Northern Rebellion.

[122] S.P.12/46/32 (February 21, 1568).

use them to secure conformity within his diocese.[123] Downman was ordered to make a visitation of Lancashire,[124] which he did during the summer at the cost of great discomfort, relieved, however, by the hospitality of the gentry and the docile obedience in religion which he reported that he experienced everywhere.[125]

The bishop, the Earl of Derby, and six other ecclesiastical commissioners cited eight prominent recusants before them in July at the manor of Latham. All had previously refused to be examined under oath: now they either denied, being sworn, those charges alleged against them, or confessed to them, but not under oath. Each of the recusants was accused (1) of not attending the legally prescribed services in his parish church; (2) of not receiving communion in his parish church; (3) of receiving one or more of certain priests — Vaux (Vause), Hargraves, Allen, Murren, Marshall, Poole, Ashbrook (Asbroock), Thomas French, Rad (? Rans) Sidhall, Dan (? Van) Banester, Nicholas Banester, Henry Crane — into his house.[126]

Francis Tunstall affirmed that he had attended the services of his parish church during the past year, without receiving communion. He admitted briefly entertaining the priest, Laurence Vaux, thinking him unobjectionable to the government.[127] John Talbot of Salesbury had neither attended his parish church nor communicated. Two years before, he had entertained the priest, James Hargraves, whom he had considered to be a respectable person.[128] John Westbye likewise had neither worshiped at his parish church nor communicated. He admitted that he had entertained his cousin, William Allen, unaware of possible governmental disapproval.[129] John Rigmaiden had attended the services of the state church but had not received communion. He had not entertained any persons named in the list, except those whom he thought to be law-abiding.[130] Edward Osbaldeston attended the prescribed ritual, but without regularity, and had failed to receive communion within the previous year. Intending no offense he had associated with Thomas French and some others mentioned by the government as objection-

---

[123] S.P.12/46/33 (February 21, 1568). [124] *Ibid*.
[125] S.P.12/48/36 (November 1, 1568).
[126] S.P.12/48/36.1 (July 31, 1568). It is to be noted that the government thought that William Allen was a priest, although actually he had not yet been ordained.
[127] S.P.12/48/36.2. [128] S.P.12/48/36.3.
[129] S.P.12/48/36.4. [130] S.P.12/48/36.5.

able.[131] Matthew Treves (or Travis) had failed to worship or communicate as prescribed by law. He had received into his house various of the "Ould Religion," including a kinsman, Smith, and with him Ashbrook, not intending to contravene the government.[132] John Towneley had worshiped at his parish church but had not communicated. James Hargraves about a year before had lodged at his house; for six years Henry Crane had lived with him, and for four of those years had served the cure of Padiham.[133] John Mollineux had worshiped at his parish church, and he had communicated once, but not the required three times annually. He had received five proscribed priests, and two scholars, Foster and Allen.[134]

All of these eight recusants were now ordered to worship only at their parish churches or other customary places of devotion; before the next All Saints' Day they were to receive communion, and always afterwards fulfill the requirement of reception three times a year; and they were commanded to attend any sermon preached in a church within three miles of their residences. They were further forbidden to support any of the persons listed as objectionable or any other nonjuring priest, and were individually bonded in the sum of three hundred marks (£200. 0s. 0d.) for their appearance before the ecclesiastical commission when summoned.[135] The Queen, through the Privy Council, had ordered leniency for those who conformed.[136] Seven of the eight accepted this offer; only John Westbye refused.[137]

This hearing, the sentences, and the submission are significant. In subsequent years all eight of these men will reappear as stanch recusants, generally unyielding in their religious faith. It proves that in the 1560's the Catholics vis-à-vis the government and vis-à-vis their church had only ill-defined principles of obedience; that civil obedience, external pressures, and fear could overcome religious obedience. It also shows that very little was being done at this time in Lancashire or probably in the rest

---

[131] S.P.12/48/36.6.   [132] S.P.12/48/36.7.
[133] S.P.12/48/36.8.
[134] S.P.12/48/36.9. The five proscribed priests were Vause, Murren, Marshall, Peele (?Poole), and Ashbrooke. Foster was a student at Oxford.
[135] S.P.12/48/36.1 (July 31, 1568). This is the report of the ecclesiastical commission; Bishop Downman's letter of November 1, 1568, to Sir William Cecil states that they were each bonded for the sum of one hundred marks (£66. 13s. 4d.) for their appearance (S.P.12/48/36).
[136] S.P.12/48/36.1 (July 31, 1568).   [137] S.P.12/48/36 (November 1, 1568).

of England to define a Catholic position or actively to keep the faith alive. The hearing also demonstrates the procedure of the government in obtaining conformity — to put pressures upon the leading persons of a county to obey the religious laws as a duty of obedience in conscience to the Queen. This was to be insured by keeping the conformist in bonds and under the supervision of the ecclesiastical commission. Here we see a defined pattern which was used repeatedly as settled policy in the future.

The punishment of these men, Bishop Downman reported to the Council, had had a salutary effect upon the county; and this had been increased by the preaching of the Dean of St. Paul's, Alexander Nowell, who had induced many to conform.[138] However, one of the most influential of the Lancashire recusants, Sir John Southworth, admitted that he had neither worshiped at his parish church nor communicated, and refused to do these when Archbishop Parker demanded his submission, although he offered not to receive or maintain priests in his house. A man of strong principles, Southworth requested that he might be permitted to live overseas in order to follow his conscience.[139]

This stringency in enforcing the religious laws in Lancashire coincided with and possibly stemmed from steps taken at Rome to prevent the conformity of Catholics in England. Two exiled theologians, Nicholas Sander and Thomas Harding, received faculties in 1566 from Pope Pius V to absolve Englishmen from schism and to declare officially that baptism, worship, and communion according to the Anglican ritual constituted schism; they were further instructed that not even the pope could dispense anyone to perform these acts other than according to the Catholic rites.[140] Laurence Vaux, the former Warden of Manchester, one of the priests singled out by the Queen's decree of February 21, 1568, received a commission from Sander and Harding to announce these decisions in England,[141] where the success of his activities attracted the attention of the government, which proscribed him in two separate declarations.[142]

[138] S.P.12/48/36 (November 1, 1568).
[139] S.P.12/47/12 (July 14, 1568), /48/36.10 (1568).
[140] S.P.12/41/1 (November 2, 1566). Letter of (?) Laurence Vaux to an unnamed person (copy).
[141] *Ibid.*
[142] S.P.12/46/32 (February 21, 1568), /48/36.1 (July 31, 1568).

The efforts of Vaux and some others to sustain Catholic morale met with a degree of success and caused a variety of rumors and suspicions to circulate — reports of oaths not to receive the Anglican communion,[143] of the reconciliation of Sir Richard Molyneux and his family upon receiving a letter from Vaux, and the reconciliation of a number of other lapsed Catholics in Lancashire also,[144] and of the celebration of the Catholic ritual by priests able to be identified.[145] Although the Bishop of Chester and the ecclesiastical commission, as we have seen, cited some of the lay recusants before them and achieved a degree of conformity, the anxiety of the Queen and her government concerning the state of Catholicism in Lancashire seems to have had little effect upon Bishop Downman, who failed to institute any consistent policy of suppressing recusancy in that county.

3. THE FUTILITY OF ACTION, 1569–1573

During the late years of the 1560's and the early 1570's a series of events fundamentally altered the position of the Catholics in England. In 1568 the Queen of Scotland, Mary Stuart, fled to England in the face of rebellion in her own realm, and in the same year the seminary at Douai in Flanders began its program of training priests to work in England. In 1569 the Northern Rebellion, which bore the tinge of a Catholic movement, broke out, continuing into the next year. In 1570 Pope Pius V solemnly declared that Elizabeth I was deposed and excommunicated and that her subjects were absolved from their allegiance to her. And in the following year, 1571, Parliament enacted a very stringent bill severely penalizing certain Catholic practices.

Very few of the Catholics, certainly none of the leading gentry families, seem to have looked upon Mary Stuart as the legitimate ruler of England in 1568, and until her death in 1587 very few Catholics of any class thought it right, morally or legally, to depose Elizabeth I in her favor. At the most they considered her to be Elizabeth's legitimate heir. The

[143] S.P.12/44/56 (December 20, 1567), /48/35 (n.d.).
[144] S.P.12/48/34 [?1568]. (?) Edmund Holmes to Mr. Glaseour (Glasor) and (?) Mr. Hurleston.
[145] S.P.12/46/32 (February 21, 1568), /48/34 [?1568], /36.1 (July 31, 1568). A postscript to the second document says: "The pryste of Kirkbye name is Sr Peater Jacson; . . . and the ij pristes at the Halle of Crosbye, the doe use to say masse commonlie."

reports of the Spanish ambassador and the contemporary documentary evidence originating in England which we have examined confirm this.[146] Only a few Catholics, never the whole body, ever plotted against the English monarch in favor of Mary Stuart; even the bull of Pope Pius V declaring Queen Elizabeth deposed did not alter the loyalty of the bulk of the Catholics. Any other frame of mind would have been unrealistic, since they had no leadership, a fact noted by the Spanish ambassador, Guzman de Silva;[147] in the end the Elizabethan Catholics had to decide for themselves their attitude vis-à-vis the state.

In the rebellion of 1569–1570 the northern leaders wished to displace, not Elizabeth, but her ministers: they intended, so we must infer from the evidence, that Mary Stuart should be appointed heir to the throne, and that the old religion, still strong in the north, should be reestablished. But the weakness of the rebellion was its sectional and feudal constitution: the great magnates of the north, the Earls of Northumberland and Westmorland and Lord Dacre, received from the classes below them a love, a respect, and an obedience to their wishes, which was a tradition inherited from centuries past. The north obviously had been less penetrated than the south by the ideas of centralized sovereignty which dissolved feudal bonds.

The government's concern during the difficult days of late 1569 was to know exactly what sections and what individuals were loyal. Sir William Cecil, the chief minister of the Queen, feared a Catholic league of princes to depose her and to set Mary Stuart in her place.[148] His policy, and that of the Queen, in the face of danger was to restrain the people of the north from taking action in the Scottish Queen's favor, to

[146] The Spanish diplomatic papers support our judgment negatively. They express a variety of opinions — that Mary Stuart had friends and supporters within the realm; that she was considered Elizabeth's rightful successor; that she was looked upon as the legitimate ruler of England instead of Elizabeth; that an uprising in her favor was a possibility. But details are lacking where the envoys reporting this information gained their knowledge; as far as we can judge their contacts within England were very limited, casting doubt on the accuracy of their opinions as reflecting the frame of mind of any large number of people. Considering all this, we must judge that the most accurate criterion of English Catholic outlook is the documentary evidence originating within the realm. See *Cal. S.P. Span.*, I, 369 (July 22, 1564), 560 (June 23, 1566), 618 (February 17, 1567), 639 (May 3, 1567), 641 (May 24, 1567); II, 48 (July 3, 1568), 75 (October 9, 1568), 85 (December 12, 1568).

[147] *Cal. S.P. Span.*, I, 370 (July 22, 1564).   [148] C.P.157/2–7 (1569).

insure by necessary alterations the allegiance of the justices of the peace and the Council of Wales, and to purge the legal profession of any members suspected of disloyalty. Immediately, the government began to implement these three steps simultaneously.

Yorkshire, despite the presence of a Protestant element and the Council of the North, had a militant core of Catholics, who hoped through the instrumentality of the Scottish Queen, if appointed Elizabeth's heir, to secure a change in the religious condition.[149] Some of the Catholics partially, some wholly, disregarded the religious laws, a situation which the government could not alter unless the magistrates performed their duties with more energy.[150] We have no statistical study of the relative strength of the northern Catholics and Protestants in 1569 and 1570 in the areas in revolt. The census of justices of the peace in 1564 showed a majority of Protestants in magisterial positions in Yorkshire, but we cannot be certain how far this accurately reflected the complexion of the county. On the other hand we do have rough estimates of the relative proportion of the two groups, made by two observers whose judgments were possibly colored by the rebellion of 1569 and who were certainly limited in making any accurate determinations statistically — Sir Ralph Sadler and Sir Thomas Gargrave, the latter a member of the Council of the North and an ardent promoter of Protestantism. Both agreed that Catholicism still retained wide adherence.[151] Sadler held that all classes were strongly Catholic;[152] Gargrave told a correspondent, presumably Sir William Cecil, that some Catholics even scrupled to pay taxes, ap-

[149] S.P.15/15/4.1 (November 2, 1569), /21/56.1 [?June 13, ?1572]. The first document, S.P.15/15/4.1, is an enclosure in a letter from Sir Thomas Gargrave to Sir William Cecil, which stated that the "papists" rejoiced and imagined that Catholicism would be restored upon hearing a rumor of a marriage between the Queen of the Scots and the Duke of Norfolk. This is further substantiated by S.P.15/14/17 (July 11, 1568), a letter from Sir Thomas Gargrave, Sir Henry Gate, and John Vaughan to Sir William Cecil, in which it was stated that the Scottish Queen was winning the affection of those who were not favorable to the Establishment. The second document, S.P.15/21/56.1, is the confession of the Earl of Northumberland, made after the collapse of the Northern Rebellion, of which he was a leader. He affirmed that the rebels only wanted Mary Stuart appointed Elizabeth's successor.

[150] S.P.15/14/15.1 (June 29, 1568), /17 (July 11, 1568), /42.1 (November [9], 1568), /15/4 (November 2, 1569), /17/64 (February 1, 1570).

[151] S.P.15/14/15.1 (June 29, 1568), /17 (July 11, 1568), /15/4 (November 2, 1569), /77 (December 6, 1569), /18/5 (March 10, 1570), /75 (June 17, 1570).

[152] S.P.15/15/77 (December 6, 1569).

parently doubting the legitimacy of the Queen's title.[153] Obedience to the pope and acceptance of his primacy were widespread, which, Gargrave pointed out, differed from the attitude prevailing under Henry VIII [154] — a tribute to the zeal of the clergy under Mary Tudor and the nonjuring priests under Elizabeth, who had apparently done much to strengthen the traditional faith. After the rebellion was suppressed the justices of Yorkshire signed a statement of loyalty and of conformity to the Establishment,[155] but the harsh repression of the rebellion did not immediately extinguish the prevailing strong Romanist pattern. Proof of this is to be found in August 1570 when Edmund Grindal, upon his appointment to the metropolitan see of York, was informed that the greater part of the gentry within his jurisdiction was Catholic, and he learned of considerable other proofs of Catholic sentiment among many of the lower classes.[156]

The evidence today extant points to the loyalty of all Englishmen outside of the areas in rebel hands. There is no better test of it than the subscription by the justices of the peace, both present and past incumbents, to a statement of their fidelity, including acceptance of the Establishment, its liturgy and communion, and rejecting all other forms of religious belief, in answer to letters sent out by the Council on November 6, 1569, to the sheriffs and justices in various parts of England.[157] With very few

---

[153] S.P.15/18/75 (June 17, 1570). This is a letter from Sir Thomas Gargrave apparently to Cecil. The penmanship is very difficult to read.
[154] *Ibid.*
[155] S.P.15/18/76 (June 21, 1570). In view of the census of 1564 and the predominance of the Council of the North in Yorkshire, the majority of the justices were probably Protestant and expressed their real sentiment in their statement of loyalty and adherence to the Establishment.
[156] S.P.12/73/35 (August 29, 1570). The archbishop mentioned various Catholic practices which had been retained despite the change in religion.
[157] The justices of the peace of Kent, as also the justices in other counties, state that their subscriptions are in answer to a letter from the Council of November 6, 1569 (S.P.12/59/37 [?November 25], 1569). S.P.12/59/37.1 [1569], the subscription of the justices of a part of Kent to the Council's request, is a model of what the letters from the justices in the various counties contained. It pledged their attendance at the rites of the Establishment, worshiping and receiving communion according to the liturgy of the Book of Common Prayer, and opposing any contempt of the Church of England. The conciliar letter of November 6 required that those who would not subscribe to the Act of Uniformity should give bonds for their good behavior and their personal appearance before the Council. There was a limitation of time set on the duration of the bonds (S.P.12/59/36, November 25, 1569).

THE DORMANT YEARS OF CATHOLICISM

exceptions all signed, even some who were most probably admitted Catholics.

In Kent William Roper, son-in-law of Sir Thomas More, declared his loyalty to the Queen, but asked not to be pressed to sign what was counter to his conscience. He was put under bond for his good behavior.[158] In Sussex William Shelley and William Scott twice absented themselves from assemblies of the justices convened to obtain their subscriptions, and William Dawtrey and James Page refused to sign because it was against their consciences.[159] In Suffolk Sir Henry Bedingfield and Thomas Rouse refused their signatures and were put under bond for their good behavior.[160] At the assembly of the justices in Berkshire the eminent barrister, Edmund Plowden, first requested time to consider whether or not to subscribe because of scruples of conscience, since he had not been informed beforehand that he must assent to such a statement.[161] Shortly afterward he refused, and bonds were taken of him for his good behavior.[162] John Yate, a former justice, did not appear, but sent in a letter of excuse and his bond.[163] Lord Chidiock Paulet in Hampshire raised an objection to the Council's demand that the signatories agree to receive communion, asking for a conference about this point. Another justice pleaded illness, and a third could not be found when summoned. Anthony Cope, an excommunicate, appeared before the justices and vehemently refused to subscribe; he was sent up to the Council.[164] James Courtney of Devonshire, who had been a justice in the reign of Mary Tudor, refused to assent, holding that his tenure of office had expired before the Act of Uniformity had been enacted. He affirmed his allegiance to Elizabeth in all civil matters, as the rightful sovereign of

---

[158] S.P.12/59/37, 37.2 ([?November 25], 1569).

[159] S.P.12/60/18 (December 4, 1569). The second assembly of the justices took bonds of Dawtrey and Page, as required by the Council, for their good behavior and for their appearance before the Council when summoned.

[160] S.P.12/60/62 (December 30, 1569), /62.2, 62.3 (December 1, 1569). A contemporary accusation charged Thomas Rouse with being an ardent Catholic and of maintaining his brother, a doctor of civil and canon law, at Rome (S.P.15/19/58 [?1570]).

[161] S.P.12/60/47 (December 22, 1569). The sheriff and the justices of the peace had assembled at Abingdon on November 17, 1569.

[162] S.P.12/60/47.2 (December 20, 1569).

[163] S.P.12/60/47 (December 22, 1569). In 1573 a prisoner, Yates, was currently confined in a London prison for religion (*A.P.C.*, VIII, 103, May 9, 1573).

[164] S.P.12/59/46 (November 28, 1569).

England.¹⁶⁵ In Cornwall Sir John Arundell of Lanherne refused to sign, stating that he would maintain this attitude until he had conferred with the Council. Sir William Godolphin, after hesitation, eventually gave his consent.¹⁶⁶

Herefordshire, the seat of ardent recusancy, witnessed few refusals. John Scudamore of Kenchurche, long a most recalcitrant Catholic, would not assent to religious conformity, but otherwise pledged his obedience and loyalty.¹⁶⁷ Thomas Havard and Henry Dudeston, both aldermen of Hereford, similarly refused their assent.¹⁶⁸ Robert Middlemore of Warwickshire failed to appear before an assembly of justices gathered to sign and sent in no indication of attitude; Thomas Throckmorton, also of that county, was not questioned because of serious illness.¹⁶⁹ In Leicestershire all the justices who attended an assembly to obtain subscription to the Council's orders signed, and one absentee, whose religious beliefs were possibly suspect, sent in a statement of willingness to comply.¹⁷⁰ In Northhamptonshire no justice dissented, including the Lord Vaux of Harrowden.¹⁷¹ Certain magistrates in Worcestershire, presumably Catholics, were absent from the county and did not sign; no one expressed dissent.¹⁷² In Gloucestershire no justice, past or present, refused to subscribe.¹⁷³ In Nottinghamshire all justices present at the assembly to subscribe assented; but some were recorded as absent and their opinions were not known.¹⁷⁴ In Derbyshire, all justices within the county signed except three, Sir Thomas Fitzherbert, John Fitzherbert, and Francis Rollestone, who had been confined to Coventry.¹⁷⁵ In Wales, no returns were sent in

---

¹⁶⁵ S.P.12/60/39 (December 16, 1569), /39.2 (December 7, 1569).

¹⁶⁶ S.P.12/60/27 (December 10, 1569), /67/57, 57.1 (April 10, 1570). Arundell was bonded for £200 for his good behavior and appearance before the Council (S.P.12/67/57.2 [?April 10, 1570]).

¹⁶⁷ S.P.12/60/22 (December 6, 1569), /22.2 (November 19, 1569). Scudamore stated that he had not taken the Oath of Supremacy when he had become sheriff of Herefordshire, but had received a pardon for this offense. Both he and Thomas Havard preferred to be imprisoned than to give bonds.

¹⁶⁸ S.P.12/60/22 (December 6, 1569).   ¹⁶⁹ S.P.12/67/24 (March 18, 1570).

¹⁷⁰ S.P.12/60/63 (December 1569). The absentee was Lord Hastings of Loughborough.

¹⁷¹ S.P.12/59/22 (November 18, 1569).

¹⁷² S.P.12/60/21 (December 6, 1569), /21.1 [?December 6, ?1569].

¹⁷³ S.P.12/66/12 (January 11, 1570). Four justices of the peace were absent from the county and did not subscribe.

¹⁷⁴ S.P.12/59/20 (November 16, 1569).

¹⁷⁵ S.P.12/59/25.1 (n.d. [?November 22, 1569]). Sir Thomas Fitzherbert was reported a prisoner in the Fleet in April 1570 (S.P.12/67/86, April 30, 1570).

THE DORMANT YEARS OF CATHOLICISM

from Flint and Caernarvon, and only one Welsh justice elsewhere, Sir Thomas Stradling, refused to subscribe.[176]

In the capital and its immediate environs, Middlesex, Essex, and Surrey, the justices manifested complete loyalty, religiously and civilly, although some justices in Surrey and Essex were absent from the county or for some other reason did not attend the meetings of the justices to subscribe their names. Lord Morley objected to subscribing because of his rank, which was possibly a subterfuge, considering his known religious sentiments.[177]

This investigation shows that in the face of overt rebellion a sense of unity pervaded most of the realm; that persons of weight in local areas, outside of the regions in revolt, some of them perhaps practicing Catholics, cast off all restraints in showing the utmost loyalty to the Queen and her government. The number of refusals was small. Both Plowden and Stradling, for instance, although they demurred from signing because of conscience, admitted that they attended the prescribed legal form of worship, receiving communion according to that rite.[178] Plowden, in fact, worshiped in the Establishment until the publication of the papal bull excommunicating Elizabeth in 1570, holding that the ritual of the Established Church had not been condemned until then.[179]

In surveying the loyalty of the other classes throughout the realm, we find no evidence of arrests for either sedition or treason in East Anglia and the southeast. There is evidence of individual Catholics practicing their rites within the counties there, but the persons and the circumstances are too obscure to prove political dissatisfaction.[180] In Hampshire, where

---

[176] S.P.12/66/19 (January 22, 1570). The Council of the Marches of Wales further reported that "the countrey is and hath been in good order."

[177] S.P.12/59/21 (November 18, 1569), /21.1 (November 14, 1569), /45 (November 28, 1569), /60/53 (December 25, 1569), /53.2 (November 2 [?December 2], 1569). Lord Morley stated that if the Queen and Council would certify to him that they intended the nobility to subscribe to the statement of loyalty, he would make an answer satisfactory to them. S.P.12/59/21.2 (November 14, 1569) lists thirteen former justices of the peace of Middlesex now living outside of the shire, including the deposed Catholic Archbishop of York, Nicholas Heath; the deposed Abbot of Westminster, John Feckenham; Lord Loughborough; William Roper; and John Story.

[178] S.P.12/60/47 (December 22, 1569), /66/19.12 (December 21, 1569). Stradling explicitly stated that he received communion according to the Anglican rites; Plowden possibly implied it in his answer affirming his regular attendance at the liturgy of the Establishment.

[179] S.P.12/144/45 (December 2, 1580).

[180] S.P.12/71/61 [?July 28 (?August), 1570], /73/10 (August 10, 1570); S.P. 15/19/58 [?1570].

from other sources we know that considerable Catholicism existed under Elizabeth I, the assembled justices reported that some persons of standing, not presently or previously members of the commission of peace, were strongly suspect of opposition to the Established Church.[181] The assembly in Devonshire stated that that county was in a state of quiet and good order.[182] Cornwall also presented the same appearance.[183] In Oxfordshire there was no sign of unrest nor of political disobedience, but the celebration of mass there caused concern.[184] During the rebellion Gloucestershire remained loyal, but in June of 1570 a group of citizens of Cirencester protested against the prevalence of Catholic practices and sentiment in their community.[185] Leicestershire, although the Council demanded a report of its state every twenty days, was in good order;[186] and Nottinghamshire evinced no sentiment of Catholic revolt.[187]

Even in northern England the rebellion was sectional, and the government did not press the question of disloyalty beyond the areas directly engaged. In the spring of 1570, when the last embers of rebellion were dying out, Queen Elizabeth did not fear hostile results when she permitted the ecclesiastical commission to continue to repress recusancy in Lancashire.[188] Less than a year later Bishop Downman of Chester was directed by the Queen and the Council to answer to the Archbishop of Canterbury concerning his negligent administration of his diocese, since reports of disorders in Lancashire had come to the attention of the government.[189] During the following spring the Archbishop of York enjoined the new Bishop of Carlisle, Richard Barnes, to make a visitation of Downman's diocese.[190] He already possessed some knowledge of it; in the previous October he had reported a considerable contrast between his own jurisdiction and that of Chester. The diocese of Carlisle was conformable; the lower classes of Westmorland and Cumberland were more so than the upper classes of Yorkshire, excepting certain individuals and the area of the Lowlands. Lancashire, however, presented the opposite picture. Recusancy, reconciliations to Catholicism, and contempt for

[181] S.P.12/59/46 (November 28, 1569). [182] S.P. 12/60/39 (December 16, 1569).
[183] S.P. 12/60/27 (December 10, 1569). [184] S.P.12/67/76 (April 28, 1570).
[185] S.P.12/71/30 (June 1570). [186] S.P.12/60/63 (December 1569).
[187] S.P.12/59/20 (November 16, 1569). [188] S.P.12/67/38 (March 31, 1570).
[189] A.P.C., VII, 399 (November 12, 1570); VIII, 5 (January 14, 1571).
[190] A.P.C., VIII, 26 (May 12-14, 1571). The Earl of Derby was directed to assist Bishop Barnes in his visitation of the diocese of Chester (*ibid.*, 28, May 12-14, 1571).

the Establishment were widespread; and the priests responsible for this were maintained by the laity.[191]

That Lancashire constituted a strong center of Catholicism the whole reign of Elizabeth attests. That the Catholics of this county flagrantly disregarded the religious laws is equally true. But despite the bishop's report, in civil matters the county always remained loyal, because no feudal loyalties bound the people to the rebel lords who elsewhere were responsible for the debacle of 1569–1570, and the enforcement of the religious laws under the regime of Bishop Downman was never severe. The question of loyalty was not raised either by the central government or by the local authorities, and there was no need to. No matter what rumors of rebellion came out of Lancashire, they never took tangible shape; and as a result we must distrust the sources of such information.[192]

Wales, far distant from the capital and under the jurisdiction of a special council, evinced loyalty and internal quiet, but also sympathy for Catholic practices. As we have seen, the justices in all counties but two, Flint and Caernarvon, obediently subscribed to a statement of loyalty during the Northern Rebellion; negligence on the part of local officials probably accounted for the failure of those two counties to return statements of loyalty. Bishop Richard Davies of St. David's twice reported, in December 1569 and January 1570, that no recusancy, neither nonattendance at church services nor nonreception of communion, existed within his jurisdiction. Many, however, lacked sincerity, some out of irreligiousness and some out of attachment to the Roman Church. The retention of Catholic practices was strongly evident, about which nothing could be done without the establishment of an ecclesiastical commission and without more conscientious enforcement of the laws by the judges of the assizes, whose example and influence over the people was great.[193] In the following November, Bishop Thomas Davies of St. Asaph sent in a statement, more optimistic in tone, concerning his diocese. It was now more obedient in religion than at the time of his appointment, although some were still of "corrupt religion" and could not be seized. The fault, as in other similar cases, lay in the remissness of the civil au-

[191] S.P.12/74/22 (October 27, 1570).
[192] *Ibid.;* S.P.15/15/113 (December 20, 1569), /19/16.1 (October 16, 1570).
[193] S.P.12/66/26.1 (January 25, 1570).

thorities, although they shared this blame with the ecclesiastical officers.[194] The Bishop of Llandaff, Hugh Jones, reported at the same time that no one in his diocese forbore to come to church or to receive communion.[195] However, the Bishop of Bangor, Nicholas Robinson, told the Council in May 1570 that a funeral service savoring of the old ritual had taken place at Beaumaris, in the previous January,[196] which should not have occasioned surprise in view of the long-standing predilection in Wales for many practices of the old church.

The capital, London, with a Protestant majority, had neither dissenting justices, as we have seen, nor sympathy for the rebellion. Some Catholic prisoners, already confined in London, were retained there,[197] and some of the captured Northern rebels were placed in the Tower,[198] showing that the government feared no popular effort would be made to rescue them in the capital.

In 1569, at the order of Sir William Cecil, an inquisition was held whether the members of the various Inns of Court attended the services of the Establishment, received communion as prescribed by law, or worshiped according to the Catholic rites.[199] In the Inner Temple five barristers, Thomas Bawde, Robert Atkinson, Arden (or Ardell) Waferer, Thomas Greenwood, and Andrew Grey, were questioned and three others absented themselves. None of these was a confirmed recusant in regard to church services. All five had had scruples about receiving communion; three — Bawde, Atkinson, and Greenwood — had previously received only when directly enjoined by the ecclesiastical commissioners; two — Waferer and Grey — had never received communion, but Grey now offered to do so. Grey also denied having worshiped according to Catholic rites; Bawde and Atkinson had not done so since being cited before the ecclesiastical commission eight or nine years previously; Waferer and Greenwood asked not to be questioned, because the offence was punishable by a penal statute.[200] Later Atkinson, Bawde and Waferer were expelled from the Inner Temple because of their recusancy. Andrew Grey, after some hesitation, conformed.[201] Three others, Lewes, Pollard, and

[194] S.P.12/74/37 (November 17, 1570).
[195] S.P.12/66/29 (February 5, 1570; endorsed according to Julian calendar, January 26, 1569). Two persons did not receive communion because "they cannot frame themselves yt to be in cherytye."
[196] S.P.12/69/14 (May 24, 1570).   [197] S.P.12/67/93 [?April 1570]
[198] Ibid.   [199] S.P.12/60/70 (1569).
[200] Ibid.   [201] S.P.12/118/69 (November 1577).

John Grey, failed to appear when summoned;[202] the first two discontinued their membership with the Inner Temple; Pollard, apparently, eventually went to the Continent.[203] In the Middle Temple four members were cited, but only Richard Palmer appeared. He denied nonattendance at the services of the Establishment, but admitted never having received communion. On oath he denied going to any Catholic rites within the previous twelve months, but he would confess to nothing further while sworn.[204] Three other members, James Gardiner, James Wyse, and William Tempest, failed to make their appearance;[205] they never conformed and were expelled from the Middle Temple.[206] In Lincoln's Inn five barristers — Roger Corham, Gerard Lother, Henry Harper, John Bown and Thomas Egerton — were questioned. Only one, John Bown, seemed at all remiss in attending the services of the Establishment. All had received communion, but Bown could produce no certificate, and another, Gerard Lother, had received only twice during Elizabeth's reign. Roger Corham refused to answer whether he had attended Catholic rites, because it would incriminate him, being prohibited by a penal statute; John Bown admitted that long before he had worshiped according to the old religion and had been shriven; Gerard Lother and Henry Harper had not worshiped in any manner to come within the purview of the law, and had never attended any Catholic services.[207] In May 1569 all five — Corham, Lother, Harper, Bown and Egerton — were disbarred by order of the Star Chamber; later Lother, Harper, and Egerton conformed and were readmitted to the practice of their profession.[208] In Gray's Inn three barristers, Walter Norton, Richard Godfrey, and Mark Oglethorpe, were questioned, and two others absented themselves. Walter Norton claimed that he was remiss in attendance at worship due to the pressure of business; Richard Godfrey attended irregularly because of a "scruple in conscience"; while Mark Oglethorpe, a new member, had always obeyed the law. Godfrey could not with certainty remember having ever received communion; Oglethorpe "by reason of certain scruples in his conscience" had not received in recent years; Norton had

---

[202] S.P.12/60/70 (1569). [203] S.P.12/118/69 (November 1577).
[204] S.P.12/60/70 (1569). Edmund Plowden, the eminent barrister and Catholic leader, was a member of the Middle Temple. Because of his known conformity, he escaped coming within the purview of this inquisition.
[205] Ibid. [206] S.P.12/118/68 (November 1577).
[207] S.P.12/60/70 (1569). [208] S.P.12/118/70 (November 1577).

communicated up to the last two or three years. Norton also affirmed that he had not heard mass since the beginning of Elizabeth's reign, and pleaded immunity to avoid a reply concerning other Catholic practices; Godfrey pleaded immunity to answering any question concerning his acts of worship according to the Catholic rites; Oglethorpe had not heard mass within the time prohibited by law, and not since he and other members of the Inns had last been questioned by the ecclesiastical commissioners concerning attendance at the forbidden ritual.[209] Later both Norton and Godfrey were expelled from Gray's Inn because of their recusancy; Godfrey, upon conforming, was restored again.[210] Two other members, Thomas Persall and Ralph Worsley, absented themselves when summoned;[211] they were later expelled from membership in Gray's Inn.[212]

The Northern Rebellion of 1569 was the only armed protest by any considerable number of Catholics against the Elizabethan regime, and they were only a portion of those still adhering to the Roman Church. Thomas Harding, a fugitive at Louvain, had praised Elizabeth in 1565 for her moderate treatment of Catholics despite bloody laws.[213] Nor did he, the most influential English Catholic writer of the decade, promote rebellion through his books, although they were devoted to a defense of papal, as opposed to royal, supremacy in religion. Reports of the Spanish ambassadors and also of others of the middle and late 1560's indicated Catholic dissatisfaction with Elizabeth's religious policy and a hope on the part of some of the English Catholics of a foreign invasion to reestablish the traditional church.[214] The diplomatic dispatches, however, fail, as always, to present definite information concerning how many Catholics supported such a course of action, especially at the end of the

[209] S.P.12/60/70 (1569). [210] S.P.12/118/71 (November 1577).
[211] S.P.12/60/70 (1569). [212] S.P.12/118/71 (November 1577).
[213] Thomas Harding, *A Confutation of a Booke Intituled An Apologie of the Church of England* (Antwerp, 1565), *2v-*3v. We have used the copy in the Bodleian Library, Oxford. Harding, a Protestant under Edward VI, had returned to Catholicism under Mary Tudor. During the reign of Elizabeth I, until his death in (?) 1568, he lived in exile at the University of Louvain, where he was a noted Catholic apologist.
[214] Cf. (as typical examples): S.P.12/44/56 (December 20, 1567), /115/43 (n.d. [?August ?1577]); S.P.15/13/25 (August 28, 1566; Isle of Guernsey); *Cal. S.P. Span.*, I, 369-370 (July 22, 1564), 662 (July 26, 1567); the ambassador was Don Guzman de Silva; II, 139 (April 2, 1569); 157 (May 31, June 1, 1569); the ambassador, Don Guerau de Spes, had an unhappy career of futile intrigues in England.

sixties. Once again we must express our doubt that the Spanish ambassador had a wide circle of contacts or that his influence was very widespread outside of London or beyond some of the upper-class adherents of the older church.

On the basis of our evidence we must conclude that neither in the Northern Rebellion nor in the unsettled years immediately following it did the majority of Catholics evince disloyalty to the Elizabethan regime on a nationwide scale. Certain areas, it is true, although never engaged in rebellion, manifested during the 1560's and later a determined intention to maintain the Roman religion, but that was the limit of their opposition to the policies of the Queen.

In further assessing the framework of Catholic political thinking it is significant to note that in 1567 Archbishop Parker questioned two imprisoned Marian ecclesiastics of standing, Bishop Thirlby of Ely and John Boxall, former Dean of Windsor Castle, about the legitimate right of subjects to rebel against their sovereigns, to which they replied in the negative.[215] And during a progress into Berkshire the next year the Queen allowed a known Marian priest to approach her and state his loyalty, pointing this out to the Spanish ambassador.[216]

The key to this pattern of fidelity lay in the fact that Elizabeth was a crowned and anointed monarch; contemporary opinion generally opposed revolt against a legitimate ruler, and the strong nationalism of the period afforded an emotional support. These seem to have been the factors which, in contemporary Catholic thinking, overrode the force of Pius V's bull, *Regnans in Excelsis,* which condemned obedience to Elizabeth as England's lawful sovereign. Many, otherwise faithful to the Roman Church, simply disregarded this decree; some, also faithful, doubted either its validity or its binding power; a few went abroad, preferring to sacrifice what they possessed than to render obedience to an excommunicated monarch.[217] But no solution could solve the dilemma which the bull created and which was to remain throughout the rest of the reign, a vexing and embittering problem — the need for a redefinition of Cath-

---

[215] *Cal. S.P. Span.,* I, 682 (November 1, 1567). Boxall had also been secretary to Mary Tudor.

[216] *Cal. S.P. Span.,* II, 51 (July 10, 1568).

[217] C.P.6/107–108 (November 2, 1571); *Cal. S.P. Span.,* II, 252 (June 11, 17, 22, 1570). A copy of the bull is at the Public Record Office, S.P.12/49/53: *Datum Romae apud S. Petrum, Anno incarnationis Dominiçe millesimo quingentesimo sexagesimo nono, Quinto Kl. Martii, Pontificatus nostri anno quinto.*

olic loyalty. Wisely, however, Elizabeth rarely pressed this point if Catholic laymen otherwise showed themselves obedient.

The leaders of the Northern Rebellion referred the question of an uprising to two theologians who advised that subjects could not lawfully rebel against an anointed prince unless he had been excommunicated by the pope.[218] An opinion given from another source held that when Elizabeth, early in her reign, had refused to receive the two papal legates, Parpaglia and Martinengo, she had automatically incurred excommunication.[219] This latter judgment, the lack of evidence attests, did not prevail among Catholics since they had never acted upon it; the first view, that of the two theologians, received additional emphasis from their further opinion that a decree of excommunication of the Queen, in order to be valid for Englishmen, had to be published within the realm.[220]

The visit of Nicholas Morton to England in 1569, bearing a papal commission to reconcile lapsed Catholics, to some degree strengthened the Catholic ranks.[221] Much or little can be made of this mission in regard to the subsequent uprising, since the evidence is not conclusive whether Morton gave assurance that a papal bull was about to be issued condemning Elizabeth or whether he promoted a rebellion. Francis Norton, one of the Northern rebels, asserted that Morton was a prime mover of the revolt;[222] the Earl of Northumberland claimed that Morton's visit was purely spiritual, that he intended only to reconcile lapsed Catholics who could not otherwise be absolved from schism due to lack of priests.[223] A certain degree of activity in reconciling Catholics through clergy in communion with Rome must be noted in the late 1560's,[224] but Nor-

---

[218] S.P.15/21/56.1 (1569, date in hand of Sir William Cecil [?June 13, ?1572]).
[219] S.P.15/21/56.1 [?June 13, ?1572].
[220] *Ibid*. This testimony of the Earl of Northumberland in (?)1571 indicates that in the immediate post-rebellion England, despite the bull, there was no definitive opinion among Catholics concerning the legitimacy of Elizabeth's title nor of the right to revolt against her, nor was there any widespread questioning of her title or desire to rise up against her.
[221] S.P.15/21/29 (April 2, 1572), /21/56.1 [?June 13, ?1572]; C.P.6/147 (November 29, 1571).
[222] S.P.15/21/29 (April 2, 1572).
[223] S.P.15/21/56.1 [?June 13, ?1572], Northumberland stated that Morton had once been at his house, and while there had mentioned no bull of excommunication and no promise of aid from the pope.
[224] The Queen's decree against priests in Lancashire and other evidence in this chapter proves this. Nevertheless, we must note Morton's lament at the lack of competent priests to whom he could give authority to reconcile persons who desired to return to Catholicism (S.P.15/21/56.1 [?June 13, ?1572]).

thumberland's strong faith at least in part was due, as was that of other Catholics, to the writings of such exiled theologians as Harding, Sander, and Stapleton.[225]

When the bull of excommunication became known in England, the government hastened to question some important Catholics concerning their opinion of it. Despite official alarm, the authorities could take consolation from the lack of clear thinking on the part of Catholics and their obvious confusion. The Earl of Northumberland pleaded inexact knowledge;[226] the Earl of Southampton followed the advice of the Scottish Bishop of Ross that the bull obligated in conscience only if the pope took steps to enforce it. This was the duty, not of subjects, but of Christian princes: until they acted, Englishmen with a safe conscience could obey Elizabeth in temporal, but not in spiritual, matters. The bull, the bishop further counseled, did not bind in conscience under prevailing circumstances.[227]

John Felton, who affixed a copy of the papal decree to the gate of the Bishop of London's palace, represented a rare exception — one of the few persons who attempted to see the purpose of the bull effected within England. The Spanish ambassador reported some arrests immediately following Felton's act,[228] and Bishop Barnes of Carlisle reported of Lancashire in 1570 that after the excommunication had become known there, persons of importance refused to worship according to the legally prescribed ritual.[229] But there is little contemporary evidence from other sources either of Catholic unrest or disloyalty due to Pius V's decree or of a harsh repression of the Catholics as a body in these first years of the 1570's.

The Elizabethan government, as time proved, acted judiciously. It did not dragoon the Catholics and press the question of the bull upon them. The Queen, too, allayed fears and perhaps strengthened the bonds of Catholic loyalty by promising to institute no inquisition into consciences for matters of religion, but asked only that her subjects be obedient to the laws concerning the Established Church.[230] During the years 1570 to

[225] S.P.15/21/63 (June 24, 1572). [226] S.P.15/21/56.1 [?June 13, ?1572].
[227] C.P.6/107–108 (November 2, 1571).
[228] *Cal. S.P. Span.*, II, 251–252 (June 11, 17, 22, 1570), 257 (June 30, 1570), 269 (August 12, 1570).
[229] S.P.12/74/22 (October 27, 1570): S.P.15/19/16.1 (October 16, 1570).
[230] S.P.12/71/16 (n.d. [?1569])

1573 this promise was kept, probably setting to rest any further thought of revolt and removing any excuse for foreign intervention. Otherwise, the pattern of the 1560's continued with no relaxation. For instance, travel abroad, as always, was restricted and those going overseas were scrutinized carefully to discover if they held Catholic or other suspected sympathies.[231] But such limitations were normal to the age, and imposed no unusual hardships on adherents of the older faith.

To prevent possible future trouble by Catholics, to plug loopholes in the existing laws, and to strengthen the hands of the authorities, Parliament in 1571 enacted certain further measures regulating Catholics, which at first were probably intended to be a threat held over their heads, rather than to inaugurate a more repressive policy. One act forbade any subject to declare that Queen Elizabeth was a heretic, a schismatic, or a usurper.[232] Another act forbade anyone to obtain, circulate, or make use of papal bulls, and prohibited any subject to reconcile others to Rome or to be reconciled.[233] Each of these laws defined as high treason the violation of its terms, and the latter defined as misprision of treason the concealment of knowledge of persuasion to reconcile or be reconciled to Rome. The penalties of the statute of praemunire were to be inflicted on those who aided offenders against the second act or who introduced certain popularly used Catholic articles into the realm.[234]

During the years 1571, 1572, and 1573, the government continued to concern itself both with repression of recusancy and with prevention of contacts between Catholics inside the realm and those abroad. Worship at the embassies remained forbidden, and the Spanish embassy was surrounded on the Feast of the Purification in 1571, but only some Spaniards were arrested.[235] In 1572 the first priests trained at Douai arrived in the realm. The following year, 1573, a second group came over; probably as a result of this, the Queen issued a proclamation enjoining conformity, and various of the bishops were ordered to effect this.[236] Although these priests were at first too few and too unobtrusive to command great attention, their presence, it is evident, caused increasing alarm to the gov-

[231] *A.P.C.*, VII, 369 (June 22, 1570), 381–382 (August 3, 1570), 384 (August 17, 1570); VIII, 105 (May 12, 1573), 118–119 (June 24, 1573), 129 (July 12, 1573), 130 (July 14, 1573), 139 (November 2, 1573).
[232] 13 Eliz. c. 1.   [233] 13 Eliz. c. 2.
[234] 13 Eliz. c. 1, c. 2.
[235] *Cal. S.P. Span.*, II, 293 (February 6, 1571)
[236] *A.P.C.*, VIII, 140 (November 8, 1573).

THE DORMANT YEARS OF CATHOLICISM

ernment, which became vigilant without being noticeably repressive. During the same year some law students of Irish birth were imprisoned for hearing mass at the Portuguese embassy.[237] At this time, too, the leading Catholics who were prisoners solely for religion were placed in the castle of Wisbeach on the Isle of Ely, because of their efforts to maintain others in their religious beliefs.[238]

The Council, busy as it was, took personal notice of individual instances of recusancy during the early years of the 1570's and more so later in the decade. It committed John Baker to the custody of the ecclesiastical commission in February 1573[239] and Lord Stourton to the care of the Archbishop of Canterbury in April, after that peer had attempted to flee the realm for religion.[240] The son of Lord Morley, a Catholic peer who had left England for the same reason, was committed at the beginning of May to the Warden of the Fleet to be kept a close prisoner, presumably because of religion or possibly as a hostage for the return of his father.[241] On the other hand, the Council during that month mitigated the conditions of the imprisonment of Sir Thomas Gerrard, a prominent Catholic layman who was laboring under suspicion of treasonable actions, permitting him to return to his house in Aldgate in order to recover his health.[242] That conciliar body also directed the ecclesiatical commission to consider the sufficiency of the submission of Dr. [?Edward] Atslow (or Atlowe), a quondam Catholic, whose imprisonment it had previously ordered.[243]

---

[237] *A.P.C.*, VIII, 110 (June 1, 1573). The students were released upon giving bonds for their good behavior.
[238] *A.P.C.*, VIII, 73 (March 11, 1571). Many of the leading Catholics, and those considered dangerous to the realm, were confined at Wisbeach Castle in subsequent years.
[239] *A.P.C.*, VIII, 84 (February 22, 1573).
[240] *A.P.C.*, VIII, 92 (March 30, 1573), 96 (April 12, 1573), 168 (December 16, 1573), 169 (December 19, 1573). Apparently, upon arrest Lord Stourton temporarily conformed (*ibid.*, 96, April 12, 1573); he was confined to the care of the Archbishop of Canterbury for further instruction. On December 19, 1573, the Council strongly demanded his conformity and took bonds of him of £2000 and the same sum of two sureties (*ibid.*, 169, December 19, 1573; 195, February 17, 1574).
[241] *A.P.C.*, VIII, 101 (April 30, 1573); S.P.12/73/42 (August 31, 1570), /89/16 [?September 29, 1572], /91/11 (March 4, 1572); S.P.15/21/58 (June 17, 1572); *Cal. S.P. Span.*, II, 247 (June 8, 1570).
[242] *A.P.C.*, VIII, 108 (May 29, 1573). Gerrard was shortly afterward allowed to walk in the adjoining neighborhood for his health (*ibid.*, 114–115, June 14, 1573).
[243] *A.P.C.*, VIII, 173 (December 26, 1573); *Dictionary of National Biography*, (New York, 1908–1909), I, 705. Doctor [?Edward] Atslow is listed as a prisoner

Between 1571 and 1573 Yorkshire, much desolated and demoralized by the late rebellion, remained quiet.[244] Archbishop Grindal took his duties at York very seriously, winning the approval of the president of the Council of the North, the Earl of Huntingdon.[245] Both of these officials recognized the need of severity to effect conformity: the archbishop advised the imposition of heavier pecuniary fines, since they would rub harshly against the northern grain;[246] the president advised a strict administration of justice, the displacement of Catholic justices of the peace, and better preaching of the Gospel.[247] The Council of the North realized the serious proportions of the Catholic problem: they sent to the justices of the peace questions for a survey of Catholicism and recusancy in the north — all recusants and known or suspected Catholics were to be reported.[248] This zeal of the president and the archbishop did not pass unnoticed on the part of the authorities in London: the long tenure of the Earl of Huntingdon in the presidency of the Council of the North and the ultimate promotion of Archbishop Grindal from York to Canterbury prove this.

Elsewhere in the north conditions were quiet, although recusancy was evident. The diocese of Durham, whose bishop held strong civil powers, continued to cause worry to the incumbent, James Pilkington. A main source of recalcitrancy, so persistent at this period as earlier in 1564, was the influence of refugees at Louvain, whose beliefs had been greatly strengthened by the theological writings and teachings at that institution, the intellectual center of Catholicism in northern Europe.[249] Carlisle, the neighboring diocese, presented little outward evidence of nonconformity except in a few areas.[250] To the south recusancy manifested itself at this

---

in 1575 (*A.P.C.*, VIII, 390, May 22, 1575; 396, June 10, 1575). Presumably Atlowe and Atslowe are variations of the same name. The Council's treatment of Catholics varied. Robert Cooke, a priest imprisoned for three years, petitioned for liberty of the place where he was confined, because close confinement had impaired his health (C.P.159/68, 1572). On the other hand, the deposed Catholic Archbishop of York, Nicholas Heath, in a letter to Lord Burghley praised the kindly treatment he had received from Queen Elizabeth (S.P.12/92/28, September 22, 1573).

[244] S.P.15/20/70 (September 6, 1571). [245] S.P.15/21/103 (December 21, 1572).
[246] S.P.12/88/5 (June 2, 1572).
[247] S.P.15/21/103 (December 21, 1572), /111 (December 28, 1572).
[248] S.P.15/21/111.1 (n.d. [?December 28, ?1572]).
[249] S.P.12/81/48 (October 15, 1571).
[250] S.P.15/20/84 (October 20, 1571), /21/65 (June 30, 1572).

time in Gloucestershire, which the Council ordered to be punished;[251] and that body took steps against similar refractoriness in Oxfordshire, ruling that books contrary to the Establishment should be seized.[252]

Of as great importance to the government in the 1570's as in the 1560's in determining sheriffs and justices of the peace was a knowledge of the religious attitudes of citizens of substance within a shire. We find evidences of such concern at this time in appointing sheriffs in Wales, where episcopal advice weighed heavily in the recommendations of the Council of the Marches of Wales, which at all costs wanted men known for "sowndnes in Religion and well affected to further the procedinge thereof." [253]

[251] *A.P.C.*, VIII, 132 (July 19, 1573). The Council did not further specify the nature of the recusancy (Catholic or Protestant) nor the recusants.
[252] *A.P.C.*, VIII, 120 (June 28, 1573). The Council did not further specify the nature of the recusancy (Catholic or Protestant) nor the recusants.
[253] S.P.12/90/3 (November 20, 1572).

CHAPTER II

THE ATTEMPTED REVIVIFICATION OF CATHOLICISM

1574–1583

1. INITIAL OFFICIAL REACTION, 1574–1577

BEGINNING in 1574 the government became stricter in its drive to eliminate Catholicism from the realm. It was cognizant of the threat represented by Englishmen, trained to the priesthood abroad, who returned home in order to revivify the ancient faith, and of the potential influence such missionaries, if very numerous, might exercise in areas and among families still strongly Catholic. These priests constituted, also, a menace to the success and even to the existence of that church which resulted from the Elizabethan Settlement of 1559. From a political viewpoint the clergy of a proscribed religion, educated in the territories of a monarch whose relations with Elizabeth were rapidly deteriorating, represented in her eyes and in the eyes of her government, a questionable and even a subversive element, deliberately undermining the Protestant orientation of the realm. Alarmed, Elizabeth and her councillors now decided that they must broaden the scope of their treatment of Catholics, and that they must make a more concerted effort to induce lay conformity: the active practice of Catholicism should be prevented; the new missionaries should be arrested and imprisoned. From 1574 onward the government ceased imprisoning and fining the lay Catholics haphazardly and began a consistent drive of penalization, which in intensity and severity lasted until the end of the reign.

As England's relations with Spain became more hostile and bitterness between England and the Holy See became more intense, Elizabeth and her Council became increasingly suspicious that the Continental-trained priests represented a traitorous group, either actually or potentially. Although they were hunted down and imprisoned or exiled or executed, the laity who were known to have received the sacerdotal ministrations of priests and to have entertained them in their houses and to have associated closely with them were rarely considered thereby to have become colored with a suspicion of treason. Very few lay Catholics suffered death upon a charge of committing a treasonable act that today might be looked upon only as an act connected with the practice of religion. The usual charge leveled against laymen, no matter how fervently Catholic, was civil disobedience, disobedience to the statutes of Parliament regulating public worship, the penalty for which was not death, but fine and imprisonment.

Neither the Council nor the Catholics had any clear idea how many adherents of the traditional church still remained in the realm. The former made repeated checks in the years to come to be more certain about this dissident group; the latter, having no other point of unity than a common faith, seem to have had little knowledge of their numbers. A privately made census of 1574, apparently of Catholic authorship but made for reasons which we can only conjecture, listed twenty-one members of noble families, forty-eight knights, and over five hundred other persons, note also being made of refugees overseas.[1] From this time onward a definite record will gradually emerge from many sources, telling us over the years more precisely who the leading Catholics were, where they lived, and what their status was.

Wherever strong concentrations of Catholics were found, Elizabeth I and her councillors drew up special instructions for their control or sup-

---

[1] S.P.12/99/55 (1574). The document is entitled "Catholickes in Inglonde 1574." That it is of Catholic authorship is proved by a reference to Protestants as "Heretikes." The list is of value because it contains both the names and the counties of residence of many known Catholics. The purpose of this census must be judged from internal criteria. *Misc.,* VIII, 86–87, suggests that it is a list of the supporters of Mary, Queen of Scots, made by one of her English adherents. Certainly, it is a private, not an official census. It is given *in extenso* in the same volume, pp. 89–138, with explanatory notes

pression. During 1574 the Council of the North was directed to assist the local bishops in enforcing the religious laws more strictly;[2] the Inns of Court were forbidden to maintain any nonconforming members;[3] the Council of the Marches of Wales was charged to see that the Welsh bishops performed their episcopal functions, since an evident laxity prevailed there;[4] and twice, in the summer and in the autumn, directives were sent for effecting conformity in Lancashire, "the very sincke of Poperie," where a considerable number of reconciliations to Rome were suspected.[5] At the end of March or the beginning of April 1574, more than likely on Palm Sunday, a raid was carried out in London at a house where mass was being celebrated: the priests were imprisoned; the lay worshipers were freed on bond.[6] Other masses and other Catholic religious activities were also reported in various places;[7] a spy related the news, very

---

[2] S.P.15/23/59 (May 1574). The Privy Council in late 1574 commended Archbishop Grindal for his efforts to induce conformity (*A.P.C.*, VIII, 317, November 22, 1574).

[3] *A.P.C.*, VIII, 246–247 (May 31, 1574).

[4] S.P.12/97/21 (June 1574). The Queen apparently suspected the religious sympathies of members of the Council of the Marches of Wales, because they were ordered to swear to the following oath if transferred to another position under the jurisdiction of that council: "You shall swear to the uttermost of your power, will, and cunning, you shall be true and faithful to the Queen's Highness, our Sovereign Lady, and to her heirs and successors, and that you do utterly testify and declare in your conscience, that the Queen's Highness is the only Supreme Governor of this realm and of all other Her Highness's dominions and countries, as well in all spiritual or ecclesiastical things or causes, as temporal. And that no foreign prince, person, prelate, state, or potentate hath or ought to have any jurisdiction, power, superiority, preheminence, or authority ecclesiastical or spiritual within this realm: And therefore, you do utterly renounce and forsake all foreign jurisdiction, powers, superiorities, and authorities."

[5] *A.P.C.*, VIII, 258 (June 28, 1574), 276–277 (July 27, 1574), 317 (November 22, 1574).

[6] *A.P.C.*, 218 (April 4, 1574).

[7] *Cal. S.P. Span.*, II, 477 (April 5, 1574: mention of three raids of houses where Palm Sunday masses were being celebrated, including the house of Lady Morley, whose husband was a refugee in Flanders); S.P.12/97/27 [?July 6, 1574], /98/10 [?August 13, 1574], /136/64 (March 17, 1580: letter from Antonio Fogaça to Duke of Guise, dated December 24, 1575, apparently written from England and referring to Catholic worship within the realm); *A.P.C.*, VIII, 270 (July 17, 1574), 314 (November 17, 1574); IX, 255–256 (December 23, 1576), 329–330 (April 22, 1577). Queen Elizabeth had granted the fines from certain Catholics to Henry Carye and a Mr. Lidcote. Those who would not pay the fines and make composition were to remain in prison. Among those arrested was Lady Browne, wife of Sir Christopher Browne (*A.P.C.*, VIII, 270, July 17, 1574), who was a known recusant in the 1560's. Apparently she conformed in 1578 (*ibid.*, X, 204, April 9, 1578). A Mistress Cawker (or Cawkon), a favorite of Queen Mary Tudor, had

unwelcome to the officials, that the deposed Archbishop of York, Nicholas Heath, would celebrate the Roman rites on a subsequent Sunday at his residence.[8]

The authorities accumulated considerable evidence during the mid-1570's of other Catholic practices — the possession of spiritual writings and of blessed objects, oftentimes smuggled in from the Continent, and the maintenance of communications between Catholics in England and on the Continent.[9] Repeated reports of Catholic beliefs persisting, which were sent in by the bishops, magistrates, and spies, reflect the strengthening of official activity and the increasing official fear of a revival of the old faith, since now it was obvious that the traditional worship was more widespread than in the previous years of Elizabeth's reign.

In 1575 and 1576 the government ordered the ejection of Catholics from the commissions of peace.[10] It took careful note of the report of Lord Chief Justice Wray that an active Catholicism existed in Suffolk and Norfolk.[11] The Privy Council, recognizing that the same condition continued to exist in the north, sent more explicit orders to the authori-

---

also had mass celebrated in her house and possessed a large library of Catholic books (S.P.12/98/10 [?August 13, 1574]). Both S.P.12/97/27 and S.P.12/98/10 are the reports of a spy, David (Davye) Jones. Lady Tregonwell was arrested in 1577 for having mass celebrated in her house (*A.P.C.*, IX, 329–330, April 22, 1577); in 1580 she and her family conformed (*A.P.C.*, XII, 132–133, August 5, 1580).

[8] S.P.12/97/27 [?July 6, 1574]. A number of reports concerning the nonjuring Marian clergy come to light at this time. Latymer, an old priest, was reported to have been in prison for fourteen years; he was currently in the Clink, one of the prisons of metropolitan London (S.P.12/97/39, July 20, 1574). The Council in August of 1574 ordered the release of three priests arrested for saying mass during the last Lent (*A.P.C.*, VIII, 287, August 26, 1574). One Woode, probably Thomas Wood, an old-time Marian priest, was in prison in 1575 (*ibid.*, 388, May 15, 1575). John Peal (or Peel or Pele), who had functioned in secret as a priest for sixteen years, went in 1576 to the seminary at Douai to refresh his knowledge of theology (*The First and Second Diaries of the English College, Douay*, Fathers of the Congregation of the London Oratory, eds. [London, 1878], 104, May 12, 1576).

[9] S.P.12/105/55 (October 17, 1575), /56 [?1575], /57 (1575), /58 [?November 10, 1575], /59 [?1575], /60 [?November 10, 1575], /108/40 (June 9, 1576); S.P.15/23/47 (March 18, 1574); *A.P.C.*, VIII, 266 (July 11, 1574), 396–397 (June 13, 1575); IX, 53–54 (November 27, 1575), 248 (December 13, 1576), 256 (December 23, 1576), 269 (January 18, 1577).

[10] *A.P.C.*, IX, 49 (November 14, 1575), 233 (November 18, 1576), 238 (December 2, 1576), 257 (December 27, 1576). These four citations from the *Acts of the Privy Council* have obvious relation to the Catholics while not specifically referring to them. Thomas Carew, who, judging from his family name, was probably a Catholic, was restored to the position of justice of the peace upon reception of communion (*ibid.*, 257, December 27, 1576).

[11] C.P.160/102 (August 2 [?1576]).

ties there concerning what measures they were to take.¹² Since priests had found refuge in the Middle Marches, carrying out their functions in districts where the Catholic population protected them and the local magistrates were lax in proceeding against them, the Earl of Huntingdon, Lord President of the North, and Sir John Forster, Warden of the Middle Marches, were enjoined by the Council to assist in apprehending these fugitives.¹³ A report concerning Lancashire laid the failure of the Establishment in that county to the need both of more justices of the peace and of justices who more sincerely adhered to the state church, to an insufficiency of ecclesiastical officials, to the partiality of the lesser magistrates in prosecuting violations of the laws, and to slackness in enforcing laws against priests.¹⁴ A report concerning Essex, naming names, gave similar information how the lesser officials disregarded the laws.¹⁵ The intent of the central government was not lost, for the Bishop of Chichester complained, probably in the spring of 1577, that harshness by the local ordinaries in Kent, Surrey, and Hampshire had caused recusants to flee into his diocese.¹⁶

The extent of official fear is shown by a proposal of Bishop Aylmer of London, alarmed, as he said, by the increase both in the number of Catholics and in the extent of recusancy; imprisonment simply reduced their household expenses and thereby enriched them. He and the Archbishop of Canterbury, after conferring with their episcopal colleagues, had decided that a more effective punishment would be a heavy fine for nonreception of communion, which, by impoverishing the Catholics, would reduce them in status and influence.¹⁷ However, the imposition of a fine for a religious offense ran into legal difficulties, since hitherto such an ecclesiastical penalty had not been clearly determined in law. An opinion

---

¹² *A.P.C.*, IX, 203 (September 13, 14, 1576); S.P.15/25/6 (March 24, 1577). The Privy Council directed the Earl of Huntingdon to send to it the names and accusations against obstinate recusants in the north; the Earl was also given directions concerning the treatment of women prisoners for religion.

¹³ *A.P.C.*, X, 79–80 (November 10, 1577).

¹⁴ S.P.12/120/21 [?1577]. The report, entitled "The imperfections of our state of Government in Lancashire," complains of "the halting of our conformable justices."

¹⁵ S.P.12/120/26 [?1577]. The report, which was anonymous, was entitled "An advertisement touching certain Papists dwelling in Essex."

¹⁶ S.P.12/112/30 (n.d. [?1577]). The Bishop of Chichester, Richard Curteys, sent several reports to Westminster, all of them indicating considerable recalcitrancy within his diocese.

¹⁷ S.P.12/114/22 (June 21, 1577).

of the attorney general, formulated after consultation with various judges, lawyers, and canonists, now held that the Act of Supremacy, vesting ecclesiastical jurisdiction in the Crown, included authority to punish crimes affecting religious law by mulct or by other means, since this appertained to the royal prerogative. Parliamentary statute also permitted the Queen to empower an ecclesiastical commission to exercise this jurisdiction.[18]

With a great deal of data about the Catholics at hand the government carefully elaborated its method of procedure. The deposed Marian ecclesiastics who were still alive had been granted a measured liberty.[19] Since some had used this freedom to effect reconciliations to Catholicism, the government now ordered them recommitted to a close imprisonment.[20] The policy toward known lay Catholics followed a twofold

[18] S.P.12/127/7 (December 3, 1578). A supplementary report stated that in canon law only the bishop could levy a pecuniary fine. A careful study of ecclesiastical and legal records is needed to determine how far these opinions were carried out.
[19] Dr. Henry Cole, deposed Dean of St. Paul's, was granted liberty but confined to London and its environs (*A.P.C.*, VIII, 218, April 4, 1574). Dr. John Young, former Vice Chancellor of the University of Cambridge, was granted a limited respite from prison (the Marshalsea) in 1574 and 1575 (*ibid.*, 253, June 13, 1574; 367, April 17, 1575). The deposed Bishop of Lincoln, Thomas Watson, was released to the custody of his brother upon bonds and sureties for his good behavior (*ibid.*, 264, July 5, 1574). The onetime Abbot of Westminster, John Feckenham, was granted temporary periods of freedom in 1574, 1575, and 1576 (*ibid.*, 269, July 17, 1574; IX, 8, July 18, 1575; 147, June 19, 1576). John Harpsfield, former Archdeacon of London and Dean of Norwich, and his brother, Nicholas Harpsfield, former Archdeacon of Canterbury, were enlarged from imprisonment in the Fleet on condition that they appear at intervals before the Star Chamber [Nicholas Harpsfield died in 1575]. *A.P.C.*, VIII, 283-284, August 19, 1574, 312, November 12, 1574, 318, November 26, 1574, 320, December 1, 1574, 339, February 11, 1575, 371-372, April 29, 1575, 373, May 6, 1575; IX, 54, November 29, 1575, 123, May 11, 1576, 161, July 11, 1576.
[20] S.P.12/114/69 [?July ?1577]; *A.P.C.*, IX, 370-371, June 24, 1577, 388, July 24, 26, 30, 1577; X, 4, July 28, 1577, 13, August 11, 1577, 16, August 11, 1577. The order committed Bishop Watson to the care of the Bishop of Winchester, Abbot Feckenham to the Bishop of Ely, Dr. Young (or Yonge) to the Dean of Canterbury, and Dr. Harpsfield to the Bishop of Lincoln (*A.P.C.*, IX, 388, July 24, 26, 30, 1577). The conditions of imprisonment directed that the Marian ecclesiastics should be confined sufficiently closely that they would have no access to anybody other than the attendants approved by the bishops who were their custodians. They were to have "a bare scholar's diet," but on special occasions could eat with their custodians. Only convinced Protestants could approach them, and only with the bishops' permission could they discuss religion. They were to be permitted to read only books of Protestant theology, and were to be encouraged to attend the services of the Establishment (S.P.12/114/69 [?July ?1577]). Dr. Young, because of his unsubmissiveness, was confined to the Queen's Bench in 1578 (*A.P.C.*, X, 168, February 18, 1578). Bishop Watson, because of his increasing blindness and lameness, asked for release from the custody of the Bishop of Winchester to the

course. Some were allowed to be free upon bonds and sureties for their good behavior.[21] Others, in increasingly larger numbers than in the past, were called in before the officials, questioned about their conformity, and if unsubmissive, committed to the custody of a bishop or other ecclesiastic for conference about points of doctrine. If these recusants continued inflexible, they were frequently imprisoned until they conformed.[22]

But the success of such steps still failed to lay ever-present fears, as shown in the significant aspects of a proposal of 1577: "How such as are backward or corrupt in religion may be reduced to conformity and others stayed from like corruption." It stated precisely that the number of recusants was large; to correct this (1) order should be taken to obtain the conformity of recusants; (2) exile or other restraint should be inflicted upon Bishop Watson, Abbot Feckenham, and any others who were recognized as the leaders and the counsellors of the consciences of Catholics; (3) a general order should be issued for the removal of "corrupted" schoolmasters throughout the realm. Each of these points was implemented by more detailed suggestions, suggestions emphasized by the assertion that the places of detention were insufficient to contain all the recusants.[23] Whether or not this document represented official thinking,

---

care of his brother in London (C.P.161/68, October 6, 1578, /69, October 7, 1578). Instead, he was given to the care of the Bishop of Rochester and somewhat later confined at Wisbeach Castle (*A.P.C.*, XI, 21, January 16, 1579, 51, February 19, 1579; S.P.12/143/17, October 16, 1580). In 1579 Abbot Feckenham was confined closely in the residence of the Bishop of Ely because of attacks on the Establishment (*A.P.C.*, XI, 290-291, October 23, 1579). In June 1580 he was confined to Wisbeach Castle (*ibid.*, XII, 68, June 26, 1580; S.P.12/143/17, October 16, 1580). The Spanish ambassador reported in 1574 that Catholic ecclesiastics and laymen were being questioned about their conformity by specially appointed commissioners (*Cal. S.P. Span.*, II, 488-489, November 28, 1574). Both this report and S.P.12/120/64 [?1577, ?1579] state that the Catholics were asked about their acceptance of various points of Protestant theology; the bulk of evidence throughout Elizabeth's reign indicates that such questions were rarely asked.

[21] Cf. *A.P.C.*, VIII, 283 (August 19, 1574), 312 (November 12, 1574), 318 (November 26, 1574), 371-372 (April 29, 1575); IX, 53-54 (November 27, 1575), 54 (November 29, 1575), 71 (January 7, 1576), 161 (July 11, 1576).

[22] In 1580 returns were sent in from the various prisons of London of those in prison for religion during the years 1577-1580. The returns are: S.P.12/140/36 (Gatehouse, July 30, 1580); /37 (Poultry Counter, July 29, 1580); /38 (Queen's Bench, July 31, 1580); /39 (White Lion, July 31, 1580); /40 (Marshalsea, July 1580). We have been able to identify the names of some, but not all, of the prisoners as Catholics.

[23] S.P.12/45/10 (July 1577). S.P.12/45/21 [?July ?1577] is largely a résumé of S.P.12/45/10.

THE ATTEMPTED REVIVIFICATION OF CATHOLICISM

it clearly demonstrates the pressures currently brought to bear upon the government to curb a renascent Catholicism.

A detailed study in this and subsequent chapters of the disposition of the cases of certain individuals will illustrate still more clearly how and why the Council proceeded against recusants of some prominence, undoubtedly, in the eyes of Queen and Council, the backbone of Catholicism. Sir Thomas Gerrard, the head of a leading Catholic family of the Midlands, had been detained for some time in London because of suspicion of treason. When freed from the Tower, he had been forbidden to travel beyond a radius of ten miles from London. That he might attend to necessary business, he now made suit to the Council for a license to go to his houses in the counties of Lancaster and Derby; and this was granted to him, June 23, 1574, until the first day of the next Michaelmas term, upon bond of £200.[24] The Council looked favorably upon this plea, stating, when it gave favorable answer to a request for renewal in mid-November, that Sir Thomas had proved himself worthy by his previous behavior. He could go to any part of England that he desired, upon giving bonds that he would not come to court nor into the Queen's presence and would appear before the Council when so ordered.[25]

When the Dean of St. Paul's, Alexander Nowell, filed a plea around December 1573, asking for the freedom of his half-brother, John Towneley, a prisoner at York, who had been committed though willing to attend the state church, but not to receive communion, the Privy Council remanded the case to the discretion of the president of the Council of the North and the Archbishop of York.[26] Towneley, however, did not conform. This caused the Privy Council to decide on July 10, 1576, that he, still a prisoner at York Castle, should be given under bond into the custody of a Mr. Assheton of Chatterton, known to be a sincere member of the Established Church, in the hope that conferences between the two might effect Towneley's conformity.[27] However, he remained obdurate, and the ecclesiastical commission at York again imprisoned him for recusancy. Subsequently, it modified this penalty, prescribing that he should live at some place easily accessible to his half-brother, Dean Nowell, in

---

[24] *A.P.C.*, VIII, 108 (May 29, 1573), 114–115 (June 14, 1573), 256 (June 23, 1574).
[25] *A.P.C.*, VIII, 315 (November 19, 1574).
[26] *A.P.C.*, VIII, 170–171 (December 22, 1573).
[27] *A.P.C.*, IX, 157–158 (July 10, 1576).

London, in order that that ecclesiastic might try to obtain his submission to the Establishment. The Council concurred in this decision, being interested in the case because Towneley stood high in the ranks of the English Catholics, and when previously confined at York, he had strengthened his belief in Catholicism by conferring with other members of that religion. The conciliar body fixed his bond while in the London area at £1000, and in order to frustrate his influence in his home county, forbade his return there.[28]

In the mid-1570's the Privy Council and also the diocesan ecclesiastical commissions inaugurated a practice, which in time became a settled policy, of calling in members of certain prominent county families, still Catholic, for questioning. If intransigent in their religious opinions, they were fined, imprisoned, temporarily released, but always subjected to suspicion and supervision. Some conformed, but others adhered with an unwavering tenacity to their beliefs. They belonged to a network, cutting across county lines, of interrelated gentry families, which sustained this alliance of blood by further marriage and by close friendship. They had risen to affluence in most cases in the fifteenth century through success in law or trade or by acquiring land; the acquisition of land had brought some out of the ranks of the yeomanry into the gentility. In almost every case in the 1570's and the 1580's the status of the male members of these families was that of knight, esquire, or gentleman; usually each one was a landholder of some substance, generally moderate; a few were of fairly considerable means. With exceptions none was a person of great wealth or of high descent. Certain individuals had been prominent in the service of Mary Tudor and some of the families had had sons and daughters who during her reign or before 1534 had been priests and nuns, which had created a tradition holding these families to the Roman Church. Much of the remainder of our study will be concerned with the members of this network of Catholic families: the first determined effort to strike at recusancy was directed, in the second half of 1575, against some of the leading Staffordshire Catholics, men of substance and influence and family tradition in their county.

On August 12, 1575, the Council summoned Brian Fowler and John Gifford, both justices of the peace, John Dracot, Erasmus Wolvesley,

[28] *A.P.C.*, X, 182 (March 10, 1578).

Francis Gatacre, Thomas Pesshall, Sampson Erdswicke, and William Maxfield.[29] All except Dracot and Pesshall appeared before the Council sitting at Worcester on August 17; Erdswicke came accompanied by his son. They admitted the charge of recusancy, and upon being examined individually, asserted that they acted according to their consciences and the example of their forefathers, who had so taught them. As they seemed willing to confer about religion, they were referred to the Bishops of Hereford, Worcester, Lichfield and Coventry, and Rochester, and other learned men to receive instructions the next day. The Council decided that, after it should receive the report of these clerics as to the attitudes of these recusants, it would then determine its further decision concerning them.[30]

On August 19 the four bishops reported that their conferences had had little effect. The Council, feeling that further consultations might produce the desired results, called in each of the prisoners separately and informed them in every case that they could not go home before making their submission in religion, since, for the sake of example, nonconformity in men of their standing would not be tolerated. Brian Fowler was assigned to the custody of the Bishop of Worcester until Michaelmas, first being given a few days' respite to pay a debt. If he yielded in religion before the terminal date of his custody he was to be dismissed; if not, the Council would then take further steps in his regard. Francis Gatacre was assigned to the Bishop of Lichfield and Coventry. Sampson Erdswicke and his father, Hugh Erdswicke, who apparently had come to Worcester without a formal summons, were assigned to the Bishop of Worcester, the former being permitted to go home to get books and notes for the conferences. William Maxfield, although ordered into the care of the Bishop of Lichfield and Coventry, was granted a leave until Michaelmas, as he had a commission to sit in the county until then. John Gifford and Erasmus Wolvesley were committed into the custody of the Bishop of Rochester; the former received a license authorizing him first to go to his house, which needed to be set in order, as the Queen had recently visited there.[31] John Dracot, who had not previously appeared, presented himself before

---

[29] *A.P.C.*, IX, 13 (August 12, 1575).   [30] *A.P.C.*, IX, 14–15 (August 17, 1575).
[31] *A.P.C.*, IX, 17–19 (August 19, 1575). No further mention is made of Sampson Erdswicke's son.

the Council on September 6, and was remitted for religious conferences to the Bishop-elect of Norwich and a Dr. Pieres.[32]

The Council intended these conferences to be conducted in a fair manner. Each recusant was to feel completely free in declaring his conscience, and could make use of any books and reasons which supported his beliefs. Nor could any advantage be taken of anything any one of them might say, with the exception of attacks on the Queen.[33]

On November 1 the Council again took up the case of Gatacre, Wolvesley, and Maxfield, who had been remanded to that body by their current custodian, the Bishop of Lichfield and Coventry, after he found that they still remained unyielding despite his efforts. As the three continued equally immovable in their bearing before the Council, they received sentence of close imprisonment, Gatacre being confined to the Fleet, Wolvesley to the Gatehouse in Westminster, and Maxfield to the Marshalsea.[34] Similarly, Fowler and the two Erdswickes did not prove amenable; and on November 10 the Bishop of Worcester turned them over to the Council, which, however, put off the disposition of their cases for a few days.[35] Three days later John Dracot was cited before the Council. As he persisted in his recusancy, he was committed a close prisoner in the Fleet. The same day John Gifford appeared and declared his conformity; but Brian Fowler, who remained unshaken in his beliefs, was committed for further conference to the Dean of Windsor; and Hugh and Sampson Erdswicke, who likewise proved intractable, were assigned to the custody of the Bishop-elect of Norwich and a Dr. Busshe.[36]

On December 7 Brian Fowler was assigned to an easy tenure in the Fleet for six weeks; if by then he had not conformed, he was to be subjected to close imprisonment. At the same time Sampson Erdswicke was ordered confined to close imprisonment under the jurisdiction of the knight marshal, and his father was ordered imprisoned in the Gatehouse under similar terms.[37]

Near the middle of the next month, January 1576, Francis Gatacre,

[32] *A.P.C.*, IX, 21 (September 6, 1575). Edmund Freake, Bishop of Rochester, had been translated to Norwich, but had not yet been formally installed. Dr. Pieres was probably John Piers, successively Bishop of Rochester and of Salisbury.
[33] *A.P.C.*, IX, 18 (August 19, 1575).
[34] *A.P.C.*, IX, 40–41 (November 1, 1575).
[35] *A.P.C.*, IX, 44–45 (November 10, 1575).
[36] *A.P.C.*, IX, 46–47 (November 13, 1575).
[37] *A.P.C.*, IX, 57–58 (December 7, 1575).

when commanded by the Council on his allegiance to conform, consented, and was released.[38] During the same month Brian Fowler became seriously ill due to his close confinement. For this reason, and since there seemed to be hope that he might conform through further conferences, the Council granted him his freedom.[39] At the same time John Dracot, in the Fleet, received permission to confer with his lawyers concerning some lawsuits which he had pending, and to walk in the prison garden for his health.[40] In March the Council allowed William Maxfield to stay under bond at Lambeth for twelve days in order to hold consultations with the Bishop of Lichfield and Coventry. If within that time he did not submit, he was to return to prison. The Council further ruled that both in prison and at Lambeth Maxfield's wife would have right of access to her husband.[41] A few weeks later, on April 19, Hugh and Sampson Erdswicke received a temporary grant of liberty until the first day of the next Trinity term, if they did not conform in the meantime;[42] and this same privilege was extended nine days later to John Dracot, that he might attend to certain lawsuits.[43]

A series of petitions praying for temporary release were filed with the Council on June 19, in behalf of John Dracot, Hugh and Sampson Erdswicke, Brian Fowler, and Erasmus Wolvesley of the diocese of Lichfield and Coventry, and Francis Eyreman, Robert Becket, and Richard Tremaine of the diocese of Exeter, all of whom were prisoners for recusancy, some of them being in prison, and others temporarily enlarged, in order to attend to lawsuits and other business matters and to participate in further religious conferences. The Council granted each of these pleas, permitting the various petitioners to return under heavy bonds to their homes until the beginning of the next Michaelmas term. Within five days after arriving there, they were to go to their local ordinary and offer to confer with him, repeating this at least once every month during the period of respite. They were not to disparage the state church in any manner, nor associate with other recusants, nor leave their residences for reasons other than those stipulated in the grant of enlargement. If they conformed, they were to remain free of prison.[44]

As far as we can infer it from the cases which we have so far observed,

---

[38] *A.P.C.*, IX, 75 (January 13, 1576).   [39] *A.P.C.*, IX, 80 (January 1576).
[40] *A.P.C.*, IX, 80–81 (January 1576).   [41] *A.P.C.*, IX, 93–94 (March 11, 1576).
[42] *A.P.C.*, IX, 105 (April 19, 1576).   [43] *A.P.C.*, IX, 110 (April 28, 1576).
[44] *A.P.C.*, IX, 145–147 (June 19, 1576).

the Council's policy toward the recusant gentry had become fixed: kindness was to alternate with severity; any evidence of weakness, even if only temporary, was to be used in order to induce conformity. Beyond this, there was no question of civil disloyalty. Thus, in February 1577, when Hugh Erdswicke petitioned to be released under bond from the Gatehouse for a short period because of illness, the Council directed that he be taken to the Dean of Westminster or some of the more capable prebends to see if their persuasion might induce him to conform, at least to the extent of attending the state church, with the imposition of no other restraint of conscience.[45] In June, however, the Council proved less exacting in the case of Erasmus Wolvesley, who had become seriously ill in the Gatehouse. He was allowed to go directly to his home under bond of £500 until the next Michaelmas Day, unless in the meantime he should conform.[46]

To prevent infection from disease, George Cotton, a prominent member of the Hampshire gentry, who was a prisoner for recusancy in the Fleet, received permission in August to go to his residence under bond of £1000, as the plague had broken out in the prison. In the middle of November he returned to his confinement.[47] For the same reason, on September 14, 1578, Cotton and John Dracot, each of whom was currently a prisoner in the Fleet, were allowed to be removed for two months under bonds of £500 apiece to some house within ten or twelve miles of the capital, if the Bishop of London, in his judgment, deemed it wise. The two were to pay their own expenses, attend the local parish church when there were sermons, and submit to religious consultations.[48] Within two weeks the Council made a different disposition of Cotton's case, turning him over to the Bishop of Winchester, at that prelate's request, for further conferences.[49]

The impact of an accumulation of proofs that Catholicism was undergoing something of a renascence became inescapably evident to the government by 1577. For some years it had been witnessing the recalcitrancy

---

[45] *A.P.C.,* IX, 295 (February 22, 1577). Apparently Erdswicke was not released, as the Council in May granted him temporary enlargement from the Gatehouse on bonds of £400 (*ibid.,* 348, May 14, 1577).

[46] *A.P.C.,* IX, 367–368 (June 24, 1577).

[47] *A.P.C.,* X, 11 (August 4, 1577), 87 (November 15, 1577), 89 (November 16, 1577).

[48] *A.P.C.,* X, 325 (September 14, 1578).   [49] *A.P.C.,* X, 329 (September 26, 1578).

of the Catholic gentry; the activities in East Anglia over a period of years of two Marian priests, Edward Jackson and Derham, chaplain to Lady Jerningham, undoubtedly were long known to the central authorities; the notorious refusal of some Catholics in the north to pray for the Queen and to participate in the services of the *Book of Common Prayer* and the labors of a Marian priest, Henry Comberforde, formerly a prebend at Lichfield, had attracted notice; the flourishing recusancy in Sussex had been recognized by the Queen; the persistent strength of Catholicism and the lack of success of the Establishment in Herefordshire had sufficiently disquieted the Council to cause it to interfere in a municipal election in the city of Hereford; and the questioning by a convert to Catholicism, Luke Atslow, of the Queen's religious supremacy, legitimacy, government and personal life was in line with the known thinking prevailing at Rome.[50] The final incident which led to a redefinition of official policy toward each of the two categories, the Catholic priests and the Catholic laymen, was the arrest of a number of Cornish Catholics on the charge of misdemeanors in religion.[51] Francis Tregian, a gentleman of considerable wealth, in whose house a priest, Cuthbert Mayne, had been seized, suffered imprisonment and sequestration of property[52] until Elizabeth's death, a harsher penalty than was generally inflicted on a layman. The priest, Continental-trained and therefore suspect, who held it to be the obligation of Catholic Englishmen to assist any prince professing the Roman faith who invaded England to recatholicize it, was executed upon a technical charge of treason.[53] From now on priests but not laymen lived under the constant fear of suffering capital punishment.

On October 15, 1577, the government, feeling itself handicapped by insufficient knowledge of the number, names, and financial resources of

[50] S.P.12/98/35 (October 21, 1574), /112/13.1 [before April 2, 1577], /117/23 (October 28, 1577); S.P.15/25/21 (May 18, 1577); C.P.160/75 (September 24, 1575); A.P.C., IX, 197 (August 30, 1576), 225 (November 2, 1576); X, 325–326 (September 14, 1578); XI, 355–356 (January 1, 1580), 357 (January 9, 1580), 363–364 (January 10, 1580).
[51] S.P.12/118/47 ([?November] 1577); A.P.C., IX, 375 (July 1, 1577), 390 (August 4, 1577); X, 276–277 (July 6, 1578).
[52] A.P.C., X, 249 (June 9, 1578), 276–277 (July 6, 1578); XI, 231–232 (August 11, 1579), 237 (August 14, 1579), 241 (August 16, 1579), 257 (September 6, 1579), 274 (October 5, 1579), 380 (January 27, 1580).
[53] A.P.C., X, 85 (November 12, 1577); S.P.12/118/46 (November 29, 1577).

contemporary recusants ordered a survey of the whole realm, diocese by diocese.⁵⁴ Each bishop was given careful directions for making a report. It is difficult to determine exactly how many of the names entered were those of Catholics and how many of Protestant nonconformists; we have listed in our footnotes as Catholics only those whose names we have been able to verify as such.⁵⁵ Archbishop Grindal, out of favor with the Queen and living under restraint, had the report for his archdiocese drawn up by an ecclesiastic and two lay magistrates. Although limited by lack of authority and insufficient information, they sent in the names of twenty-four recusants of substance.⁵⁶ The remainder of Kent, comprising the diocese of Rochester, reported seven.⁵⁷ Chichester, where a strong concentration of Catholics existed, returned the names of twenty-two recusants.⁵⁸ Winchester, comprising Hampshire and Surrey, reported seventy-nine (or eighty) recusants.⁵⁹ Bristol reported the prevalence of insincere conformity, and sent in four names.⁶⁰ Exeter reported thirty recusants in Cornwall (but some had fled or were only suspected).⁶¹ The Bishop of

⁵⁴ *A.P.C.*, X, 87–88 (November 15, 1577); S.P.12/117/9 (October 24, 1577). The letters from various bishops to the Council state that the date of the Council's directive ordering the census was October 15, 1577. The complete returns are given in *Misc.*, XII, 1–114.

⁵⁵ *Misc.*, XII, 1–114, the episcopal reports, contain explanatory notes identifying some of the Catholic recusants. We have supplemented these from other sources. This still leaves a margin of possible error, due to the lack, at the present time, of a definitive list of Catholic recusants.

⁵⁶ S.P.12/117/5 (October 21, 1577), /5.1 (October 1577), /9 (October 24, 1577). The agents of Archbishop Grindal stated that an inquisition was necessary for exact information; due to the shortness of time allowed for sending in a return, the census was based upon recusants presented in the courts and those of "public fame." The Archbishop and the commissioners sent in their own estimates of the financial condition of the persons returned. So far as we can determine five of these recusants were Catholics.

⁵⁷ S.P.12/117/2 (October 20, 1577). We have identified four of the recusants as Catholics.

⁵⁸ S.P.12/117/15 (October 26, 1577), /118/51 (November 29, 1577). We have identified seventeen of these recusants as Catholics.

⁵⁹ S.P.12/117/10 (October 24, 1577), /10.1 (October 1577), /14 (October [?25], 1577), /14.1 (October 1577). We have identified fifty of those named as Catholics. In Hampshire there were fifty-six recusants (or fifty-seven, depending on the reading of the document), of whom thirty-eight were Catholics; in Surrey there were twenty-three recusants, of whom twelve were Catholics. One of the recusants included in Surrey was reported dead and his widow had remarried.

⁶⁰ S.P.12/118/72 [?November ?1577]. The four names included in the report for Bristol are also contained in the report for Bath and Wells. We have identified two of the names as those of Catholics.

⁶¹ S.P.12/117/25 (October 28, 1577), /25.1 (October 28, 1577). We have identified twenty-two of the thirty Cornish recusants as Catholics.

THE ATTEMPTED REVIVIFICATION OF CATHOLICISM

Bath and Wells reported eight recusants in Somersetshire,[62] and one, a Catholic, in Dorsetshire, which county he had been asked to investigate, although outside his jurisdiction.[63] Salisbury sent in fifty-seven names, forty-seven (or more) in Berkshire,[64] the other ten being in Wiltshire.[65] Gloucester sent in two reports: the first contained thirty-nine names;[66] the second contained seventy-seven names.[67] The Bishop of Worcester, John Whitgift, reported that there was much evidence of recusancy in his diocese, but the recency of his appointment prevented him from reporting more than forty-nine names for Worcester and Warwick.[68] Hereford reported fifty-two names and also evidence of insincere and even contemptuous conformity.[69] Coventry and Lichfield reported one hundred and twenty-six recusants.[70] In Wales the Bishop of Llandaff sent in thirteen names, implying that if he had more exact knowledge, he prob-

---

[62] S.P.12/117/11 (October 24, 1577), /118/16, 16.1 (November 9, 1577). We have identified four of the names as those of Catholics. Depending on the reading of the document there may be nine recusants in Somersetshire.

[63] S.P.12/117/11 (October 24, 1577), /21 (October 28, 1577).

[64] S.P.12/117/17, 17.1 (October 26, 1577). Twenty-two of those named are identifiable as Catholics. The number of recusants actually is somewhat larger than the number of names (forty-seven), as the daughters (no names or number indicated) of John Yate are mentioned.

[65] S.P.12/117/26.1 (October 28, 1577). All of the Wiltshire recusants seem to be Catholics; six of these ten both refused to come to church and to receive communion.

[66] S.P.12/117/12 (October 24, 1577), /12.1 (1577). We have identified ten of these names as those of Catholics. The exact number of recusants is indeterminate, due to the unqualified "and familie" appended to Thomas Bradforde.

[67] S.P.12/118/32, 32.1 (November 20, 1577). Twelve of those named were Catholics. However, the exact number of recusants is indeterminate, due to the unqualified "and his familie" appended to George Feltoe.

[68] S.P.12/118/11 (November 5, 1577), /11.3 (October 30, 1577), /11.4 (episcopal visitation report of 1577), /11.5 (November 5, 1577). Six of those named definitely are Catholics, and four others are possibly so. Bishop Whitgift wrote to the Council: "For in that Visitation [of his predecessor earlier in 1577] there was not one gentleman, nor person of wealth presented, for not coming to hear divine service: and yet it is well-known that there are both men and women of great countenance and revenues, within my diocese, guilty therein" (S.P.12/118/11, November 5, 1577).

[69] S.P.12/118/7 (November 2, 1577), /7.1 [?1577]. Thirty-four of the recusants were Catholics. The exact number of recusants is indeterminate, due to the unqualified "and maydes" appended to Katherine Mornington.

[70] S.P.12/118/17 (November 10, 1577), /17.1 (November 14, 1577). One recusant, Sir Thomas Fitzherbert, is listed twice. It is difficult to determine exactly how many of those named were Catholic; we conjecture about seventy-five. A second, very full report of the diocese of Coventry and Lichfield (Staffordshire, Derbyshire, and Shropshire) was sent in on February 1, 1578 (S.P.12/122/28.1, February 1, 1578).

ably could send in about two hundred other names;[71] the Bishop of St. David's reported only one Catholic recusant;[72] in St. Asaph there was none;[73] in Bangor only a priest was reported as a proven recusant, although there was considerable evidence of further recusancy in isolated areas.[74] A posthumous list was sent in compiled by the late Bishop of Chester, William Downman, naming sixty-nine recusants (of whom seventeen were doubtfully charged);[75] but the ecclesiastical commissioners, laymen, sent in corrected lists of seven recusants in Cheshire,[76] and of thirty-five recusants in Lancashire.[77] The commissioners openly stated that the deceased ordinary had been lax in securing conformity and that nonconformity to the Establishment was widespread.[78] Durham reported eight recusants, with indications that there were more unreported.[79] York showed that, despite the repression of the Northern Rebellion seven years before, Catholicism, alive and active, existed in the north.[80] Archbishop Sandys listed one hundred and sixty-nine names of recusants in the archdiocese,[81] sixteen persons of the diocese of Chester presented for recu-

[71] S.P.12/118/11.2 (October 25, 1577). Six of the thirteen names were those of Catholics. The list also contained those persons excommunicated for unchastity. The bishop in his covering letter complained of the laxity of the local sheriff in prosecuting recusancy.
[72] S.P.12/118/11.1 (October 28, 1577). The bishop reported that some others who came to church favored the Roman Church.
[73] S.P.12/118/10 (November 4, 1577).
[74] S.P.12/118/8 (November 3, 1577). The priest, Humphrey Barker, was one of the nonjuring Marian clergy.
[75] S.P.12/118/49 (1577). Thirty-four of those named are definitely identifiable as Catholics. Bishop Downman died on December 3, 1577.
[76] S.P.12/118/48.1 (November 29, 1577). One and possibly more of the Cheshire recusants was a Catholic.
[77] S.P.12/118/45.1 (November 28, 1577). Twenty-nine of the Lancashire recusants were Catholics.
[78] S.P.12/118/45 (November 28, 1577; report of ecclesiastical commissioners for Lancashire), /48 (November 29, 1577; report of G. [or E.] Fytton to Sir Francis Walsingham).
[79] S.P.15/25/42, 42.1 (October 24, 1577). Probably all of the eight recusants were Catholics; six are identifiable as such and the other two would also seem to be. The Privy Council, aware of the extent of recusancy in the diocese of Durham, wrote to Bishop Barnes concerning certain priests functioning there, shortly after receiving his census report (*A.P.C.*, X, 79, November 10, 1577), and also to the Earl of Huntingdon, Lord President of the Council of the North, about the same problem (*ibid.*, 79–80, November 10, 1577).
[80] S.P.12/117/23 (October 28, 1577).
[81] S.P.12/117/23.1 (October 1577). Ninety of the persons named were Catholics. The mention without qualification of dependents makes the total figure of recusants somewhat larger than one hundred and sixty-nine.

THE ATTEMPTED REVIVIFICATION OF CATHOLICISM

sancy at York,[82] and fifteen in Nottinghamshire.[83] The large diocese of Lincoln, extending over much of eastern England, reported at least thirteen recusants with indications that there were probably more.[84] Peterborough reported six recusants in its first return, all Catholics;[85] the second list, adding two more names, indicated that one of the first list had conformed.[86] Ely reported nine recusants.[87] Norwich reported forty-seven recusants in the county of Norfolk (or forty-nine, including two recusants also included in the diocese of Ely).[88] The Vice Chancellor of Cambridge University, Richard Howland, reported no evidence of recusancy either in the university or in the city of Cambridge.[89] Oxfordshire sent information about seventy-one recusants (and one doubtful case) and the families and dependents of some of them, including both university men and townspeople; the report furnished grounds of suspicion of a close connection between some Catholics there with the Continent.[90] A second report sent in a few weeks after the first listed one hundred and fifty-nine

---

[82] S.P.12/117/23.2 (October 28, 1577). All of these persons apparently were Catholic. The mention of dependents without further qualification makes the total figure of recusants larger than sixteen.

[83] S.P.12/118/2.2 (October 30, 1577). None of these recusants was identifiable as a Catholic.

[84] S.P.12/117/13 (October 25, 1577), /22 (October 28, 1577), /118/9 (November 3, 1577), /34 (November 21, 1577), /50 (November 29, 1577). Only four of the recusants would appear to be Catholics. The inclusion of dependents not otherwise qualified, doubtful recusants and a person also listed in the diocese of Peterborough makes the figure larger than thirteen, but indeterminate. Depending upon the interpretation of one of the documents, the figure may be fourteen.

[85] S.P.12/117/16 (October 26, 1577).

[86] S.P.12/118/29 (November 18, 1577). A Mr. Slade of Rushton in Northamptonshire had conformed. A Mr. Standish absented himself frequently in Lancashire and could not be reached; many others also shifted their dwellings whenever the bishop sent for them.

[87] S.P.12/117/28.1 (October 30, 1577). Five of the recusants were Catholic. The Bishop of Ely, Richard Cox, reported that recusants within his diocese by various means evaded summonses to appear before him (S.P.12/117/28, October 30, 1557).

[88] S.P.12/117/27.1 (October 29, 1577). Twenty-nine of the recusants were Catholics. The basis of the schedule sent from the diocese of Norwich to the Council was an old certificate and the religious condition of some of those contained in the certificates had altered in the meantime (S.P.12/117/27, October 29, 1577).

[89] S.P.12/118/35 (November 22, 1577).

[90] S.P.12/118/37.1 (November 24, 1577). About thirty-five of the recusants would appear to be Catholics. The exact number of recusants is indeterminate due to the mention of dependents without further qualification; the total of seventy-one depends upon the inclusion or exclusion of certain names as properly included among the Oxford recusants.

names for Oxfordshire, exclusive of the university.[91] Bishop Aylmer of London gave one hundred and sixty-seven names to the Council,[92] and sixteen more recusants were added for the archdeaconry of Colchester in Essex.[93]

The Council was especially concerned about the considerable amount of "Poperie" in the Inns of Court and the Inns of Chancery in the capital; the Lord Keeper was directed to report concerning the former, the Lord Chief Justice concerning the latter.[94] The four Inns of Court sent in very detailed reports, enumerating the religious preferences of the various members about whom there was any question. One would infer from the certificates of the Inns that all or most of the names reported were Catholic recusants or Catholics who had conformed, but we cannot verify this from existing lists of Catholics.[95]

The Middle Temple reported twenty-six barristers. Fifteen were known recusants, including Edmund Plowden of Berkshire and Edward Vavesor of Yorkshire; three others were fugitives overseas at Louvain; eight were adherents of the Establishment.[96] The Inner Temple sent in sixty-two names. Four — Robert Atkinson, Thomas Bawde, Arden Waferer and James Braybrooke — had been disbarred because of their refusal to renounce the traditional church. Thirty-two, some of them bearing recognizably Catholic names, either absented themselves from the Inner Temple or had discontinued membership: some of them were among the more important recusants whom the Council constantly kept under surveillance — Francis Waferer of London (who later became a priest), Thomas Copley of Surrey, (?Francis) Yate of Berkshire, Michael, Robert

---

[91] S.P.12/119/5.1 (December 7, 1577). Approximately fifty of those named were Catholics. The covering letter indicates considerable recusancy in the diocese of Oxford (S.P.12/119/5, December 3, 1577). This second census report contains one hundred and twenty recusants, twenty-one others who would attend church but not receive communion (some had promised conformity in this regard), and ten who occasionally attended church (some had promised full obedience in this matter).

[92] S.P.12/118/73 (November 1577). About thirty-five of the recusants were Catholics. The listing of dependents without further qualification increased the number of recusants in the diocese of London, making the total indeterminate.

[93] S.P.12/118/44 (November 27, 1577). Five of the recusants were identifiable as Catholics.

[94] A.P.C., X, 94–95 (November 17, 1577).

[95] We have counted as Catholics only those persons listed for whom we have evidence of their religious beliefs. Despite this, in some cases our judgment could only be approximate.

[96] S.P.12/118/68 (November 1577).

and William Hare of Suffolk, Sampson Erdswicke of Staffordshire, Henry Shelley of Sussex, and Henry Everard of Suffolk. Richard Carewe of Devonshire was recorded as a recognized recusant; seven were categorized as doubtful; eighteen were adherents of the Establishment.[97] Lincoln's Inn reported forty members. Two, Roger Corham and John Bown, had been permanently disbarred because of religion; eleven were suspect in religion; ten adhered to the Establishment; one had been expelled from the Inn because of refusal to receive communion; and sixteen had been sequestered from membership because of religion, among them William Roper and his son, Thomas, of Kent, Richard Tremaine of Devonshire, and Mark Curle of Hampshire.[98] Gray's Inn reported fifty-four names. Fifteen adhered to the Establishment; three had given up their profession and become Jesuits; twelve had been sequestered from membership for nonconformity, including Nicholas Tirwhitt, Walter Norton of Suffolk and Richard Culpepper and John Wyburne of Kent; twenty-four were known to be recusants, among them Henry Darrell of Sussex and (?William) and John Yaxley of Suffolk and (?John) Bedingfield of Norfolk.[99] Six of the Inns of Chancery reported twenty-five names out of their total membership; one, Francis Eyreman, was a Catholic, and some others would appear to be. Two of the Inns, Clement and Lyon, reported no recusants.[100]

Such a census, formulated too hurriedly to be other than incomplete in information,[101] gives only an approximate picture of nonconformity, chiefly of nonconformity among the wealthy. It does show that a considerable number of persons, both those listed and an unknown number indicated but otherwise unlisted, did not adhere to the Queen's proceedings in religion almost a generation after she had ascended the throne. In the counties in the north and northwest and in Wales laxity or conniving on the part of local authorities must account for the unevenness in the number of names reported in some sections where other evidence

[97] S.P.12/118/69 (November 1577).   [98] S.P.12/118/70 (November 1577).
[99] S.P.12/118/71 (November 1577).   [100] S.P.12/118/38.1 (November 24, 1577).
[101] Various of the covering letters complain of the lack of time to secure complete information concerning the number and names of the recusants and their economic status. Typical examples are the covering letters for the archdiocese of Canterbury (S.P.12/117/5, October 21, 1577) and for the archdiocese of York (S.P.12/117/23, October 28, 1577). A detailed contemporary summary of the census is contained in S.P.12/119/20 (December 1577), and is given *in extenso* in *Misc.*, XII, 6-9 (our totals for the various dioceses, counties and Inns of Court do not always agree with the "corrected totals" given in this volume).

exists and was recognized contemporarily that Catholicism was still being practiced widely.¹⁰² It raises, too, the interesting question of how many of those believing in and to some degree practicing Catholicism conformed sufficiently not to be considered recusants. That occasional conformity was widespread is proved by the efforts of the priests trained abroad on the Continent to discourage it in the next few years.

The leading Catholic gentry of some dioceses frequently were not summoned before the ecclesiastical commission, or were cited irregularly, and great laxity prevailed on the part of the officials, lay and clerical, who undoubtedly avoided challenging the power of the local magnates. These administrative weaknesses and the prevalence of a quasi-feudal social structure in the north were also responsible for the fact that there, more than in the rest of England, the lower classes were strongly subject to the influence of the upper. In the remainder of the realm, where Protestantism was stronger and the greater concentrations of population existed, in many cases the persons mentioned were of some wealth and social position or belonged to certain ranks of the educated, who stubbornly clung to the traditional religion because of belief or because of the cultural pattern prevailing in their families or among segments of their class. It would seem from this that the limited evidence of Catholics in most of England other than the west and northwest (and Sussex) reflected the considerable diminution of Catholic numbers in the rest of the realm. Bearing all these facts in mind, the general picture given by the census is true if by no means completely accurate.

2. THE PROCEDURES OF OFFICIAL POLICY, 1577-1580

The census of 1577 served to confirm to the government that Catholicism was being kept alive, not only by an older generation of priests, but also by a small but steady stream of newly ordained English-born priests trained on the Continent.¹⁰³ The hardening of official policy because of

---

[102] There are no reports for the diocese of Carlisle and for Suffolk in the diocese of Norwich. The reports for Durham, Lincoln and Chester were inadequate when compared to those of other dioceses; that of Chester subsequently had to be corrected.

[103] Scattered evidence confirms that both the older generation of Marian priests and the newer, seminary-trained priests were performing sacerdotal functions in England: *A.P.C.*, X, 174-175 (February 23, 1578), 178 (March 7, 1578), 317 (August 28, 29, 30, 1578), 325-326 (September 14, 1578), 348-349 (October 17, 1578),

the latter now proceeded apace. Before the end of the 1570's two priests, Cuthbert Mayne and John Nelson and a seminarian, Thomas Sherwood, who questioned the legitimacy of the Queen's title, were executed. Wherever discovered, priests were now as a matter of course imprisoned,[104] and the utensils needed for mass or for administering the sacraments or otherwise pertinent to Catholic spiritual life were seized and usually destroyed.[105] And, as in the past, watch was kept to prevent any secret communications with the Continent in matters pertaining to religion.[106] Conformity, however, wiped away penalties incurred either by a priest or a layman for previous violations of religious laws, even if the act had entailed suspicion of the accused person's loyalty.[107] This determination embodied the tenor of official policy: the Council and those carrying out the ecclesiastical laws under its direction strove to convince the subject that due obedience to the ruler embraced complete conformity to all of the Queen's directions, which in religion, as in other matters, it was her prerogative to determine.[108]

The government at Westminster, forced to deal with local situations through local officials, found that more than ever a continuing worry, dating back to the survey of the justices of the peace in the early 1560's, was the number of reports from some areas of the laxity of these officials

---

400 (November 27, 1578), 403 (November 28, 1578); XI, 33 (January 29, 1579), 57 (February 23, 1579), 293–294 (October 30, 1579); C.P.161/59 (September 20, 1578), /117 (April 15, 1579); S.P.12/118/37.1 (November 24, 1577), /136/16 (n.d. [?1580]). S.P.12/136/16 is a short treatise concerning attendance at the services of the Establishment.

[104] Contemporary prison lists of London indicated the policy of imprisoning priests: S.P.12/140/36 (July 30, 1580; Gatehouse), /37 (July 29, 1580; Poultry Counter), /38 (July 31, 1580; Queen's Bench), /40 (July 1580; Marshalsea).

[105] *A.P.C.*, X, 143 (January 13, 1578), 246 (June 8, 1578), 426 (December 15, 1578; XII, 256 (November 1, 1580); S.P.12/143/33 (October 24, 1580).

[106] *A.P.C.*, X, 227 (May 18, 1578), 282 (July 7, 1578), 289 (July 20, 1578), 295 (July 30, 1578), 309 (August 23, 1578), 348 (October 17, 1578), 355 (October 26, 1578), 426 (December 15, 1578), 432–433 (December 21, 1578); XI, 289 (October 20, 1579), 297 (November 4, 1579); C.P.10/23 (August 5, 1578); S.P.12/143/33 (October 24, 1580), /165/55 (n.d. [?1580]); *Cal. S.P. Span.*, II, 649 (February 18, 1579); Oratorians, *Diaries,* 170–171 [?September 18, 1580].

[107] This frequently occurred. A typical contemporary case was that of Robert Blades, who had communicated with a Catholic fugitive on the Continent (*A.P.C.*, XI, 103, April 17, 1579).

[108] The Privy Council wrote to the Bishop of London in January 1578 that the justices of the peace who were recusants "dishonored God, infringed the laws, and [gave] evil example . . . to the common people" (S.P.12/45/16 [?January 1578]).

and of their connivance to help Catholics to evade prosecution,[109] and evidence of the almost unhindered protection of priests by influential persons in various localities.[110] In the late 1570's greater pressures were now brought to bear upon recusant justices of the peace to conform, and more so than in the previous decade, perhaps, the recalcitrants were ejected from their magistracies.[111]

A comprehensive memorandum which the Council sent to Bishop Aylmer of London stated that the Queen in a progress made a short time previously through various shires had learned that a considerable number of justices of the peace during recent years were known recusants. To correct this, the Council had sent letters to the justices, reminding them of their conscientious duty in this regard, and directing them to hold conferences with the Bishop of London, which had proved unsuccessful. The Council (although not yet fully informed of this failure) had received specific information concerning magisterial nonconformity in certain shires. Bishop Aylmer was directed to discover what justices within his jurisdiction were nonconformists and their economic and social conditions and proof of their recusancy.[112] Letters were also sent to the justices of the assizes to administer the Oath of Supremacy to the justices of the peace within their circuits.[113] In accordance with this, the oath was administered in various of the counties:[114] it is significant that some of the justices absented themselves when summoned, excusing themselves because of illness or invalidity or presenting no reason at all.[115] Such nonjurors, however, were to be proffered the oath whenever they could be reached.[116]

In September 1578 the Council sent directions to the Earl of Pembroke and the Bishop of Salisbury directing them how to deal with nonadher-

---

[109] C.P.161/82 (October 16, 1578). This is also stated or implied in the reports of various of the bishops in the census of 1577: Bangor (S.P.12/118/8, November 3, 1577); Worcester (S.P.12/118/11, November 5, 1577); Llandaff (S.P.12/118/11.2, October 25, 1577); Chester (S.P.12/118/45, November 28, 1577; /48, November 29, 1577); Oxford (S.P.12/119/5, December 3, 1577).

[110] C.P.161/59 (September 20, 1578); *A.P.C.*, X, 317 (August 28, 29, 30, 1578), 348–349 (October 17, 1578), 400 (November 27, 1578); XI, 57 (February 23, 1579).

[111] S.P.12/45/16 [?January 1578]; *A.P.C.*, X, 168–169 (February 19, 1578); XI, 178 (July 1, 1579), 208 (July 27, 1579).

[112] S.P.12/45/16 [?January 1578].   [113] *A.P.C.*, XI, 178 (June 28, 1579).

[114] S.P.12/133/10[?December ?1579], /11, 12 [?1579], /13 (1579).

[115] S.P.12/133/11 [?1579].

[116] S.P.12/133/13 (1579); *A.P.C.*, XI, 292 (October 25, 1579).

THE ATTEMPTED REVIVIFICATION OF CATHOLICISM

ence to the Establishment in the diocese of Salisbury.[117] The obstinacy of the recusants, probably in part, at least, Catholics, in Gloucestershire, beyond the efforts of the local ecclesiastical commission to cope with, caused the Council to order that three or four of the principal offenders be sent to it.[118] In the following June it thanked the sheriffs and justices of Devon and Cornwall for their success in obtaining conformity.[119]

The two universities also continued to be a source of concern to the government. In April 1578 proceedings against religious malpractices at Cambridge, possibly referring in part to some Catholic activities, were directed to be instituted,[120] and in the ensuing weeks similar steps were ordered to be taken against Catholics at Exeter College, Oxford.[121]

Wales, especially, remained a sore spot. An inquisition into the activities of Hugh Owen, who had escaped abroad, turned up evidence of pronounced Catholic sympathies there.[122] Later during that year, Welsh recusants were ordered to be subjected to severe penalties, perhaps to compensate for leniency in the past; and certain Catholics in Flint and Denbigh openly practicing their religion were directed to be brought to trial.[123] A commission to apprehend "massing priests," sent to the Bishop of Llandaff, led him to write to Sir Francis Walsingham that some officials had apparently leaked news of this to two priests, who were protected by Catholics of the diocese.[124] He protested, in the same tone he had used two years previously to denounce religious violations,[125] about a Marian priest, George Morris, who continued practicing his sacerdotal functions, although a hunted fugitive.[126] In April 1579 the Privy Council sent further instructions concerning repressing recusancy to the Council of the Marches of Wales.[127]

---

[117] *A.P.C.*, X, 330 (September 28, 1578).

[118] *A.P.C.*, XI, 37 (February 3, 1579). The text does not give the names or other indications concerning these recusants. Gloucestershire had a Catholic population of indeterminate size; the county was adjacent to an area with a considerable concentration of Catholics.

[119] *A.P.C.*, XI, 152 (June 4, 1579).   [120] *A.P.C.*, X, 217–218 (April 27, 1578).

[121] *A.P.C.*, X, 221 (May 4, 1578), 295 (July 29, 1578). Exeter College had a considerable reputation for Catholic leanings.

[122] S.P.12/123/1 (March 2, 1578), /11 (March 24, 1578).

[123] *A.P.C.*, X, 331–332 (September 28, 1578); XI, 29 (January 25, 1579), 48 (February 15, 1579).

[124] S.P.12/129/30 (February 3, 1579).   [125] S.P.12/118/11.2 (October 25, 1577).

[126] S.P.12/129/30 (February 3, 1579).

[127] *A.P.C.*, XI, 97 (April 9, 1579). In a report of the Bishop of St. David's during the following summer a considerable aggregation of Catholics was mentioned in a section of Carmarthen (S.P.12/131/42, July 24, 1579).

The drive against nonconforming Catholic justices of the peace, whom the Queen had learned about during a progress through East Anglia,[128] led immediately to action against them and other leading Catholics of that area — Catholics, it must be noted, of differing family names, but frequently related by blood or marriage. In answer to a summons from the sheriff of Norfolk, Humphrey Bedingfield, Robert de Grey, John Downes, Robert Downes, John Drury, and (?Edward) Rockwood appeared individually before the Council, sitting at Norwich (because of a royal progress to that city), on August 22, 1578; and each was charged with recusancy contrary to his duty as a good subject. All of them admitted the charge and refused to conform. The Council then consulted with the Bishop of Norwich, who was present, concerning how many of them had previously participated in conferences or had otherwise been dealt with to induce conformity. Rookwood, who had taken part in such conferences in the past, and had been excommunicated for contumacy, was called back, and then ordered imprisoned in the gaol of the county. The terms governing his confinement were quite severe. He was to be kept secluded from all contacts except with someone designated by the bishop to discuss doctrinal differences and with his agent, in order to direct him concerning the care of his family and his property. Robert Downes, who had remained obdurate despite previous conferences, suffered similar treatment, being confined in the gaol at Norwich.[129]

The bishop had not previously prosecuted Humphrey Bedingfield, Robert de Grey, John Downes, and John Drury for recusancy. Each one was now required to furnish bonds of £200 insuring that he would not depart from his appointed lodgings in Norwich, and would confer with the bishop or his deputy. That prelate was authorized to free any of these recusants who conformed, and to imprison under the same severe regulations as (?Edward) Rockwood and Robert Downes those ordered to remain in Norwich but not confined in prison, if they did not submit by the feast of St. Michael.[130]

---

[128] S.P.12/45/16 [?January 1578]; *Cal. S.P. Span.*, II, 610–611 (September 8, 1578); Oratorians, *Diaries*, 149 (February 15, 1579).

[129] *A.P.C.*, X, 310–311 (August 22, 1578). Rookwood's Christian name is not given. These proceedings against the recusants in East Anglia are contained, in more abbreviated form, in S.P.12/142/43 [?1580]; this report is entitled "A Note of the names of such as were committed for Papistry in the Counties of Norfolk, Suffolk, and Cantabr."

[130] *A.P.C.*, X, 311–312 (August 22, 1578).

THE ATTEMPTED REVIVIFICATION OF CATHOLICISM

On the day following these drastic decisions the Council summoned Thomas Lovell, Robert Lovell, and Ferdinando Paris, all members of the Norfolk gentry, and accused them of recusancy. As they remained firm in refusing to change, they were confined to their lodgings in Norwich under bond, on the same conditions as Humphrey Bedingfield and the others. Similar regulations were also imposed on two other Norfolk Catholics, Sir Henry Bedingfield and Edmund Windham, a doctor of civil law.[131] The Council considered Sir Henry's case too grave to refrain from pursuing it further at this point. It directed the Bishop of Norwich or his deputies and two justices of the peace to go to the knight's house and discharge all his recusant servants. Neither he nor their friends could maintain them, wherever they should settle, and Sir Henry was strictly forbidden to hire any suspected recusants as servants in the future.[132]

Despite the stanchness of certain of the Norfolk Catholics, others proved less steadfast when cited before the Council during its sessions at Norwich. William Gibbon, James Hubbard, and Philip Awdley conformed when subjected to examination, and the Council dismissed their cases.[133] This, indeed, must have been a shock to the adherents of the traditional church and a victory for the Establishment, because the three had been cited as recusants in the census of Norfolk nonconformists in 1577,[134] and their Catholicity was of prominence in their county.

That body also summoned recusant members of the Suffolk gentry before it. Edward Sulliard was directed to remain at Ipswich until Michaelmas, participating there in religious conferences; and the same order, with the substitution of Bury for Ipswich, was enjoined upon Edmund Bedingfield, Henry Everard, William Hare, and Thomas Sulliard. Several others endured the infliction of harsher punishment. Roger Martin, Michael Hare, and Henry Drury were subjected to close imprisonment at Ipswich, without benefit of any conference; and John Daniel was committed to close confinement at Bury. However, another of the persons under examination, Thomas Bateman, conformed.[135]

The Council committed Evans Fludd of Cambridgeshire to the custody of a Dr. Ithell, who in September was directed to place him in some residence in Cambridge, confer with him until the next Michaelmas, and

---

[131] *A.P.C.*, X, 312 (August 23, 1578), 315 (August 24, 1578).
[132] *A.P.C.*, X, 315–316 (August 24, 1578).   [133] *A.P.C.*, X, 312 (August 23, 1578).
[134] S.P.12/117/27.1 (October 29, 1577).   [135] *A.P.C.*, X, 313 (August 23, 1578).

see that he was brought to the local parish church to hear the sermons.[136] Rooke Greene of Essex was committed to the custody of the treasurer of Walden, to live there at his own expense, in order that he might confer with two preachers, Lawson and Harrison. Either the treasurer or his servants were to be responsible for bringing Greene to the local parish at the hour of sermons and any other occasion of preaching. If by Michaelmas he had not conformed, he was to be subjected to close confinement in the county gaol of Essex.[137] The Council meted out a similar penalty to a Mr. (?Thomas) Crawley of Manudon, Essex, who was confined to a house at Colchester unless he, too, conformed by Michaelmas. Three other Essex recusants, when summoned at this time, conformed, and their cases were dismissed.[138]

The Bishop of Norwich informed the Council on September 14 that he had induced the conformity of Thomas Lovell, and in early October he added the names of (?Edward) Rookwood and John Drury, each of whom had now been set free under bond. The other recusants at Norwich, proving obstinate up to the terminal date of their partial custody, had been imprisoned; and the Council directed that they should so remain until they conformed. Robert Downes, though unwilling to conform, consented to hear sermons, if commanded. He was ordered to remain in his present place of restraint, continue attending conferences, and hear sermons in the local church. The lawyer, Edmund Windham, on the other hand, proved extremely obstinate, and the Council commanded that he be sent to them so that they might use severer measures.[139]

In the latter part of October Evans Fludd, after some weeks in Dr. Ithell's custody, conformed, and was released on bond to continue his new intention.[140] However, the recusants retained at Bury for conferences refused to yield. The Council thereupon empowered the Bishop of Norwich to imprison them and all other obstinate recusants either in jail at Ipswich or in the other places within his jurisdiction, except

---

[136] *A.P.C.*, X, 320 (September 4, 1578). Dr. Ithell, although not otherwise identified, most probably was the Master of Jesus College, Cambridge, of that name.
[137] *A.P.C.*, X, 313 (August 23, 1578), 323–324 (September 11, 1578), 327 (September 19, 1578).
[138] *A.P.C.*, X, 327–328 (September 19, 1578).
[139] *A.P.C.*, X, 333 (September 29, 1578), 342 (October 12, 1578).
[140] *A.P.C.*, X, 359–360 (October 29, 1578).

Sir Henry Bedingfield, who was to be sent at once to London to the Council.[141]

Sir Henry, once he had started out, became too ill to continue his journey. The Council, which frequently mitigated its severe attitude in cases of necessity, excused his attendance if he were unable to come and directed him in that case to return to his former place of custody until that body should send him further orders.[142] In the middle of the following January (1579), since Sir Henry still remained indisposed, the Council excused him from going to Norwich to confer about religion, but ordered him to come to London for such conferences on Our Lady's Day.[143]

Another member of the same family, Edmund Bedingfield, likewise received a degree of leniency because of illness. When he sued in November 1578 for permission to reside at the house of a Mr. Browne in Suffolk until he had recovered his health, the Council granted his request on condition that Bishop Freake appoint a preacher to confer with him there and report the results within twenty-eight days, so that the Council could decide on further steps.[144] In the following May, Bedingfield became so seriously ill that he was permitted to go under bond to Bath for his health.[145]

Rooke Greene, whose unyielding attitude had now resulted in his imprisonment in Colchester Castle, in June sued for enlargement because of his ill-health and pressing suits-at-law caused by the death of his father-in-law. The Council, when it granted his request, based its decision partly on the hope that Arthur Harris, who was to supervise Greene's acts during his period of freedom, might induce his conformity.[146] Similarly, when Lord Wentworth in the same month requested that Edward Sulliard, then a prisoner at Ipswich, be delivered into the custody of Philip Wentworth, the plea was granted until Michaelmas on condition that both custodian and ward give bonds that the latter be forthcoming when wanted.[147]

Earlier that year, in mid-February, the Council inquired if Michael

---

[141] *A.P.C.*, X, 372–373 (November 4, 1578).
[142] *A.P.C.*, X, 408 (December 1, 1578).   [143] *A.P.C.*, XI, 15–16 (January 15, 1579).
[144] *A.P.C.*, X, 385 (November 11, 1578).   [145] *A.P.C.*, XI, 116–117 (May 4, 1579).
[146] *A.P.C.*, XI, 174–175 (June 28, 1579). Greene's leave was to last until November 1.
[147] *A.P.C.*, XI, 166 (June 15, 1579).

Hare, Roger Martin, Henry Drury, and John Daniel, who had been committed during the previous summer to private custody at Ipswich and Bury, had been induced by means of conferences to conform. If they had not, they were to be confined to close imprisonment in the common gaols of Norfolk.[148] It is not clear to what extent this order was carried out at this time. Somewhat later, during the summer, when the recusant prisoners at Bury petitioned for release to avoid an epidemic of the plague, the Council permitted them to be moved temporarily elsewhere and subsequently directed the Bishop of Norwich to commit Henry Drury, Michael Hare, and Thomas Sulliard to private custody, giving similar directions to the sheriff of Suffolk concerning John Daniel.[149] Henry Everard, a man of small income whose wife was dying and who had fourteen children, now received a mitigation of sentence to attend to personal affairs.[150]

The year 1579 brought to an end a decade which had witnessed an increasingly more stringent official policy against Catholics. By 1580 rumors, based on fact, were coming to the government that the pope was sending over to England an ecclesiastical mission, composed of the aged Marian Bishop of St. Asaph, Thomas Goldwell, long an exile on the Continent, some lesser clergy and some Jesuits. Simultaneously, a small, ill-timed and ill-fated papal army entered Ireland to assist a rebellion there. This combination of forces, threatening the religious status and the security of the realm, caused the Queen and her government to resolve even more rigorously to secure lay conformity. The new policy of the government was to immobilize the practice of recusancy by selecting castles in various counties in which the more notorious nonconformists of the upper classes were to be incarcerated.[151]

---

[148] *A.P.C.*, XI, 47–48 (February 15, 1579).

[149] *A.P.C.*, XI, 165–166 (June 15, 1579), 204 (July 26, 1579), 253–254 (August 26, 1579), 254 (August 27, 1579).

[150] S.P.12/126/39 [?October ?1578], /131/53 (August 6, 1579); *A.P.C.*, XI, 253–254 (August 26, 1579).

[151] S.P.15/27/21 [?June ?1580]; *A.P.C.*, XII, 124 (July 26, 1580). News of this apparently was not publicized; the King of Spain was informed in early August that it was under consideration, but had not been decided upon (*Cal. S.P. Span.*, III, 45, August 7, 1580). The castle of Framlingham in Suffolk was chosen for the confinement of the recusants of Norfolk and Suffolk (*A.P.C.*, XII, 82–83, July 5, 1580). Wisbeach Castle continued to be the place of incarceration for the most important Catholics. In 1580 eight Catholics were recorded as imprisoned there — Bishop Watson, Abbot Feckenham, Dr. Young, Dr. Windham, Dr. Oxenbridge,

Next, the Council, at the order of the Queen, directed that a certain number of leading recusants were to be sent out of each shire to the custody of the Bishop of London and his fellow ecclesiastical commissioners.[152] The prison lists for London, dated "1580," include a considerable number of Catholics from various counties of the realm; however, some of these, chiefly clerics, had been incarcerated for many years.[153]

Hampshire, facing the Catholic south of Europe, added to the government's alarm and forced it further to toughen its Catholic policy. In August 1580 the Privy Council ordered the ecclesiastical commission of the diocese of Winchester to imprison some Catholic recusants "of very lewde demeanour"; that this was an inadequate step became evident in December when Elizabeth Sander, a nun and sister of the most militant opponent of the Elizabethan regime living abroad in exile, Nicholas Sander, and William Hoord, a well-known recusant since 1559, were apprehended on suspicion of possessing a Catholic propagandistic writing.[154] This latter incident, it seems probable, moved the authorities to make a tentative decision about the intransigence of female recusants, who usually in the past had been left unbothered. The Bishop of Winchester was directed to see that conformist husbands of recusant wives were held responsible for obtaining their spouses' conformity by keeping the latter isolated until that was effected. To spur it, these husbands were also forced to pay weekly a "convenient mulcte."[155]

These decisions of the government serve merely as an introduction

---

and three secular priests, Mettam, Wood, and Bluet. Complaints were placed against them because of their continued refusal to conform (S.P.12/143/17, October 16, 1580).

[152] S.P.12/141/34 (August 22, 1580); S.P.15/27/21 [?June ?1580]; *A.P.C.*, XII, 156–157 (August 15, 1580). The Privy Council requisitioned the London house of the Archbishop of York at Battersea to be a prison for recusants (S.P.12/141/34, August 22, 1580).

[153] S.P.12/130/43 (July 31, 1580; Fleet), /140/36 (July 30, 1580; Gatehouse), /37 (July 29, 1580; Poultry Counter), /38 (July 31, 1580; Queen's Bench), /39 (July 31, 1580; White Lion), /40 (July 1580; Marshalsea), /141/1 (August 1, 1580; Counter in Wood Street). Reports to the Spanish king speak of a considerable number of Catholics being imprisoned or ordered to report to prison at the time of the missionary activity of the Jesuits, Campion and Parsons (*Cal. S.P. Span.*, III, 38, June 26, 1580; 43, July 23, 1580; 54, October 16, 1580; 62, October 23, 1580).

[154] *A.P.C.*, XII, 133 (August 5, 1580), 270 (December 1, 1580); S.P.12/144/31 (November 18, 1580).

[155] S.P.12/144/36 (November 22, 1580).

to a host of other acts which make even more manifest official apprehensiveness. The Bishop of London received directions to inquire into the conformity of the physicians of the capital.[156] The sheriffs of Wilts and Berks were each sent a list of known recusants, excommunicates, who had previously escaped apprehension through official negligence; they were to seize them without fail.[157] The diocese of Chester and within it especially Lancashire, distant from the capital, difficult to penetrate, and notoriously Catholic, persistently attracted the government's attention after 1580, as in the 1570's, since the religious laws were difficult to enforce in view of the obstacles of geography and the scattered population, which also permitted fugitive priests and hunted laymen to find refuge there. The Queen granted the fines levied upon certain recusants to Nicholas Annesley, partly, so it was declared, to terrify the recusants and partly to moderate the penalty by an easy composition with him. The recusants, however, refused to compound, preferring to be imprisoned. The Council did not consider this adequate punishment and prescribed that all persons making a refusal in the future were to be sent before it for further proceedings.[158] This directive proved to be of little value. Although Annesley was able to secure the conviction of some poorer recusants before the diocesan commissioners for ecclesiastical causes, the recusants of higher standing ignored any summons to appear. To force their appearance, he secured distraints to be executed against their lands, which the Council supported with its authority.[159]

Other evidences of an active practice of Catholicism, increasing the government's nervousness in 1580, kept cropping up repeatedly throughout Lancashire. In May the officials at Westminster learned that masses were openly celebrated and attended. Although the worshipers were

[156] *A.P.C.*, XII, 129 (August 1, 1580). Spies' reports were probably responsible for some of the government's nervousness. Typical was a detailed spy's report of the late 1570's about Catholics in London (S.P.15/25/118, n.d. [?October ?1578]).

[157] *A.P.C.*, XII, 90–91 (July 8, 1580). Further orders for the seizure and prosecution of Catholic priests and laymen, actively practicing their religion, were issued by the Council again later in 1580 (*ibid.*, 211, September 26, 1580; 289, December 20, 1580).

[158] *A.P.C.*, XI, 446 (April 14, 1580).

[159] *A.P.C.*, XII, 103–104 (July 15, 1580). Later in Elizabeth's reign the grant of recusants' fines to some individual, either as a reward or in payment of a royal debt, was more widely practiced and became a settled policy in the reign of James I. Annesley's grant was probably also an attempt to enforce in Lancashire an almost unenforceable law.

indicted, their attitude toward such legal proceedings was one of contempt.[160] The Bishop of Chester, the Earl of Derby, and the Earl of Huntingdon, because of their standing, were among those appointed to an ecclesiastical commission for that county to investigate recusancy and secure conformity;[161] almost immediately they were directed to punish recusants by "mulcte," which by limiting their financial ability tended to lessen their influence in the community of their residence. The Council in London also made the further decision to imprison recusants at the castle of Halton in Cheshire.[162]

The archdeaconry of Richmondshire, also within the jurisdiction of the Bishop of Chester, which had been one of the centers of sympathy for the Northern Rebellion, still caused worry to the northern officials.[163] On August 2 the ecclesiastical commission sat at Richmond. A "slender audience" attended the opening sermon, and following it a jury was impanelled. Only a minority of the recusants who were summoned appeared; to them the Bishop, William Chaderton, gave a word of warning to submit. The first defendant, William Wycliffe of Wycliffe, asserted his conformity. Since he refused to communicate in the Establishment, he was granted a respite for further consideration. Three others declared their conformity, but Lady Sedgewick of Richmond, who remained obstinately a recusant, was imprisoned. Twelve others, having fled away or pleading such excuses as illness, failed to appear and answer the summons.[164]

The despair of the Bishop of Chester at the situation in his diocese is shown in a letter which he sent to the Earl of Leicester, recounting considerable conformity in Lancashire, balanced by considerable recusancy, especially among many of the gentlemen of the county, who both failed to answer summonses to appear before the ecclesiastical com-

---

[160] S.P.12/138/18 (May 16, 1580).   [161] S.P.12/45/75 (June 7, 1580).
[162] A.P.C., XII, 77 (July 3, 1580).
[163] The Earl of Huntingdon, Lord President of the North, complained to the Earl of Leicester that recusancy was reportedly flourishing more than in the past. He intended to test the religious sentiments of the gentlemen of the archdeaconry by having them receive communion with him on Whitsunday (S.P.15/27/14, May 19, 1580).
[164] S.P.12/141/3 (August 2, 1580). A typical case was that of Francis Wycliffe of Snape, who was reported to have moved. The maids at his house "shamefully reviled" the messenger bringing the summons and refused to accept it. He left it in the hall. The policy of the Council in 1580 apparently was opposed to imprisonment for refusing to receive communion (S.P.12/144/26, November 14, 1580).

mission and obstinately maintained their refusal to adhere to the Establishment, despite heavy fines. They influenced the lower classes to follow their example, and these latter were further encouraged by the priests laboring in the county and by the want of an able ministry of the Establishment there.[165] Reports of the diocesan ecclesiastical commission, which made a perambulation in October 1580 and in late November and early December sat at Manchester, and contemporary indictments for recusancy further attest both to outright violations of the religious laws and to partial conformity — participation in the liturgy of the *Book of Common Prayer,* except in the communion service.[166] Richmondshire, Bishop Chaderton complained in alarm, was seething with a rebellious spirit inimical to the welfare of the realm.[167] Although the letters of the ordinary indicate that he tended to take an extreme view of affairs, in this case we must accept his judgment since it was based on hearings by the ecclesiastical commission in the archdeaconry. The patience of the Privy Council became exhausted by late 1580 and it directed the imprisonment of obdurate recusants throughout the diocese of Chester.[168]

During the summer of 1580 the ecclesiastical commission held a perambulation throughout the Archdiocese of York, starting at the cathedral city. On Monday morning, July 18, a session was held in the cathedral, all prisoners for religion being present. A sermon was preached in which the prisoners were exhorted "to foresake their vayne and erronious opinions of popery, and conforme them selves with all Dutifull obedience to true religion now established." Some, however, stopped their ears; others coughed and by other noisy behavior avoided hearing what was being said. They further refused to recite the Lord's Prayer, when requested, for spiritual enlightenment in matters of religion. In the subsequent judicial hearing, held in the common hall of York, forty-three

---

[165] S.P.15/27/28 (August 8, 1580).
[166] S.P.12/143/7 (October 4, 1580), /143/11 (October 8, 1580); S.P.15/27/61 (December 2, 1580).
[167] S.P.12/141/3 (August 2, 1580).
[168] *A.P.C.,* XII, 282 (December 16, 1580). A contemporary report praises the devoted obedience of the gentlemen of Cheshire (S.P.15/27/47, October 3, 1580). The nonconformity of Cheshire is partially explained by a report of the 1570's, apparently during the incumbency of Bishop Downman, listing thirteen active Catholic recusants and stating that the bishop was responsible for appointing unworthy and unlearned clergy in his diocese, and for consorting with known Catholics without visible results of converting them (S.P.15/27/94, n.d.: probably before 1577).

THE ATTEMPTED REVIVIFICATION OF CATHOLICISM

men and women, priests and laity, most of them already prisoners, were recommitted after refusal to submit, following a conference with the archbishop. Nine persons conformed, agreeing also to receive communion, and certain of them were also bound to effect the submission of their families. The second session was held on Friday, July 29, at which a man and a woman separately refused to conform; two men and a woman conformed, the men also being bound to effect the submission of their families. The third session was held at Beverley on Friday, August 5. Nine men conformed and bound themselves that their families (except for one who was unmarried) would be brought to make submission. Seven prisoners at Hull of a total of forty-one incarcerated there for religion were summoned before the commissioners; they were recommitted after they rejected the religious arguments presented to them and refused to alter their beliefs. Christopher Monckton, who obdurately refused to attend the state church, was committed to prison at Hull; five others, four acting for their families as well as for themselves, conformed. The fourth session was held at Old Malton on Monday, August 8. Eight persons gave bonds for their own or for their family's conformity. Two who resolutely refused to change their creed were imprisoned. The fifth session was held at Ripon on August 10. There thirteen conformed, but Christopher Marten of Ashton refused and was imprisoned. The sixth session was held at Skipton on August 12. Seven recusants submitted and no one else who was questioned refused conformity. The seventh session was held on the fifteenth and sixteenth of August at Wakefield. Seven persons and their families gave pledges of conformity; no one else who was questioned refused.[169]

In neighboring Lincolnshire Catholicism also flourished to some degree, leading to recusancy and to proselytizing. This, the Council directed, was to be investigated and punished.[170] Similarly, when the celebration of masses within Oxfordshire was reported and other evidence of Catholicism there occasionally appeared, such as suspicions about the prevalence of "papistry" at Balliol College, the Council directed that an

---

[169] S.P.12/141/28 (July 18, 1580–August 16, 1580). This very interesting document, which embodies the procedures of the ecclesiastical commissions to secure conformity, is found *in extenso* in Hughes, *Reformation in England*, III, 428–440.

[170] A.P.C., XII, 70 (June 26, 1580). Evidence of a conformed Marian priest, a parson in Lincolnshire, who urged people to return to the Roman Church is contained in S.P.12/144/48 (n.d. [?December 12, 1580]).

inquiry be held in order to determine the truth and to take necessary corrective steps.[171]

Before 1580 the question of attendance at the services of the Establishment had been unsettled and bothersome to the Catholic conscience, and this it was destined to remain for many years to come. Before 1580, however, there was no unifying force able to bind the Catholic conscience around one course of action. Up to that year the priests working in England, both the Marian survivals and those trained on the Continent, had disagreed whether or not Catholics could attend the legally prescribed ritual. In Scotland and on the Continent, on the other hand, tolerance of worship at Protestant services, when required by law, was the accepted practice.

A committee of the Council of Trent and another of the Inquisition had condemned any degree of conformity in England, although we are at a loss to know how far these judgments were made known within the realm and how far they were considered binding. The widespread violation of this ruling leads one to conclude that before 1580 knowledge of it was limited, or if known it was frequently not considered obligatory. In the chaotic condition of Catholicism in England in the 1560's and 1570's communication with the Continent was haphazard; the ministrations imparted by a dwindling number of Marian priests and the increasing, but always small, number of priests trained abroad were uneven, depending upon the frequency with which one might labor in a locality or whether he resided permanently in a neighborhood. The moral judgments of these priests concerning the immediate problems facing the English Catholics, determined individually by each of these clerics according to his knowledge and experiences, lacked any uniformity or guidance. The eminent barrister, Edmund Plowden, worshiped, as we have seen, according to the rites of the Establishment until Pius V's condemnation of the Queen and her policies, after which he ceased.[172] Lord Montague, acting on the advice of his chaplain, worshiped for years, so it was asserted, according to the legal prescriptions, on the grounds that expediency justified him in conscience.[173] And very influential in the late 1570's was a book written by a William Clithero, then

[171] *A.P.C.*, XII, 211 (September 26, 1580); S.P.12/146/10 [?1580 ?1582].
[172] S.P.12/144/45 (December 2, 1580).
[173] *Misc.*, II, 180; *Misc.*, IV, 4–5, note. The Jesuit, Robert Parsons, in "Domesticall Difficulties" (reproduced in *Misc.*, II) stated (p. 180) that Lord Montague went to

THE ATTEMPTED REVIVIFICATION OF CATHOLICISM

a layman and later a priest, permitting attendance at the services of the state church as a matter, at the most, of slight sin.[174]

The Jesuits, Campion and Parsons, in 1580 and 1581, strongly combatted Clithero's opinion in speech and writing. They held a small synod of priests at Southwark, both survivals of the Marian period and later ones trained on the Continent, which reaffirmed the Tridentine prohibition of worshiping according to the Establishment. Although not completely successful, the two Jesuits strengthened the resolve of many lay Catholics to refuse conformity. Their books, printed and circulated in considerable numbers, were known to the government. When copies were seized, the publication was continued in secret by means of a roving press.[175]

The effect of this intensive effort to shore up a dwindling faith reacted unhappily on the passive Catholic laity. We have observed the strengthening of the official policy begun in 1575 of keeping the leading recusants in prison or under constant surveillance; we can now very clearly observe its effectiveness in regard to some of the more important of the Catholics.[176]

---

mass, but had the liturgy of the *Book of Common Prayer* celebrated for his servants. Bishop Richard Smith in "The Life of Lady Magdalen, Viscomtesse Montague" (quoted in footnote, *Misc.*, IV, 4–5) stated definitely that Lord Montague went to the Anglican services because his chaplain considered it permissible out of expediency.

[174] *Misc.*, II, 28, 179–181; *Misc.*, IV, 5. The book (or pamphlet) of Clithero is possibly S.P.12/144/69 (n.d.), an erudite, but confusing and diffusely written, work. The arguments in this book were sufficiently cogent to raise doubts in the mind of a Catholic about the binding power of Rome's prohibition against worshiping in the Establishment.

[175] These books are polemical in nature. Campion's chief writing, a pamphlet, *Decem Rationes*, was apologetical. Parsons wrote *A Brief Discovrs contayning certayne Reasons Why Catholiques Refuse to Goe to Church* (1580) and *A Brief Censvre vppon two bookes Written in Answere to M. Edmonde Campions offer of disputation* (1581). For a recent treatment of Campion and Parsons see Hughes, *Reformation in England*, III, 304–315.

[176] It is interesting to take notice of a contemporary document, S.P.12/136/16 (n.d.), which apparently had little circulation, since the imprisoned Catholic recusants did not make use of it in defense of their acts. It is entitled: "A breife advertisement howe to Answere unto the Statute for not coming to Church both in Law, and Conscience, Conteining three Principall Points." The three divisions are: "The first what is to be said in Law to that common demand, Doe you, or Will you goe to the Church. The Second whether the matter of the statute for not coming to Church can be found by Inquisition of a Jury. Thirdly if any Person being denied the advantage of all Exceptions by Law, how to Answere with most Safety according to the duty of a Catholicke." This is a carefully thought-out analysis of a difficult question, going into the legal and moral aspects of the case.

Evans Fludd, who had previously been induced to conform through conferences, was confined to the Castle of Cambridge after he had returned to the practice of Catholicism. Although the government viewed his actions with a hostile eye, it released him under bond of £100 for four months in order to regain his health, on condition that he reside in surroundings where he might again be induced to conform. As his health did not improve, this respite was later extended.[177] Gilbert Hussey, a notoriously obdurate Catholic imprisoned in the Gatehouse, received less favorable consideration on account of health. He was released only for twenty days to the custody of Charles Morrison, with the condition that if after conference during that time he had not conformed, he was to return to the Gatehouse.[178] Robert de Grey, who had been prosecuted in the late summer of 1578, continued to remain in custody, although recently the Bishop of Norwich had permitted him to appear before the Court of Wards.[179] Edmund Bedingfield, also still a prisoner, received a temporary release under bond to attend to his business affairs, and the Council later extended this in order that he might make arrangements for the marriage of his son.[180]

The intractability of various Catholic gentry in Staffordshire caused them again to be summoned before the ecclesiastical commission in London, to explain why they had used the bonds they had given for their continued good behavior as an excuse for refusing to appear and answer concerning their recusancy.[181] John Gifford, one of the wealthiest and most influential Catholics in this county, who had repented of his recent abjuration of the ancient faith, was subjected for some time to very close confinement; the Council preferred to stay a civil suit at the assizes in Staffordshire, in which his absence might prejudice his rights, rather than release him. He was later set free for a short period upon posting very heavy bonds.[182]

Two of the very small group of Catholic recusants who belonged to

---

[177] *A.P.C.*, XI, 378 (January 27, 1580); 380 (January 27, 1580); XII, 51–52 (June 10, 1580).
[178] *A.P.C.*, XII, 298 (December 31, 1580). [179] S.P.15/27/4 (February 4, 1580).
[180] *A.P.C.*, XI, 390 (February 14, 1580); XII, 38–39 (May 26, 1580).
[181] *A.P.C.*, XI, 415–416 (March 11, 1580).
[182] *A.P.C.*, XII, 356–357 (March 13, 1581); XIII, 7 (April 2, 1581), 42 (May 8, 1581). Gifford apparently had been confined to the Marshalsea (*A.P.C.*, XII, 357, March 13, 1581), but was later placed in his own house in London under charge of the knight marshal (XIII, 7, April 2, 1581; 42, May 8, 1581).

families of the peerage, Lord Paget and John Talbot of Grafton, Worcestershire, could never hope to escape the close scrutiny of the highest authorities. The Queen, anxious to secure the conformity of Lord Paget, whose family also contained other recusants, directed the Council to examine him about his adherence to Catholicism. After some weeks of restraint he temporarily conformed.[183] John Talbot, who stood close to the earldom of Shrewsbury, was cited before the Council for recusancy in August 1580. In extenuation of his behavior he stated that he did not want to be forced suddenly to change the religion in which he believed and had been raised, until he might be convinced otherwise by conference with some learned man. At the same time he assured the Earl of Leicester of his loyalty as a subject. The Council committed Talbot to close confinement in the custody of the Dean of Westminster, who was to discuss religious questions with him.[184] In the following March, as he had not conformed, the Council refused to grant him leave to attend to a property suit at the assizes at Chester, preferring to stay the suit in order to prevent prejudice to his title.[185]

John Gage and William Shelley of Sussex were confined as close prisoners in the Fleet because of their intransigence in religion, and for the same reason Edward Gage and Richard Shelley of the same county were given into the custody of the knight marshal.[186] Ralph Sheldon, whom the Catholics considered one of the stanchest of their coreligionists, was imprisoned, but after a time released to the care of the Dean of Westminster, while ill. Though it was left to his option whether or not he wished to confer with his host about religion, Sheldon chose to do so and conformed at the beginning of January 1581.[187] If Sheldon's conversion proved that the astuteness of the government in applying to the recusants

[183] *A.P.C.*, XII, 157 (August 15, 1580); S.P.12/144/29 (November 17, 1580).
[184] *A.P.C.*, XII, 169 (August 24, 1580); S.P.12/141/29 (August 17, 1580). Talbot complained of the mental torment he was undergoing because of the conflict between his loyalty to the Queen and his obligations of conscience in matters of religion.
[185] *A.P.C.*, XIII, 4 (March 28, 1581).
[186] *A.P.C.*, XII, 152–153 (August 13, 1580). William Shelley's wife complained that during her husband's long imprisonment much of their joint property had been distrained; she petitioned for a return of her share (S.P.12/148/39, n.d.: probably during the 1580's). Edward Gage's wife begged that her long-ailing husband should be released from imprisonment in order that he might recover his health (S.P.12/159/59, n.d.: probably during the 1580's).
[187] *A.P.C.*, XII, 254–255 (November 1, 1580), 301–302 (January 8, 1581).

a mixed policy of harshness, moderation, and cautiousness would eventually bear fruit, an even stronger proof was the temporary conformity of Sir George Peckham, a more important person, who had been given a grant of land in America as a refuge for recusants and who had sheltered Campion and had distributed money to imprisoned recusants.[188]

John Towneley, who had suffered imprisonment in the preceding decade, was subjected to stricter supervision because he was steward of certain crown manors in Lancashire and reportedly had considerable influence over many of the royal tenants. It was known that he had used his freedom from imprisonment to encourage the Catholics in various sections of Lancashire. The Council in June 1580 ordered that he be temporarily suspended from his stewardship until the ecclesiastical commission for the diocese of Chester could determine if he had conformed or should be prosecuted as a recusant.[189] Towneley refused to alter his religious views and was still a prisoner in Lancashire in 1584 when Robert Cecil suggested that he be moved to London for his health.[190]

The well-connected Tyrwhitt family proved to be a source both of trouble and of satisfaction to the government. Its members exhibited pro-Catholic sympathies while under the influence of Sir Robert Tyrwhitt, although his attitudes occasionally seemed equivocal; away from his influence his son-in-law and daughter, Lord and Lady Sheffield, and a son, John Tyrwhitt, conformed. Another son, William, in prison in London, refused to change his beliefs.[191] In January 1581 he and his brother Robert, both of whom were confined in the Tower for recusancy, received a command from the Council to confer with William Wickham, Dean of Lincoln. This came to nothing; but on June 13 the two young men, acting at the direction of their father, accepted the conditions prescribed on May 7, 1581, for releasing recusants from prison and agreed to hold further conferences with the Dean of Lincoln after their release.[192] This was very possibly only an excuse to obtain their discharge

---

[188] *A.P.C.*, XII, 282–283 (December 18, 1580), 296 (December 28, 1580), 325–326 (February 7, 1581), 346 (March 1, 1581); S.P.12/144/56 (December 20, 1580), /57 ([?December 21], 1580), /58 (December 21, 1580), /146/40 (n.d.: probably in early 1580's).
[189] *A.P.C.*, X, 182 (March 10, 1578); XII, 57 (June 13, 1580).
[190] S.P.12/168/28 (February 28 [?1584]).
[191] *A.P.C.*, XII, 91–92 (July 10, 1580), 105–106 (July 16, 1580).
[192] *A.P.C.*, XII, 306 (January 11, 1581); XIII, 41 (May 7, 1581), 75 (June 13, 1581), 79–80 (June 14, 1581).

from the Tower, for in October the Bishop of Lincoln complained that the two Tyrwhitts, after returning home, had strengthened the faith of certain Catholics inclined toward conformity and had shaken the Protestant beliefs of some others.[193] Obviously this alarmed the bishop, who had just succeeded in effecting the conformity of some recusants within his diocese, apparently Catholics, judging from the circumstances.[194]

3. CATHOLICISM CONTAINED, 1581-1583

Judging from what we know today, the activities during the 1580's of the priests, both the seculars and the Jesuits, by no means proved to be a widespread evangelizing movement. Their efforts constituted, in reality, a haphazardly conducted drive to strengthen what remained of Catholicism in England; looking today at the extant data and considering the total population of the realm of Elizabeth I, inexact as our knowledge may be, conversions were comparatively few. One of the chief obstacles to the priests' success was the plots fostered by Catholic princes and ecclesiastics on the Continent, including the pope, to attack England by military force. This rendered suspect to the government any adherent of the papal church within the realm; and the whole body of Catholics was even more suspect because refugees who had fled abroad, some of them blood kin of wealthy and influential recusants at home, advised these attacks.

From the acts of the Queen and of the Council we can now determine that they met this peril to their official policy by resolving to destroy the Catholic priesthood through execution, exile, and imprisonment; by repressing Catholic religious activities through stricter laws; by continuing control of the lay Catholics through fine and imprisonment. Essentially, Westminster still wished only to secure the conformity of the laity; when the authorities had no evidence of nor reason to suspect treason, they prosecuted no layman upon wild charges, although the Council probably always feared possible Catholic adhesion to an enemy in case of invasion.

Parliament in 1581 enacted further stringent regulations of Catholic activities.[195] To celebrate or hear mass now involved one in a crime

---

[193] *A.P.C.*, XIII, 238 (October 17, 1581).
[194] *A.P.C.*, XII, 92 (July 10, 1580), 105-106 (July 16, 1580), 271 (December 1, 1580).
[195] 23 Eliz. c. 1.

punishable by fine and imprisonment; to reconcile or be reconciled to Rome became high treason; to fail to attend the services of the Establishment entailed a monthly fine of £20. These provisions hung more heavily over the heads of the lay Catholics than previous laws, and the recusants were very cognizant of this increased severity. So worried were some of them that they got in touch with William Allen, the future cardinal, who was the leader of the disaffected Catholic exiles abroad, and pleaded with him not to speak of the Queen other than honorably, lest it should increase their troubles.[196] Most of the laity continued to accept the religious alteration of 1559 as something to be endured temporarily, hoping that in time the traditional church would be restored or some degree of toleration would be granted. One senses this as being implicit in the intransigence of some recusants, in the protestations of loyalty of such men as Sir Thomas Tresham, and in the answers, when under examination, of the influential members of the Catholic gentry. It is manifest also in the frustration and despair which the Catholics felt in the aftermath of the crisis of the 1580's.

The government, on its side, acted on the premise that it was the legitimate government of England, with full legal powers to rule. It considered itself to be acting justifiably in maintaining its settled religious policy and in repressing any subversion by internal or external forces. It now simultaneously intensified its program to secure conformity, as we have seen, and strengthened the Establishment and gradually made it more attractive by removing abuses and improving the quality, and thereby the zeal, of its clergy.

Nonconformity, the Queen and Council decided, was to be treated as a matter of degree. On May 7, 1581, in order to distinguish the less from the more intransigent Catholics, they provided that those in prison or in the custody of private individuals should be released upon giving bonds guaranteed by sureties and accepting certain prescribed regulations:

The condition is suche that if the within bounden A. B. doe not at anie tyme hearafter departe owt of this Realme into anie of the partes of beyond the seas without her Majesties speciall licence to be graunted unto him in that behalf, and doe also continew and remayn at his dwelling house called ———, in the countie of ———, or within three myles compas of his said

[196] *The Letters and Memorials of William Cardinal Allen (1532–1594)*, Fathers of the Congregation of the London Oratory, eds. (London 1882), 92–93 (April 17, 1581).

howse, until he shall have conformed and yelded him self unto the Orders for Religeon and for coming and resorting to Divine Service established by Act of Parliament within this Realme, and that the same his conformitye shall by his meanes and procurment bee notefyd by the Ordinarie of the Diocesse where he shall be dwelling unto the Lords of her Majesties honnorable Privie Councell; and also doe not at anie tyme hearafter willinglie suffer or admitt the repaire and accesse of anie Jesuite, Massing Preist, Semmynary Preist, or of anie other person what soever knowen to him to bee a Recusant in not cominge to the churche according to the lawes of the Realme, and doe also from hencefourthe forbeare to haunt or resorte aswell unto the howse as to the societie of anie such personn or personns as now is or hearafter shalbe known to the said A. B. to bee a Recusant in not coming to the churche; and also if the said A. B. doe not reteine or keape anie servauntes or sojoner [*sic*] in anie of his howses that shall, contrary to the lawes of this Realme, forbeare to resorte and come to the churche . . .[197]

This bonded pledge facilitated the government's treatment of the Catholic problem, since it could now handle the more tractable recusants with less supervision. Many of them, weary of the harassments of laws which prevented them from living normal lives, grasped at this concession to alleviate their situation.

Brian Fowler of Staffordshire, currently a prisoner in the Fleet, accepted the conditions on May 7 and obtained his release.[198] As these terms became more widely known, other imprisoned recusants willingly followed suit. On May 18 three prisoners in the Marshalsea, on May 23 two in the same prison and one in the Fleet, and on May 25 a woman in the Marshalsea, on May 28 a man in the same prison, on May 30 a prisoner in the Gatehouse and one in the Marshalsea, and on May 31 another in the Marshalsea, accepted these new conditions.[199] On June 13 two sons of Sir Robert Tyrwhitt, imprisoned in the Fleet, and a prisoner in the Gatehouse, obtained freedom by accepting these provisions,[200]

---

[197] *A.P.C.*, XIII, 41 (May 7, 1581). A different form of recognizance was ordered at York in the previous December, providing for the attendance of all members of a recusant's family at the local parish church and reception of communion as provided by law. This was to be attested by the curate and churchwardens and forwarded to the ecclesiastical commission for York. A conformist bound by such a recognizance was to apprehend any priest or any other recusant of whom he had knowledge and deliver him over to the ecclesiastical commission (S.P.15/27/67, December 1580).

[198] *A.P.C.*, XIII, 42 (May 8, 1581).

[199] *A.P.C.*, XIII, 59–60 (May 18, 1581), 61–62 (May 23, 1581), 62 (May 25, 1581), 64 (May 28, 1581), 67 (May 30, 1581), 68 (May 31, 1581).

[200] *A.P.C.*, XIII, 75 (June 13, 1581).

and on June 14 this concession was extended to another prisoner in the Fleet and to two others in the Gatehouse, one of them a woman.[201] On the same day the Council directed the Bishop of Norwich to offer them to the recusant prisoners within his jurisdiction. If they refused, they were either to attend the state church under guard or be subject to indictment and conviction.[202] During the next two weeks a recusant prisoner in Dorset, another in Shropshire, and the prominent Berkshire lawyer, James Braybrooke, received release from imprisonment on these terms.[203] From the spring of 1581 to the end of the reign the offer of them to lay recusants became a fixed policy of the government, except, perhaps, to those who were more recalcitrant or were considered to be the most dangerous. Since some of those who accepted the conditions of May 7 were later imprisoned, the government either revoked its concession because of violations of the terms or for other reasons the individual had come under the suspicion or the ill will of the authorities.

However, nonacceptance of these conditions did not mean loss of temporary respites from imprisonment to attend to necessary business. Frequently they were granted as a favor in order to incline the recipient toward conformity;[204] undoubtedly they were given in some cases because the councillors had personal knowledge and even familiar acquaintance with individual recusants, especially if men of prominence and wealth, and such a concession came as a matter of course. Edward and John Gage and William Shelley of Sussex were temporarily released from custody in June under heavy bond, without taking this pledge and the particular bond required by it,[205] but John Gage, by accepting the conditions of May 7 on August 4, was freed from further imprisonment at the end of his respite.[206] John Gifford of Staffordshire and Francis Eyreman of Middlesex, who had returned to prison after a temporary respite, received their release upon assuming the obligations of the

[201] *A.P.C.*, XIII, 76 (June 14, 1581).   [202] *A.P.C.*, XIII, 80–81 (June 14, 1581).

[203] *A.P.C.*, XIII, 94 (June 20, 1581), 106 (June 26, 1581).

[204] For example, Lady Stonor was permitted to live in her residence in order to confer about religion as she had apparently signified a willingness to do this (*A.P.C.*, XIII, 264–265, November 27, 1581), and John Cotton was granted a similar respite for a similar reason (*ibid.*, 396, April 25, 1582; 454–455, June 26, 1582). Sir William Catesbie was respited from prison to prosecute certain lawsuits because it was felt such a favor would further an inclination which he had signified of conforming (*ibid.*, 436–437, June 5, 1582).

[205] *A.P.C.*, XIII, 93–94 (June 20, 1581), 105 (June 26, 1581). Each of the three prisoners had to post a bond of £1000.

[206] *A.P.C.*, XIII, 149 (August 4, 1581).

pledge of May 7; each one, however, was dispensed for a time from adhering to the terms, the former in order to recover his health, impaired by his imprisonment, the latter in order to attend to business affairs.[207] In July the Council demonstrated this same spirit of measured liberality in the case of Sir Thomas Fitzherbert, who was permitted to go to his home for the summer on condition that he fulfill only a part of the May pledge, the agreement not to associate with recusants.[208] In June 1582 after having returned to prison, he was again enlarged and subsequently granted a further extension because of serious illness,[209] and two other recusants, Sir William Catesbie and William Tyrwhitt, who were already at large, were released from custody for a further period to attend to private affairs.[210]

The Council dealt with these individuals, instead of referring their cases to lesser authorities, because from its viewpoint their very considerable influence in their local communities needed limiting. This is borne out by a study of extant prison lists of London, which show that a number of the more prominent Catholic recusants were confined in the capital, under the watchful eye of the central authorities.[211] From the viewpoint of Westminster, it was now more than ever imperative to keep attention constantly focused on the areas of concentration of Catholic strength. A series of censuses of recusants in the realm at large,[212] in the north[213] and in certain counties,[214] and repeated appraisals of their

[207] *A.P.C.*, XIII, 7 (April 2, 1581), 42 (May 8, 1581), 110–112 (June 28, 1581), 129 (July 11, 1581); S.P.12/140/38 (July 31, 1580).
[208] *A.P.C.*, XIII, 138–139 (July 26, 1581). [209] *A.P.C.*, XIII, 449–450 (June 18, 1582).
[210] *A.P.C.*, XIII, 436–437 (June 5, 1582), 446–447 (June 15, 1582). The Tyrwhitt family was very ardently Catholic. It was stated that a member of the family was married privately at a Catholic nuptial mass, but publicly by a simple declaration of espousal, without a Protestant minister or the local pastor being present (S.P.12/165/28 [?1583]).
[211] S.P.12/149/81 [?1581], /83 ([?1581] lists of prisoners in various London prisons), /150/74 ([?1581] Newgate), /77 ([?1581] Tower), /94 (December 1581; White Lion, Southwark), /159/28.1–36 (1582–1583; various prisons in London). These prison lists are given *in extenso* in *Misc.*, II, 219–231.
[212] S.P.12/154/25 ([?1582] list of recusants free on bond), /156/42 (1582), /157/90 (1582). Another listing of Catholics, S.P.12/157/88 [?1582], is apparently a spy's report.
[213] S.P.12/155/35 (August 31, 1582; covering letter), /35.1 (1582; census list). According to the covering letter the census was inefficiently administered. The census was to be of the principal recusants convicted in the assizes of 1582, and the annual rental value of their lands and tenements. Yorkshire reported five recusants; Durham, five; Cumberland, two; Lancashire, four; Westmorland, none; Northumberland, none.
[214] S.P.12/151/11 ([?1582] London), /154/44.1 ([?1582] Berkshire), /160/26 (1583, Hampshire).

property and income,²¹⁵ brought in considerable information to shape the future policies of the Queen and her councillors.

Random samplings taken from 1581, 1582, and 1583 will further indicate how ubiquitously the government at a critical period spread its attention in implementing its Catholic lay policy. In Southwark Henry Shelley and Peter Titcheborne, who did not accept the conditions of May 7, 1581, could obtain only a temporary respite from the White Lion prison to attend to private business;²¹⁶ and Gervase Pierpoint, a pillar of recusancy up to the end of the reign, who had been in the custody of the new sheriff of Middlesex, was ordered to be given over to the knight marshal if he did not conform.²¹⁷ In Lancashire Sir John Southworth, who had lived for many years under the government's oversight, was ordered into the custody of the Earl of Derby by March 25, 1582; if he continued his refusal to conform, the earl could recommit him a prisoner at Manchester.²¹⁸ Although this could be ruinous to a landlord, great or small, Southworth showed no signs of yielding, and he was again in prison in April 1582, where the gaolers complained of his continued intractability in religion.²¹⁹

In Staffordshire Hugh Erdswicke and his son, Sampson, were notorious for their antipathetic attitude toward the Establishment. The father violently attacked a messenger sent in April 1581 by the ecclesiastical commission in London to attach him, contemned the warrant which he presented, and spoke insultingly of the Bishop of London. The Council cited him at once to appear before it to make an explanation of his act, but this apparently affected neither his conduct nor his influence in Staffordshire, as a grand jury in December failed to indict him for recusancy; and in May 1582 the Council again summoned him to appear and explain his activities.²²⁰

Much more detail filled the government's dossier from hints and direct accusations against individuals sent in by neighbors or spies, not all of it, by any means, being substantiated. Suspicion or fact about the

²¹⁵ S.P.12/142/33 [?1580], /155/35 (August 31, 1582; covering letter), /35.1 (1582; census list).
²¹⁶ *A.P.C.*, XIII, 129 (July 11, 1581).   ²¹⁷ *A.P.C.*, XIII, 194 (September 5, 1581).
²¹⁸ *A.P.C.*, XIII, 98–99 (June 22, 1581), 335 (February 28, 1582).
²¹⁹ S.P.12/153/6 (April 13, 1582).
²²⁰ *A.P.C.*, XIII, 30–31 (April 19, 1581), 270–271 (December 4, 1581), 425 (May 25, 1582). The Council stated (p. 425) that it had received information that Sampson Erdswicke had been married at a mass.

THE ATTEMPTED REVIVIFICATION OF CATHOLICISM

relations between the laity and the priests, and about the performance of priestly ministrations,[221] and details, real or false, about the education of children beyond the seas,[222] were repeatedly reported to the authorities, forcing them to an alert attention.[223] Undoubtedly, they came more and more to consider the order of May 7, 1581, to be a wise decision, which simplified their duties.

Three papers, generally complementing each other, well express the government's thinking at this time. The first dealt with the ability of recusants to pay fines in full or only in part on a sliding scale, and recommended that conformist husbands should be held responsible for their recusant wives.[224] The second treated the manner of executing certain decisions of the Privy Council concerning recusants. Justices of the assizes were to prosecute all those of the gentle classes who already stood indicted, both men and women, and were to deal in an undefined way with those of the lower classes; and these justices were also to inquire how faithfully the sheriffs and justices of the peace were carrying out their duties in suppressing nonconformity. All classes of recusants at liberty were to be proffered the conditions of May 7, 1581, with the further prohibition against their moving from their dwellings without official consent; refusal to accept these conditions entailed imprisonment.[225] The third paper approved a more intensive use of existing procedures and, partially corroborating the second paper, suggested that recusants at liberty should be bound to remain in their houses or suffer imprisonment.[226] This last paper certainly indicates that the government had become satisfied in general with the effectiveness of its program.

In June 1582 a new form for certifying recusancy, carefully worked

---

[221] S.P.12/140/43 [?July ?1580], /147/2 (January 5 [?1582]), /8 (January 1581), /97 ([?1581] document is faded and partly illegible; some of the contents must be reconstructed by inference), /151/5 [?1581], /12 [?1581], /21 [?1580's], /152/54 (February 1582; *in extenso* in C.R.S., V, *Unpublished Documents Relating to the English Martyrs*, Vol. I: *1584–1603*, J. H. Pollen, ed. [London, 1908], 26–27), /153/14 (April 19, 1582), /78 ([?May] 1582), /154/76 [?July ?1582], /155/27 (August 24, 1582), /155/59 [?1582], /165/22 [?1583], /72 (August 13, 1581). S.P.12/140/43, /147/97 are the interrogations of certain priests, contemporaries of Campion and Parsons in 1580–1581. The examinations of other priests are similar.

[222] S.P.12/150/95 (1581; document is faded and defective), /152/3 (January 10, 1582). S.P.12/146/137, a very comprehensive list, is apparently to be dated ca. 1578.

[223] The data in footnotes 221 and 222 were chosen at random from records of 1581, 1582, and 1583.

[224] S.P.12/136/17 (after January 1580).   [225] S.P.12/154/14 [?1582].

[226] S.P.12/157/52 [?1582 ?1583].

out by lawyers in order to remove any doubt of the meaning or intent of the law, was ordered to be used:

―――, Esquire, one of the Queen's Majesty's Justices of the Peace, within the County of ―――, do hereby certify unto our said sovereign Lady the Queen, into Her Highness' Court, commonly called the King's Bench, that ―――, late of ―――, in the said County, gent. and, ―――, late of ―――, in the said County, yeomen, etc.: every of them being of the said County and above the age of XVI years, on the last day of March in the XXIII year of the reign of our said sovereign Lady the Queen's Majesty, have not by the space of 12 months next, after the same last day of March, repaired to any Church, chapel, or usual place of common prayer. But they and every of them have forborne the same by the said space of the said twelve months, contrary to the form of divers statutes in that case made and provided. In witness whereof, I, the said ―――, have set my hand. Given the ――― day of, etc.[227]

A little over a year later, in October 1583, the antirecusant policy was further intensified when the Council directed the ordinaries to have the ministers within their dioceses warn the parishioners on the first Sunday of each month of their duty to worship at their parish churches. The parish clergy were also to inform the bishop or other qualified authority of the names of recusants in order that they might be indicted; those who escaped indictment through official laxity were to be excommunicated.[228]

We have selected certain dioceses and certain counties spread throughout the realm, an analysis of which will enable us, at the risk of some repetition, even better to judge the degree of success and of failure which attended the drive toward conformity during the earlier years of the 1580's. In the dioceses of Chester and Lichfield and Coventry, where both the ordinaries and the officials at Westminster were keenly aware of large aggregations of Catholics, the Council directed the bishops to search out and prosecute certain obstinate recusants.[229] The Council further provided, in December 1581, that recusants of the diocese of Chester imprisoned at Chester Castle were to be moved to the castle of Manchester,

---

[227] S.P.12/154/15 (June 1582).   [228] S.P.12/163/17 (October 23, 1583).
[229] *A.P.C.*, XIII, 122–123 (July 4, 1581). Between May and July 1581 the Bishop of Chester had been occupied with the case of a very recalcitrant Catholic, James Apsden, a "person of verie lewde demeanour" (*ibid.*, 57–58, May 18, 1581; 122, July 4, 1581).

THE ATTEMPTED REVIVIFICATION OF CATHOLICISM

where the people were more loyal to the Establishment.[230] The Catholic prisoners in Salford gaol, in the very heart of Lancashire's recusancy, proved very refractory, and hope of inducing their conformity remained slight due to want of a preacher.[231] In York, under the watchful eye of the Earl of Huntingdon, Lord President of the Council of the North, intensive efforts were made to prevent lay contacts with priests; and in November 1582, the better to accomplish this, the earl and the northern council were directed to assist the clergy of the Establishment in performing their duties.[232] In some others of the northern counties the remissness of sheriffs in prosecuting recusancy forced the Privy Council to take corrective measures there.[233] This was supplemented by a complaint contained in a census of recusants in the northern counties of the difficulty of bringing in some of them for trial.[234]

In July 1582 the Council demanded a complete report from the Bishop of Salisbury of the recusants in Wiltshire and Berkshire, who had been convicted, but still remained nonconformists.[235] At the University of Oxford Catholicism was known still to exist and consequently remained a worry to the government,[236] although its strength was problematical. A grand jury in Staffordshire which failed to indict certain well-known recusants, despite the bishop's certificate, was ordered to answer for this before the next assizes in the county.[237] The incumbent sheriff of Hereford and his two predecessors received a summons to appear before the Privy Council and answer for their favoritism toward certain prominent recusants.[238] That body also ordered an investigation of recusancy in Herefordshire in December 1581, because, so its instructions stated, Catholicism was very strong there and steps to suppress it needed to be taken.[239] The Council directed the prosecution of those

---

[230] A.P.C., XIII, 279–280 (December 6, 1581).
[231] S.P.12/153/45 (May 13, 1582), /155/76 (October 13, 1582). Among those imprisoned was the ardent Catholic, Sir John Southworth. Another, John Finch, proved to be very unyielding in his examination (S.P.12/163/2, October 1, 1583). The extent of conciliar supervision of the northwest is shown in the order to the sheriff of Chester to apprehend John Whitmoor, "a verie daungerous practising Papist" (A.P.C., XIII, 447, June 15, 1582).
[232] S.P.15/27A/128.1 [?November 21, ?1582].
[233] A.P.C., XIII, 433 (May 29, 1582).   [234] S.P.12/155/35 (August 31, 1582).
[235] S.P.12/154/44 (July 1, 1582).   [236] S.P.12/161/13 (June 25, 1583).
[237] A.P.C., XIII, 271 (December 4, 1581).
[238] A.P.C., XIII, 192–193 (September 5, 1581).
[239] A.P.C., XIII, 286–288 (December 12, 1581).

who had escaped indictment for nonconformity in the diocese of Winchester,[240] and in April 1583 it had a complete census made of recusants in Hampshire, both in and out of gaol.[241]

To the east of the capital the Lord Chief Justice Wray found only a little proof of recusancy in Buckingham, Bedford, and Cambridge, none in Huntington, but considerable in Norfolk and Suffolk.[242] To the south of London in Surrey the Council charged the local authorities in February 1582 with obtaining the indictment of all imprisoned recusants who continued in their refusal to attend church.[243] Early in 1581 the Lord Mayor of London received instructions to dismiss any Catholic holding a position in the municipal government,[244] and in December the sheriff and justices of the peace in Middlesex were directed to investigate evidences of slackness in the prosecution of recusancy within their jurisdiction.[245]

Although the term "recusant" referred both to Catholic and to Protestant nonconformists, the strong drive currently waged against the traditional church is manifest proof that its adherents were in part, probably in large part, intended in these various reports. We can therefore well understand that, to the officials, nothing was more acceptable than the optimistic note sounded in a series of reports indicating a slow, but steady, increase in conformity. The Establishment in Westmorland in 1582 was found to be generally well accepted; in neighboring Northumberland conformity, especially among some members of the lower classes, proved fairly easy to accomplish.[246] Wales, although there there had been little effective effort to convert the people to the Elizabethan church, exhibited only a nonmilitant Catholicism, recognizable in the persistence of various practices, although attempts, in secret, were being made to reinvigorate it.[247] But how well the government was

[240] A.P.C., XIII, 203 (September 11, 1581).
[241] S.P.12/160/26 (April 1583).
[242] C.P.162/51 (July 26, 1582). The context of this report shows that it referred to both Catholic and Protestant nonconformists.
[243] A.P.C., XIII, 337 (February 29, 1582).
[244] A.P.C., XII, 315 (January 18, 1581). This order had followed upon the dismissal of a very active Catholic, Eden, from service in the municipal government.
[245] A.P.C., XIII, 298–299 (December 24, 1581).
[246] S.P.12/155/35.1 (1582). A number of recusants had been indicted in Northumberland.
[247] S.P.12/153/66 (May 28, 1582), /162/29 (September 16, 1583), /165/1 (1583), /3[?1583]; A.P.C., XIII, 427–428 (May 27, 1582). The Bishop of Bangor complained that his life had been threatened for taking steps to suppress Catholic practices (S.P.12/153/66, May 28, 1582).

aware of the moribund state of Catholicism in Wales is hard to determine.

The Bishop of Winchester received the approval of the Council in September 1581 for the favorable results of his efforts to induce conformity.[248] The neighboring Bishop of Salisbury obtained the adherence of Henry Clerke, a prominent Catholic of Berkshire.[249] Thomas Vavasour, whose surname indicates a family with a wide reputation for stanch recusancy, at first under questioning evinced an ardent allegiance to the Roman Church, even to asserting his unwillingness to fight against the pope if he should invade England; eventually he submitted, petitioning Sir Francis Walsingham for his freedom.[250] Six men and a woman implicated in the case of the Jesuit, Campion, were freed of the charges against them by conforming.[251] Thomas Roper again became one of the Council's concerns at this time, because of his reputation for recusancy and his standing as a lawyer. It committed him to close imprisonment in the Fleet and permitted only the Bishop of Rochester or other persons appointed by him to confer with Roper about religion. Quick success attended this decision, for he conformed within a few weeks.[252] At Wisbeach Castle, where only the most refractory of Catholics were incarcerated, and of these only a few were laymen, Andrew Oxenbridge, a lawyer of some standing and erudition, at length could no longer withstand pressures constantly applied. He signed a pledge which showed how far one of the better minds among the Catholics was willing to go in defining the fine line between civil loyalty to the Queen and spiritual allegiance to Rome:

I, Andrew Oxenbridge, Doctor of the Laws, do frankly and from my heart, acknowledge [and] avow the most gracious Lady Elizabeth, now Queen of England, to be most rightful and lawful Queene thereof *de jure*, as whereof she is most justly possessed [since the] first day of her reign till now. And to Her Majesty alone, as to my most just sovereign magistrate, I owe all my loyalty, service, and whole duty of subjection next under God. And ever so will I repute Her Majesty during life, against the Bull (if any be) of Pius V, Gregory, or any other Pope henceforth . . . Furthermore, if

---

[248] *A.P.C.*, XIII, 203 (September 11, 1581).
[249] *A.P.C.*, XIII, 223–224 (October 7, 1581).
[250] S.P.12/140/43 [?July ?1580], /149/83 (n.d. [?1580's]), /165/20 [?1583]. There was a Thomas Vavasour, a contemporary Catholic physician in Yorkshire.
[251] *A.P.C.*, XIII, 260–261 (November 24, 1581), 290–291 (December 15, 1581).
[252] *A.P.C.*, XIII, 148 (August 2, 1581), 158–159 (August 6, 1581), 196 (September 5, 1581).

any man, pretending Catholic Roman religion be [of the] mind that the pope for one cause or other, may depose her or [?dispense] with subjects' oath and [?of] loyalty, I hold it a traitorous article ... But, contrarily, am ready and vow to spend my life and goods [?for the] peace and quiet of Queen Elizabeth and this present state against [?whatever] invader, disturber, or underminer, by what authority, bull, or direction he shall do it, of Prince, or priest, potentate or prelate, ... by what jurisdiction, power, or name be it soever he command.

And as touching matter of religion, to avoid all show of obstinate holding [?anything] by me once received, I promise that if in conference, with any learned [?person], which, being sent by authority, I will willingly admit he can convince me by [?the] only Scripture of the Old and New Testament to hold any error, I will [?yield] me to better reason, and thank God.

All this I protest simply and plainly according to the plain show of these words, abhoring all hidden sophisticated, and dissembled reservation of private sense or secret interpretation, which may never so little impeach, qualify, or modify, the express, most common and readiest taking of the very words, as [?they] lie and offer themselves without forced understanding.[253]

The concessions derogating from an unswerving allegiance to Rome which Oxenbridge made in this pledge show how far the efforts of the secular priests and the Jesuits to sustain the traditional beliefs were being thwarted by the reality of the situation within England. We see this also in an almost identical declaration made contemporaneously by another highly respected Catholic lawyer, Edmund Windham:

I have evermore heretofore acknowledged, accepted and honored the Queen's Majesty that now reigneth over us ... Queen Elizabeth, as my Sovereign Lady, lawfully succeeding in the estate of the said crown, as heir and next of blood to Her Majesty's sister and immediate predecessor, Queen Mary of honorable memory ... and by all extern means and duty shall be ready to my power always to show the same ... notwithstanding any Bull of Censure, or supposed deprivation, or of other sentence whatsoever, either already passed or that hereafter may pass, and come forth from the See of Rome ...[254]

Obviously the Catholic renascence was failing. A gradual attrition was cutting away Catholic numbers and their helplessness is evident in the

---

[253] S.P.12/160/44 (May 14, 1583; the document is torn and somewhat defective, but the sense is integral); *A.P.C.*, XIII, 133 (July 17, 1581).

[254] S.P.12/172/5 [?June 2, ?1583; ?August 2, ?1583; ?July 2, ?1584]. There are two copies, no. 5 (which we have used) and no. 6, a copy. The dating differs in the two, and no. 5 is somewhat difficult to read due to defects. Windham's declaration was signed at Norwich.

very few cases of violent or even tacit opposition to the government; plots implicating Catholics during this decade concerned not the whole body, but only a few. With a high degree of statesmanship the Queen and her Council persisted in their refusal to consider the adherents of the older church as a body as traitorous; instead, they were still judged only to be disobedient. The influential element among the Catholics, the gentry, seem at this distance generally to have been passive, either neutral or openly, but not usually effusively, loyal toward the governing regime. The majority of them were neither connected with nor sympathetic to foreign intervention. Essentially, they remained unorganized, scattered, and leaderless, and from all we can judge, their relations with the priests were restricted to the spiritual plane. Their political thinking was shaped by the society in which they lived, with its nationalism and antiforeign sentiments and ingrained habits of civil obedience, characteristic of the times. Never did they have the opportunity, nor did they ever show the inclination, to unite into a bloc to obtain an amelioration of their condition or to formulate a program of action.

During these years Edmund Plowden and Sir Thomas Tresham were the most influential of the Catholic laity. The former was a leading barrister, the builder of the Middle Temple. The latter became spokesman for an undefinable section of the English Catholics. Plowden represented the earlier transitional years from the Catholic days of Mary Tudor to the Protestant regime under Elizabeth; Tresham symbolized Catholic accommodation to the middle and last years of the Elizabethan era. Plowden, at the time the two Jesuits, Campion and Parsons, came to England, embodied the spirit and the thinking of the older generation now passing away. Until the papal condemnation of 1570 he had considered partial conformity to be justifiable in conscience; after that date, he refused any such compromise. He was accused in his day of responsibility for the presence of Catholicism in the Middle Temple;[255] it has also been claimed that his religion was the sole bar to his appointment to the chancellorship.[256] He is a typical example of the sixteenth-century urban professional man who held to his conscientious beliefs despite the disadvantages it entailed.

---

[255] S.P.12/144/45 (December 2, 1580).
[256] We owe this information to the kindness of Mr. Richard O'Sullivan, Q.C., of the Middle Temple.

On the other hand, throughout the major part of Sir Thomas Tresham's life two currents run parallel: his complete devotion to Catholicism and his undiluted patriotism. From the beginning of the 1580's onward he became the foremost Catholic spokesman pledging unswerving loyalty to the Queen and appealing for relief for his suffering coreligionists. Despite his ardent love of country the government was either too distrustful of him or considered him too prominent to relieve him of the penalties of recusancy. Throughout the Queen's reign he suffered frequent periods of imprisonment and an almost continuously circumscribed liberty, and without audible protest impoverished himself by paying the monthly fine of £20.

Certain facts in Sir Thomas's life, which will become evident between 1580 and 1603, probably explain these conflicting situations: he was a typical member of the gentry class with its consciousness of status and with its limitations of breadth of experience and knowledge; and his religious convictions show a kinship to those of the contemporary *politiques* in France, or perhaps they resulted from a parochialism — a lack of contact with his coreligionists, so that religion was an individual, not a social, thing for him.[257] His strong love of country led him to fear any foreign foe; his patriotism led him to discard and oppose dynastic and religious claims which threatened Elizabeth's right to the English throne.

In 1581 Tresham was imprisoned in the Fleet, after the Jesuit, Campion, according to the Council's assertion, claimed to have been entertained in Sir Thomas's house. Apparently Tresham was uncertain if this were true and refused to swear to it on the grounds that he kept open house and many people came there whose names he did not learn.[258] On September 1 he assured the Council of his loyalty to the Queen, and on the same day he wrote, probably to the Earl of Leicester, that he prayed for her and willingly would spend his life and property in her defense. Significantly, he added that Queen Elizabeth allowed many people, including him, to have liberty of conscience, provided that they did not transgress

---

[257] H.M.C., *Report on Manuscripts in Various Collections,* III (London, 1904), vii, states that Tresham was a convert to the Catholic Church, joining it in 1580. This is the opinion of other writers, but a review of available evidence makes this writer hesitant to agree. Tresham wrote to the (?) Earl of Leicester on (?) September 1, 1581, that he did not know the Jesuit, Campion (p. 17), which would remove the possibility of conversion by the Jesuits.

[258] H.M.C., *Var. Coll.,* III, vii–viii, 17.

her laws.²⁵⁹ But imprisonment, though a new experience, did not shake his faith; and in November he refused to take the Oath of Supremacy because of his religious convictions, although his civil loyalty remained unchanged. The conditions of Tresham's imprisonment had been very strict, and in a letter to Sir Christopher Hatton he pleaded with the favorite of the Queen to obtain his release.²⁶⁰ When this was granted, its terms proved extremely rigid. He had to post bonds of £2000 not to come within four miles of London and was confined to a designated house, which he was forbidden to leave, being deprived even of the customary circuit in which a person in custody had liberty of movement. Moreover, he was not only bound to good behavior, but also the exceptions of religion and conscience, which were sometimes granted, were refused.²⁶¹

About the middle of 1583 the government allowed Sir Thomas to remove to Hoxton. The two years of his imprisonment had had serious effects, and release came as a blessing. His health had suffered grievously; he had been separated from his family; and he had been deprived of the opportunity to supervise his children's upbringing.²⁶²

Although the official reason for the severity of Tresham's strict imprisonment was Campion's accusation, it undoubtedly was also connected with his recusancy. This is the only charge which the government subsequently ever placed against him; it hung over him constantly, and he never escaped official surveillance, especially since the Council dealt with him as the spokesman and the leader of the Catholics.

---

²⁵⁹ *Ibid.*, 16 (September 1, 1581), 18–19 (September 1, 1581).
²⁶⁰ S.P.12/150/66 (November 22, 1581; the document is defective, although the sense is apparently integral); H.M.C., *Var. Coll.*, III, 18 (September 1, 1581), 27 (January 16, 1583).
²⁶¹ H.M.C., *Var. Coll.*, III, 28 (May 27, 1583).
²⁶² *Ibid.*, 28–29 (May 27, 1583), 32 (October 1, 1583).

CHAPTER III

THE DECLINE OF CATHOLICISM
1584-1603

1. MOUNTING TENSIONS, 1584-1587

By 1584 the attempted revivification of Catholicism was very evidently beginning to fail. Although the Continental seminaries continued to send contingents of priests each year to England and some of the religious orders had members working there, the aggregate of seculars and regulars was far from equal to the challenge of thoroughly evangelizing any substantial part of the realm. The priests, usually carefully chosen and given both a well-planned spiritual formation and a good training in Catholic theology, nevertheless were showing the strains of the times; nothing emphasizes this more than the number who abjured or temporized in the face of torture or death or whose faith was shaken in conference with clergy of the Establishment. Except in a few areas there could be no widespread practice of or numerous conversions to Catholicism when its very existence was prohibited by law and repressed by a vigilant officialdom; a secret existence meant haphazard ministrations of religion, a situation made worse by the lack of a resident ecclesiastical authority with adequate power to direct and govern.[1] Persistently conformity cut into the

[1] An examination of relevant sources proves that the number of secular priests and members of religious orders working at any time in England never totaled more than a few hundred. Their labors, although motivated by high ideals, were haphazard due to the absence of any ecclesiastical authority within the realm. A contrasting situation of heroic efforts and scandalous situations prevailed: a certain number of priests abjured; others offered secretly to give information to the government, if thereby they could gain immunity from arrest and prosecution.

ranks of the laity, as we shall so frequently see; during the last nineteen years of Elizabeth's reign the Roman Church dwindled to a leaderless and powerless minority.

The gifted Jesuit, Robert Southwell, bore witness in July 1586 to the condition of his coreligionists in a letter to the Superior-General of his order in Rome, in which he admitted that the strength of the government's repression had brought about wavering even among the stanchest. The Catholic cause, he added significantly, was much weakened by the scarcity of priests: many persons received no ministrations, and some counties had no priests.[2]

Events of the year 1584 explain much which lay behind the harsh enactments of Elizabeth's fifth Parliament of 1584–1585 and of her sixth Parliament of 1586–1587. The number of lay Catholics in prison, whether for recusancy or for other grounds connected with their religion, increased.[3] The abundant data extant in the public records of the period is proof that the government, from various sources of information, kept check on the Catholics, and confessions of suspected persons often served to confirm the fears and the suspicions of the Queen and the Council.[4]

---

[2] S.P.12/191/29 (July 25, 1586). The letter is signed "Father Robert," presumably the Jesuit, Robert Southwell. Some of this information is also to be found in an anonymous letter (probably by Robert Southwell) to William Allen, the Cardinal (S.P.12/191/26, July 23, 1586).

[3] The prison lists showing lay Catholics and priests in prison between 1584 and 1587, the year before the Armada, are very numerous. 1584: S.P.12/169/23, 24, 26, 30; /170/8–15. 1585: S.P.12/178/74, /179/62, /180/64. 1586: S.P.12/190/13, 13.1, 22–27, 29, 32, 33, 42, 44[?1586], 55; /191/37; /193/64, 66, 67; /195/30, 32, 34, 51, 72, 73, 74. 1587: S.P.12/199/91 [?1587], /202/61. Most of these lists and some others are in *Misc.*, II, 232–278.

[4] Much of the government's intelligence concerning the Catholics came from spies' reports, which were frequently of limited reliability. Information was also given by persons of more respectable character, and much of the more trustworthy evidence comes from reports of public officials and ecclesiastical authorities. Some priests and some laymen under examination revealed facts about their relations with persons abroad which alarmed the government, the confession of Gervase Pierpoint and eight others being an example (S.P.12/167/59, January 3, 6, 10, 1584). The government, of necessity, made detailed tabulations of the names and whereabouts of the priests and of laymen (S.P.12/168/33, 34, 35 [?1584], /183/15 [?1585]), of London and some of the counties (S.P.12/184/10, November 7, 1585), of receivers of priests (S.P.12/195/115 [?1586], /201/53, May 31, 1587), of legal action taken against various recusants (S.P.12/200/59 [?April 30, ?1587]), of recusants under bond (S.P. 12/205/13, November 7, 1587), of suspected recusants in sections of London (S.P.12/206/60, December 1587), of Norfolk (S.P.12/208/16, January 22, 1588; /16.1 [?1588]).

The Catholics, on their part, either endured their lot passively, or without indication of disloyalty tried to evade prosecution by various shifts which by now had become a recognized pattern — a temporary change of residence, the cultivation of the favor of local officials in order to forestall indictment and trial, the recourse to pleading such acceptable excuses as being "out of charity" with one's neighbor to avoid attending the services in the local parish church. The government countered the resort to such evasions both by refusing reappointment to conformist justices of the peace whose wives remained Catholic, as far as it was feasible,[5] and by prosecuting women, oftentimes neglected in the previous two decades, as far as the terms of the law, by no means clear, permitted.[6]

An inquisition into recusancy in the county of Norfolk during April 1584 investigated attendance at mass and some other facts about recusancy and conformity, and looked into the use of beads.[7] Shortly afterward two gentlemen of the county, Robert Sutton and Charles Ratclyffe, were convicted for publishing a book upholding the Catholic faith.[8] A search was made throughout London in August for Catholics, Catholic books, and Catholic articles used in worship;[9] another very comprehensive search of the capital was undertaken two years later, on August 10, 11, and 13, 1586.[10] The government had reason for concern. A contemporary report dealing with Catholics in the capital stated that they both contemned the Establishment and vigorously defended their traditional beliefs, and listed in detail their disobedience to the laws governing religion.[11] In the north convictions were still hard to obtain. During the perambulations of the ecclesiastical commission of the diocese of Chester through Lancashire, recusants were presented only at Manchester, although, according to the report of the commission, such nonconformists were quite numerous throughout that county.[12]

[5] S.P.12/206/85 [1580's].
[6] Three examples of the current treatment of women are S.P.12/167/40 (January 22, 23 [?1585], Lancashire), /195/116 [1580's, Bedfordshire]; *A.P.C.*, XVIII, 45 (August 17, 1589).
[7] S.P.12/170/49 (April 23, 1584). In Norwich persons attending mass were apprehended by the mayor; the use of beads, an index of belief, was also reported (S.P.12/167/30, January 17, 1584).
[8] S.P.12/170/48, 49 (April 23, 1584).
[9] S.P.12/172/102–115 (August 27, 1584 [?1585]).
[10] S.P.12/192/35 (August 10, 11, 13, 1586).
[11] S.P.12/172/105 [?August 27, ?1584 (?1585)].
[12] S.P.12/167/40 (January 23, 1584). This document and S.P.12/168/16 (Febru-

Repression, however, was a negative approach, positive action — zealous preaching of the doctrines of the Establishment — best promised to destroy recusancy.[13] The Archbishop of York, in order to make certain that the rising generation in a section of north Lancashire might be educated in the Established Church, founded a grammar school at Hawkshead;[14] the Earl of Huntingdon assured Walsingham that, even though recusancy flourished in the north, experience had taught him that the people proved conformable if they were ministered to by a "preaching pastor," and laid some of the blame for recalcitrancy on neglect of duty by Archbishop Sandys.[15] On the other hand, certain of the news about the northern Catholics proved heartening to the authorities. The forwardness of the gentlemen and others of lesser social status in Cheshire, Lancashire, Cumberland, Westmorland, and Yorkshire in signing the "Association for the defense of Her Majesty's person" proved the civil loyalty of many and eased official fears a little.[16]

The problems that had become intensified since 1580, and which the examples cited from 1584 indicated were serious and unrepressed, were dealt with drastically in the statute of 1585, forbidding either the Jesuits or the seminary priests to be within the realm unconformed, and making it a felony, punishable by death, to receive, house, or otherwise aid them. Education of children abroad was prohibited; the penalty of praemunire was to be inflicted upon anyone holding communication with priests on the Continent or sending financial support to a religious college or seminary there; those who within twelve days did not disclose their knowl-

---

ary 15, 1584) and S.P.12/175/21 ([?November] 1584) are lists of recusants, both men and women, in Lancashire. The recusants in gaol at Salford are in S.P.12/167/41 [?1584]. In 1585 Bishop Chaderton of Chester requested the renewal of the ecclesiastical commission of his diocese as a necessity (S.P.12/178/67, May 23, 1585).

[13] A paper of (?) 1582, "The Manner of Proceeding with the Recusants," perhaps written by Sir Francis Walsingham, listed as the causes of defection from the Establishment (1) the "dispersing of the Jesuits," (2) the evil example of the recusants, (3) the negligence of the bishops, (4) the corruption of the court (S.P.12/157/51 [?1582]). Another paper of the same year recommended the installation of good preachers, the augmentation of church livings, the removal of scandalous ministers, the instructing and catechizing of youth, and the "reformation of non-residents." (S.P.12/157/89 [?1582]).

[14] S.P.15/29/73 [?1585].   [15] S.P.15/28/101 (November 22, 1584).
[16] S.P.12/175/4 (November 7, 1584); S.P.15/28/101, 102, 108, 109 (November 22, 30, December 22, 1584).

edge of a priest's whereabouts to the authority were to suffer fine and imprisonment at the Queen's pleasure.[17]

Deficiencies in the stringent "Act to retain the Queen's Majesty's subjects in their due obedience," enacted by Elizabeth's fourth Parliament in 1581,[18] were now corrected by the sixth Parliament, which met from October 29, 1586, to March 23, 1587.[19] Wherever the monthly fine of £20 had accumulated arrears by Easter term and Michaelmas term, the whole sum was to be paid; if not, the government, at its discretion, was empowered to levy a distraint upon all the goods and two-thirds of the real property of the defaulter, leaving him one-third for his own support. The laws of 1581 and 1586 provided the framework within which much of the subsequent history of Elizabethan recusancy was embraced; their purpose, accomplished successfully, was to provide a control over, but not to destroy, the recusants financially and socially.

We have already seen how the dangers of the first half of the 1580's accelerated the drive against the Catholics. With the enactment of the statute of 1585 the tempo of this was further intensified. In Hampshire, on the vital southern coast, at each judicial term indictments for recusancy numbered at least seven score, and those who could not pay their fines or had been outlawed and afterward apprehended were imprisoned.[20] Steps to prevent the landing of priests in that county were ordered, since their labors there and the example of the lay recusants had been instrumental in effecting conversions and confirming others in their traditional beliefs. Certain of the more influential, as examples, were directed to be sent to the Council for questioning.[21] Simultaneously, the Council wrote to the Earl of Leicester offering to send two hundred recusants from Hampshire and Surrey, who were physically well-fit, to the Netherlands to perform the necessary chores for his army there.[22]

---

[17] 27 Eliz. c. 2. With the passage of this law, plans for effecting it were considered. A contemporary paper, apparently a memorandum for consideration by the government, listed five types of subversion on the part of recusants—their offense by example; their corruption of others by persuasion; their aid to Jesuits and seminary priests both at home and abroad; their education of their small children "in errronyous Religion"; their corruption of their servants and tenants. Various corrective measures were recommended (S.P.12/195/114 [?1586]).
[18] 23 Eliz. c. 1.   [19] 28 and 29 Eliz., c. 6.
[20] S.P.12/185/83 [?1585].   [21] A.P.C., XIV, 123–125 (May 25, 1586).
[22] A.P.C., XIV, 125 (May 25, 1586). The Bishop of Winchester, the diocese which comprised Hampshire and Surrey, suggested to the Council the offer of the two hundred men to Leicester.

On the same day, May 25, 1586, that it made this offer, the Privy Council also wrote to the Council of the Marches of Wales about the active practice of Catholicism in Hereford, Gloucester, and some of the Welsh counties, and about conversions there which took place because of the negligence of the justices of the peace.[23] The problems of Hereford were familiar, and so too were the reforms which were suggested — an increase in the number of preachers, the displacement of recusant justices of the peace, the designation of substitutes who adhered to the Establishment, the appointment of justices in areas where there were none, and the selection of constables firmly attached to the official religion, since many of the incumbents, being "somewhat popishly given," permitted freedom of activity to priests. Two other suggestions indicated much of the source of trouble — that convicted recusants enjoyed considerable liberty and little restraint, and that juries and too many of the officials were intentionally negligent in prosecuting recusancy. Sir Francis Walsingham received further information that the number of recusants in Hereford amounted to an active two hundred, against whom a most effective penalty would be excommunication, with its consequent penalties both religious and civil.[24]

Many of the same conditions were also to be found nearby in Monmouthshire; at Uske, for instance, a priest, Powell, notoriously had been laboring under the protection of the local population. Some corrective steps, however, had already been initiated in that county.[25] In the Midland counties of Northampton, Rutland, and Leicester this same problem, the protection of priests by the laity, simultaneously necessitated clearly defined measures of correction.[26]

Three census reports of priests and laymen were drawn up (possibly by spies) in 1586, the first, in July, listing the Catholics, who, it was feared, might aid a foreign invader,[27] and Lord Burghley drew up two subsequent memoranda in February 1587 of recusants to be restrained in view of the increasing imminence of a Spanish invasion.[28] In another,

---

[23] A.P.C., XIV, 124–125 (May 25, 1586).
[24] S.P.12/195/45 (December [?3], 1586), /46 [?December 4, ?1586].
[25] S.P.12/195/86 [?1580's], /197/44 (January 28, 1587).
[26] A.P.C., XIV, 140 (June 1, 1586).
[27] S.P.12/191/22 (July 20, 1586), /193/13 (September 4, 1586), /193/47 (September 15, 1586). The latter two, nos. 13 and 47, may have been drawn up in connection with the Babington Plot.
[28] S.P.12/198/18 (February 7, 1587), /198/29 (February 10, 1587). Lord Burghley

undated, memorandum he recommended that the Earl of Huntingdon keep watch over the recusants in Yorkshire; the Earl of Derby, those in Lancashire; the Lord President of Wales, those within his jurisdiction.[29]

Lord Burghley, in these memoranda, listed the Catholics whom he considered most influential and whom he feared to be potentially the more dangerous. Therefore, they and some others were continued under the surveillance in which they had been living, which, however, did not prevent individuals or others acting for them from pleading for leniency, although by no means certain of receiving a favorable answer. Sir Thomas Cornwallis, when questioned about recusancy (since the Queen was aware that he had once conformed), pleaded conscience and asked not to be prosecuted because of age.[30] Mark Curle, expelled about twelve years previously for "papistry" from Lincoln's Inn and now a prisoner in the Marshalsea, petitioned for release on condition that he live quietly.[31] Petitions were sent to Sir Francis Walsingham, despite his known anti-Catholicism, to use his influence with the Council to secure the transfer of John Towneley from his prison in Lancaster to another that was more salubrious, because of his health.[32] Erasmus Wolvesley, for years one of the most obdurate recusants in Staffordshire and one of the most influential of the gentry in bringing others over to Catholicism, remained in custody; having grown old, his son now sued for his freedom and the privilege of immunity from prosecution for recusancy.[33]

Favorable consideration of such requests for clemency was predicated partly on the gravity of the offense and partly on the social status of the offender[34] and the degree to which he was personally known to the

---

considered, later that year, of making another register of recusants (S.P.12/204/2, October 3, 1587). The recusants are listed by name and by county in S.P.12/198/18 (the document is illegible in places). S.P.12/198/29 mentions "The names of some special persons of note: Lord Vaux, Sir Thomas Tresham, Sir William Catesby, Sir John Arundell, William Tyrwhitt, Thymelby, John Talbot, Sir Thomas Fitzherbert, Sir John Southworth, George Cotton, Philip Dracott, Erdswyck, John Scudamore, Robert Rockwood, Robert Downes, Philip Parry, Robert Gage, Edward Gage, Hare, Thomas Vachell, Gilbert Wells, Nicholas Langford."

[29] S.P.12/185/81 [?1585].   [30] S.P.12/172/17 (July 9, 1584).
[31] S.P.12/172/56 (August 6, 1584).
[32] S.P.12/168/28 (February 28 [?1584]), /169/8 (March 1584). No. 28 is a request from Robert Cecil that Towneley be removed to London to obtain the services of a physician.
[33] S.P.12/184/44 (November 25, 1585).
[34] Although most of the recusants whom we are considering were of the gentry, some were not. Richard Higges, a husbandman of Berks, was imprisoned in the

THE DECLINE OF CATHOLICISM

Queen or the Council. Elizabeth, as we shall see from time to time, occasionally intervened in cases. In the summer of 1585 she freed both Lady Lovell and her son, Robert, from prison and granted them immunity from further prosecution for recusancy.[35] The Council, however, generally dealt with nonconformity, retaining the more important cases for its own consideration and referring the others to subordinates. It proved lenient even in critical times, when it thought the reasons to be sufficient or when the accused was personally known to some of the councillors.

Sir John Southworth, long a prisoner for recusancy, was released upon bond from the gaol at Westchester in March 1586 to go to Bath for his health until the end of September. This was revoked in May, as he had associated with Catholics and had caused the conversion of several Protestants, instead of proceeding to his destination. In July 1587 the Council again was amenable to freeing him, that he might make arrangements to pay his debts to the Queen, but the length of time for this respite was left to the discretion of the Earl of Derby, Lord Lieutenant of Lancashire and Cheshire.[36]

Richard Cliborne, an elderly, sickly, and very ardent Catholic, long a prisoner for recusancy in the Clink, was granted liberty to go to Bath for his health until May 1. He received an extension until August 1, and in the summer the Council lengthened this to the beginning of the next Michaelmas term.[37]

John Gifford, once again a practicing Catholic, had now been restrained to London and its environs because of his recusancy. Nevertheless, because of illness, he received permission to go to either of two health resorts and to his home in Staffordshire and elsewhere for business, provided that his stay in his county should be limited to a month while the Queen of the Scots was there, and that he should not depart

---

Marshalsea after admitting that he and his family had neither attended church nor communicated for seven years, and that he had had his child baptized by a priest and not in his local parish church (S.P.12/193/17, September 6, 1586, /193/45.1, September 5, 1586).

[35] S.P.12/181/62 (August 25, 1585).

[36] *A.P.C.,* XIV, 27 (March 14, 1586), 125–126 (May 25, 1586); XV, 163 (July 16, 1587).

[37] *A.P.C.,* XIV, 75–76 (April 27, 1586), 194 (July 25, 1586); S.P.12/173/73 (October 12, 1584), /186/38 [?January 31, 1586].

from the realm without the Queen of England's license. In the summer of the Armada, however, he was committed to close confinement.[38]

William Tyrwhitt, who had been circumscribed within a limit of five miles of his custodian's house in Kent, received a respite of a month and a half to attend to personal business in Lincolnshire, and this was later prolonged by two months. Somewhat after this he was permitted to move to Sussex, under the same geographical limitation of freedom and allowed to come to London to deposit a bond in the Exchequer guaranteeing payment of arrearages of his recusancy penalties. Shortly afterward, the Council granted his suit, because of illness and business necessities, to go to Lincolnshire until the next Michaelmas term.[39]

John Talbot of Grafton (in Worcestershire) had given a bond of £500 to remain in a certain private house in Surrey and not to go beyond two miles of it. The Council now granted him the liberty of London and its environs and the right to pass between the capital and his Surrey residence at his pleasure, and to go temporarily to his home county in order that he might settle business affairs. In December 1588 the danger from the Armada having passed, he was granted greater freedom in order to go for a time to his sick wife; and this was further extended in January 1589 upon the heavy bond of £2000 because of his own illness. In May of that year, due to his continued bad health, he was granted freedom within an area of six miles around his place of custody in which to move about and improve his health; the Council declared its willingness to do this, although again requiring him to post a bond of £2000, because of his good behavior and his care not to abuse previous grants of enlargement. In August the Council permitted him to return to his home in Worcestershire with the right to remain until October, in order that he might attend to business affairs and also sell all or part of his armor, apparently because he was in need of money.[40]

But not all the recusants were as fortunate as Cliborne, Gifford, Southworth, Talbot, and Tyrwhitt. Some found that they could expect no consideration because of the nature of the charges against them or because of their lesser social status and lack of prestige, being little known to the

[38] *A.P.C.*, XIV, 19 (March 3, 1586); S.P.12/211/60 (June 27, 1588).
[39] *A.P.C.*, XIV, 34-35 (March 19, 1586), 192 (July 21, 1586); XV, 119-120 (June 8, 1587), 151 (July 9, 1587).
[40] *A.P.C.*, XV, 102 (June 3, 1587); XVI, 389 (December 9, 1588); XVII, 40-41 (January 22, 1589), 198-199 (May 19, 1589); XVIII, 9-10 (August 2, 1589), 45 (August 17, 1589).

Council. John Daniel, three times returned as a recusant in Suffolk, was subjected in November 1585 to further investigation by the Council.[41] Francis Yeates was restrained to his house at Highgate because of his unyielding attitude; a subsequent investigation of his residence turned up such religious articles as relics and books dealing with Catholicism.[42] And with a view to sequestration, the goods of (?Thomas) More of Haddon in Oxfordshire were ordered inventoried after priests had been apprehended in his house.[43]

During the critical years of the second half of the 1580's, years surcharged with strong feelings of nationalism and of an intense devotion to Queen Elizabeth, the steady progress of conformity continued. It was never on a mass scale, any more than it had been in the past, but year by year individuals and small groups gave up their traditional faith for the church of the Settlement of 1559. In Hereford three important recusants openly pledged acceptance of the Establishment[44] and in Worcestershire three others included in a conciliar schedule of recusants were found already to have made profession of their conformity.[45] The Earl of Huntingdon reported additional evidence from the north,[46] and the Earl of Derby supplied proofs within his jurisdiction in the northwest.[47] In Staffordshire, where the leading gentry frequently showed great recalcitrance, conformity during the 1580's also made some headway.[48] And a partial acceptance of the Establishment on the part of some men was to be found both in strongly Protestant Kent and in Catholic Lancashire.[49] It is difficult to estimate how far such examples, whether of whole or of partial acceptance of the Elizabethan church, influenced others, but given the deep respect of the lower classes for the upper and the ardent patriotism of the times, it is safe to conclude that there were further cases of conformity contained only in local records, which, if extant, have not yet been investigated.

An unnumbered group of Catholics, more than likely very small and

[41] S.P.12/184/19 (November 11, 1585).   [42] S.P.12/198/12 (February 12, 1587).
[43] A.P.C., XV, 72 (May 7, 1587). The Council's report does not give More's Christian name. The family of Thomas More of Adderbury owned a house at Haddon (*Misc.*, XII, 109, note).
[44] S.P.12/189/2 (May 2, 1586), 190/4 (June 4, 1586).
[45] S.P.12/190/11 (June 9, 1586).   [46] S.P.15/29/157 (November 18, 1586).
[47] S.P.12/184/20 (November 12, 1585).   [48] S.P.12/184/44 (November 25, 1585).
[49] S.P.12/170/53 (April 29, 1584), /175/21 ([?November] 1584; list of Lancashire recusants and those who attended the Establishment, but had mass at their houses for their wives), /193/9 (September 3, 1586).

certainly not constituting a well-defined bloc, now looked to Sir Thomas Tresham for leadership and considered him to be their spokesman. Apparently he was chiefly responsible at this time for two documents, one, a memorandum studying the feasibility of petitioning the Queen for relief for the Catholics, drawn up most probably either late in 1584 or very early in 1585, the other, a petition to the Queen belonging to the beginning of 1585.

The first, the memorandum, stated that the chances for success of a petition for mitigation were small, since in the past, when times were less severe and the Catholics had more friends, such supplications had been rejected. Now there was no one who would favor or promote this suit. On the other hand, Catholics had no other means to approach the Queen, who "is most mercyfull and hathe used great clemencie even now to the priestes," and who, if she understood the true thoughts and attitudes of the Catholic body, would extend her favor to them. Even if she did not see the supplication, the Council and others who did would think better of the Catholics.[50]

In determining the content of the supplication, it was decided that a detailed recital of Catholic sufferings would be avoided as tedious and difficult to collect. However, because past experience showed that obnoxious laws had been repealed upon suit, the supplication would include a request to repeal or modify the statute of recusancy, even though it was objected that the government would not grant this and that it was not enforced with equal severity against everyone. The loyalty and obedience of the Catholics to "her Majestie our undoubted Queene" would be stated and amplified to explain their attempts to prove their sentiments to her, the reasons for their recusancy, and a justification of their conversations with priests, traitors in the eyes of large numbers. As all Catholics were guided in conscience by the laws of God, the supplication, in protesting obedience and loyalty to the government, though signed by a few, would represent the convictions of all.[51]

The resultant petition[52] expressed the same loyalty that the memorandum suggested, stating that Catholics were bound to render Elizabeth obedience as their lawful ruler and repudiating the traitor, Parry, and

[50] H.M.C., *Var. Coll.*, III, 34.   [51] *Ibid.*, 34–35.
[52] The relation between the memorandum and the petition is not certain, but it seems very probable that the latter resulted from the former.

all his accomplices.⁵³ It denied that the pope or a cardinal had power to authorize anyone to commit a mortal sin or any other act contrary to the divine law, including the "false, develishe and abominable" act of regicide.⁵⁴

The chief accusation laid against the Catholics was their refusal to attend the state church. This had deprived them of the Queen's favor; yet recusancy was not committed out of willful disobedience to the laws or for treasonable reasons, but solely because of conscience and the fear of offending God — a man who did otherwise was the worst possible type of subject. Catholics, in fact, would be willing to attend the rites prescribed by the state, if convocation could give logical proofs sufficiently forceful to learned Catholics to convince them that conformity was morally justifiable.⁵⁵

Now, an even greater calamity threatened the Catholics than the disgrace, imprisonment, and impoverishment which they had previously borne with. In the eyes of the law and of the government priests were considered traitors, and those persons harboring them brought suspicion of treason upon themselves. To the Catholics, priests were absolutely necessary as ministers of the sacraments and as the true advisers and guides to immortal life; therefore, they could not avoid receiving them into their houses.⁵⁶

Tresham and the other sponsors of the supplication gave positive assurance that all the priests with whom they had had relations recognized the Queen to be the rightful sovereign of England both *de jure* and *de facto,* and that they prayed for her and taught obedience to her. If, however, any priest were guilty of treason or civil disobedience or irreverence toward the Queen, the petitioners promised on an irrevocable oath that they would be the first to apprehend and accuse him. They begged Elizabeth — which was the main purpose of the petition — not to permit the enactment of a law ordering the priests to be banished and rendering the harboring of them to be traitorous.⁵⁷

⁵³ H.M.C., *Var. Coll.,* III, 37. Dr. William Parry was executed as a traitor after having made the claim that he had papal approval to assassinate Queen Elizabeth.
⁵⁴ *Ibid.,* 39. The reference to a cardinal is to the papal Secretary of State, the Cardinal of Como, who was also implicated in the Parry Case.
⁵⁵ *Ibid.,* 38–39.   ⁵⁶ *Ibid.,* 39–41.
⁵⁷ *Ibid.,* 40–42. We can conclude that the petition belongs to 1585 because the clause appealing against the enactment of a law banishing priests from England opposes the terms of a law passed that year by Parliament (27 Eliz. c. 2).

The government did not act upon this petition. It came when the authorities were cognizant of a possible foreign attack from Catholic sources and the sponsors were undoubtedly too few to alter official fears. What especially worried the Queen and the Council was the possibility that the Catholics within England might aid an invader. To prevent this the authorities in the various counties were ordered, probably in late 1585, to summon the Catholics before them, question them under oath about their possession of armor and require their surrender of it.[58] This was not allowed to become a dead letter; it was carried out with little waste of time by the county officials.[59]

2. THE CRISIS, 1588

The Armada was an attempted invasion by a Catholic power, Spain, backed by the Papacy, to restore England to the traditional church. Queen Elizabeth and her councillors, cognizant that a substantial grouping of Catholics remained within the realm, balanced their policy toward the laity between preventing them from being a potential source of aid to the enemy and putting a hesitant trust in their professions of loyalty, so that they were not treated with an undue harshness. Sound policy, the authorities felt, demanded that the more influential ought either to be incarcerated or persuaded to conform; to effect one or the other of these became a definite plan of the government. Early in 1588 an order went out that all persons of standing who remained obdurate in their Catholic belief were restrained and compelled to surrender their arms, if they still possessed them; these were to be sold to well-affected subjects needing armor, the proceeds to be returned to the original owners. The more obstinate of the recusants were to be placed in close confinement; those less so were to be assigned to private homes where their conformity might be induced; a few, where the government thought leniency to be advisable, were permitted to remain in their homes under restrictions.[60] Indict-

---

[58] S.P.12/185/82 [?1585].
[59] S.P.12/186/77 (February 28, 1586; Lincolnshire), /187/5.1 (March 2, 1586; Lancashire-Cheshire), /194/52 (October 19, 1586; Staffordshire).
[60] S.P.12/208/15 (January 20, 1588; Berkshire), /16 (January 22, 1588; Norfolk), /19 (January 22, 1588; Bedfordshire), /37 (January 30 [?1588]; Staffordshire), /209/86 (April 12, 1588; Hertfordshire, Essex); *A.P.C.*, XV, 348 (January 28, 1588), 400 (February 25, 1588); XVI, 38-39 (April 12, 1588). S.P.12/208/15, 16, 19, 37 obviously represent a general order of the Council for the whole realm taken sometime in January 1588.

ments, past and present, were the source for determining those to be restrained, but local officials were given discretion in deciding the more and the less obstinate. Schedules of the recusants were then filed with the Council by the local officials. Despite the care of the authorities in London difficulties immediately arose, because some, apparently having foreknowledge, absented themselves from their homes to avoid receiving the order to surrender themselves, or otherwise evaded imprisonment. Since the directives applied to men only, recusant wives were able to escape incarceration.[61] Although one would infer — because the evidence is not very clear — that at times practicing Catholics not yet convicted of recusancy suffered some disabilities including a measure of surveillance or restraint, the stringency of early 1588 did not cause the government to panic; no one was proceeded against because of suspicion, but only after the legal process of indictment, trial and conviction had been completed.[62]

In April the Council ordered an investigation of the landed Catholics who lived in Middlesex, but had property in other counties, to determine their contribution to the recent levy of horses[63] and the amount which they had paid in recusancy fines.[64] This insured that Catholics of wealth with wide distribution of landholdings did not escape paying their full share of taxes and did not evade certifying all their sources of living to the government.

In June, with danger imminent, the Council resolved to commit the principal Catholics to the Tower; others of quality were to be committed to one of four places — Quinborough, Hartford, Maidstone, or Leedes Castle. This was broadened, because of lack of space, to include various episcopal residences, and the palace of Ely was requisitioned for some of the more important.[65]

By late July the national welfare necessitated definite knowledge about

[61] S.P.12/208/15 (January 20, 1588; Berkshire), /16 (January 22, 1588; Norfolk), /19 (January 22, 1588; Bedfordshire), /37 (January 30 [?1588], Staffordshire), /40 (January 31, 1588; Kent), /58 (February 8, 1588; Cambridgeshire, Huntingdonshire), /58.1 (February 8, 1588; Cambridgeshire), /58.2 (February 8, 1588; Huntingdonshire), /66 (February 12, 1588; Leicestershire), /66.1 (February 1588; Herefordshire). The rule concerning women was not uniform. Both Ferdinando Paris and his wife, Frances, were committed to custody at Lynton in Cambridgeshire (S.P.12/208/58.1, February 8, 1588).
[62] S.P.12/208/34 (January 28, 1588). [63] S.P.12/200/61 [?1587].
[64] A.P.C., XVI, 35 (April 12, 1588).
[65] S.P.12/211/22 (June 1588), /67 (June 30, 1588); H.M.C., *Var. Coll.*, III, x-xi, 53-54.

Catholics who were traitors, who were doubtful, and who were loyal. Order was taken to repress persons possibly troublesome.[66] The harsh penalties of the statutes punishing priests were carried out against them, not only during the critical summer months but throughout 1588, with greater severity than during any other year of Elizabeth's reign.[67] Laymen of necessity had to be prudent; those who heard mass at this trying period could not avoid bringing suspicion and punishment on themselves.[68]

Catholics, caught up in the emotions of a great national crisis, had two alternatives. They could continue to adhere to their religion and suffer the consequences or they could conform. Throughout 1588 a certain number chose the latter.[69] As in the past, those who did so conformed individually or in small groups, but the number was convincing proof that the force of nationalism or the ignominy and distress of enduring the repressive hand of the government and the suspicion of one's neighbors could outweigh the convictions of one's conscience, given truly trying circumstances.

The only vocal Catholics at the height of the crisis were the more prominent: in unison they proclaimed their loyalty to Elizabeth. The less prominent apparently adhered to the same sentiments or were silently neutral. When the news of the Spanish preparations reached England in 1587, Sir Thomas Tresham, Lord Vaux (the sole peer under a cloud for his Catholicism and not for some other cause),[70] and other leading rec-

[66] *A.P.C.*, XVI, 170 (July 23, 1588; order to Lord Strange concerning northern England). The government received information, true or false, which tended to keep it suspicious. Some of the data were verifiable; others depended upon the veracity of the informer: *A.P.C.*, XV, 361–362 (February 7, 1588; comment on official report dealing with northern England); XVI, 95–96 (May 29, 1588; rescue of priest in Wales), 249 (August 25, 1588; reported laxity of treatment of prisoners in Norwich gaol); S.P.12/209/39 (March 29, 1588; disaffected recusant), /215/79 (August 1588; anonymous report concerning priests and those harboring them), /219/77 ([?1588]; Catholics overseas and their friends in England).

[67] S.P.12/208/66.1 (February 1588), /214/51 (August 9, 1588), /215/19 (July 2, 1588: content of document shows that date is erroneous; it probably should be July 4, 1588); *A.P.C.*, XVI, 4 (March 25, 1588), 235–236 (August 14, 1588), 286 (September 22, 1588). A list of Catholics, including the priests, executed in 1588 is in C.R.S., V, *English Martyrs*, 10–12.

[68] *A.P.C.*, XVI, 260 (September 2, 1588).

[69] S.P.12/208/58.1 (February 8, 1588), /214/51 (August 9, 1588); *A.P.C.*, XV, 362 (February 7, 1588); XVI, 228–229 (August 11, 1588).

[70] The quasi-conformist Lord Montague pledged his loyalty (S.P.12/213/11, July 23, 1588). Lord Morley, long an exile abroad for his Catholicism, wrote to the Council pledging his loyalty (S.P.12/211/68, June 30, 1588).

usants had been committed to the custody of the state clergy to destroy any illusion which the Spanish might hold that they could hazard an invasion expecting internal help. The prisoners were assured that Queen Elizabeth and the Council understood and appreciated their faithfulness and their desire to fight in their country's defense, to which they — all the leading Catholics — replied that they were willing to be placed in custody wherever the Council saw fit for the best interests of their ruler and the realm, but that they especially desired to fight in the front ranks against the enemy. The government, however, insisted that their confinement was of more importance than their assistance in battle, and their leading member, Tresham, who was their spokesman, remained in the custody of the Bishop of Lincoln. In July 1588 with the Armada approaching the English shores, all these recusants were incarcerated in the Bishop of Ely's diocesan palace. There, again, they expressed their earnest desire to fight, asking the lord lieutenant of the county, Lord North, to appeal to the Council on their behalf for an opportunity to prove their loyalty, but no such concession was granted to them.[71] Instead, the Queen's policy during the critical month of August was to subject all recusants known for their obstinacy to very close confinement and toward the middle of that month a census of all the recusants in London prisons was ordered to be taken, with a view to proceeding against them, especially the priests, according to law.[72] But the government was not wantonly vindictive. The treatment of the leading laymen proves this, and it is further manifest in the case of a relapsed conformist who was enjoined to submit to two or three conferences a week again to secure his conformity.[73]

Feeling at Ely ran high against the prisoners during the period of crisis; and after it was over there was still more danger for them, since in the thinking of the public Catholics were traitors, and demands for their execution were loudly voiced.[74] In October the Council determined to gain exact knowledge of their attitudes before freeing them, either by inducing their conformity, or if that failed, by having them sign a statement of civil loyalty. All the prisoners at Ely made a very loyal protestation of their fidelity to the Queen. The Council then ordered that they

---

[71] H.M.C., *Var. Coll.*, III, x–xi, 53–54.
[72] *A.P.C.*, XVI, 165 (July 14, 1588), 235–236 (August 14, 1588), 241–244 (August 18, 1588).
[73] *A.P.C.*, XVI, 246–247 (August 21, 1588), 278–279 (September 18, 1588).
[74] H.M.C., *Var. Coll.*, III, xi, 54.

be enlarged, to be assigned by the Archbishop of Canterbury to new residences within ten miles of London.[75] Elsewhere, however, certain other recusants received contrary treatment. Humphrey Bedingfield, Robert de Grey, Edward Downes, Robert Lovell, Walter Norton, and Ferdinando Paris, who were felt to have abused the liberty of the common gaol in Norfolk, were transferred to Wisbeach Castle.[76]

Sir Thomas Tresham was released before the others at Ely, due to bad health.[77] His Catholicism had proved expensive to him, not only in terms of personal liberty, but also in money payments to the Queen, by 1589 aggregating more than £2,800, including his fine (paid irregularly) of £20 per month for recusancy.[78] This did not embitter him, at least openly, and his loyalty to the state remained as ardent as ever. At the end of the Armada year he thanked Lord Burghley, on behalf of himself and his fellow prisoners, for helping them to obtain their liberty; and a few weeks later he wrote the Master of the Rolls that he would willingly give as much of his lands as the Queen should wish "in this so just and honourable a cause as is the defending of her Majesty's realm my native country from all hostile invasion . . ."[79]

Toward the end of the year John Talbot and William Tyrwhitt were permitted to go to their homes.[80] In January 1589 the Council granted Thomas Hale of Essex an indefinite period of enlargement from custody upon bond, because of financial distress and ill health, after he had declared his allegiance to the Queen and his loyalty to the state.[81] Richard Biddolphe was given into the charge of his father on condition that he sign a statement of loyalty similar to that made at Ely.[82] Michael Hare, whose health had become impaired during his imprisonment, was allowed in May 1589 to live in the environs of London and to have the freedom of a three-mile radius of his residence, although the actual date of his release seems confused; in July he was permitted to go to his home in

---

[75] *Ibid.; A.P.C.*, XVI, 313 (October 16, 1588), 370 (December 1, 1588).
[76] *A.P.C.*, XVI, 317 (October 18, 1588). The keeper of the gaol at Norwich and the sheriff of Norfolk were accused of permitting too great liberty to the recusants imprisoned at Norwich (*ibid.*, 249–250, August 24–25, 1588).
[77] *A.P.C.*, XVI, 362 (November 29, 1588).
[78] H.M.C., *Var. Coll.*, III, 46 (February 20, 1589).
[79] *Ibid.;* S.P.12/219/50 (December 31, 1588).
[80] *A.P.C.*, XVI, 389 (December 9, 1588).
[81] *A.P.C.*, XVII, 30–31 (January 16, 1589).
[82] *A.P.C.*, XVII, 57 (January 28, 1589).

Suffolk.[83] Edward Sulliard of that county was set free in June for three months in order that he might go to his home to raise money for the payment of his recusancy fines; his estate had become seriously impaired through heavy charges for recusancy.[84] Sir William Catesbie, Sir Thomas Cornwallis, John Dracot, Sir Thomas Fitzherbert, Richard Owen, and Thomas Welles, were enlarged during the summer of 1589 until the next term.[85] The government felt so certain of Cornwallis's loyalty that in October 1589 it permitted him to remain at his current place of residence without any present bother, as he was old and his sole fault was his recusancy.[86] Catesbie, however, at his own request was committed into the custody of the Dean of Windsor.[87]

Those who were free did not thereby escape surveillance. In July William Tyrwhitt was ordered confined to a specified residence in Surrey, where he had previously been in custody, and a circuit of six miles about it after the first day of Michaelmas term, 1589;[88] and at the same time George Cotton of Hampshire received a release until the same date.[89] Sir Alexander Culpepper, John Gage, Gervase Pierpoint, and Nicholas Scrope were allowed to go to their home counties until the first day of the next Michaelmas term.[90] Sir John Arundell, who had been confined to his own house, was now granted the freedom of a six-mile circuit around it, for the use of which he had to post bonds.[91]

3. THE REACTION AFTER THE ARMADA, 1589–1594

The history of English Catholicism after the Armada is a paradox. An invasion intended to restore the disestablished traditional church had just been thwarted; the force of English nationalism had been mobilized to ward off the attack; nothing measurable in the way of sympathy or internal help for the invader had been manifested in any quarter. The slow, steady stream of the conformity of previous years continued. Yet, Catholicism continued to be practiced openly in some sections and secretly in others, with no feeling of disloyalty on the part of its adherents.[92]

[83] *A.P.C.*, XVII, 231 (May 31, 1589), 383 (July 13, 1589).
[84] *A.P.C.*, XVII, 281 (June 18, 1589).　[85] *A.P.C.*, XVII, 319 (June 29, 1589).
[86] *A.P.C.*, XVIII, 170 (October 6, 1589).
[87] *A.P.C.*, XVIII, 172–173 (October 6, 1589).
[88] *A.P.C.*, XVII, 351–352 (July 7, 1589).
[89] *A.P.C.*, XVII, 357 (July 7, 1589); S.P.12/225/17 [?July 7, ?1589].
[90] *A.P.C.*, XVII, 383 (July 13, 1589).　[91] *A.P.C.*, XVII, 410 (July 19, 1589).
[92] William Sterrell (alias Henry Saintmain), apparently a spy, reported in 1591

Less than a year after the Armada, in the diocese of Bangor in Wales, pilgrimages were held; offerings to saints were made; chapels continued to be dedicated to them; beads were used for private prayer; the sign of the cross was a frequently witnessed religious act; and medieval burial customs persisted.[93]

In 1590, hardly two years after the Armada, two complementary studies of religion in Lancashire showed the continuing existence of a very active Catholicism.[94] Previous to the issuance of the last commission for recusants to be presented at the quarter sessions and assizes, of the 941 persons listed over 700 were indicted, and since the last commission 800 had been presented, resulting in the indictment of over 200 of them.[95] Such a degree of recusancy and evidence that it was possibly increasing greatly alarmed the Bishop of Chester, who was conscious of the open contempt expressed for the authority of the Establishment, especially since he had personally experienced disrespect at Wigan. After thirty years, both he and the authorities in London were still unable to rectify the negligence of the magistrates of Lancashire in enforcing the laws governing religion and their slackness in carrying out the judgments of the ecclesiastical commission, which resulted both in backsliding and in the known activity of Catholic priests.[96]

To forestall the various devices used by recusants to escape trial, a new model indictment was carefully drawn up in which, it was hoped, loopholes could not be found, and justices of the peace were directed to con-

---

that the Catholics loved the Queen, but hated the Council and especially Lord Burghley, holding that these advisers of Elizabeth were responsible for their troubles. The Catholics were anxious that the pope and their ruler should come to some agreement. Sterrell, it is interesting to note, pointed out that the Catholics had no recognized leader (S.P.12/239/120, August 2, 1591).

[93] S.P.12/224/74 [?May ?1589]. The Council in 1592 ordered an inquiry into the activities of refugee priests in Wales, who had effected conversions; and in 1593 ordered that the Welsh be prevented from worshiping at the sites of one-time shrines. (*A.P.C.*, XXII, 543–544, June 19, 1592; C.P. 203/138, February 12, 1593).

[94] S.P.12/235/4 [?1590], /235/68 [?1590]; *A.P.C.*, XIX, 335–342 (July 25, 1590). S.P.12/235/4, a very valuable document, lists data concerning the dwellings, status, and attitude of persons of standing in Lancashire, both justices of the peace and others.

[95] S.P.12/235/4 [1590]. *A.P.C.*, XIX, 335–337 (July 25, 1590) partially confirms S.P.12/235/4, stating that there were over 200 unconvicted recusants in Cheshire and over 700 unconvicted recusants in Lancashire.

[96] S.P.12/235/68 [?1590]; *A.P.C.*, XVII, 309–310 (June 25, 1589); XIX, 312 (July 9, 1590), 335–342 (July 25, 1590).

tinue indictments at each quarter session. As a further preventive the Bishop of Chester was ordered to arrange for the instruction of recusants; the leading ones, who had not conformed one year after conviction, were to be bound for their good behavior and disarmed.[97]

Contemporaneously the archdiocese of York had 707 convicted recusants.[98] Its chief geographical component, Yorkshire, could report only slow progress, at least in some parts, in obtaining conformity, due to the defective state of the Establishment within the archdiocese. There was not only a dearth of preachers, but also a need of preachers of better quality. The lack of sufficient financial support for them explained a great deal: the Crown had seized much of the ecclesiastical revenue, rendering the ministry within the archdiocese undesirable to men of education and to those with families to maintain.[99]

Because of the need to keep the records of the recusants up-to-date, the Council continued to make tabulations of their numbers, condition, and activities.[100] In March 1590 it wrote to the deputy lieutenants of all the counties except those in the Marches of Wales, sending them the names of some prominent recusants at liberty, into whose means of livelihood they were to inquire and report back. The same information was to be sent concerning any other recusants of whom they knew; and a similar inquiry was to be made into those of the lower classes who paid no fines, in order that steps might be taken to disarm them.[101] Shortly afterward the Council ordered the indictment of certain unconvicted recusants in Derbyshire and Staffordshire and of the unconvicted recusant wives of conformist husbands there. This stringency, that body held, was necessary because of the doubtful times.[102]

In view of the possibility of another Spanish attack in 1590, the Council sent a letter to the Archbishop of Canterbury, directing him to sum-

---

[97] *A.P.C.*, XIX, 337–339 (July 25, 1590).
[98] S.P.12/235/25 [?1590's]. This document states that in the ecclesiastical province of York there were 1,948 recusants: archdiocese of York, 707; diocese of Durham, 339; diocese of Carlisle, 57; diocese of Chester, 845.
[99] S.P.12/234/35[?1590].
[100] Among the reports of Catholic activities in the first two years after the Armada were: recusants on bail (S.P.12/226/72, September 27, 1589); prisoners in the Tower (S.P.12/227/37, October 24, 1589); partial financial census (S.P.12/235/24 [?1590]). During the summer of 1590 a report was made of pensioners of Spain (S.P.12/233/32, August 1590).
[101] *A.P.C.*, XVIII, 406–407 (March 8, 1590).
[102] *A.P.C.*, XVIII, 413 (March 13, 1590).

mon certain of the wealthier and more influential Catholics who were in the vicinity of London, and to explain that they were being imprisoned to prevent their helping the enemy.[103] Sir Thomas Tresham and sixteen others were confined to the episcopal palace at Ely, although one, Thomas Gawen, was kept there only temporarily. Another group of sixteen, among them Sir William Catesbie, Sir Thomas Fitzherbert, and John Talbot of Grafton, were committed to the charge of Richard Fiennes, to be held either at Banbury or Broughton.[104] Suspect because of their large numbers of retainers and dependents, six of the leading Catholics of Norfolk and Suffolk — Humphrey Bedingfield, Robert de Grey, Robert Downes, Robert Lovell, Roger Martin, and Walter Norton — received severer treatment, confinement in Wisbeach Castle.[105]

Tresham, conscious that he was spokesman for a segment of the Catholic body, wrote to Archbishop Whitgift protesting the loyalty of his co-religionists. As in 1588, so now again Sir Thomas affirmed that "we Catholics, for number not few, for calling, degree and antiquity not of the basest or vulgarest sort, and for faithful deserving to the State and just demeaning ourselves towards all men (without vaunt be it said) censured not the unworthiest members in this Commonwealth" and acknowledged that the government acted toward them from motives of justice. The Catholics had always conducted themselves, despite adverse

[103] *A.P.C.*, XVIII, 414 (March 13, 1590). A memorial of Lord Burghley of 1590 or 1591 proposed for consideration "that all Papists . . . which by their wealth and credit may seem dangerous, be restrained and punished according to the laws" (S.P.12/231/103 [?1590, ?1591]).

[104] *A.P.C.*, XVIII, 415 (March 13, 1590). Those confined at Ely were Sir John Arundell, Henry Carvell, George Cotton, Thomas Crawley, John Dracot, Sampson Erdswicke, Samuel Erdswicke, John Gage of Firle, Michael Hare, Richard Owen, William ap Pryce, Edward Rookwood, Sir Thomas Tresham, Gilbert Welles, Thomas Wilford, and Thomas Gawen, who was reassigned to the Fleet (*ibid.*, XX, 62, October 28, 1590). Those confined at either Banbury or Broughton were William Browne, Sir William Catesbie, Sir Alexander Culpepper, Henry Drury, Sir Thomas Fitzherbert, John Gage of Haling, Samuel Loame (?Love), Thomas Newdigate (or Nudigate), Ferdinando Paris, Gervase Pierpoint, Edward Sulliard, John Talbot of Grafton, John Thimelby, Thomas Throckmorton, John Towneley, William Tyrwhitt (*ibid.*, XVIII, 415, March 13, 1590). Conciliar directions provided that they were to receive the right to keep servants and were to be treated courteously, but had to pay a considerable share of their own expenses. Social intercourse with each other and with outsiders was limited and supervised (*ibid.*, 415–417, March 14, 1590). The conditions at Ely proved unhealthy, necessitating corrections ordered by the Council (*ibid.*, XIX, 387–388, August 14, 1590; 409, August 21, 1590).

[105] *A.P.C.*, XIX, 10 (April 5, 1590).

circumstances, as the most faithful of subjects, solely because of the allegiance and love which they owed to the Queen. Although they willingly submitted again to imprisonment, in order to frustrate any Spanish hope of internal aid, they would prefer to fight to preserve English freedom from foreign enslavement and to remove any charges of disloyalty. Their recusancy, their only fault, resulted from adhering to the religion in which most of them had been born and bred, and to which their ancestors had belonged.[106]

When it was feared that Sir William Stanley, who was in the service of Spain, intended to attack the Isle of Anglesey, the Earl of Derby, as lord lieutenant of the two adjoining counties of Cheshire and Lancashire, was directed to remove all potentially dangerous persons of means to some safe place. His prompt and thorough obedience shortly afterward elicited the thanks of the Council.[107] Another maritime area, Hampshire, with a considerable number of influential recusants, came under the government's scrutiny, because of its strategic location. A schedule was sent to the Marquis of Winchester and the Bishop of Winchester of those to be confined at Farnham Castle, and they were given discretion to add to this list; certain others in the schedule, considered dangerous, were to be lodged in local gaols; the rest were to be free under bond.[108] The number of recusants in Hampshire continuously worried the Council; it held that the laxity of the undersheriff was partly responsible, and that various devices, such as concealment, also accounted for the considerable number (three hundred or more) of those who escaped prosecution.[109]

When in 1590 fear of exterior attack did not materialize, the government again relaxed its severity. Fines and repeated imprisonment during recent years had now brought a number of the propertied recusants to the verge of bankruptcy, and others had a variety of pressing financial problems which needed settlement. They could deal with these only if they had freedom of action, and if the Council proved amenable in granting them enlargement.

Those who, in October 1590, still remained at Ely or in the custody of Richard Fiennes at Broughton were reassigned to the Archbishop of Canterbury, to be placed by him, under bond, wherever he thought fit;

---

[106] H.M.C., *Var. Coll.*, III, 51–58 (March 25, 1590).
[107] *A.P.C.*, XIX, 155–156 (May 24, 1590), 270 (June 23, 1590).
[108] *A.P.C.*, XIX, 26–27 (April 7, 1590).   [109] *A.P.C.*, XIX, 105–109 (May 5, 1590).

and the same terms were applied to Thomas Gawen who was imprisoned in the Fleet.[110] The suit of Thomas Throckmorton's wife that he be permitted to go to London to take care of certain lawsuits pending there was granted on condition that he post bond of £500.[111] Sir Thomas Tresham received repeated grants of enlargement upon deposit of heavy bonds, beginning in May 1590, to help his brother-in-law, Lord Vaux, a man of poor financial ability, manage the affairs of his estate. In July, for instance, this was extended for a month, with the proviso that he remain at his residence except when the exigencies of Vaux's affairs demanded his presence; and this was extended three times in August. Finally, in October, the Council made this respite indefinite, in order that Sir Thomas might wind up the affairs of his brother-in-law's estate.[112]

John Talbot, who needed to collect evidence concerning a disputed land title, received permission to go to his home at Grafton after depositing bonds of £1000;[113] John Gage, imprisoned at Broughton, was released at the intercession of the lord admiral, Baron Howard of Effingham, to prevent any prejudice to his inheritance from his recently deceased mother;[114] and John Thimelby was granted a temporary enlargement to execute his father's will and enter upon his inheritance.[115] John Dracot's debts had become so onerous that he was freed until the beginning of the next term to sell lands in Lincolnshire and Shropshire to meet his obligation.[116] Rooke Greene, who had remained in prison for the past three years because of recusancy, asked, in consideration of his age and ill health, for freedom that he might go to his home and set his affairs in order, which was granted.[117] William Tyrwhitt and Edward Sulliard were allowed temporarily to go to their homes to better their estates; and Tyrwhitt received a further extension to tend to matters of property when his mother died intestate.[118] Lord Montague's brother, William Browne, was permitted in April 1591 to go to his children in Norfolk until the

---

[110] *A.P.C.*, XX, 16 (October 5, 1590), 62 (October 28, 1590).
[111] *A.P.C.*, XIX, 102–103 (May 4, 1590).
[112] *A.P.C.*, XIX, 139 (May 20, 1590), 313 (July 9, 1590), 365 (August 6, 1590), 400 (August 17, 1590), 416 (August 26, 1590); XX, 9 (October 5, 1590).
[113] *A.P.C.*, XIX, 159 (May 24, 1590).   [114] *A.P.C.*, XIX, 194 (June 7, 1590).
[115] *A.P.C.*, XX, 6–7 (October 4, 1590).   [116] *A.P.C.*, XX, 96 (November 30, 1590).
[117] *A.P.C.*, XX, 129–130 (December 22, 1590).
[118] *A.P.C.*, XX, 142–143 (December 20, 1590), 252 (February 1, 1591).

end of Trinity term because of his ill health, age, and poverty; and in June he was granted another respite, which was indefinite in duration.[119] Another East Anglian recusant, Walter Norton, currently a prisoner in the custody of the sheriff of Norfolk, was released to attend to suits over the titles of certain of his lands called into question by the government.[120]

During the 1590's the tensions, despite a few scares, were never of the proportions of those of the 1580's. That the government recognized this is obvious, because its fixed pattern of treatment of the Catholics remained the same, increase or mitigation of intensity being a matter of intermittent official discretion, as in the past. Obviously Elizabeth and her ministers never fully trusted the Catholics and were never willing to discard an established policy built up and tested over a period of years.

Certain principles designed even better than past methods to control recusancy were laid down in October 1591: commissioners were to be appointed to enforce the religious laws in each county, each one to have a certain section as his jurisdiction; the local bishop and his chancellor were to certify the names of recusants to the commissioners, and the law clerks were to inform them of all current proceedings against recusants; and the commissioners were, secretly, to gather information about those harboring priests. Certain other provisions were of special note, indicating the thinking of the Elizabethan government: persons were not to be questioned concerning religion, other than about the reception of priests into their homes, about attendance at the rites of the Establishment and about their attitude toward the pope and the King of Spain; and suspected persons were to be interrogated concerning who had influenced them to adopt a pro-Spanish attitude. Recusancy, it was made clear in the report, could cause suspicion of disloyalty.[121]

The Council followed this up by sending schedules of recusants to the justices of the peace, with orders to descend without warning upon the houses of the leading offenders and impound their armor and weapons, which were to be retained until they conformed. Agents were also to be appointed to disarm the lower classes. No one was to escape; the justices

---

[119] *A.P.C.*, XXI, 77 (April 26, 1591), 211 (June 18, 1591).

[120] *A.P.C.*, XXI, 189 (June 13, 1591). The Council added that it wished to be lenient because these suits might work grave injury to Norton, whose financial condition was already badly distressed, his goods and two-thirds of his lands having been distrained for recusancy.

[121] S.P.12/240/43 (October [?18], 1591).

were to proceed equally against those recusants in the schedule and those not in it.[122]

Fines for recusancy had been systematically itemized in the exchequer to facilitate obtaining commissions to extend recusants' property;[123] now their annual revenues (derived chiefly from property) were to be certified to the Council.[124] As a further measure all those who recently had been confined to Ely and Broughton and at present (August 1592) lived at home were to be recommitted to either of these places or to Banbury at their own expense and other recusants of the same social status were to be confined with them.[125] The Council made some exceptions, perhaps for the sake of convenience. Recusants in Bedfordshire, Nottinghamshire, and those under the jurisdiction of the Earl of Derby in the northwest were to be placed in custody in the areas of their residence, and the Council of the North was to act similarly in regard to those within its charge.[126]

These orders were carried out during the late summer and the autumn of 1592, although temporary exceptions were again permitted.[127] In February 1593, perhaps as a prelude to the meeting of Parliament and the enactment of further legislation against the Catholics, a few of the most important, free on bond, were again confined at Ely.[128]

The new law, the "Act against Popish Recusants," enacted in the spring of 1593, directed that every Catholic over sixteen years of age convicted of recusancy was to be confined to his residence and to a five-mile radius around it. Any violation of this measure incurred, as a pen-

[122] S.P.12/243/103 [?1592]. [123] S.P.12/241/66 (February 26, 1592).
[124] S.P.12/243/103 [?1592]. The annual revenues of the wives were also to be certified.
[125] A.P.C., XXIII, 106–108 (August 7, 1592).
[126] A.P.C., XXIII, 110–112 (August 7, 1592, Earl of Derby's jurisdiction, Bedfordshire), 202–203 (September 19, 1592, Nottinghamshire); S.P.12/242/105 (August 13, 1592, jurisdiction of Council of the North).
[127] A.P.C., XXIII, 198 (September 17, 1592), 215–216 (September 30, 1592), 329–330 (November 30, 1592); XXIV, 17 (January 21, 1593); S.P.12/243/59 (November 7, 1592).
[128] A.P.C., XXIV, 76 (February 21, 1593). The recusants were Sir William Catesbie, Thomas Gawen, John Talbot of Grafton, Sir Thomas Tresham, Thomas Throckmorton. Government policy towards recusants was influenced at this time by a report compiled by the Earl of Huntingdon, "Jesuits, Seminaries, and Old Priests," which included the names of lay persons who had masses celebrated in their houses in London and listed five Marian priests still functioning covertly (S.P.15/32/64, January 20, 1593).

alty, the sequestration of all the offender's goods and chattels, and during his life the sequestration of his lands.[129]

This law simplified the treatment of the Catholics, putting the surveillance of them on a more efficient plane; its ease of application made it most useful to the government, which intended it to be a method of control but not a substitute for imprisonment.[130] It was undoubtedly the precondition for the temporary release of the prisoners at Ely. In March of 1594, however, those who had previously been there and at Broughton were recommitted to one or other of these places of confinement;[131] the explanation is to be found in a memorandum of the lord treasurer of March 1594, who reasserted the necessity of restraining them to prevent their aiding a future invader.[132]

Lord Burghley, in the memorandum of March 1594, also urged an inquiry into the legal status of the whole body of the recusants to determine how many had been indicted and convicted and if their property had been distrained.[133] This proposal represents the collective viewpoint, also, of the Council where Lord Burghley, after the Queen, was the recognized policymaker. It accounts for a series of investigations conducted before the midpoint of the decade.

A very comprehensive census was undertaken in 1592. Recusants were listed by counties, subdivided into dioceses, and further divided into various categories — those committed to prison, those remaining at liberty as distinguished from those at liberty under bond; those at liberty under bond were further subdivided into those free under the general condition of May 7, 1581, and those free for a time in respect of sickness, or till the Queen's pleasure should be known. Returns were given for the counties of Chester, Cornwall, Cumberland, Derby (no entries), Devon,

---

[129] 35 Eliz. c. 2.
[130] In June of 1593 recusants in custody in various parts of England petitioned for release and permission to live in their houses according to the terms of the statute of 1593 (*A.P.C.*, XXIV, 296, June 7, 1593). Six husbands petitioned for the release of their wives from prison into their custody, citing the statute as a further precaution against their wives abusing their enlargement and as an inducement to their possible conformity (*ibid.*, 317–318, June 19, 1593). The Council, in granting freedom to a spinster, Catherine Radcliffe, cited the statute as an insurance against abuse of freedom (*ibid.*, 318).
[131] *A.P.C.*, XXV, 517 (March 5, 1594).
[132] S.P.12/248/9 (March 6, 1594). The memorandum is only partly in the hand of Lord Burghley.
[133] *Ibid.*

Dorset, Durham, Essex, Gloucester, Hereford, Kent, Lancaster, Lincoln, Middlesex and the city of London, Norfolk, Oxford, Shropshire (no entries), Somerset, Southampton, Stafford, Suffolk, Surrey, Sussex, Wales, Westmorland (diocese of Carlisle), Worcester, and York. No recusants were listed as at liberty under bond in certain counties and dioceses — Bristol, Chester, Devon, Durham, Gloucester, Lancaster, Norwich, Suffolk, Surrey, or Worcester, and none was listed as being in prison in Bristol, Chester, Dorset, Durham, Gloucester, or Kent.[134]

Twice during the following year the Council decided that it needed further detailed information concerning the recusants. In August 1593 it directed the ordinaries, deans, and other officers of the various dioceses to report concerning the wives and servants of recusants and the standing of the husbands.[135] In the following December it ordered the lord lieutenants of the various counties to certify the children of gentlemen recusants and others suspected in religion who had gone beyond the seas within the last seven years and by what license they had received permission. If any were found to have crossed over unlicensed, their parents had to give bonds for the children's personal appearance in court by a certain day.[136]

The Archbishop of Canterbury was required in January 1594 to draw up a schedule of recusants of substance currently at liberty on bond, and to have similar certificates sent to him by the bishops and ecclesiastical commissioners throughout the realm. This was to enable the government to know accurately how many recusants there were; it was also to facilitate disarming them and suspending them from any public office.[137] These and other measures of the government by no means proved wholly successful, and their tenor was repeated in November 1595, with the seeming imminence, once again, of foreign dangers. The Council then directed the Archbishops of Canterbury and York to have inquiries instituted within their metropolitan jurisdictions by the local ordinaries of the extent of recusancy and of religious instruction in every parish and of the status and financial condition of each individual recusant, and to certify this to the central authorities.[138]

Census reports could point out, but not remedy, the great weakness

[134] C.P.138/237-252 (1592). [135] A.P.C., XXV, 513 (August 26, 1593).
[136] A.P.C., XXV, 515 (December 31, 1593).
[137] S.P.12/247/5 (January 7, 1594).
[138] A.P.C., XXV, 85-86 (November 26, 1595).

in Tudor government, the lack of an articulated structure, integrating local government closely with the central organism at Westminster. Local government depended upon nonsalaried officials, in the more remote parts of the country too distant adequately to be supervised.[139] This was but too true in the diocese of Chester where the ecclesiastical commission lacked competency and the magistrates exhibited laxity in proceeding against friends and relatives.[140] In Northumberland laxity and evasion flourished; when the ecclesiastical commission sat at Newcastle-upon-Tyne in December 1592 no person who had been cited appeared before it and no official gave it any cooperation.[141] Durham, despite a vigorous bishop and dean, also experienced considerable evasion — fifty-three men and women had either fled or kept themselves in hiding.[142] The laxity of the ecclesiastical commissioners of the diocese of Lincoln, including three lay peers of the realm, brought about a rebuke to them from the Council.[143] In Leicester, Nottingham, and Monmouth sufficient evidence of recusancy existed to attract conciliar supervision.[144] This was also true of Herefordshire, still a hotbed of Catholic nonconformity, where nine recusants deliberately absented themselves from their homes and did not appear before the ecclesiastical commission, although they had been summoned.[145] In Northampton, Rutland, and Wiltshire the Council, feeling

---

[139] Tobie Matthew, Dean of Durham, wrote to Lord Burghley that conformity was harder to effect in counties and dioceses at a distance from the capital than in those closer at hand (S.P.15/32/89, October 16, 1593).

[140] S.P.12/240/138 [?1591], /139 [?1591]. The ecclesiastical commission of Chester became more active after the Earl of Derby became associated with it (*A.P.C.*, XXII, 324, March 8, 1592; 369–370, March 25, 1592; XXIV, 26, January 23, 1593; S.P.12/243/51, October 30, 1592). S.P.12/240/138 is a report about Lancashire and Cheshire. It repeated the familiar evidence of the low quality of the clergy and the poor instruction of the laity.

[141] S.P.12/243/59 (November 7, 1592); S.P.15/32/50 (September 23, 1592), /59 (November 11, 1592), /59.2 (November 7, 1592), /62 (January 5, 1593), /62.1 (December 16, 1592).

[142] S.P.12/244/8, 8.1 (January 13, 1593). In no. 8.1 forty-two men and women were listed as imprisoned, and twelve men and women bound to appear upon notice. The Bishop of Durham was Matthew Hutton; the dean was Tobie Matthew.

[143] *A.P.C.*, XXIII, 289 (November 13, 1592). The peers were the Earl of Lincoln, Lord Willoughby of Eresby, and Lord Sheffield.

[144] *A.P.C.*, XXII, 342–343 (March 19, 1592); XXIII, 191–192 (September 14, 1592), 227 (October 3, 1592).

[145] *A.P.C.*, XXII, 342–343 (March 19, 1592); XXIV, 45–46 (February 11, 1593). The nine recusants were Richard Abingdon, Richard Clark, Richard Hill, William Minors, Christopher Roper, John Scudamore, Thomas Scudamore, John Seborne, and Michael Vaughan. They were ordered to be apprehended and sent to the Council.

that severity was needed, commanded that recusant men of importance were to be imprisoned and that recusant wives of Protestant or conformist husbands, who were known to influence their families or others, were also to be incarcerated.[146]

Warwickshire, especially, has a very rich record still extant of the extent of recusancy in the early 1590's, rivaling Lancashire in the fullness of data available to us. A considerable part of the population still adhered to the traditional church, largely due to the effective work of both Marian and seminary priests, and, apparently, of a system of messengers who carried letters around to various families. Catholic numbers were further kept intact by recourse to the familiar means of evading prosecution. The investigation inquired into known and suspected recusants as well as priests, and listed, parish by parish, persons indicted as well as those in prison or in private custody, or free upon bonds and under surveillance.[147]

In London, where a large transient population permitted influences of many kinds to radiate out into the counties, a temporary committee was set up and continued in existence for some time, to investigate recusant prisoners there and in confinement in a perimeter of ten miles around the capital.[148] Another committee, an ecclesiastical commission to deal only with certain religious matters, was already in existence in Surrey, to the south of the capital, investigating the activities of priests and the extent of recusancy.[149] Norfolk, to the east of the capital, because some of the more affluent Catholics resided there, aroused similar concern and the diocesan ecclesiastical commissioners were ordered to keep recusants under observation, since any evidence of Catholic activities tended to cause suspicion and a concerted effort to secure conformity was meeting with success.[150]

---

[146] *A.P.C.*, XXIII, 192–193 (September 14, 1592), 215–216 (September 30, 1592).
[147] S.P.12/243/76 (November 1592).
[148] *A.P.C.*, XXIV, 145 (March 30, 1593). An example of Catholic activities which aroused conciliar concern was the arrest both of a priest celebrating mass near Gray's Inn and of the worshipers. The priest was committed to the Gatehouse (*ibid.*, XXII, 92, November 28, 1591).
[149] C.P.168/115 (May 29, 1592). The head of the committee was Lord Howard, the lord admiral.
[150] *A.P.C.*, XXII, 365–366 (March 25, 1592). The Council's letter to the ecclesiastical commission of the diocese of Norwich does not indicate the religious complexion of the recusants who had conformed. Undoubtedly a certain number were Catholics, since some of the more important Catholics, under constant pressures to conform, lived in Norfolk.

THE DECLINE OF CATHOLICISM

Two pressing problems, about which the government hitherto had not formulated any consistent policy, demanded a conclusive decision in the early 1590's — the religious affiliations of the justices of the peace and the disposition of recusant wives. Since the mid-1560's the trend of official policy was to pass over the Catholics in filling vacancies in the commission of peace. But this probably was not always feasible, due to local circumstances. The officials at Westminster with reason suspected that the attitudes of such justices hindered the enforcement of laws inimical to their beliefs, and this same suspicion carried over to magistrates whose wives or children were Catholic. In October 1592, the Queen and the Council laid down the decision that recusants and conformists with recusant wives or sons living at home were henceforth debarred from the commission of peace,[151] and this was now put into effect.[152]

The question of the legal penalties to be imposed on women convicted as recusants was not definitively determined during Elizabeth's reign. By their recusancy they had broken the law and had to bear the responsibility for their acts. The question of spinsters and widows was simple; they could be fined and imprisoned, as were men. But the number of such was few and the law was clear in their regard. The more important question was the recusant wife. If her husband were a recusant she might be simultaneously imprisoned with him or be allowed to remain at home to administer the property and care for the children. The decision what to do was left to the discretion of the authorities. The knottier problem was the responsibility of a conformist husband for a recusant wife's fines and for her behavior. Here law conflicted with public policy. The common law subordinated the wife to her husband; her property was vested in him. He was responsible for what were termed her "temporal debts" but not for her "corporal acts" unless he was an accessory to them, which generally meant that he could not coerce her conscience nor be

---

[151] *A.P.C.*, XXIII, 255–256 (October 20, 1592).

[152] According to a document of the late Elizabethan or early Jacobean period public office was closed to those whose wives or first-born were Catholics (C.P.109/137, n.d. [?1606]). This obviously applied to others besides justices of the peace. In 1593 Roger Bodenham of Herefordshire was ordered by the Council to be ejected from the commission of lieutenancy because of his wife's recusancy. The conciliar order stated that this was the usual practice in such cases (*A.P.C.*, XXIV, 278, May 31, 1593). In 1599 a member of the Tregonwell family, a Protestant, considered for captain of petronels in Dorsetshire was refused appointment because his wife was a recusant, until Sir Robert Cecil had ruled on the case (C.P.70/42, May 21, 1599).

held responsible for her decisions in matters of conscience.[153] Public policy demanded that the mistress of a household should not be allowed to influence others, especially her children (which would create another generation of Catholics); but if the strict letter of the law demanded her imprisonment, public policy viewed the interests of the state as being better served by not rendering family life inoperable and depriving an obedient husband of the obligations due him by his wife. He would be made to pay a penalty for a situation which he possibly could not control; it could render him embittered and secretly opposed, no matter what his exterior acts and professions, both to the Establishment and to the Elizabethan regime.[154]

The Act of Uniformity of 1559 had penalized nonconformity, but not in particularly harsh terms; Parliament had left the work of implementing the enforcement of this statute to future sessions. The question of recusant wives did not assume serious proportions until the 1580's and 1590's; even then it was viewed as an annoyance rather than as a grave threat by the governing authorities. It was never considered necessary to regulate it by parliamentary legislation; the discretion of the officials and the terms of the common law regarding women were the norms guiding the solution of individual cases. Here, however, difficulties arose. The authorities did not follow a consistent pattern, but settled each question according to the circumstances of the time; lawyers found the common law uncertain in this particular question, since traditional legal principles did not envisage the responsibility of a husband for his wife's conscience and worship but for her acts apart from religion.

Various facts will illustrate this confusing situation. In 1591 the Council, referring to the release from prison of some recusant wives in the north into the custody of their conformist husbands, stated that it was customary to take bonds of such husbands for the good behavior of their

[153] S.P.12/281/37, possibly to be dated 1601 or 1602 (the date and authorship are not given in the document and the script is not clearly Elizabethan), is the chief source for our general discussion of the responsibility of the conformist husband for his recusant wife.

[154] The case of Edward Lloyd of the Inner Temple is a typical example of the dilemma facing a husband. He had been ordered to appear in the Queen's Bench for his wife, or, if he failed, to suffer imprisonment or outlawry. If he appeared for his wife he faced ruin. He had the other alternatives, divorce or legal separation from his wife. He asked, if made answerable for his wife's financial penalties, to be assessed according to his ability to pay, leaving the exact determination of the sum to Sir Robert Cecil (C.P.1116 [probably between 1596–1603]).

THE DECLINE OF CATHOLICISM

recusant wives.[155] The Council in September 1592 directed the imprisonment of five or six recusant wives of standing in Northamptonshire as a public example and ordered this to be the lot of the more militant in Wiltshire.[156] When the Council in March and again in September 1592 was asked to determine the responsibility of the conformist husband for his wife's fines and behavior, it referred both requests to the law courts for a decision.[157] No definitive ruling came from the judges because in June 1593 the Council referred the question of the responsibility of such husbands for wives released under the conditions of the statute of 1593 to the attorney general and the solicitor general, who were directed to obtain the opinions of judges and other leading lawyers.[158] There is no record of an answer and within a few weeks some recusant wives in Yorkshire were released to the custody of their conformist husbands.[159] Nor was there a ruling by 1594 when Lord Burghley recommended that the husbands of women convicted of recusancy were to be held responsible for their fines or to be made to suffer imprisonment until their wives conformed.[160] Obviously no real need for a decision arose because five years later Sir Arthur Throckmorton, apparently an alarmist, wrote to Sir Robert Cecil that it was necessary to disarm and restrain conformist husbands of recusant wives.[161] Until the end of the reign, so far as we have evidence, no definitive ruling was given in this matter, and practice remained inconsistent.[162]

The post-Armada years witnessed an increasing willingness upon the part of the Council, although its practice was by no means uniform, to

[155] A.P.C., XXI, 152–153 (May 24, 1591).
[156] A.P.C., XXIII, 192–193 (September 14, 1592), 215–216 (September 30, 1592).
[157] A.P.C., XXII, 324–326 (March 8, 1592); XXIII, 182 (September 10, 1592). The first request, that of March 8, 1592, was presented by the commissioners for recusancy of Lancashire, including the Earl of Derby. The second request, that of September 10, 1592, was presented by the commissioners for recusancy of Dorsetshire, including Viscount Howard. The Earl of Derby raised the question again the following November in a report to the Council about his anti-recusant activities (S.P.12/243/71, November 1592). In January and May of 1593 the Council directed the Earl of Derby to proceed against recusants without enumerating any exceptions (A.P.C., XXIV, 26–27, January 23, 1593; 234, May 14, 1593).
[158] A.P.C., XXIV, 296 (July 7, 1593).
[159] A.P.C., XXIV, 317–318 (June 19, 1593).
[160] S.P.12/248/9 (March 6, 1594: memorandum partly in hand of Lord Burghley).
[161] C.P.72/61 (August 12, 1599).
[162] S.P.12/281/37 [?1601, ?1602]; C.P.109/137 [?1606].

grant more or less prolonged periods of enlargement to those individuals, now aging and declining in health, who had long been subjected to conciliar surveillance. The qualifications, as always, were the posting of bonds and the proof of adequate reasons; the privilege was withdrawn in times of crisis. In some cases permanent enlargement was permitted. Those who received these degrees of favor undoubtedly had demonstrated their loyalty in some way during the recent critical years, but we must note that they, also, were the very persons responsible for maintaining the existence of the Roman Church within the realm for many years.

Rooke Greene received a concession of indefinite enlargement in June 1591 because of his advanced age and debilitated health.[163] Almost simultaneously John Gage of Sussex was permitted to go to his home county for as long a period as necessary to care for family matters, and Sir Alexander Culpepper received an indefinite respite to attend to personal affairs.[164] Both Edward Sulliard and Ferdinando Paris received an indefinite respite in order to sell lands and woods to pay to the Queen an unstated sum, probably their recusancy fines.[165] In the late summer of 1592 John Talbot was excused from recommitment to prison, although he was later confined at Ely. As he had been chosen an umpire to adjudicate certain matters in controversy between the Earl of Shrewsbury and some of his relatives, he was twice granted further extensions of his enlargement to settle this affair.[166] Edward Gage was released to take care of pressing matters and to attend the funeral of Viscount Montague, of whose will he was an executor. The Council limited his respite first to one month and subsequently to two months, but granted him considerable freedom after returning to custody.[167] Sir Thomas Tresham received a three-month leave to assist Lord Vaux further in his business affairs.

---

[163] *A.P.C.*, XXI, 236 (June 27, 1591).

[164] *A.P.C.*, XXI, 402–403 (August 18, 1591); 415 (August 26, 1591). In May, 1593 John Gage was removed from custody and confined to his house and a restricted area because of his health upon posting bond of £500 (XXIV, 229, May 13, 1593).

[165] *A.P.C.*, XXI, 458 (September 19, 1591 [name is given as Edmund Sulliard, which is an obvious error]), 474 (September 30, 1591).

[166] *A.P.C.*, XXIII, 198 (September 17, 1592); XXIV, 76 (February 21, 1593), 304–305 (June 10, 1593), 344 (June 29, 1593). Later Talbot was granted freedom for two months to go to Bath for his health (*ibid.*, 476, August 19, 1503).

[167] *A.P.C.*, XXIII, 329–330 (November 30, 1592); XXIV, 17 (January 21, 1593), 148–149 (April 1, 1593).

At the latter's request this respite was later extended, and Sir Thomas was licensed to go beyond the statutory five-mile limit prescribed for recusants.[168] Similarly, Thomas Throckmorton found the Council lenient both in granting him freedom to attend to his suits-at-law pending in the courts at Westminster and in granting him a release temporarily because of his health.[169] Michael Hare, whose wife had died about the time of his commitment, causing chaos in his personal and family affairs, also received similar consideration, being enlarged for two months to set them in order.[170] Supervised freedom was the lot of Edward Eccleston, a young Lancashire recusant imprisoned in the Gatehouse at Westminster, whose father, rated an esquire in his county, was a suspected conformist; the son was given into the custody of his parent to escape the contagion of the plague, raging in the prison.[171] Obviously, there was no suspicion of treason of such persons, and a considerable confidence in their loyalty.

4. THE ELIZABETHAN CATHOLIC POLICY UNCHANGED, 1595–1599

The second half of the 1590's was, for the Catholics, a monotonous repetition of the first half; it marked also, in 1599, the completion of forty years, nearly two generations, of the Elizabethan settlement of religion. It must have become evident to even the least discerning among the Catholics that, as long as the Queen lived, there was no hope of obtaining an alteration of their condition which would give them a status similar to that proposed a number of times for the Huguenots and finally realized under the Edict of Nantes.

The possibility of further trouble with Spain continued to disturb the English government even after 1595, during the declining years of Philip II. In 1596 fear of renewed hostilities again caused the Catholics to be brought under stricter surveillance. At Wisbeach Castle, those incarcerated were subjected to considerably more stringent regulations. Access to priests confined there, since they were considered dangerous to the state, was restricted early in the year, and the prisoners and those who frequented their company out of friendship and sympathy or for spiritual

---

[168] *A.P.C.*, XXIV, 159 (April 1, 1593), 328 (June 24, 1593), 354 (July 2, 1593).
[169] *A.P.C.*, XXIV, 221 (May 11, 1593), 399 (July 15,1593).
[170] *A.P.C.*, XXIV, 468 (August 15, 1593).
[171] S.P.12/235/4 [?1590]; *A.P.C.*, XXIV, 282–283 (June 5, 1593).

guidance were ordered to be examined.[172] For this reason the Suffolk squire, Edward Rookwood, and certain other recusants were cited in February to appear before the Star Chamber at its next session, and in connection with the same charge the Council in May ordered the apprehension of various persons who had refused to appear before the justices of the peace in Cambridgeshire and other counties, when summoned.[173] This vigilance persisted into the next year. Even illness, which was a sufficient excuse for freeing recusants imprisoned elsewhere, could not obtain liberty for those confined at Wisbeach. In September 1597, when an epidemic of sickness infected this prison, the Council ordered that those who were ailing should be removed only to the keeper's house.[174]

In November 1596 the apprehension that the government felt of a possible Spanish attack moved Lord Burghley to counsel the restraining of recusants, both men and women, and the sequestration of their horses and arms.[175] The Council thereupon directed that recusants free on bond from confinement at Ely and Banbury and others who gave cause of suspicion were to be committed to one or other of those places of detention and the enforcement of this was entrusted to the Archbishop of Canterbury.[176] The seriousness of the Council's intentions during the period of crisis became manifest in the following February, when it drew up a new set of regulations for those confined at Banbury and Ely, which seriously limited communication with the outside world.[177] Already the Council had instituted an alteration of its original plans. Some of the recusants

---

[172] *A.P.C.*, XXV, 154–155 (January 11, 1596), 174–175 (January 18, 1596). Edward Hall, porter at Wisbeach Castle, sent to Sir Edward Coke, the attorney-general, a description of the persons visiting the priests there and gave information how they were maintained (S.P.12/256/116, March 31, 1596).

[173] *A.P.C.*, XXV, 252 (February 29, 1596), 418–420 (May 24, 1596). On February 8, 1596 five long-prominent Catholic recusants, George Cotton of Hampshire, Henry Drury of Suffolk, John Gage of Sussex, and Rooke Greene and his son, William, of Essex, were cited before the Council to be placed in custody (*ibid.*, 208, February 8, 1596). Greene, who was old and blind, was permitted to remain at home (S.P.12/256/76, March 5, 1596); Cotton's and Gage's claims of illness for staying their immediate imprisonment were ordered to be investigated by a competent physician (*A.P.C.*, XXV, 234, February 25, 1596; 294, March 14, 1596).

[174] *A.P.C.*, XXVIII, 6 (September 20, 1597). The strictness imposed at Wisbeach brought about real deprivation, since the friends of the priests there feared to give aid to them (C.P.53/93, August 1, 1597).

[175] S.P.12/260/92 (November 4, 1596), /101 ([?November 10, ?1596] not clear if Lord Burghley is author); *A.P.C.*, XXVI, 375–376 (December 19, 1596).

[176] *A.P.C.*, XXVI, 322–323 (November 21, 1596).

[177] *A.P.C.*, XXVI, 522 (February 25, 1597).

could not appear for confinement because of age and illness and their eldest sons were ordered to be substituted in their place.[178] Certainly nothing manifested better that the most militant generation of Elizabethan Catholics, that of the first thirty years of the Queen's reign, was now about to disappear through death.

In January of 1597 the Council granted a temporary respite to Sir Thomas Tresham, who the month before had been confined at Ely, in order that he might prosecute certain suits-at-law. It felt moved to concede this because of a number of petitions presented by various persons who had purchased land from him, asking that he be released in order to complete the contracts.[179] On February 27 John Talbot of Grafton was set free for two months from Banbury, when the rigors of his imprisonment increased his bad health. Troubles had accumulated for him rapidly during his incarceration; his presence had now become necessary at his home because of the death of his wife and the pressing needs of his estate.[180] On the same day Richard Tremaine, the prominent Cornish recusant, who with various members of his family had long endured much because of religion, petitioned that he be transferred from his present confinement near Plymouth to his own house or to some other suitable place, in order that he might better provide for his own and his family's needs. The Council granted this, leaving the decision of his residence to the justices of the assizes in Cornwall.[181] The Council proved equally amenable only a few days afterward to a Mistress Dorrell, permitting her to go to her home in Kent during the delivery of her child, despite the fact that she, her husband, and their servants had been taken into custody for harboring priests and there was a standing accusation that treasonable words had been uttered in their household.[182]

When the danger of attack lessened during March of 1597, the conditions governing the confinement of the foremost recusants were greatly ameliorated. Early in that month the wife of Thomas Throckmorton was permitted access to her husband at Banbury whenever necessary, to confer about private matters. In April he was released for that year's Easter and Trinity terms, in order to attend to lawsuits, after which he

---

[178] *A.P.C.*, XXVI, 363–364 (December 12, 1596).
[179] H.M.C., *Var. Coll.*, III, xix; *A.P.C.*, XXVI, 428–429 (January 16, 1597).
[180] *A.PC*, XXVI, 523–524 (February 27, 1597).
[181] *A.P.C.*, XXVI, 526 (February 27, 1597).
[182] *A.P.C.*, XXVI, 422–425 (January 2, 11, 1597), 531 (March 2, 1597).

returned to custody. When he again applied for enlargement during Michaelmas term, the Council hesitated, fearing the inconveniences that might result from granting freedom to recusants at that time. It decided, however, to set Throckmorton free under bond, the length of which was to be at the discretion of the Archbishop of Canterbury, because of the pressure of his business affairs and various suits-at-law.[183]

On April 30, 1597, the Archbishop of Canterbury was directed to grant John Talbot of Grafton, upon expiration of his period of enlargement, such further freedom as the prelate thought desirable in order to improve his health.[184] In June the primate received a directive to take bonds of Michael Hare, confined at Ely, who was permitted a six-week period of liberty to attend to some important lawsuits.[185] In September, for the same reason as in the case of Thomas Throckmorton, the Council was at first averse to granting freedom to John Arundell, imprisoned at Banbury. However, to prevent incarceration from prejudicing his interests in certain business matters and lawsuits, the Council set him free, the length of his respite being left to the judgment of the Archbishop of Canterbury.[186]

By November, with the disappearance of the foreign danger, the Council proved very lenient and granted an indefinite extension of freedom to Arundell, Hare, Talbot, and Throckmorton, all of whom were temporarily enjoying liberty. One caution, however, was prescribed: they and others subsequently to be respited were to be warned by the Archbishop of Canterbury that they must continue to pay their recusancy fines to the Queen.[187]

Sir Thomas Tresham, back in prison, ran into difficulties when he applied for another discharge to attend to lawsuits and other personal affairs. His first request was granted and then revoked. On November 13 the Council reversed its attitude and sent an order to the primate to grant Tresham his liberty for the remainder of the current judicial term.[188] He returned on November 25; on December 3 he and two other prisoners at Ely, Edward Rookwood and Edward Sulliard, and two prisoners

---

[183] *A.P.C.*, XXVI, 538–539 (March 9, 1597); XXVII, 64 (April 24, 1597); XXVIII, 14–15 (September 25, 1597).
[184] *A.P.C.*, XXVII, 80 (April 30, 1597).   [185] *A.P.C.*, XXVII, 229 (June 19, 1597).
[186] *A.P.C.*, XXVIII, 18–19 (September 23, 1597).
[187] *A.P.C.*, XXVIII, 102 (November 6, 1597).
[188] *A.P.C.*, XXVIII, 118 (November 13, 1597).

at Banbury, Thomas Crawley and Thomas Wilford, were released.[189] The next day nine other recusants at Ely were ordered to be discharged, among them John Dracot, Thomas Gawen, Ferdinando Paris, and John Thimelby, with a proviso regulating certain debts incurred while in prison.[190]

The last of the Spanish scares took place during the summer of 1599. The leading recusants were again confined at Ely and Banbury and disarmed. The danger lasted but a few weeks, and at the beginning of September the prisoners were released.[191]

Obviously, to many of these recusants the fortieth anniversary of the Queen's accession, 1598, and the fortieth anniversary of the inauguration of the Establishment, 1599, caused little rejoicing. We can see it in the continued militancy of those areas, now nearly two generations after the religious change, where for years there had been strong aggregations of Catholics; elsewhere, too, scattered individuals and small groups still worshiped at mass or otherwise evinced Catholic beliefs.[192]

In the years just preceding the end of the century, in the diocese of Winchester, both on the mainland and on the isle of Jersey, Catholics

---

[189] *A.P.C.*, XXVIII, 167 (December 3, 1597).
[190] *A.P.C.*, XXVIII, 172 (December 4, 1597). The other five were Henry Carvell, Samuel Love, Philip Paris, Gervase Pierpoint, Robert ap Rece.
[191] *A.P.C.*, XXIX, 740 (July 20, 1599), 741 (September 3, 1599); C.P.72/46 (August 10, 1599).
[192] Some random evidences of Catholicism during the 1590's show its practice by individuals in areas where Catholics were generally a dwindling minority or interferences made it difficult to practice the Roman rites: 1592: accusation of entertaining priests in London (?) (*A.P.C.*, XXIII, 24, July 9, 1592); spy's report of Catholic activities in London (S.P.12/241/35 [?January ?1592]); 1593–1594: stanch adherence to Catholicism of Wiseman family of Essex (S.P.12/244/7, January 12, 1593; /247/3, January 2, 1594; /248/68.1, April 14, 1594; /103, May 12, 1594); 1595: priests and recusants in Derbyshire, Leicestershire, London, Northamptonshire (S.P.12/251/14, 19 [?1595]); 1596: Richard Topcliffe's report concerning priests in prison in and around London (C.P.43/41, August 1, 1596); lapsed conformist, London (C.P.45/48–49, October 6, 1596); refusal of conformity by William Stanney, prisoner in Marshalsea and suspected priest (S.P.12/260/24, September 25, 1596); use of Catholic articles (*A.P.C.*, XXV, 351, April 15, 1596; 505, June 27, 1596); 1597: pursuivant injured in searching for priest in Shropshire (*A.P.C.*, XXVI, 442–443, January 23, 1597); harboring of priest in Devonshire (*A.P.C.*, XXVII, 75, April 18, 1597); 1599: suspected harboring of priest in Derbyshire (C.P.73/11, August 23, 1599; /25, August 25, 1599). The State Papers for the 1590's have considerable data concerning the labors of priests in various parts of the realm, including the capital, London. One valuable example is the series of confessions of the Jesuit, Henry Walpole (S.P.12/248/78, /91, /112; /249/4, /12, /13, /14, /16, /44, /45, April 27, 1594–July 1594).

maintained the practice of their religion; and as was so often the case, official connivance accounted for the lack of severity in punishing nonconformity.[193] Bishop Bilson of Worcester, ordinary of a fairly small diocese, reported in 1596 a surprising degree of recusancy, including both men and women of all social ranks, Catholics and Protestant nonconformists, who were under the influence of certain persons of wealth and prominence, and related by blood and marriage. A lack of legal authority beyond the power of excommunication prevented effective countersteps being taken, which only an ecclesiastical commission, at present wanting, could satisfy. For better consideration of the problem Bishop Bilson sent on to the Council the names and status of the leading recusants of both sexes.[194] Monmouthshire, too, reported the prevalence of recusancy, which limited the choice of dependable law-enforcing officials.[195]

The Council of the North, cognizant that Catholicism was still widely practiced within its jurisdiction, took vigorous steps, indicting many, imprisoning some, and executing a few.[196] Some areas, such as Ripon, the neighborhood of Whitby, and the archdeaconry of Richmond, continued notoriously to set the example of a militant recusancy in the north which did not eschew evasion and even violence, scorning the repressive efforts of the government. But the majority of Catholics, although firm in their faith, were more peaceable.[197]

The Queen, alarmed at this evidence of continued northern opposition to the Establishment, removed Archbishop Hutton from the presidency of the Council of the North, putting in his place the second Lord Burghley, son of her greatest minister, and gave him very specific orders to repress recusancy, prevent further defection from the state church, and render the ecclesiastical commission a more efficient and effective body.[198]

---

[193] S.P.12/248/11 (March 7, 1594 [?1599]), /256/102.1 (March 22, 1596 [?1597]), /273/23 (November 5, 1599), /23.1 (September 20, 1598), /23.2 (October 5, 1598), /23.3 (September 28, 1599).

[194] C.P.42/51 (July 17, 1596).   [195] C.P.65/98 (November 24, 1598).

[196] A.P.C., XXVII, 91–92 (May 5, 1597); C.P. 176/66 (January 18, 1599); S.P.12/262/65 (March 12, 1597). A layman, Ralph Grimston (or Grymstone), was executed at York in 1598 for maintaining a seminary priest (C.P.70/82, June 6, 1599; document implies that date of execution was 1599; C.R.S., V, *English Martyrs*, 14, dates execution in 1598).

[197] C.P.61/30 (May 20, 1598), 69/103 (May 4, 1599); S.P.12/263/52 (May 24, 1597), /270/99 (April 27, 1599), /10 (May 29, 1599), /271/9 (June 14, 1599), /9.1 (June 13, 1599), /70, 71 (July 3, 1599), /72 (July [?3], 1599), /272/7 (August 3, 1599).

[198] C.P.73/9 (August 22, 1599); S.P.12/272/7 (August 3, 1599). Archbishop Hut-

He energetically conducted an inquisition, personally supervising the questioning of both men and women recusants. The extent of recusancy, he wrote to his half-brother, Sir Robert Cecil, was alarming and the obstacles were considerable in overcoming it.[199]

Durham, the neighboring diocese, had the same problems; boundary lines did not erase long-ingrained sentiments. The obstinacy of the Catholic nonconformists, many of them persons of status, was very pronounced: it extended to baptism and marriage by Catholic rites, and the education of the children of Catholic parents otherwise than in the common schools; and, on the part of some, it even was manifested by a refusal to join in prayers for the Queen. The number of those indicted in Durham did not correspond to the actual number of Catholics within the diocese. The larger part of them, when they appeared before the High Commissioner, refused conference, so that conformity of individuals among them was infrequent. As elsewhere, manifest evasion to avoid prosecution was evident; much of the cause of it, one must conclude, still lay in the lackadaisical officials of some sections and in the favor leaders of a community showed one another, being closely related in blood.[200]

Carlisle, a sparsely settled diocese, still had a considerable degree of recusancy, but the problem seemed to be reaching something of a solution through the migration of recusants elsewhere. The incumbent bishop, Henry Robinson, like the bishops in other dioceses, blamed the poor quality of the local clergy, holding that a better class of men was not attracted to the ministry due to the poor conditions of living and the risks involved, and he blamed his predecessor, John May, who had been lax in the qualities which he demanded of the clergy whom he ordained.[201]

---

ton seems to have undergone a breakdown which altered his character at the time of his translation from Durham to York, becoming more amiable and less energetic.

[199] S.P.12/272/112 (September 12 [?1599]), /273/14 (October 21, 1599). Continuing causes of the weakness of the Establishment were the poor quality of instruction of the people and the need of a better clergy (C.P.61/30, May 20, 1598; 73/9, August 22, 1599; S.P.12/263/52, May 24, 1597).

[200] S.P.12/262/11 (January 16 [?1597]), /25 (February 1, 1597), /263/55 (May 26, 1597), /81 (May 1597), /268/57 (September 16, 1598); C.P.30/78 (February 20, 1596).

[201] S.P.12/273/56 (December 26, 1599). S.P.12/262/22 (January 1597) is a list of forty-seven recusants within the diocese of Carlisle who had been presented to the grand juries at the assizes for the previous five years. Bishop May of Carlisle stated in 1597 that he had only one dependable pursuivant within his diocese, Thomas Lancaster (C.P.53/28, July 11, 1597).

Substantially, the religious pattern of the diocese of Chester, and within it especially Lancashire, showed, at the fortieth anniversary of the religious alteration, no significant change from earlier years; but here, as elsewhere in the north, the picture was uneven. The Establishment still had need of able preachers; evasion, official connivance and favoritism, deleterious to the Elizabethan Church, negated the efforts of the bishop and sheriff to apprehend recusants. Violence occasionally broke out against those enforcing the religious laws, and the prevention of such outrages was difficult, given the prevailing sentiments of the local population. It followed that conviction by jury trial for violation of any religious law was difficult to obtain when juries were so patently biased. Balancing all this to some degree, certain officials attempted conscientiously to enforce the laws; and — a sign of greater severity — husbands were liable to be held responsible financially for their wives' recusancy.[202]

One must keep in perspective the ratio between the population of these areas of Catholic concentration and the population of the rest of the realm: the former were, for the most part, the less densely populated, peripheral counties (with the exception of certain areas in East Anglia and sections of a few other counties, where there were aggregations of Catholic families). In Herefordshire, Lancashire, Yorkshire, and Wales, where priests (whose numbers cannot be accurately determined today) functioned with something of openness, they kept up the spiritual strength of some and reclaimed others who had fallen away. But in the larger urban districts, without churches, without a fixed schedule of religious services, and with the danger of spies and the known hostility of the law-enforcing officers, it was difficult for Catholics to gather together in other than small groups. This made any extensive proselytizing impossible; in general, those who had lapsed and had voluntarily sought reconciliation to Rome could be reclaimed in urban centers, since there were always some priests there. But despite claims by the government and by contemporary Catholics of considerable defection away from the Establishment to Rome, the data at hand cause one to discount it other

---

[202] S.P.12/266/18 (January 14, 1598 [?1599]), /18.1 (January 12, 1598 [?1599]), /18.2 (January 6, 1598 [?1599]), /18.3 (January 1598 [?1599]), /32 (January 29, 1598 [?1599]), /80 (February [?1599]), /270/60 (March 19, 1599); C.P.58/103 (January 11, 1599), 179/98 (November 23, 1599); A.P.C., XXIX, 604–607 (February 25, 1599).

than on a small scale and only in certain areas. The internal power of Catholicism to expand had ceased; it had become static.

In the past only individuals and small groups had come over to the Establishment at any one time. This continued to be true during the 1590's; in the areas where we have seen recusancy, we shall also see conformity, either recent or of longer duration. It was reported in Hereford, Leicester, Monmouth,[203] Norfolk,[204] Northampton,[205] Rutland,[206] Warwickshire[207] and Wiltshire.[208] The energetic activity of Matthew Hutton, when Bishop of Durham, led to a piecemeal conformity within his jurisdiction;[209] he continued this course, but less militantly year by year, as Archbishop of York.[210] The second Lord Burghley, however, compensated by his own energetic repression of recusancy after his appointment as president of the Council of the North.[211] The neighboring Bishop of Carlisle could report some progress also.[212] Lancashire, too, presents an interesting picture. Reports about some of the justices of the peace and some other men of prominence show that a very considerable proportion of them were conformists, even if their families were recusants; an opening wedge threatening Catholicism had been entered, no matter what the degree of sincerity of the individual. At intervals other cases of conformity were also reported.[213]

Some of those who openly came over to the Establishment during the 1590's — Miles Gerrard; Sir Thomas Gerrard; Nicholas Longford of Derbyshire; John and Thomas Shelley of Sussex; Anne Sherborne, the daughter-in-law of Sir Richard Sherborne, an ecclesiastical commissioner of the diocese of Chester; Richard Turberville (apparently the son of a

---

[203] A.P.C., XXII, 342–343 (March 19, 1592).
[204] A.P.C., XXII, 336 (March 15, 1592).
[205] A.P.C., XXIII, 192–193 (September 14, 1592).
[206] A.P.C., XXIII, 216 (September 30, 1592).
[207] S.P.12/243/76 [?November 1592].
[208] A.P.C., XXIII, 215–216 (September 30, 1592).
[209] S.P.12/244/8 (January 13, 1593). Apparently, after Bishop Hutton's departure for York conformity became more difficult to obtain (S.P.12/262/11, January 16 [?1597]).
[210] A.P.C., XXVII, 85 (May 5, 1597); C.P.55/78 (September 28, 1597), 73/9 (August 22, 1599); S.P.12/272/7 (August 3, 1599).
[211] S.P.12/272/112 (September 12 [?1599]), /273/14 (October 21, 1599).
[212] S.P.12/273/56 (December 26, 1599).
[213] S.P.12/235/4 [?1590], /240/139 [?1591], /270/8 (January 8, 1599); C.P.63/22 (August 3, 1598: not clear if document refers to Lancashire or to Cheshire); A.P.C., XXIV, 36–37 (January 31, 1593).

prominent Catholic family of Glamorganshire); and Sir William Vavasour of York — had for years been widely known as Catholics.[214] When persons of this standing and longtime recusancy conformed, the Elizabethan government had won a signal triumph.[215]

And the authorities could then afford to be generous. After a test period to prove the sincerity of adherence to the Establishment, if the magistrates had no further doubt that the change in religion was sincere, the new conformist was pardoned of all past faults, even treason, no matter whether he was priest or layman.[216] Conformity, which could save life, property, and social status, was indeed a compelling pressure weighing on the Catholic recusant at the end of the sixteenth century.

5. THE ULTIMATE MEASURE OF DISESTABLISHMENT, 1600–1603

The very last years of the century that had witnessed the English Reformation and the first years of the seventeenth century, which were the last of Elizabeth's reign, saw the rise to power of new men, whose formative years had followed the religious change. Archbishop Whitgift was one of the few elder statesmen left; he had attained high position in the middle of the reign, in the 1580's, and was influential chiefly in ecclesiastical matters. Sir Robert Cecil was the most important of the younger statesmen. He had succeeded his father as the chief royal adviser

---

[214] *A.P.C.*, XXIII, 368 (December 14, 1592); XXIV, 36–37 (January 31, 1593), 334 (June 25, 1593), 410 (July 22, 1593); XXVI, 310–311 (November 19, 1596), 378 (December 25, 1596); C.P.29/23 (December 7, 1594), 55/78 (September 28, 1597); S.P.12/235/4 [?1590], /240/139, 140 [1590's], /250/29 (Docquet: S.P.38/4; November 11, 1594).

[215] Varying types of persons conformed for motivations which are not always clear: Henry Marshall, apparently a Catholic, who had lived beyond the seas for ten years, returned to England and conformed (*A.P.C.*, XXIII, 236, October 24, 1592); Hugh Scrivenour of Herefordshire had been educated overseas, most likely in a seminary for priests (XXIV, 454–455, August 12, 1593); John Doulande, a musician of distinction, who had lived abroad, returned to Protestantism after resettling in England (C.P.172/91, November 10, 1595); Miles Dawson, an irregularly ordained priest, became a preacher for the Establishment (C.P.55/78, September 28, 1597); the son of William Tyrwhitt of Lincolnshire by being a conformist received back his dead father's sequestrated armor (*A.P.C.*, XXIX, 592–593, February 24, 1599).

[216] *A.P.C.*, XXIII, 368 (December 14, 1592); XXIV, 36–37 (January 31, 1593), 410 (July 22, 1593); S.P.12/248/48 (Docquet: S.P.38/4; March 30, 1594), /249/19 (Docquet: S.P.38/4; June 30, 1594), /250/29 (Docquet: S.P.38/4; November 11, 1594), /259/88 (Docquet: S.P.38/4; August 3, 1596), /263/101 (Docquet: S.P.38/5; June 13, 1597).

and he continued the great Lord Burghley's policies. The Bishop of London, Richard Bancroft, was another rising figure. Eventually to succeed to the primatial see of Canterbury, he represented the trend to strengthen the structure and the doctrine of the Establishment along traditionalist lines. Fully aware of the complexities of the Catholic problem, Bishop Bancroft was highly instrumental in diminishing whatever prestige and respect still attached to the ancient faith.

These newer statesmen had no intention of altering a religious policy, which they had learned during their formative years to consider necessary to the maintenance of the established order. It is true that a little before the Queen's death the government and some of the English Catholics attempted to work out a modus vivendi, which would have permitted some measure of toleration, even if unofficial, to be granted to the adherents of the Roman Church. But this came to nothing — and its whole context is so vague that we know nothing definite of what either party proposed. Instead, the longstanding pattern of Catholic life continued uninterrupted up to Elizabeth's death.

The capital, London, still exhibited evidences of some adherence to the traditional church, but how extensive it was cannot easily be determined. In 1600 twenty-two men and twenty-six women of various classes, some of them members of families of standing, were taken while listening to a sermon preached by a Scots Capuchin, Campbell, in the Marshalsea. The priest was committed to close ward; the lay persons were handed over to the Bishop of London and others for examination and then either committed to prison or fined or released on bond.[217] In 1602 ten worshipers were arrested while hearing mass at Newgate.[218] Such flagrant exhibitions of illegal practices still caused alarm to an ever-fearful government, since contact between priest and layman, it felt, meant the influence of the former over the latter, which boded ill to sound obedience.[219]

In 1600 two Londoners were convicted of recusancy and one the next year;[220] in 1602 eleven priests and lay recusants confined in various London prisons were attested by Bishop Bancroft to be immovable

[217] S.P.12/274/50 (February 25, 1600), /54 (February 29 [?1600]).
[218] S.P.12/285/59 (November 19, 1602).
[219] A.P.C., XXX, 539–540 (July 27, 1600).
[220] S.P.12/283/50 [?December ?1601]. Francis Parkins and William Roper were convicted in 1600 and Henry James in 1601.

against persuasions to conformity.[221] Since one source of this recalcitrancy was religious books smuggled in from abroad, further regulations to prevent their circulation were decided upon in 1602.[222]

The diocese of Winchester, strategically situated on the southern coastline in case of enemy attack, as was realized in the days of the Spanish danger, continued to cause alarm to the government because of the standing of some of the local Catholics.[223] Nevertheless, there were no signs of disaffection in 1603, when Elizabeth died.[224] The vigor with which the ecclesiastical commission of the diocese of Salisbury had restrained recusancy and punished it accounted for the progress of the Establishment within that jurisdiction,[225] where some well-known Catholics of local prominence and influence had long been recalcitrant. In Warwickshire and Staffordshire the old religion still flourished limitedly, nourished in the latter county by the poor quality of the local ministry.[226] In Exeter, at the turn of the century, a temporary increase of Catholic recusancy occurred, especially in the remoter sections, due largely to the lack of a diocesan ecclesiastical commission.[227]

At the end of Elizabeth's reign and in that of James I the largest aggregations of Catholics were still probably in the west country, Wales, and the northern counties. There the pattern of Catholic life and sympathies was slow in dying. The militancy of Elizabethan Hereford was to be found also in the early years of the new monarch; the Catholic alliances — blood and friendship — of the magistrates, some of them conformists, continued to account, as in the past, for their remissness; the hot temper of the Catholics still could not be restrained from rioting; and a fully empowered ecclesiastical commission was necessary to control the traditional church.[228] In this county and in Monmouth, Shropshire, and Wales, masses were celebrated and a corps of messengers carried around the articles needed for performing the Catholic rites, while

---

[221] S.P.12/284/62, 62.1 (July 6, 1602).
[222] C.P.184/82 (August 21, 1602). Evidence of Catholic books being smuggled in or otherwise obtained is in C.P.89/75 (November 6, 1601), 91/109 (February 8, 1603).
[223] S.P.12/274/34 (February 6, 1600); C.P.92/39, 40 (March 16, 1603).
[224] C.P.92/39, 40 (March 16, 1603).   [225] C.P.185/23 (October 8, 1602).
[226] C.P.83/49 (July 19 [?1604]), 113/114 (December 29, 1605).
[227] C.P.141/217 [?1600], 182/5 (April 28, 1601). An ecclesiastical commission effected considerable conformity in Exeter (C.P.192/130, September 23, 1606).
[228] C.P.188/87 (March 11, 1605), 190/93 (June 1, 1605).

responsible officials closed their eyes. Recusancy flourished, and the usual picture of a state clergy of little competence persisted.[229] During the Queen's last illness, in the tensions caused by apprehension for the future, the number of Catholics in Wales, their status, wealth, and arms, caused real concern to the local officials in case of a Catholic uprising or of an exterior attack,[230] but this proved groundless and the transition to the new regime came about peaceably.

Queen Elizabeth, worried about the extent of Catholicism in Yorkshire in 1600, commended Lord Burghley's stringent policy of control. Catholics, although probably a minority, were admittedly numerous, and their ranks had swelled after the regime of the Earl of Huntingdon, a very stern lord president of the North, had been followed by the more gentle administration of Archbishop Hutton. Obeying the Queen, Lord Burghley, now lord president, did not relax his enforcement of the laws until her death; his severity was so marked that Catholics openly complained. Some fled away; one poor farmer, Anthony Bates (or Battie), was executed for harboring a priest.[231]

It was disconcerting to the government, in the last years of Elizabeth's reign and in the first years of James I's rule, to find that obedience to the religious laws and exterior conformity were in many cases superficial, especially in the north. The triumph of the Establishment, although very widespread and very real, was not complete. Any leniency, however slight or ill-founded, bred hope among the Catholics that toleration might be granted; and when the pressure of the law was relaxed, as at the beginning of James I's reign, an immediate return to Catholicism on the part of many in the north was noticeable.[232]

The diocese of Durham, at the beginning of the new century, had in Bishop Toby Matthew a militant administrator of much the same stamp

---

[229] C.P.83/97 (March 4, 1601), 89/35 (October 31, 1601), 89/116 (November 18, 1601), 92/48 (March 19, 1603), 96/94 (December 5, 1602), 96/133 (December 21, 1602), 188/87 (March 11, 1605), 190/93 (June 1, 1605).

[230] C.P.92/31 (March 13, 1603), 92/48 (March 19, 1603), 99/64 (March 30, 1603; conditions in Wales immediately after Elizabeth I's death).

[231] S.P.12/274/16 (January 14, 1600), /281/28 (July 27, 1601), /284/52 (June 29, 1602); C.P.68/66 (March 1, 1600), 80/32 (June 14, 1600), 85/106 (March 24, 1602), 94/45 (July 18, 1602), 118/36 (November 1, 1603), 180/96 (May 21, 1600), 182/56 (June 17, 1601), 187/116 (October 19, 1603), 190/30 (January 16, 1606); C.R.S., V, *English Martyrs*, 16.

[232] C.P.94/45 (July 18, 1602), 118/36 (November 1, 1603), 187/116 (October 19, 1603), 190/30 (January 16, 1606).

as the second Lord Burghley; he, too, had to deal with many of the same problems. Success would have been difficult but for the ability of a pursuivant, Henry Sanderson, whose efforts in Northumberland, his home county, to some extent counterbalanced the laxity of the local sheriff and other officials. Nevertheless, to enforce conformity there presented immense difficulties: the geography of that county permitted evasion; some Catholics used force to ward off apprehension; the hold of the traditional religion over many was still considerable. In the end, only unrelenting pressures, chiefly that of the ecclesiastical commission, insured successful control of recusancy.[233] Nor did boundary lines erase problems. Bishop Robinson of Carlisle unhappily found himself face-to-face with an aggressive recusancy nourished by priests and by threats of violence. He, too, needed a fully empowered ecclesiastical commission in order to enforce the Establishment.[234]

A stream of reports concerning Lancashire kept the officials in London aware that no substantial change had taken place in that county. Despite some progress in securing conformity and the piecemeal introduction of a better-trained clergy of the Establishment,[235] Catholicism retained a firm footing wherever influential persons, with the connivance of friendly officials, dominated a locality. Priests also bore a share of the responsibility, encouraging a spirit of not yielding, and the bad turn of the war in Ireland added to a growing feeling (fostered by the priests) that things would soon change.[236] So notorious had recusancy become that some who fled Lord Burghley's rigorous rule in York felt safe in Lancashire.[237] The worried Privy Council took initiatory steps to extend a more effective control over that county,[238] but the first years of James's reign

[233] C.P.103/111 (January 14, 1605), 180/127-129 (June 27, 1600); S.P.12/278/53 (February 12, 1601); A.P.C., XXXI, 26-28 (December 14, 1600).

[234] S.P.12/275/66 (September 20, 1600), /278/7.1 (January 20 [?1601]); C.P.85/95 (March 19, 1602), 85/153 (April 14, 1601).

[235] C.P.68/44 (February 20, 1600), 78/4 (March 28, 1600), 91/125 (February 16, 1603), 181/140 (April 16, 1601), 183/26 (August 27, 1601), 185/39 (October 18, 1602). Some, but not all, of the preachers maintained by Queen Elizabeth to secure conformity in Lancashire proved conscientious (C.P.183/130, January 15, 1603).

[236] S.P.12/274/25 (January 31, 1600), /282/74 (n.d. [?November ?1601]), /287/9 (January 18, 1603); C.P.77/54 (March 14, 1601), 78/4 (March 28, 1600), 180/96 (May 21, 1600), /100 (May 28, 1600), 183/145 (February 15, 1603), 250/99 (November 3, 1600); A.P.C., XXX, 368-370 (June 13, 1600).

[237] C.P.180/96 (May 21, 1600).

[238] A.P.C., XXX, 368-370 (June 13, 1600), 542-543 (July 29, 1600). The progressive formulation of the government's policy toward Lancashire indicates that there

THE DECLINE OF CATHOLICISM

indicate a continuation of the longstanding picture. We see this militancy of the Lancastrian Catholics both in their arming of themselves at the time of Elizabeth's death[239] and in a study of the parish of Prescott and the chapels dependent on it, which in the first decade of the seventeenth century still stoutly opposed the religious change. Priests and landed gentlemen were chiefly responsible for the prevalence of nonconformity, although the number of women recusants was about double that of the men. Some of the inhabitants had not scrupled to wound or even to slay the Queen's messengers carrying out prosecutions against recusants. As elsewhere a decline from conformity became noticeable when the powers of the ecclesiastical commission ceased, for then the laws were not enforced and priests functioned unhindered.[240] But again we must keep in mind that such evidences of strong Catholic recalcitrancy and violence were only in scattered areas, distant from the dominant pressure points of contemporary English politics.

The newer officialdom, as anxious as their predecessors to obtain the conformity of the more prominent Catholics, continued the longstanding pattern of alternating the imprisonment of these persons with temporary or prolonged respites from prison. John Towneley at the beginning of 1600 was in confinement along with other recusants at Norton in Lincolnshire. Due to his advanced age and increasing infirmities, his half-brother, Alexander Nowell, the Dean of St. Paul's, successfully sued for his release and he was removed to his home in Lancashire.[241] Edward Rookwood petitioned for a respite from custody to attend to pending lawsuits gravely affecting his estate. The Council empowered the Archbishop of Canterbury to grant his plea and to determine the conditions

---

was a larger volume of correspondence between the officials at Westminster and in Lancashire than is contained today in the State Papers, the Cecil Papers and the *Acts of the Privy Council.*

[239] C.P.99/113 (May 13, 1603), 190/134 (July 14, 1605). The first document is an investigation by the justices of the peace of Lancashire into the sale of armor and gunpowder during the spring of 1603. Everywhere those suspected made denials, the truthfulness of which we are justified in doubting. The pattern of recusancy and the occasional resort to violence in Lancashire and the exigencies of early 1603 would undoubtedly lead those who could to stock up with arms.

[240] C.P.141/281 (May 17, 1604). There were 207 recusants, 73 men and 134 women. In an attempt to effect conformity a well-trained pastor, a bachelor of divinity, had been placed at Prescott. The Bishop of Chester certified that in 1604 there were 2,400 recusants in the diocese, 917 men and 1,483 women. More than 600 had been induced by the bishop to conform.

[241] A.P.C., XXX, 67–68 (February 10, 1600).

governing it.²⁴² Likewise the Bishop of Norwich was directed to release Humphrey Bedingfield from confinement and also to permit him to live for a time with his son-in-law, since that longtime recusant was ill and unable properly to take care of himself in his own residence. His petition was furthered by the justices of the peace of Norfolk, where he resided, who confirmed his reputation as a well-behaved subject.²⁴³ But the number of such requests, which formerly could be drawn out at some length, was less than before the turn of the century because the oldtime recusants whom the government had so long watched were either dead or incapacitated.

Certain other contemporary cases also deserve our attention because they illustrate the force of special circumstances and indicate the extent of the discretionary powers of the authorities. Sir George Carew, currently one of Elizabeth's most efficient officials in Ireland, successfully obtained the release of his brother, Richard, a man of few means and an unsuccessful lawyer, who had been convicted of recusancy and penalized while managing Sir George's private affairs during his absence from England.²⁴⁴ Sir Robert Cecil stayed further proceedings in the diocese of Carlisle against one of the most convinced Catholics of Westmorland, Thomas Pickering, who had, it would appear, manifested a very obedient attitude in civil affairs.²⁴⁵

Queen Elizabeth had long been lenient to friends of many years who continued to adhere to the Roman Church. The Cornwallis family especially had experienced her kindness and also that of the Cecils, both Lord Burghley and his son, Robert. Lady Anne Stourton was another friend who had always been dispensed from prosecution under the recusancy laws. In 1601, when she was indicted through the medium of an agent of the chief pursuivant, Thomas Felton, at the assizes in Dorsetshire, she petitioned the Queen for a continuation of her former privilege. Proof was also given to the Queen that she did not shelter Catholics inimical to the state and that her conviction and the consequent distraint of two-thirds of her lands would impoverish her completely. Elizabeth I, once she had learned of Lady Stourton's troubles and the

---

²⁴² *A.P.C.*, XXX, 216–217 (March 30, 1600).
²⁴³ *A.P.C.*, XXX, 356 (June 6, 1600).   ²⁴⁴ S.P.12/278/4 (January 16, 1601).
²⁴⁵ C.P.85/153 (April 14, 1601).

reasons presented for staying the indictment, ordered that it should be dismissed and that none of the lady's lands should be distrained.[246]

Sir George Peckham, who suffered intermittent restraint because he had returned to Catholicism after a brief conformity, received release from imprisonment (apparently in the summer of 1602) in order that he might recover his health while living in the country with his wife. However, he ran into difficulties when presenting his suit. Thomas Arundell (the future Baron Arundell of Wardour), with whose family Lady Peckham was residing, firmly opposed any visit by her husband, because his reputation for ardent recusancy might cast suspicion on those with whom he mingled. Shocked at this frustration Peckham appealed to Cecil, begging him to write Arundell to ask him to alter his decision.[247]

But if Thomas Arundell were afraid to receive a recusant guest, the Lord Warden of the Cinque Ports, Lord Cobham, did not fear to further the petition of a Catholic to the government.[248] This as much as anything demonstrates the anomalous position of the Catholics in late Elizabethan England, and we could supply still further proofs by citing more cases involving special circumstances and manifesting a discretionary magnanimity on the part of the authorities. All of this evidence forms a pattern which shows, as the whole reign of Elizabeth manifests, that the Catholics were leaderless and that their well-being depended completely upon the policy of the government and the frame-of-mind of individual officials. Thus, the mitigation of the treatment of some did not mean that all escaped the full weight of the recusancy laws. George Cotton, who had suffered repeated terms of imprisonment in the past, was again ordered into custody in March 1603 despite claims of illness, which for some time had obtained him his freedom. Another Hampshire Catholic, Thomas Welles, at the same time was directed into confinement, while two other recusants of that county were singled out, with the implied suggestion that they should be investigated.[249] Richard Tremaine was reimprisoned in 1602 after a respite while awaiting a hearing at the assizes; he continued to suffer financial distress because of the distraint

---

[246] *A.P.C.*, XXXII, 28–29 (July 6, 1601); C.P.91/3 (1601).
[247] C.P.94/65 (July 24, 1602).   [248] C.P.80/41 (June 20, 1600).
[249] C.P.92/39 (March 16, 1603).

levied upon two-thirds of his property fourteen years before.²⁵⁰ In Staffordshire, although the aged John Dracot was ordered to be left in peace, despite being under suspicion of harboring priests, his recusant son, Philip, suspected of the same charge, was directed to be confined in close custody, and his house was to be searched for any extraordinary supply of horses and arms.²⁵¹

By 1600 and after a multitude of factors, some of them new, coalesced, further weakening the Roman Church. The limitations hindering an active Catholic spiritual life and the interferences preventing close relations with revitalized Catholic institutions on the Continent were now rendering conformity less onerous in conscience. The Establishment, too, was on a firmer basis; its clergy in the more populous areas was better trained; scholars, most notably Richard Hooker, were appearing, ready to defend the Anglican Church on learned grounds; and such able leaders as Archbishop Whitgift and Bishop Bancroft, as far as the secular-minded Queen gave them scope, were making the Elizabethan Church a more positive force in the nation's religious life and more attractive to Catholics weakening in their faith.

And other means at the government's disposal were also wearing down Catholic resistance — raids by pursuivants which could jeopardize property and even personal safety, the refusal to recognize both the validity of marriages not celebrated by the Anglican rites and the legitimacy of births not registered in a parish of the Establishment, difficulties in educating children in surroundings not inimical to Catholicism, social and political advantages in being a Protestant, and the ever-present fear of imprisonment. Conferences between Catholic laymen and the clergy of the Established Church proved, perhaps, the most successful single means in inducing conformity. For one to maintain his religious convictions against the learned arguments of the later Elizabethan higher clergy necessitated a good training in theology and intellectual strength. The average layman, when faced with the explanations of an Oxford- or Cambridge-trained dean or bishop, could hardly hope with meagre knowledge gleaned from a few books smuggled in from the Continent and occasional instructions given by itinerant priests to uphold doctrinal

---

²⁵⁰ C.P.93/168 (July 3, 1602); *Recusant Roll. No. 1, 1592-3*, M.M.C. Calthrop, ed., C.R.S., XVIII (London, 1916), 16, 17, 19.
²⁵¹ *A.P.C.*, XXXI, 471-472 (June 21, 1601).

positions concerning intricate points of theology. It is no wonder, then, that Catholics ran into difficulties during a conference about religion and rejected their faith.

Some boys who had been taken at Wisbeach Castle, where they were attending certain priests while receiving a Catholic education, are a case in point. When subjected to questioning two conformed and were placed with friends who were devoted to the Establishment; two others who did not evince the same willingness were ordered to be placed in the charge, in one case, of a prebend at Lichfield, in the other, of the Archbishop of Canterbury.[252]

In the north the pressures of Lord Burghley's rigid control continued to reap a harvest of conformity.[253] This was true of parts of Lancashire, where not only some members of the upper classes, but also elements among the lower classes, were falling into the habit of attending the local parish.[254] The vigorous efforts of the Lord Warden of the Middle Marches, Sir Robert Carey, acting under the direction of the Ecclesiastical Commission for the North Parts, had the same effect and resulted in the apprehension and subsequent conformity of certain recalcitrant recusants in Northumberland, while others gave the impression of a willingness to conform.[255] In Wales and Herefordshire, where the Roman Church was but slowly dying out, occasional conformity or even a more full adherence to the Establishment now characterized the gentry and the ranks of the justices of the peace.[256] The rate of conformity in Wales was more easily accelerated after the execution of the Earl of Essex (February 25, 1601), according to a spy's report. Due to that peer's influence some of the gentry families had never been indicted, insuring them an immunity which permitted their houses to be used undisturbed as priests' residences and as chapels for the celebration of mass and the administration of the sacraments.[257]

The sincerity of some, at least, of the individuals who changed over

---

[252] S.P.12/272/107, 107.1 (September 7, 1599); *A.P.C.*, XXX, 201 (March 25, 1600). In December 1600 the prisoners at Wisbeach Castle were transferred to Framlingham Castle, Suffolk (XXXI, 63, December 26, 1600).
[253] C.P.68/66 (March 1, 1600), 182/56 (June 17, 1601).
[254] C.P.93/22 (May 5, 1602), 183/26 (August 27, 1601).
[255] S.P.12/278/53 (February 12, 1601).
[256] C.P.83/97 (March 4, 1601), 190/93 (June 1, 1605), 191/69 (November 13, 1605).
[257] C.P.83/97 (March 4, 1601).

to the state religion may be questioned, because there was a certain amount of backsliding in the first years of James I, but we lack sufficient data to know the exact numbers of those who returned to the traditional religion and the length of their previous conformity.[258] A few cases selected because of their local importance illustrate the varying motivations causing contemporary conformity. Thomas Sandford, who had for some time borne a reputation of irregularly attending the state church while insisting that he was a Catholic, continued his contradictory behavior into the last years of the Queen's reign in order to escape further impoverishment, since he had dissipated his estate.[259] In the county of Montgomery a conformist son of a Catholic family, suspected only casually of adhering to the state church, intrigued strongly in the fall of 1602 to secure his own selection as sheriff in order to prevent the conviction of his wife and his mother as recusants.[260]

Odd as it may seem, one of the persons most responsible for some recusant riots in Lancashire, Edward Norris of Speke in the hundred of Derby, whose house Bishop Vaughan of Chester considered a veritable nursery of Catholicism, was an occasional conformist. After he was accused in 1600 of inciting certain disturbances and had been summoned before the Council, he conformed in earnest to escape further punishment. Early the following year he testified before that body that he was working sincerely to win over his tenants and other dependents to the Established Church. The Council, unwilling to press further a case where pressures and fears had reacted so much in its favor, licensed Norris to return home upon bond to continue his efforts.[261]

The importance of a case such as Norris's is that it illustrates the progressive weakening of an occasional conformist's Catholicism, once he was willing to compromise with his conscience. The government and most Protestants looked upon this type of Catholic as extremely danger-

---

[258] C.P.103/111 (January 14, 1605), 110/90 [?April 19, ?1605], 118/36 (November 1, 1603), 187/116 (October 19, 1603).

[259] S.P.12/263/56 (December 26, 1599); C.P.182/130 (August 2, 1601). Sandford was a fairly firm recusant until he had persuaded his wife to adopt that practice, whereupon he lapsed into occasional conformity to save his property. Reputedly he maintained a priest in his house.

[260] C.P.97/82 ([?November], 1602). The conformist, in this case, apparently also wanted to use the influence of the office of sheriff in his own favor in certain lawsuits.

[261] C.P.180/100 (May 28, 1600); A.P.C., XXX, 368-369 (June 13, 1600), 542 (July 29, 1600); XXXI, 137 (February 1, 1601).

ous due to the secret nature of his beliefs and the state's inability to keep check on his convictions. Such a judgment resulted from unfounded fears, for he who would compromise with his conscience lacked integrity of belief; and faith, if subjected to adjustments, frequently became shallow and eventually disappeared. Although the government did not realize it, an occasional conformist was a lost Catholic, a fact increasingly true as Elizabeth's reign progressed.

Those Catholics after the turn of the century who refused to conform continued to determine their attitude toward the Queen and also toward their native realm according to personal conscience and family tradition, but also, very probably, according to the degree of harassment by officials which they felt that they endured and their numerical strength within a local area. The newer officialdom, like the old, distinguished between the priests and the laity, looking upon the latter generally as guilty of civil disobedience, but no more. The major problem bothering the Catholic layman (and every priest more so) was fear bred of uncertainty. He never knew when the enforcement of the laws might become harsher; always facing him under the most usual circumstances was a possible loss of liberty, property, and status. He was aware that the ultimate severity of the law rarely touched the layman, but that under particular circumstances it might: eight of the laity had been executed between 1600 and 1603 for acts connected with Catholic practices or activities. But the Catholic layman also was aware that the government showed a degree of forbearance even towards those suspected of harboring priests or worshiping at mass; that class background weighed a great deal in determining punishment; and that the maximum penalties for most were fines and temporary imprisonment.

We can see how overwhelmed the priests and the laity felt themselves to be with a multitude of severe restrictions in two documents, written separately but which concur in content, summarizing the picture from a contemporary and partisan viewpoint. In all of England there was no place, private or public, where Catholics could legally participate in the rites of their religion. Those who refused to attend the Protestant services, if solvent, paid a heavy fine; if insolvent, were confined in prison or endured heavy losses of lands and goods. Almost all prominent Catholics were already held in some kind of custody, severe or light. Capital punishment faced those who were reconciled to Rome, accepted absolution for their sins from priests, or assisted the priests in any way. The status of Catholics in society and in the state was very degraded, for they were disfranchised from holding high public office, limited in the scope of their activities, and subject to excommunication by the Establishment[262] — the implication of the mention of this last penalty being that it entailed not merely religious consequences, but also serious civil disabilities. The significance of these two documents is the extent to which chaos had come to pervade Elizabethan Catholic life, rendering almost impotent the onetime dominant church, now over forty years disestablished.

[262] *The Archpriest Controversy,* T. G. Law, ed., Camden Society, n.s., LVIII (London, 1898), II, 117–118; C.P.109/137 (n.d. [?1606]). The ever-recurrent question of worshiping in the Established Church was treated, apparently by a Catholic theologian, according to current principles of casuistry, in S.P.12/279/90 (May 23, 1601). Despite the date the document is written in a Caroline hand and refers "to his Majesty."

CHAPTER IV

THE SOCIAL AND ECONOMIC STATUS OF THE ELIZABETHAN CATHOLICS

Between 1577 and 1603 Queen Elizabeth and the Council had appraisals made of the wealth of the Catholics and imposed special taxes upon them that give us the most informative picture available of their economic and social status. In assessing this mass of data we must remember that before the late 1570's the government prosecuted the Catholics only haphazardly; that many escaped indictment and trial because the machinery of local government was not particularly competent or honest; and that a certain number — a growing number, once the law was enforced with more rigor — escaped prosecution by some degree of conformity. During the 1590's and the three-and-a-quarter years of the Queen's reign after the turn of the century the number of Catholics progressively diminished and financial penalties cut into their property, destroying any hope of a stable picture of that decade. It is chiefly from the 1580's that we have fairly abundant and accurate data: in the period when the devotion of the Catholics to their creed and to the pope was stanchest; the number of uncompromised Catholics was largest; their affluence and standing were yet fairly intact; but also when the laws against them were hardening without yet having attained their final, fixed pattern.

Our sources are (1) the census of the recusants of 1577 that included the value of their property and goods; (2) the three levies of horses of the 1580's; (3) the returns required of the Catholics in 1586–1587, reporting their wealth and ability to pay impositions; (4) the Recusant Roll of 1592–1593; (5) the administration of the Act of 1586 that regulated distraints levied on the property of recusants defaulting in the payment of fines; (6) the levy of horses of 1598.

Obviously questions can be raised about the validity of these sources; possibly more extensive research in county and other local records could give us additional proofs. It is our opinion, evident throughout this study, that the government at Westminster was well aware of the names, social status, and economic condition of the leading Catholics: the returns of the levy of horses of the mid-1580's were made to a teller in the Exchequer, Robert Freake, personally, for auditing;[1] another official, Thomas Moryson, clerk of the pipe in the Exchequer up to about 1591 or 1592, had personal charge of keeping a special record of the financial condition of individual recusants;[2] the master sheet tallying the values of individual recusants of 1586 was subjected to checking and verification and therefore must be considered in large part accurate; the records of distraints levied upon the estates of recusants were based upon official investigations. In sum total Elizabeth's government had a corpus of data about the leading Catholics built up from a great wealth of detail.

1. THE ASSESSMENT OF CATHOLIC WEALTH IN THE 1580's

As one goes through the State Papers he finds a number of instances where persons or classes or districts were assessed a levy of horses. Obviously these were imposed to meet a special need arising from the unsettled condition of the international scene or of Ireland: it would have been useless and uneconomic otherwise to place such a levy. In terms of the sixteenth century the person assessed could not necessarily consider such an exaction to be a penalty, since it was not uncommon in England or on the Continent to require those most affected by the turn of events to bear a large share of the burden. But official statements show that the levies of the 1580's, although imposed on various groups within Elizabethan society, were considered in regard to the Catholics specifically to be a test of loyalty.[3]

Not all Catholics of substance were included in the levies of horses and

[1] S.P.12/184/40 (November 21, 1585), /184/48 (November 26, 1585).
[2] S.P.12/241/66 (February 26, 1592).   [3] S.P.12/172/72 (August 15, 1584).

SOCIAL AND ECONOMIC STATUS OF CATHOLICS

the various calculations of landed wealth. There are significant omissions of names that have recurred at intervals in this study; possibly the inclusion of some of them would raise our estimate of the wealth of the Catholics as a body. It is very likely, however, that the recusants who were omitted had conformed, at least temporarily, or were the recipients of special royal favor (such as the Cornwallis family) that exempted them from inclusion in the lists of those who, in the eyes of the law, must bear the financial impositions attached to the status of recusancy.

What is much more striking, since the financial records of the 1580's contain a very comprehensive cross section of the Catholics whom Westminster considered especially worth its attention, is the almost total lack of the great family names of the Tudor era. No more significant evidence exists that such events as the Northern Rebellion and the attrition of time had cut away the ranks of the Catholics of high status; that by-and-large even the leading Catholics were of most secondary importance. The very lenience of the government during the various crises of the 1580's proves that, as a body, the laity adhering to Rome lacked the substance to cause real fear in the authorities; that a sufficient test of the loyalty of the Catholics and a sufficient restraint upon possible subversiveness on their part lay in economic controls and periodic imprisonment.

Some words of caution are necessary about the purpose of this chapter. We are concerned primarily with determining the general pattern of Catholic wealth and status, not with the effect upon that group of sixteenth-century economic conditions. We must also keep in mind that very possibly a goodly number of the recusants whose financial resources we have investigated might have had hidden sources of wealth that are not now apparent and might, if known, throw more light on how they maintained both their standing in society and their style of living. Generally, but by no means in all cases, estates were scrutinized in only one county, most probably where the owners designated legal residence; there would be the main source of income from lands and the environment from which social status was derived. We know from the Recusant Roll of 1592–1593 that some owned property in more than one county, but this would have been recorded for tax purposes at Westminster in the 1580's only if a careful system of cross-referencing were in use, something that we cannot judge from the evidence at hand. Defects both in the method of determining property values and in the keeping of local records, because of inefficiency in recruiting, paying, and supervising local officials (even without considering the many opportunities for dishonesty), prevented full and exact computations. The round figures usually reported for property assessments and for income (frequently marks that we have converted into pounds, shillings, and pence) prove the difficulty in arriving at exact calculations; the estimate by a sixteenth-century man of substance of his own wealth in all good faith could easily have been inaccurate.

But granting all the possibilities of error, of fraud, and of unintentional inaccuracy, it is our considered judgment that the care exercised by the central government, its detailed corpus of information, and its constant surveillance of the leading Catholics, insures a fairly correct picture of Catholic wealth emerging from the data that we use in this chapter. We must therefore take note that the Catholics of most affluence were to be found in those counties where, in Tudor days, the wealth from commerce or sheep raising or from well-run great estates was concentrated. In other words, Catholic wealth roughly followed the geographical pattern of the distribution of wealth in the realm, and Catholic wealth and Catholic numbers were not necessarily correlative. Thus, the sizable and devoted aggregations of Catholics in Lancashire and Herefordshire represent less wealth than the fewer Catholics in Protestantized East Anglia and London and its environs. The Council kept more of the leading Catholics of the latter districts (and of parts of the Midlands, an area of great estates) under its direct surveillance, leaving most of the Catholics toward the west and north to be dealt with by local jurisdictions. Nothing proves better than this policy the relative distribution of the Catholics of importance in the eyes of Elizabeth's government.

During the 1580's a levy of horses was imposed at least three times on selected recusants, the first apparently during the troubled year of 1580[4] and extended into the next year, judging from a complaint sent to Sir Francis Walsingham by the Bishop of Coventry and Lichfield in June 1581.[5] The other two were in 1584 and 1585; the administration of the

[4] S.P.12/142/33 [?1580]. The date of this document is uncertain; we ascribe it to 1580 because it mentions Archbishop Heath, the last Catholic metropolitan of York, with no evaluation of his lands or goods and no assessment of lances or light horses placed against him. This would seem to indicate that he had recently died (the date of his death was 1579).

[5] S.P.12/149/37 (June 11 [?1581]).

latter ran on for some years, as the government found it necessary to recheck or alter the assessments. In the State Papers there are two schedules of those to be charged, S.P.12/142/33 [?1580] and S.P.12/183/15 [?1585], and one chart summarizing both assessments and payments, S.P.12/200/61 [?1587]. These three documents were composed after the contents had been sifted and checked by the central authorities, certifying at least their approximate accuracy; the second schedule bears assessments of individual wealth in the hand of Lord Burghley which is still another proof that the highest authorities knew well the condition of the recusants.

The first schedule, S.P.12/142/33, was based roughly and with exceptions on the ratio of one lance or one light horse per 100 marks (£66. 13s. 4d.) or fraction thereof of the annual rental value of land, the principal measurement of a man's financial worth. Goods were occasionally assessed along with lands; the ratio was established, but not always followed, of one horse or lance per £200 or £300 (or even more) of goods. In a considerable number of cases the appraisals of wealth made in the census of 1577 were used in 1580. Twenty-two of the dioceses of England and Wales were the areas designated to bear the levy. The total number of individuals bearing charges was 256 according to the schedule, but 261 by our calculation. Not all were rated equally, but according to ability to pay: 274 persons were assessed lances (283 by our calculation) and 200 were assessed light horses (213 by our calculation). Further proof that the number of Catholics of any considerable wealth or even of local standing was small is the fact that only a few dioceses had more than a most minute handful of recusants judged to be able to meet the levy. In Hereford sixteen persons were assessed sixteen lances and fifteen light horses. In London sixteen persons were assessed twenty-one lances and six light horses. Seventeen recusants of Chester were required to furnish ten lances and twelve light horses. York, with the same number of persons, was required to furnish five lances and twenty-eight light horses. Coventry and Lichfield had twenty persons assessed a total of thirty-two lances and seventeen light horses. Salisbury had twenty-three recusants listed, required to furnish thirty-five lances and nineteen light horses. Winchester had twenty-four persons listed, who had to furnish twenty lances and fifteen light horses. Norwich, a diocese containing perhaps the most affluent Catholics, had thirty-two persons charged with furnishing forty lances and twenty-two light horses. Oxford, with the same number of recusants, was required to furnish twenty-five lances and twenty-three light horses. The city of Oxford was separately recorded: it had eight persons assessed a total of eleven lances and six light horses.

The assessments in the other dioceses show a small Catholic population. Bath and Wells had only two recusants who were charged; they had to supply a total of four lances and one light horse. Canterbury, in strongly Protestant Kent, but where there were still a few Catholics of some standing, had twelve persons assessed twelve lances and seven light horses; the remainder of the county, the diocese of Rochester, had only two persons assessed, being charged a total of two lances and one light horse. Chichester had nine recusants assessed a total of thirteen lances and four light horses. Durham with five persons included in the levy had to furnish eight light horses. Ely, a strong center of Protestantism, had only five persons listed, who were ordered to furnish eight lances and one light horse. Exeter had eight names listed, with a requirement of furnishing nine lances and ten light horses. Gloucester had only one recusant listed, who was required to furnish two light horses. Lincoln, the residence of some fairly affluent Catholic families, had four names listed, charged with supplying five lances and five light horses. The one recusant charged in Llandaff was apparently deceased. In Peterborough the one recusant who was charged had to furnish two lances. In Worcester, which contained Warwickshire with a considerable Catholic remnant, six recusants were required to furnish thirteen lances and eleven light horses.

The schedule of the levy of 1585, S.P.12/183/15, included only eleven dioceses, half the number assessed in 1580. The data, however, is more diversified and more informative. Of the 206 persons listed, 189 were assessed a lance or light horse and 202 were assessed according to wealth, on the basis that one lance or light horse was the equivalent of £50 or less in money. Since those charged a lance or a light horse had the possibility of rendering personal service, we have checked their status: three were knights; forty-seven were esquires; 135 were gentlemen. The rural landed gentry, to which class all other evidence also shows the leading Elizabethan Catholics belonged, thus predominated. Apparently the plan was to have 109 lances and 109 light horses furnished and these are the totals given in the schedule; our calculation, however, shows that the assessment was for 108 lances and 110 light horses. There was, it is obvious, a certain amount of duplication. In Chester twenty-two persons were required to furnish nine lances and fifteen light horses; in Coventry and Lichfield nineteen had to furnish thirteen lances and ten light horses; in Ely two lances were charged, one to each of two recusants; in Hereford eight had to furnish three lances and six light horses; in Llandaff two had to furnish a total of three light horses; in London thirty-two had to furnish fourteen lances and nineteen light horses; in Norwich forty-one had to furnish forty-six lances and twelve light horses (three persons being given an alternative of one or the other); in Salisbury nine had to furnish two lances and seven light horses; in Winchester thirty-eight had to furnish eight lances and thirty-one light horses; in York sixteen had to furnish eleven lances and seven light horses.

The schedule of 1585 also assessed recusants according to their financial ability to meet the levy. As far as we can determine the government measured the ability of each recusant to pay according to one's ready cash at hand, rents, liquid assets and the total value of one's property, or at least that part of it which could be used as security for a quick loan. The notations on the schedule made in the hand of Lord Burghley assure the accuracy of the assessments and point up the government's detailed knowledge of the financial condition of individual recusants. The total charged was £8333. 6s. 8d., which correctly, according to our calculation, should be £9163. 6s. 8d. Ten recusants were charged the maximum, £100; five were charged £66. 13s. 4d.; thirty-four were charged £50; and 153 were charged the minimum, £40. In Chester twenty-four persons were assessed a total of £1106. 13s. 4d., one being required to pay the maximum and sixteen the minimum. In Coventry and Lichfield, containing the strongly Catholic Staffordshire gentry, twenty were charged a total of £1010, two being assessed the maximum and fourteen the minimum. In Ely the total, £80, represented the minimum charge being levied against each of two, and this was true also of Exeter and Llandaff. In Hereford eight persons were charged a total of £330, one being assessed £50 and seven the minimum, £40. In London the total, £1480, represented the minimum charge levied against thirty-seven recusants. In Norwich the total, £2010, represented payments by forty-one, four paying the maximum and twenty-five the minimum. In Salisbury the total, £360, represented the minimum payment by nine persons. In Winchester forty-one were charged a total of £1870, three being assessed the maximum and thirty-three the minimum. In York sixteen were assessed a total of £576. 13s. 4d.; one was charged £66. 13s. 4d.; nine were charged £50; and six were charged £40. Recusant wealth, it is manifest even in the pattern of a selective assessment such as this, lay in Norwich, London, and Winchester, which corresponds to the pattern of the wealth of the realm, but it is surprising that Chester, not then a rich diocese, was charged more and presumably was considered able to pay more than Coventry and Lichfield, a diocese of substantial landed gentry, and more than York, where the Catholic gentry ought to have been more affluent.

The chart of 1587, S.P.12/200/61, summarized the final charges and payments of the long drawn-out levy of the mid-1580's which had shifted from an optional payment of money or the furnishing of a lance or light horse solely to the payment of money. As in 1585 the basis was the ability of a recusant to meet a stipulated charge — £100, £75, £50, £25. By 1587 the government had a mountainous volume of data concerning numerous individual recusants, collected over the years and summarized and verified in the assessments of wealth and the proposals for composition made in 1586 (although some of the assessments of 1587 seem not to have considered the information returned in 1586). It was based, as far as we can determine, upon income and especially ready cash, rents, liquid assets, and that property which could be used as security for a quick loan. Twenty-eight counties, not dioceses as in the past, were the areas of assessment. The 218 recusants listed were charged a total of £6822. 10s. 0d. (or, according to our calculation, £6672. 10s. 0d.), of which only about half was paid, £3319. 3s. 6d. (or, according to our calculation, £3369. 3s. 6d.). The maximum charge, £100, was levied against four, £75 was levied against five; £50 was levied against thirty-six; £25 was levied against 169; lesser amounts were levied against four others. Possibly 106 made payment, although we cannot be certain about seven, which, subtracting them, would reduce the total to ninety-nine; 112 did not pay. In Berkshire five were assessed a total of £150; two made payments totaling £50. In Buckinghamshire nine were assessed a total of £350, of which four paid £150. In Cheshire three were assessed a total of £100, of which two paid the total sum of £75. In Derbyshire three were assessed a total of £100; one paid £25. In Devonshire two were charged £75; there was no payment. In Dorsetshire one person was charged, but did not pay, £25. In Essex five were charged £150, of which three paid the total of £75. In Gloucestershire three were charged £100, of which one paid £50. The sloppiness and lack of clarity with which this chart was made out, so different from the care usually to be found in official Elizabethan documents, causes confusion in regard to Southamptonshire: fourteen were charged a total of £350; the sum recorded as paid was £275; but we can identify with certainty only £50. In Herefordshire five were assessed a total of £125, but only one paid £25. In Hertfordshire one person was assessed but failed to pay £50. In Huntingdonshire two were charged a total of £75; one paid £50. In Kent seven were assessed a total of £250; four paid the total sum of £175.

There are two returns for Lancashire, one more complete than the other: twenty-one persons were charged a total of £550; thirteen (of which there were two pairs of two each) paid a total of £350. In Leicestershire one recusant was charged and paid £75, and this was true also of Lincolnshire. In London-Middlesex twenty-nine persons were assessed a total of £975; £675 was paid by nineteen, but two of these paid in another county; one paid half of the assessment; and one was discharged of his obligation but included in the return as having paid. In Norfolk thirteen were charged a total of £400, of which six paid altogether £175, one paying in part. In Northamptonshire five were charged the total sum of £125, but only one paid his assessment, £25. In Oxfordshire some confusion obscures an accurate picture. The number assessed, eighteen, were charged, according to the chart, £397. 10s. 0d., which according to our calculation correctly should have been £403. 10s. 0d.; of these eight paid a total of £126. 13s. 6d., which according to our calculation should have been £126. 2s. 6d. In Staffordshire ten were charged a total of £250, which, according to our calculation, should have been £350; only four made payment of a total of £125. In Suffolk the total charged, £600 (which according to our calculation should correctly have been £500), was levied against fifteen, of whom nine paid a total of £275, one paying half of his assessment and one being discharged of his obligation although included in the return as having paid. In Surrey, where as in London recusants from other counties were at times confined, ten were assessed £400, of which four paid a total of £225. In Sussex twelve persons were assessed a total of £350, of which six paid £140, two paying only in part. In Warwickshire three were assessed a total of £75, of which two paid, but only in part, the sum of £27. 10s. 0d. In Wiltshire four were assessed £100, but only one paid his charge, £25. In Worcestershire six were charged £150, of whom one paid his assessment, £50. In York ten were charged a total of £250, of whom only two paid the sum of £50.

In each of the three levies the number of persons charged, a carefully selected group of representative Catholics, was less than three hundred. They were at the most of moderate affluence and the levies, added to the regular recusancy fines, constituted a heavy burden. Lord Burghley knew this in 1585 when the majority were charged the minimum assessment, obviously the most that he felt they could pay. In 1587, with the danger of war impending, the government was more rigid both in enforcing the payment of the recusancy fines and in distraining the property of delinquents; nevertheless, the levy of that year was predicated on ability to pay, and not motivated by a vindictive intent to force the recusants into bankruptcy. By far the larger number were charged the minimum sum; a few were permitted to pay only a part; others were listed in the levy but not assessed. And at a time when a suspected minority had every reason to assert its loyalty, over half of those charged had enough confidence in the government's tolerance to admit inability to pay. The maximum charge, £100, was placed against only two persons in London-Middlesex and one in Staffordshire and one in Surrey; £75 was charged against one in Buckinghamshire, one in Leicestershire, one in Lincolnshire, one in Surrey, and one in Worcestershire; £50 was charged against one or more persons in nineteen counties; £25 was charged against one or more persons in twenty-five counties. What especially strikes us, looking at these figures, is how much the traditional church had dwindled in membership in one generation; only a fluctuating number, comparatively small, were of sufficient importance to attract more than the passing glance of a busy government. In terms of the expenses of Elizabeth's government, the total assessment placed against the recusants in 1585 and 1587 and the total amount paid by them in the latter year was but a fraction of the annual costs recorded each year in the Exchequer.

Although there is an absolute paucity of data other than S.P.12/142/33 to explain the levy of 1580, and there is very little information recorded of the levy of 1584, we have a wealth of evidence about the levy of 1585

SOCIAL AND ECONOMIC STATUS OF CATHOLICS

and its administration for some years to come, supplementing the schedule, S.P.12/183/15, and culminating in the chart, S.P.12/200/61. By 1585 the government, as we have seen in Chapters II and III, had defined its anti-recusant policy in very specific terms and was gathering abundant details about the numbers, wealth, and status of the Catholics. Perhaps the most authoritative census upon which it based the levies of 1584 and 1585 was that of the convicted recusants of 1582, S.P.12/156/42. According to the census report the total was 1,939.

London and Middlesex	64
Essex	105
Kent	22
Suffolk	43
Norfolk	51
Devon	6
Cornwall	23
York	327
Durham	10
Cumberland, Northumberland, Carlisle	31
Worcester	71
Warwick	7
Southampton	132
Surrey	65
Oxon	73
Hereford	163
Somerset	11
Shropshire	30
Derby	64
Stafford	72
Chester	41
Lancaster	428
	1,839

The levy of horses of 1584, imposed on selected Catholics within various counties for the support of the wars in Ireland,[6] consisted of a specific sum, usually £25, to be paid for the furnishing of a light horse or the supplying of a properly armed horse. Those charged (the assess-

[6] S.P.12/172/72 (August 15, 1584). This is the covering letter sent to each county.

ment was made in late August) were given until a specific date in the following September to remit the money or horses, with a remission of £1 if they paid immediately upon notification; otherwise they were to write out their excuses which the local officials were to send on to the Queen.[7] Apparently, judging from the evidence, the levy of 1584 was pressed much less vigorously than that of 1585, into which it was probably merged.

With war clouds gathering the levy of 1585 was designed to aid the English forces in the Netherlands.[8] The sum originally suggested to be contributed in money by the recusants was £5000;[9] obviously this was soon raised, judging from S.P.12/183/15, which became the general schedule of those to be charged and the amount which they were to pay.[10] Separate schedules were then sent to the local authorities;[11] at least some of the persons who had been required to contribute the previous year were again charged.[12]

The willingness with which some, and the slowness with which others, paid their assessments; the obvious shifts to which some resorted to avoid this imposition; the pleading for special consideration on the part of some because of financial inability — all these make clearer the economic condition and the political outlook of the Catholics of the mid-1580's.[13] In Huntingdonshire, of two recusants assessed one agreed to pay, the other lived outside the county.[14] The sheriff of London at-

[7] S.P.12/172/72 (August 15, 1584). In S.P.12/172/81 (August 17, 1584) the sum is specified to be £20.
[8] S.P.12/183/72 ([?October] 1585).   [9] S.P.12/185/64 [?1585].
[10] S.P.12/183/15 [?1585; possibly October 12] and S.P.12/119/26 (usually attributed to 1577) are almost identical. In comparing them we have found only five differences, chiefly minor, and a different set of totals. It is our opinion that these are variations of the same schedule, probably sent out nearly simultaneously.
[11] S.P.12/183/23 (October 17, 1585), /29 (October 20, 1585), /32 (October 20, 1585), /32.4 (October 1585), /33 (October 20, 1585), /184/2 (November 1, 1585). These are typical examples of the orders sent to the sheriffs of various counties designating the recusants to be taxed.
[12] S.P.12/183/33.3 (October 20, 1585): Thomas Vachell, esquire, Berkshire, is an example of a number of persons assessed both in 1584 and 1585.
[13] In reporting the returns from the various counties we have not followed a geographical pattern, but instead in most cases have given the various sheriffs' answers according to the order of their listing in the State Papers, which is chronological. The advantage of this is that it shows the length of time required by authorities in the various counties to obtain data and file their answers, and it emphasizes the relative speed (or dilatoriness) of these officials in discharging an important function in a time of relative crisis.
[14] S.P.12/183/21 (October 15, 1585), /184/6 (November 4, 1585).

tempted to get in touch with the persons whose names were given to him. Very few could be found; of these some — and they were among the most prominent recusants in the realm — promised to contribute either in money or light horses; others refused or excused themselves.[15] A second report stated that a very considerable number who had been assessed were in prison, or could not be found, or had not been heard from, or were elsewhere. Seventeen so listed agreed to pay; nine pleaded their inability; two not listed agreed to remit; one whose wife was a recusant pleaded nonrecusancy for himself.[16] The sheriff of Leicester replied that George Sherley had prepared three geldings and that he had surrendered his armor.[17] The sheriff of Buckingham reported that he was able to get in touch with only three of nine names sent him; two of these, one of whom pleaded nonrecusancy, offered to fulfill their obligation; a third begged to be excused because of insolvency; another was unknown in the county.[18] The sheriff of Oxfordshire could not find six of the persons whose names were sent to him; nine agreed to pay, a tenth being added later; and five others pleaded inability due to their financial condition.[19] Staffordshire reported two recusants willing to pay and one, no longer resident in the county, offered to meet this obligation; another pleaded financial inability; others in the schedule were out of the county. A supplementary report added further information concerning collections and certified the inability of one recusant to pay.[20] A somewhat similar pattern to that first sent in from Staffordshire was returned by Sir Fulke Greville, sheriff of Warwickshire.[21] In Yorkshire much difficulty attended the levy. Two recusants agreed to pay; seven others were only vaguely known and were not easy to reach; and one proved unwilling.[22] The sheriff for Surrey and Sussex reported that in the former county only four recusants named in the schedule sent to him were resident in the county. They were willing to pay; five others

[15] S.P.12/183/23, 23.1, 23.2, 23.3, 23.4 (October 15–17, 1585).
[16] S.P.12/183/71, 71.1 (October 31, 1585).
[17] S.P.12/183/29 (October 20, 1585).
[18] S.P.12/183/32, 32.1, 32.2, 32.4 (October 16–20, 1585).
[19] S.P.12/183/33, 33.1, 33.2 (October 20, 1585). In subsequent reports those willing to pay numbered ten (S.P.12/184/61, November 1585; /206/8, December 4, 1587).
[20] S.P.12/183/34 (October 21, 1585), /185/8 (December 6, 1585).
[21] S.P.12/183/35, 35.1 (October 21, 1585).
[22] S.P.12/183/37 (October 21, 1585), /184/2 (November 1, 1585).

were not resident in the county; and one pleaded error, asserting his conformity.[23] In Sussex four recusants were willing to pay; one pleaded error, not being a recusant; three were either nonresidents or out of the county; one was deceased; and four pleaded inability to fulfill their obligation. A subsequent report of the sheriff concerning both Sussex and Surrey stated that he had collected £250 from nine persons, who were assessed differing amounts.[24]

In Kent only two recusants paid; there was a probable confusion in the identity of two others; and three others were absent from or nonresidents of the county.[25] The return for Wiltshire showed only one recusant able to pay; three others named in the Council's schedule were out of the county or nonresidents.[26] In Chester two recusants offered to pay; a third was dead.[27] The sheriff of Gloucester was unable to find any of the recusants in the schedule sent him, except one who was in London and who offered to supply two horses.[28] Southampton reported one recusant willing to pay, one unable to pay, one dead, one difficult to identify, and three residing outside the county. Five others, not yet assessed, were reported as able to pay.[29] In Northamptonshire a number of the recusants either were not at home or not in the county; one pleaded inability to furnish either a horse or money; another was unknown; a third denied being a recusant.[30] Three recusants offered to pay in Worcestershire; one pleaded inability to do so; two were not resident in the county.[31] In Devonshire two recusants charged were not in the county.[32] Suffolk, home of several prominent Catholic families, reported ten who were willing to pay, one who was dead, one who had conformed, one who pleaded inability to pay, and six who could not be found.[33] Three recusants of Herefordshire, greatly impoverished through imprisonment and loss of property, pleaded inability to pay, which the sheriff confirmed as true. A fourth, the longtime recusant, John Scuda-

---

[23] S.P.12/183/38, 38.1 (October 22, 1585).
[24] S.P.12/183/38.3–9 (October 1–23, 1585), /184/45, 45.1 (November 25, 1585).
[25] S.P.12/183/40, 40.1–3 (October 22, 1585).
[26] S.P.12/183/41 (October 22, 1585).   [27] S.P.12/183/43 (October 22, 1585).
[28] S.P.12/183/44 (October 22, 1585).
[29] S.P.12/183/45, 45.1–2 (October 23, 1585), /184/8 (November 6, 1585).
[30] S.P.12/183/46, 46.2 (October 18, 23, 1585).
[31] S.P.12/183/51, 51.1–3 (October 22–24, 1585).
[32] S.P.12/183/52 (October 24, 1585).
[33] S.P.12/183/53, 53.1, 53.2, 53.4 (October 20, 25, 1585).

SOCIAL AND ECONOMIC STATUS OF CATHOLICS

more, was willing to furnish a horse, if his lands distrained for non-payment of his recusancy fines were returned to him in order to provide the means; otherwise, he could not do so because of poverty. Later, probably under pressure from the sheriff, he made a positive offer of a horse.[34] Two recusants, both men of standing, could not immediately be found in Lincolnshire, but a relative voluntarily substituted himself for one of them.[35] In Lancashire various of those to be taxed were absent from their residences; thirteen agreed to pay the assessment; one was deceased; one was doubtful; one boldly refused; one pleaded inability; and four pleaded error, affirming their conformity.[36] One of the recusants charged in Derbyshire offered to pay in full; another was in London; a third denied that he was a recusant.[37] In Berkshire two agreed to pay the levy; a third pleaded inability.[38] Two recusants of Essex agreed to pay an assessment of £25 each.[39] A Dorset recusant of distinguished family was found to be of little means and living outside of that county.[40] In Norfolk those who had been approached by the sheriff agreed to pay; one, however, could pay only part of the levy assessed against him.[41] Two separate schedules were sent to Somersetshire, one for the hundreds in the eastern, the other for the hundreds in the western, part of the county, and these were clearly not restricted to Catholics.[42]

Other evidences of hardships were mentioned in some of the returns. A certain number could not furnish armor because it had been sequestrated the previous year.[43] John Gifford claimed that his wealth had been overvalued and that he had been overassessed; he pointed out that

---

[34] S.P.12/183/57, 57.1-4 (October 23, 25, 26, 1585), /184/39 (November 21, 1585).

[35] S.P.12/183/60 (October 27, 1585). The two missing recusants were William Tyrwhitt and John Thimelby. William Fitzwilliams substituted himself for his brother-in-law, Tyrwhitt.

[36] S.P.12/183/61, 61.1 (October 27, 1585).

[37] S.P.12/183/62, 62.1 (October 28, 1585).

[38] S.P.12/183/63 (October 28, 1585; original document is slightly damaged).

[39] S.P.12/183/73 (October 1585). The recusants were Rooke Greene and Thomas Crawley.

[40] S.P.12/184/4 (November 3, 1585). The recusant was James Marten, son of Lady Tregonwell.

[41] S.P.12/185/3, 3.1 (December 3, 1585). Robert Downes could pay only part of the assessment against him.

[42] S.P.12/187/36, 37 (March 14, 1586 [?1587]).

[43] Richard Lyngen, Sir John Southworth, John Talbot, John Towneley, John Westbye, William Haddocke, and William Heskett stated that their armor had been sequestrated.

he was supporting his eldest son in attendance upon the Earl of Leicester in the Low Countries.[44] Thomas Gawen, whose poverty became chronic in subsequent years, pleaded inability to contribute, since his property had already been distrained because of recusancy.[45] Richard Tremaine offered to pay £25, adding the complaint that all his lands had been distrained for nonpayment of recusancy fines.[46] Four men of considerable importance — Lord Vaux of Harrowden, Sir Thomas Gerrard, Erasmus Saunders and a noted lawyer, Arden Waferer — pleaded inability to pay.[47] Robert Jetter, after more than twenty years still an intransigent Catholic, asserted that he could not meet his requirement because he was in prison and his property had been distrained because of recusancy.[48] The seventy-year-old Richard Lyngen had been assessed in September 1584, but he was too impoverished to pay because of recusancy fines, long imprisonment, and the seizure of his armor.[49]

Although the Anglican bishops and deans[50] and also Protestant recusants had been included in the levy, we have confined our analysis to the Catholics. In London the Exchequer constantly checked both the accuracy of the returns from each county and what individuals had paid or had refused to pay, and a number of additional schedules were subsequently made out of recusants previously overlooked or who by some means had escaped or evaded payment.[51] In November 1585 an inventory of those willing to pay the assessment was drawn up in detail.[52] The total amount specifically turned in by the recusants (Catholic and Protestant) at that time was £729. 3s. 4d., paid to Robert Freake, a teller in the Exchequer.[53] By July 1586, that official reported the receipt of £9,654. 6s. 8d.,[54] and by March 1587, £10,589. 13s. 0d., of which

[44] S.P.12/183/23.2 (October 15, 1585).   [45] S.P.12/183/23.3 (October 15, 1585).
[46] S.P.12/183/23.4 (?October 1585).
[47] S.P.12/183/71, 71.1 (October 31, 1585).
[48] S.P.12/183/53.1 (October 20, 1585).   [49] S.P.12/183/57.3 (October 25, 1585).
[50] In a tabulation of money received by March 1587 the Anglican bishops and deans had paid in over twice as much as the recusants (S.P.12/199/74, March 30, 1587).
[51] S.P.12/183/71 (October 31, 1585; London), /184/6 (November 4, 1585; Huntingdonshire), /8 (November 6, 1585; Hampshire), /195/2 (November 3, 1586; Hampshire); A.P.C., XIV, 86–88 (May 4, 1586; Hampshire); XV, 414–415 (March 10, 1588; Hampshire). There was also correspondence between the authorities in London and various local officials about individual recusants.
[52] S.P.12/184/61 (November 1585).
[53] S.P.12/184/48 (November 26, 1585). A briefer report had been sent in five days earlier (S.P.12/184/40, November 21, 1585).
[54] S.P.12/199/33 (March 14, 1587).

SOCIAL AND ECONOMIC STATUS OF CATHOLICS

the recusants (without distinction of religion) had contributed £3,129. 3s. 4d.[55] Two more tabulations were made during 1587, confirming and correcting any previous errors.[56]

Although recalcitrancy was evident on the part of some Catholics in meeting the terms of the levy, the government obviously considered that this was trivial and that the Catholics had both proved their willingness and had attested their loyalty. As a reward the Queen promised officially to consider an amelioration of the penalties for nonconformity, a promise which she had previously made for prompt cooperation in meeting the levy of 1584. She required that the recusants in each county named in a schedule and others to be determined by the sheriffs and the justices of the peace should offer in composition such proportion of their income to be paid yearly that the remainder would leave them sufficient for a decent living. The sheriffs and justices were to appraise the sufficiency of all offers.[57]

Throughout the year 1586 and into 1587 meetings between commissioners especially appointed for the purpose and recusants were held, individually and in groups, or where this was not feasible, composition was worked out by correspondence.[58] Difficulties arose, similar to the assessment for horses just studied. Recusants were out of the county, or in prison, or too poor to offer anything substantial, or for some reason could not go abroad out of the neighborhood of their houses, and some simply evaded making any declaration.[59] But a very large

---

[55] S.P.12/199/74 (March 30, 1587), /206/8 (December 4, 1587).

[56] S.P.12/200/61 [?1587], /206/8 (December 4, 1587: document which retabulated and confirmed the total collected the previous March).

[57] S.P.12/172/72 (August 15, 1584), /186/83 (February 25, 1586): *A.P.C.*, XIV, 8 (February 20, 1586: letters to special commissioners for composition with schedules of names). S.P.12/186/81, 82 apparently were drafts to be sent out to the sheriffs and magistrates of the various shires. S.P.12/186/83 was directed to the sheriff of Bedford.

[58] *A.P.C.*, XIV, 8 (February 20, 1586). The reports concerning the dealings between various officials and recusants fill a considerable portion of a number of volumes of the State Papers. The data is so extensive that we can only cite selections. Examples of conferences between the commissioners and recusants are: Berkshire, S.P.12/187/45 (March 18, 1586); London and Middlesex, S.P.12/187/48 (March 19, 1586); Essex, S.P.12/187/64 (March 27, 1586); Norfolk, S.P.12/188/9 (April 10, 1586); Wiltshire, S.P.12/188/15 (April 12, 1586); Hampshire, S.P.12/188/16 (April 13, 1586); Staffordshire, S.P.12/188/29 (April 18, 1586); Buckinghamshire, S.P.12/188/32 (April 20, 1586); Suffolk, S.P.12/188/38 (April 23, 1586); Cornwall, S.P.12/188/42 (April 27, 1586); Lincoln, S.P.12/188/51 (April 1586); Herefordshire, S.P.12/189/2 (May 2, 1586).

[59] The various reasons for avoiding composition are a constant theme throughout

number took advantage of the offer, usually strongly protesting their loyalty to the Queen, although, very surprisingly, a tone of bitterness runs through some of the answers, indicative of underlying sentiments of frustration and resentment at the lot of the writers.

No body of data is so rich in facts concerning the economic condition and social status of individual recusants as were the answers sent in by individuals and in county groups and summarized in May 1586 in the master sheet, S.P.12/189/54, 55, "Collection of the Certificats of thoffers of the Recusants to be dismissed of the Penaltie of the Statut." (It is our assumption, although we cannot verify it, that all the names in the master sheet were those of Catholics.) The corpus of evidence accumulated in the Exchequer concerning the more important recusants and the certifications sent in by the authorities of some of the counties attesting the veracity of answers[60] are both proofs of the reliability of at least a part of the data. Some of the answers, however, arouse suspicion about their truthfulness, and quite a number obviously manifest special pleading to avoid the burden of the recusancy taxes. An analysis of the answers shows that the Catholics formed no unified bloc in making them; that there is no evidence of planned fraud, as was to be found, two centuries before, in the returns of the poll tax of 1380–1381.

In the master sheet, our principal guide, twenty-five counties were listed, with 406 persons of varying conditions, those of affluent standing numbering one peer, seven knights, forty-eight esquires and seventy-six gentlemen; one of the women was a peeress of ancient lineage. The wealth of only eighty-one recusants was valued, chiefly, but not solely, in terms of income from land; in accordance with the custom of the day the evaluation was approximate and in round numbers (frequently marks, which we have rendered in pounds, shillings and pence), due to the difficulty of being more exact. The maximum annual income of any

---

the answers. Examples are: Berkshire, S.P.12/187/45, 45.2 (March 18, 1586); London and Middlesex, S.P.12/187/48, 48.2 (March 19, 1586); Norfolk, S.P.12/188/9 (April 10, 1586); Hampshire, S.P.12/188/16 (April 13, 1586); Staffordshire, S.P.12/188/29 (April 18, 1586); Buckinghamshire, S.P.12/188/32 (April 20, 1586); Cornwall, S.P.12/188/42 (April 27, 1586); Lincolnshire, S.P.12/188/51 (April 1586); Durham, S.P.12/187/49, 49.1 (March 19, 1586); Hereford, S.P.12/189/2 (May 2, 1586), /190/4 (June 4, 1586); Leicestershire, S.P.12/189/17 (May 13, 1586).

[60] The local authorities certified wholly or partly to the veracity of returns in Essex (S.P.12/187/64, March 27, 1586), Staffordshire (S.P.12/188/29, April 18, 1586), Leicestershire (S.P.12/189/17, May 13, 1586).

SOCIAL AND ECONOMIC STATUS OF CATHOLICS

Catholic was £1000; the minimum was £2; the certified total was £11,924. 3s. 4d. (or, according to our calculation, £13,049. 3s. 4d.). A smaller aggregation of affluent merchants or of the higher gentry or of the leading peers would have been worth much more. A majority, 347 recusants, offered compositions; fifty-nine did not: the maximum, £100, was far below the £240 per year required by the law of 1581; the minimum, 5s., was obviously an unsatisfactory sum. The total of the offers of composition, £3,198. 5s. 4d., would barely have met the more minute expenses of Elizabeth's government. In only five counties — Buckinghamshire, Middlesex, Suffolk, Surrey and Wiltshire — was any individual worth £500 or more annually; and only in four counties — Middlesex, Norfolk, Suffolk, and Surrey — was the total certified annual value of the Catholics above £1000. Catholics felt that they could offer as much as £50 or more in composition (in lieu of the required £240) only in eight counties — Buckinghamshire, Herefordshire, Kent, Middlesex, Norfolk, Suffolk, Surrey, and Sussex; in only ten counties was the sum total of the offers over £100 — Berkshire, Buckinghamshire, Herefordshire, Kent, Middlesex, Norfolk, Oxford, Suffolk, Surrey, and Sussex. A defect in the master sheet, which limits an adequate picture of Catholic wealth, was the failure of Berkshire, Cornwall, Dorsetshire, Gloucestershire, Herefordshire, Kent, Leicestershire, Lincolnshire, and Northamptonshire to report the value of recusant wealth, possibly due to a misunderstanding on the part of the commissioners charged with compounding or to their laxity or to lack of time to get correct information, although each of these counties reported offers of composition.

To determine more precisely the economic and social status of the Elizabethan Catholics, we have selected 128 recusants, 110 men and eighteen women, living in twenty-two counties, who were listed in the master sheet of 1586, S.P.12/189/54. These individuals represent a sufficient diversification of area of residence, degree of wealth, and social standing, and enough of them were known to the officials at Westminster, that they form an accurate cross section of the Catholics then considered typical.

Very considerable difficulty faces us in assessing accurately the mass of data concerning Catholic wealth which was reported in 1586. The terminology used both in official and private reports was not uniform; and to the twentieth-century reader the context of many of the terms is lacking in precision, which prevents clear definition. We have analyzed the values of the individual recusants that were entered on the master sheet, S.P.12/189/54, 55, the values contained in the reports sent in from the counties and by individuals, the statements by individuals of their debts, fines, charges in the levies of horses, and any other encumbrances, and the offers of composition. Elizabeth, we must remember, did not intend that an offer of composition should impair an estate; certainly she did not intend that an offer of composition should entail sale of lands. Our conclusion is that the recusants in 1586 reported what we term income in this study, because its use is convenient. More correctly what the recusants reported was their annual financial worth: ready money, rents, property that could be used as the basis for loans (because loans in the Elizabethan days were very common to tide persons over when the payment of rents or debts owed them was delayed), and possibly some kinds of services that could be converted into money. Obviously not all these elements were components of the income of each of the recusants. In twelve cases persons reported only the actual amount of money which they received each year from land and other sources. Although it is difficult to be certain, some seem to have reported the total value of all their property or of their lands; others seem to have reported the potential rental value per annum of their lands. Even where actual receipts of money were reported, the recusants normally would have had to resort to loans because rents were often in arrears and the sale of cattle or of products of the soil encountered such difficulties as fluctuations in prices and the problem of finding purchasers; therefore money income was not certain and the government knew that it would have to be supplemented from other sources from time to time. Where the total value of lands and other property or the potential rental value of lands was reported, the government realized that the mention of these was to give assurance of a basis for obtaining loans or for future exploitation of land for income in order to pay the composition. We feel justified in grouping all the statements of value in 1586 under the generalized term "income," although our terminology is open to question, because we find that an attempt to be more precise threatens to lead to confusion: "income," as we are using it, sufficiently expresses the worth of the Elizabethan Catholic of 1586.[61]

[61] Our study of the economic and social status of the Elizabethan Catholics is

SOCIAL AND ECONOMIC STATUS OF CATHOLICS

We can arrive from a variety of sources at the incomes of eighty-five of the 128 recusants in 1586; the values of nine others are not clear; thirty-four have no record of their worth in that year. However, 125 of the recusants made offers of composition, thereby showing some income or exterior aid, such as loans or charity (of the three who did not offer any composition, two were too poor to do so and one was deceased). Where possible we make the financial picture of each individual clearer by using data from the census of 1577 and the schedules of the levies of 1580 and 1585 and the chart of the levy of 1587. We can ascertain the values of sixty-one in 1577; the worth of five others who were named is not recorded. Fifty-nine were included in the schedule of 1580 and thirty-nine in the schedule of 1585; eighty-five were assessed and four others were named but not charged in the chart of 1587. Our main criterion, however, by which we measure the Catholics of wealth and their social status is S.P.12/189/54, 55; within its framework we place our study of the 128 recusants.

One of the problems difficult to explain is the fluctuations in the values reported of the recusants between 1577 and 1587. The latter evaluations were, of course, more precise and more accurate. We cannot prove fraud and we doubt that most, at least, of the 128 recusants reported falsely because they were under government scrutiny, sometimes for many years. But fraud cannot be dismissed altogether, both because a report probably of Sir Francis Walsingham dealt with fraudulent conveyances of property by recusants[62] and because the sixth Parliament of Elizabeth in 1586 recognized the existence of some fraudulent dealings by recusants in its legislation (28 and 29 Eliz. c. 6). Other explanations also throw light on the fluctuations in the worth of various recusants, such as the devising of property (nonentailed) on younger children, if the parents were elderly and the children were adults and of a status demanding income-bearing property. Acquisitions of property by purchase or inheritance cannot be ruled out, and can be proved in some cases; further, a study of the Recusant Roll of 1592–1593[63] bears out

---

placed within the framework of sixteenth- and seventeenth-century English economic conditions and social status explained in W. K. Jordan, *Philanthropy in England, 1480–1660: A Study of the Changing Pattern of English Social Aspirations* (New York, 1959).
[62] S.P.12/151/72 [?1580's].
[63] We have been able to identify 85 of the 128 recusants in the Recusant Roll of 1592–1593, but not all of the names with certainty.

that the disfranchised condition of the Catholics by no means prevented the buying, selling and inheriting of property. Sale, especially to pay recusancy fines or the levy of horses or to provide dowries for daughters, and loss of some property through neglect due to imprisonment or to financial reverses and loss of income through distraint of property for nonpayment of recusancy fines also played a part.

The determination of status, so very important in the sixteenth century, is very elusive. Where it was not recorded in the master sheet, we have had to determine it from other sources, where it is by no means always clear. The rank of a peer or of a knight was not open to question; birth, income, landholdings, the society in which one mixed, determined if one belonged to the gentle class; education was the criterion of a professional man. But there seemed to be no clear line of division between an esquire or a gentleman, into which categories most of the 128 Catholics fell. And, although status was by no means well defined, its designation was of real importance. It was the opening to preferments on the local and national level; an error about status could under certain circumstances invalidate an indictment;[64] the wrong title could be considered an insult, engendering bitter resentment. In all but three cases we have been able to determine the status of the 128 recusants.

Berkshire reported fifty-three recusants, of whom one was an esquire and three were gentlemen. Their individual incomes were not recorded in the master sheet, but all of the fifty-three personally or through others made a total of forty-one offers of composition, twelve persons being included in ten joint offers. The maximum was £13. 6s. 8d.; the minimum was £2; the total was £138. 6s. 8d.[65] That Berkshire was not a county of Catholic affluence is borne out by the two recusants, a husband and wife, whom we have chosen for further investigation. James Braybrooke, ranked both as an esquire and as a lawyer, was one of the very few Catholic lawyers of prominence contemporary with Edmund Plowden in the early years of Elizabeth's reign. A onetime utter barrister of the Inner Temple, he had been sequestered for religion from active membership, and during the earlier 1580's had suffered considerable imprisonment. His worth both in 1577 and in 1580 was £266. 13s. 4d.; in the

[64] C.P.83/49 (July 19 [?1604]).   [65] S.P.12/189/54, 55 (May 1586).

latter year he was assessed two lances and two light horses; in 1587 he was charged and paid the minimum, £25. He made two offers of composition, one of £13. 6s. 8d. for himself, and another of £1 for his wife, Martha, which was also to include his daughter, Dorothy. His estate was small for one of his status and education; his small composition can be explained by heavy expenses and a deterioration of his earning power.[66]

Buckinghamshire, which appears to have been made out carelessly, reported eighteen recusants, two ranking as esquires and five as gentlemen. The income of four recusants was given: the maximum was £666. 13s. 4d.; the minimum was £66. 13s. 4d.; the total recorded in the master sheet, £300, correctly should have been £900. There were twelve offers of composition (of seventeen persons, five being included in four joint offers): the maximum was £100; the minimum was 10s.; the total was £171. 10s. 0d.[67] We have selected four recusants as representative of the county. Augustine Belson, gentleman, had no estate of any kind, most likely having devolved it on his son, Robert, a conformist; in 1587 the father was charged £25, which he was unable to pay. The son offered £6 in composition for his father, to include also three other members of the family.[68] Edward East, gentleman, was worth in 1580 £66. 13s. 4d. annually in lands and £200 in goods, and he was assessed one lance. In 1587 he was assessed and paid £25. His income in 1586 was £66. 13s. 4d.; his offer of £13. 6s. 8d. bears out that his estate was small.[69] Henry Mansfield, esquire, had an income of £100 in 1586 derived from lands held jointly with his wife; in 1587 he was charged and paid the minimum, £25. His offer of composition, which included his wife, was small, £13. 6s. 8d.[70] Thomas Throckmorton, esquire, member of a family prominent in the Elizabethan era, was one of the wealthier Catholics. It is not clear if his worth were appraised in 1577; in 1586 his income was £666. 13s. 4d.; in 1587 he was charged and paid

---

[66] S.P.12/117/17.1 (October 26, 1577), /140/36 (July 30, 1580), /142/33 [?1580], /154/38 (June–July 1582), /159/31 (March 1584), /36 (March 23, 1584), /170/9 (April 8, 1584), /187/45.1 [?March 18, 1586], /189/54 (May 1586), /200/61 [?1587].
[67] S.P.12/189/54, 55 (May 1586).
[68] S.P.12/188/32.5 (April 15, 1586), /189/54 (May 1586), /200/61 [?1587].
[69] S.P.12/142/33 [?1580], /188/32.2 (March 19, 1586), /189/54 (May 1586), /200/61 [?1587].
[70] S.P.12/188/32.3 (March 19, 1586), /189/54 (May 1586), /200/61 [?1587].

£75. His offer of composition, £100, was one of four proposing that sum, which constituted the maximum any of the Catholics could pay.[71]

Cheshire had eight recusants listed, three being esquires, and four, gentlemen. The incomes of only three persons were reported: the maximum was £240; the mimimum was £13. 6s. 8d.; the total was £273. 6s. 8d. Six made offers of composition, the maximum being £30, the minimum, £2; one of the two not paying was listed as "reformed." The total of offers was £72.[72] We have selected six recusants for further study. Lady Edgerton had no values placed on her wealth, either in 1577 or in later years, probably because she had devised her estate to her heirs; in 1587 she was charged and paid £50; her offer of composition, £30, would indicate an annual income sufficient to maintain an elderly gentlewoman in dignified comfort in an area where the expenses of upperclass status were not too pressing.[73] William Hesketh, gentleman, recently a prisoner in London, had lands worth £20 annual rental value in 1577, but he was "poore" in goods; in 1586 his income was £13. 6s. 8d. The question arises if he may have had assets invisible to us but known to the government, since in 1585 his assessment was £40 or one light horse, and in 1587 he was charged and paid £25. His offer of composition was half of his certified income, £6. 13s. 4d.[74] Henry Latham, gentleman, had an income in 1586 of £20; his offer of composition was roughly one-seventh of this, £3. 6s. 8d.[75] Richard Massey, gentleman, had an annual living of £10 in 1577. Since there is no evidence of property or of goods in 1586 and since his offer of composition was "nil," he must have become totally impoverished.[76] John Talbot, esquire, of Salesbury in Lancashire (although reported under Cheshire), had an estate hardly equal to his rank as a member of a cadet branch of the Talbots, the earls of Shrewsbury. In both 1577 and 1580 his lands were appraised at £133. 6s. 8d. annual rental value and his goods were worth £300; in the latter year he was assessed one lance and one light horse; in 1585 he was assessed £50 or one lance; in 1587 he was charged and paid £50. The last assess-

---

[71] S.P.12/118/11.5 (November 5, 1577), /188/32.13 (April 16, [?1586]), /189/54 (May 1586), /200/61 [?1587].
[72] S.P.12/189/54, 55 (May 1586).
[73] S.P.12/189/54 (May 1586); /200/61 [?1587].
[74] S.P.12/118/45.1 (November 28, 1577), /159/28 (March 22, 1583), /36 (March 23, 1584), /183/15 [?1585], /189/54 (May 1586), /200/61 [?1587].
[75] S.P.12/189/54 (May 1586).
[76] S.P.12/118/48.1 (November 29, 1577), /118/49 (1577), /189/54 (May 1587).

ment undoubtedly was based on his income in 1586, £240. His offer of composition must have reflected his current expenses because it was only one-twelfth of his income, £20.[77] John Whitmore, esquire, was valued in 1577 and 1580 at £66 in annual rental value of lands. His assessment in the levy of 1580 was one lance and he was charged the same in 1585 with the option of paying £50. We have no other evidence of his wealth, but his offer of composition was small, £10, which, since there was no report of him in 1586 or 1587, probably represents as much as he could pay.[78]

In Cornwall only Richard Tremaine, gentleman, and his mother jointly were able to make an offer of composition; all other recusants were in prison, out of the county or too poor to pay. Tremaine held lands jointly with his wife worth £50 annual rental value and goods worth £100 in 1577; the same value was assigned to his lands in 1580, when he was required to furnish one light horse; in 1585 he was assessed £40; in 1587 he was charged and paid £25. No value was recorded of him in 1586. During the earlier 1580's he had suffered imprisonment in London; he had paid £140 in recusancy fines and still owed £180. In 1586 his and his mother's joint offer of composition was £10.[79]

Devonshire had two persons listed, but one was apparently a resident elswhere. James Courtney, esquire, of distinguished family, possessed only a small income, £30, in 1586; in 1587 he was charged but did not pay £25. His offer, £10, characterized the decayed estate of a once prominent family.[80]

Dorset listed five recusants with no recorded status. Only two made offers, one of £6. 13s. 4d., the other of £2. One of the delinquents offered nothing and two could not be found. The total, £8. 13s. 4d., was small and reflected a county which figures little in the history of Elizabethan Catholicism. There was no recusant of sufficient importance for us to investigate further.[81]

Essex listed four recusants, including two esquires and one gentleman.

[77] S.P.12/118/45.1 (November 28, 1577), /142/33 [?1580], /183/15 [?1585], /189/54 (May 1586), /200/61 [?1587].
[78] S.P.12/118/48.1 (November 29, 1577), /142/33 [?1580], /183/15 [?1585], /189/54 (May 1586).
[79] S.P.12/117/25.1 (October 28, 1577), /140/38 (July 31, 1580), /142/33 [?1580], /159/33 (1584), /36 (March 23, 1584), /183/15 [?1585], /188/42, 42.1 (April 27, 1586), /189/54, 55 (May 1586), /200/61 [?1587].
[80] S.P.12/189/54, 55 (May 1586), /200/61 [?1587].
[81] S.P.12/189/54, 55 (May 1586).

The maximum value reported was an income of £236. 13s. 4d.; the minimum was £40; the total of the certified incomes was £419. 6s. 8d. All four of the recusants made offers: the maximum was £40; the minimum was £2; the total was £78. 13s. 4d.[82] We have selected three of the four persons listed. Thomas Crawley, esquire, was worth (jointly with his wife) in 1577 £120 in annual rental value of lands and £100 in goods. He was charged £40 or one light horse in 1585, and £25 in 1587, which he paid. In 1586 his income was £142. 13s. 4d. His offer of £30 evidently was reasonable.[83] Rooke Greene, esquire, had an income in 1586 of £236. 13s. 4d.; in 1587 he was charged the minimum, £25, which he paid. His debt structure, which included seven unmarried children, was heavy; his offer of £40 was probably reasonable.[84] Thomas Hale, gentleman, was worth in 1577 jointly with his wife £40 annually in lands and their goods were worth £20; his income in 1586 was £40; in 1587 he was charged and paid £25. His offer of composition, £6. 13s. 4d., probably represented all that he could pay in view of eight unmarried children and debts of £300.[85]

Gloucester listed one family, Henry Cassey, his wife and son. He ranked as an esquire and made a total offer for all three of £20. We have not investigated him further; he was not listed either in 1577 or in the Recusant Roll of 1592–1593.[86]

Hereford (which was made out in a different hand and sloppily in S.P.12/189/54) contained twenty-two recusants, whose status and wealth were not given in 1586. Nineteen offered £129. 16s. 8d., of which the maximum was £50, the minimum, £1. Hereford was indeed a problem now as throughout the reign. The recusants were scattered throughout the county and "very many in number and daily increase more and more." Some failed to appear when summoned to determine composition; the three who failed to make offers were men of importance who openly

---

[82] *Ibid.*

[83] S.P.12/118/44 (November 27, 1577), /140/36 (July 30, 1580), /39 (July 31, 1580), /183/15 [?1585], /187/64.4 (March 24, 1586), /189/54 (May 1586), /200/61 [?1587].

[84] S.P.12/187/64.1 (March 24, 1586), /189/54 (May 1586), /200/61 [?1587]. It is not clear (but seems likely) that Rooke Greene was the Robert Grene worth £60 annually in lands and £40 in goods in 1577 (S.P.12/118/44, November 27, 1577).

[85] S.P.12/118/73 (November 1577), /187/64.2 (March 24, 1586), /189/54 (May 1586), /200/61 [?1587].

[86] S.P.12/189/54, 55 (May 1586).

conformed when cited before the magistrates—Anthony Elton, son-in-law of the ardent, indeed notorious, recusant, John Scudamore, Richard Brydge, and John Gage.[87] The six recusants whom we have investigated made small offers of composition and some did so with contingencies attached. Richard Davis (or Davies), status undetermined, had been in prison for over four years and was currently under indictment for further recusancy and charged with a suit for unpaid recusancy fines. He possessed no lands and had sold his goods to protect himself and his family from need; his debts were heavy and pressing on him because he had need of his resources to care for his family. He proposed, as long as he was granted liberty, to pay 20s. a year with the help of friends, notwithstanding his various expenses.[88] John Gomond, gentleman, complained that although young and bearing the expenses of a large family and of other debts, his living had been distrained in 1583 to the amount of £13. 6s. 8d. As a result, in the levy of the next year, 1587, he was not able to pay the £25 levied against him. His annual income, which is not easily determinable, was about £25–£30; his offer of composition was about half of the income, £15.[89] Edmund Jones, gentleman, had been imprisoned five years before when he was fifty-five. In 1577 and 1580 his goods, apparently then his only property, had been assessed at £300 and in the latter year he had been charged one light horse. In 1587 he was unable to pay the charge of £25. He reported in 1586 that his lands, a small tenement, and his goods, worth altogether £48, had been distrained, leaving him little. In the hope of further liberty he offered composition of £2 yearly.[90] John Scudamore, esquire, perhaps the most prominent recusant in Herefordshire, exhibited real bitterness in his answer. He was currently imprisoned; he had been fined for recusancy; and because of nonpayment his property, two manors (former monastery lands) had been distrained for £52. 13s. 4d., at a rent of £2 per year. In 1577 and 1580 his annual living, held jointly with his wife and son, amounted in lands to £266. 13s. 4d. and in goods to £666. 13s. 4d.; in the levy of 1580 he had been charged three lances. In

[87] *Ibid.;* S.P.12/190/4 (June 4, 1586), /195/45 (December [?3, 1586]), /46 [?December 4, ?1586].
[88] S.P.12/189/2.7 (May 1586), /189/54 (May 1586).
[89] S.P.12/189/54 (May 1586), /190/4.2 (June 4, 1586), /200/61 [?1587].
[90] S.P.12/118/7.1 [1577], /142/33 [?1580], /189/54 (May 1586), /190/4.3 (June 4, 1586), /200/61 [?1587].

1585, barring an error in the records, he had been assessed £40, or both one lance and one light horse; in 1587 he had been charged and had paid the minimum, £25, not in money, but by contributing a horse. His estate, inherited from his parents, had been partly bequeathed to his son, Thomas, partly to a brother, very possibly to escape impositions; he had also set up annuities amounting to £13. 6s. 8d. to provide dowries for married daughters. Of what was left and subtracting what had been distrained, he had less than £50 left in income from lands. From prison he offered composition of £33. 6s. 8d., if the Council decided that he must remain incarcerated and if he won a pending court action. However, not only if he won this suit, but also if he were granted freedom and the right to occupy his house and to farm his lands, he would pay annually £50. If this were insufficient Scudamore asked the Council to appraise his property and determine the composition.[91] His son, Thomas, making no effort to hide his resentment against years, past and current, of imprisonment and of fines, offered "in prison, discharged of other troubles and officers — 20 marks [£13. 6s. 8d.]; at liberty — £20." We cannot determine the value of the property which his father had bequeathed to him, but the charges against it apparently were heavy, since he complained that both his recusancy fines were large and that his debts amounted to over £400.[92] William Woode, a physician, was currently imprisoned and had suffered distraint of all his lands and goods, except a farm, with little hope of return. He supported his family inadequately out of an uncertain income derived from a somewhat unsuccessful medical practice and from some other sources, while trying to pay off £50 of unpaid recusancy fines. He offered to pay £1. 6s. 8d. while at liberty, pledging that he would not persuade anyone, even his wife, to embrace Catholicism.[93]

Kent reported twelve names, of whom one was a knight, three were esquires, and two were gentlemen. No value was given of property, but five (one of whom was subsequently reported "non inventus") made offers, the maximum being £80, the minimum, £10; the total of offers was £190. Of the seven who made no offers, two could not be found;

---

[91] S.P.12/118/7.1 [1577], /142/33 [?1580], /183/15 [?1585], /189/54 (May 1586), /190/4.6 (June 4, 1586), /200/61 [?1587].
[92] S.P.12/189/54 (May 1586), /190/4.1 (June 4, 1586).
[93] S.P.12/189/2.6 (May 1586), /54 (May 1586), /190/4.12 (June 4, 1586).

one was dead; one was non-resident; three were prisoners.[94] We have selected three of the names reported for investigation. Sir Alexander Culpepper long lived under surveillance since he had married into the great family of the Dacre of the North, which had a blotched record of loyalty. The annual value of his lands in 1577 and again in 1580 was £400; in the latter year he was required to furnish four lances (which means that he was not charged the full amount for which he might have been liable). In 1587 he was assessed and paid £50. There is no record of his income in 1586, but his offer of composition, £40, was small.[95] His cousin, Richard Culpepper, esquire, was worth £100 in goods in 1577 and £100 in lands in 1580, when he was charged for one lance. In 1587 he was assessed, but did not pay, £25. His offer of composition, which would seem to reflect his estate, was small, £10.[96] William Tyrwhitt, esquire, of Lincolnshire but confined to Kent, has no recorded value. In 1587 a William Tyrwhitt was charged £75 in Lincolnshire and £25 in London (probably a place of detention); the charge was paid in both places. Tyrwhitt's offer of £80 in composition clearly indicated a very moderate estate for a member of so prominent a family.[97]

Lancashire furnished nine names, including one knight, three esquires and one gentleman. The value of six was given, the maximum being £133. 6s. 8d., the minimum, £26. 13s. 4d. The total reported of the value of recusants' property was £933. 6s. 8d., which according to our calculation should be £453. 6s. 8d. The same number, six, made offers of composition: the maximum was £40; the minimum was £3. 6s. 8d.; the total was not large, £96. 13s. 4d. The three who made no offers were listed as conformists, an indication of the trend of the times in one of the remaining centers of the traditional church.[98] We have investigated the six who admitted their recusancy. Richard Blundell, esquire, until his death in prison an ardent Catholic, had a small estate. His income in 1586 was £66. 13s. 4d. derived from lands; his offer of composition, reflecting his small value, was £10.[99] William Haydock, gentleman, had lands

[94] S.P.12/189/54, 55 (May 1586).
[95] S.P.12/117/51.1 (October 1577), /142/33 [?1580], /189/54 (May 1586), /200/61 [?1587].
[96] S.P.12/117/51.1 (October 1577), /142/33 [?1580], /189/54 (May 1586), /200/61 [?1587].
[97] S.P.12/189/54 (May 1586), /200/61 [?1587].
[98] S.P.12/189/54, 55 (May 1586).   [99] S.P.12/189/54 (May 1586).

of £20 annual value and was "poore" in goods in 1577; his certified income was £26. 13s. 4d. in 1586; he proposed £3. 6s. 8d. in composition.[100] Elizabeth Kigheley, a widow whose name figures considerably in reports in Lancashire recusancy, had a small estate, although it is possible that she had devised most of it to her children. In 1577 and 1580 she was valued at £40 annually in lands and £200 in goods; in the latter year she was charged one light horse. In 1587 she was charged the minimum, £25, jointly with another, and paid her share. In 1586 her income was £26. 13s. 4d.: all the facts concerning her would make her offer of composition, £10, seem reasonable.[101] John Rigmaiden, esquire, in both 1577 and 1580 had an estate valued at £133. 6s. 8d. annually in lands and £300 in goods; in the latter year he was assessed one lance and one light horse. In 1585 he was assessed £50 or one lance; in 1587 he was charged and paid £50. His income in 1586 was certified at £100 annually; his offer of composition, £20, would seem to be reasonable in view of his expenses.[102] Sir John Southworth, throughout Elizabeth's reign a very intransigent Catholic, was valued in 1577 and 1580 at £200 annually in lands and at £300 in goods; in the latter year he was charged, jointly with his son, Thomas, for two lances; in 1585 he was assessed £100 or one lance and one light horse; in 1587 he was charged and paid the minimum, £25. In 1586 his certified income was £133. 6s. 8d.; in view of his long troubles with the government his offer of composition, £40, would seem to be a fair proposal.[103] John Westbye, esquire, like Southworth, had long been a very intransigent Catholic. In 1577 and 1580 his lands were appraised at £66. 13s. 4d., his goods at £200; in the latter year he had been assessed one lance. In 1585 he had been charged £100 or two horses (part of the charge being in Lancashire and part in Yorkshire); in 1587 he paid a levy of £25. The latter, the minimum charge, was probably a true picture of his wealth because his certified income in 1586 was £100 and his offer of composition was small, £13. 6s. 8d.[104] Lancashire, we must conclude, had few Catholics of any wealth

[100] S.P.12/118/45.1 (November 28, 1577), /189/54 (May 1586).

[101] S.P.12/118/45.1 (November 28, 1577), /142/33 [?1580], /189/54 (May 1586), /200/61 [?1587].

[102] S.P.12/118/45.1 (November 28, 1577), /142/33 [?1580], /183/15 [?1585], /189/54 (May 1586), /200/61 [?1587].

[103] S.P.12/118/45.1 (November 28, 1577), /142/33 [?1580], /183/15 [?1585], /189/54 (May 1586), /200/61 [?1587].

[104] S.P.12/118/45.1 (November 28, 1577), /142/33 [?1580], /183/15 [?1585], /189/54 (May 1586), /200/61 [?1587].

and none of national standing. Its strong Catholicism was a very localized matter.

Leicestershire had seven recusants listed, no status being given, of whom only two offered composition; the five delinquents comprised one who did not make an offer, three who could not be found and one who was listed as "reformed." The two offers were small, £5 apiece.[105] We have investigated Walter Whitehall (or Whythall), gentleman, who had an annual income in 1586 of £20, out of which he supported his wife and four children. He asked to be permitted to pay his small offer of composition, £5, in two installments a year because of his straitened circumstances.[106]

Lincolnshire listed only one recusant, John Thimelby, esquire, in the final report, omitting Robert Tyrwhitt, included in the original return, whose living of £40 had been distrained. Thimelby declared that his income had been greatly reduced by various charges and heavy debts, including the care of his children and others. His living was an annuity from his father; the only other evidence of his financial worth is that he was named in the levy of 1587 but no assessment was placed against him. His composition, £20, is evidently all that he could currently pay.[107]

London and Middlesex reported twenty-four recusants, but quite a number were confined there out of other counties. The one Catholic peer, Lord Vaux of Harrowden, four knights, three esquires and two gentlemen were among the most important, but not necessarily the wealthiest, Catholics. The income of only seven was given, the maximum being £800, the minimum, £100; the certified total was £1910. Two failed to propose any composition; twenty-two sent in offers, of which the maximum was £100, the minimum, £1; the total was £849. 13s. 4d.[108] We have selected twenty-two for further investigation. Sir John Arundell, the leading Catholic magnate of Cornwall, had recently been imprisoned and had been fined one thousand marks (£666. 13s. 4d.) in the Star Chamber for receiving priests into his house, having masses celebrated there, and for having gone to confession. Besides having to pay this, he had the care of a large family. In 1577 and 1580 his property, held jointly with his wife, amounted to £1000 annual rental value of

---

[105] S.P.12/189/54, 55 (May 1586).
[106] S.P.12/189/17.3 (April 8, 1586), /54 (May 1586).
[107] S.P.12/188/51, 51.1 (April 1586), /189/54, 55 (May 1586), /200/61 [?1587].
[108] S.P.12/189/54, 55 (May 1586).

their lands, and £2000 in goods; in 1580 he was assessed four lances and four light horses. He was charged £100 in 1587, which he paid. We do not have his worth in 1586, but he proposed a composition of £100, which indicated greater affluence than most of the Catholics, but encumbrances so great that he could not afford the annual recusancy fine of £240.[109] Rowland Barker of Shropshire, ranked both as a gentleman and as an esquire, had been confined to London and a radius of two miles about it since his recent release from prison. Deeply in debt, with interest charges and family obligations to meet, he had recently sold part of his lands; the rest were up for sale through an agent, since he could not leave London, to his financial loss. He had been listed, with no value recorded, in Shropshire in 1577; a subsequent report, sent in to London by the Bishop of Coventry and Lichfield, reported him as living chiefly at London and as worth annually in lands, £66. 13s. 4d., and in goods, £100. He possibly was the "Mr. Barker, gent.," charged £40 or one lance in 1585; in 1587 he was assessed and paid £25. In 1586 his income, derived from rents and shared partly with his mother, amounted to £32; his offer of £10 would seem reasonable.[110] Francis Bastard of Norfolk, lawyer and gentleman, was appraised in 1577 and 1580 at £40 annual value of land and in 1577 at £66. 13s. 4d. in goods; in 1580 he was charged one light horse and in 1585 £40 or one lance. His goods, worth £8. 17s. 4d., had been distrained in 1585, but had been returned to his wife and now were held in her name. Bastard's only certain living was a lease of a tenement for four years, worth £2 annually after subtracting other charges. He offered £1 in composition.[111] Katherine Bellamy, whose family connections undoubtedly raised a question about her loyalty, pleaded widowhood, age, illness, the care of her family, and a burden of debt amounting to about £260, which would permit her to offer only £10 in composition. She had devised all her property, other than £30 in rents, upon her son, Thomas; in 1587 she was unable to

---

[109] S.P.12/117/25.1 (October 28, 1577), /142/33 [?1580], /178/74 (May 27, 1585), /187/48.2 (March 14, 1586), /48.4 (March 10, 1586), /189/54 (May 1586), /200/61 [?1587].

[110] S.P.12/117/17.1 (November 14, 1577), /122/28.1 [?1577], /183/15 [?1585], /187/48.2, 9 (March 14, 1586), /189/54 (May 1586), /200/61 [?1587].

[111] S.P.12/117/27.1 (October 29, 1577), /142/33 [?1580], /170/14 (April 8, 1584), /183/15 [?1585], /187/48.2 (March 14, 1586), /48.12 (March 18, 1586), /189/54 (May 1586).

SOCIAL AND ECONOMIC STATUS OF CATHOLICS

pay a levy of £25.[112] Humfrey Cumberforde, gentleman, of Staffordshire, being a younger son possessed only a small estate yielding £10 annually in 1586; against it he had a heavy load of debts and distraints had been levied against his property (but possibly not yet enforced). He had been convicted of recusancy a number of times and had been in prison in the Gatehouse at Westminster from 1580 to the present. He offered £4 in composition.[113]

Sir Thomas Fitzherbert of Staffordshire and Derbyshire, long one of the most notorious recusants of the Midlands, was valued annually in lands (with goods included) in 1577 at £666. 13s. 4d. A subsequent appraisal in 1577 and again in 1580 placed his worth at £666. 13s. 4d. annually in lands and at £1000 in goods; in the latter year he was assessed four lances; in 1585 he was charged £100 or two lances; in 1587 he was able to pay only £50 of the £100 levied against him. His certified annual income in 1586 was £200, but his personal estimate was somewhat higher, £263. 5s. 9d., out of which he had to meet a debt structure of £203. His offer of composition, £40, manifestly reflected his ability to pay.[114] Thomas Fryer (or Freer), a physician, reported that he had an uncertain income derived from a declining practice of medicine, the rent, 40s. annually, from a tenement, and a house in London, out of which he supported his wife and eight children. The only other indication of his financial worth is the census of 1577 which records "Doctor ffriar, a Phisition," worth £100 in goods. He offered £4 in composition.[115] John Gage, esquire, a leading Sussex recusant confined to London, had been assessed in both 1577 and 1580 in lands at £266. 13s. 4d. annual rental value, and in goods, at £500; in the latter year he had been charged two lances and two light horses. In 1587 he paid £50. His income had increased over the years; by 1586 it amounted to £800 annually and he was worth £1000 in goods, but

---

[112] S.P.12/187/48.2 (March 14, 1586), /48.13 (March 18, 1586), /189/54 (May 1586), /200/61 [?1587].

[113] S.P.12/140/36 (July 30, 1580), /159/31 (March 1584), /36 (March 23, 1584), /170/9 (April 8, 1584), /187/48.2 (March 14, 1586), /48.10 (March 18, 1586), /189/54 (May 1586), /190/25 (June 12, 1586).

[114] S.P.12/118/17.1 (November 14, 1577), /122/28.1 [?1577], /142/33 [?1580], /183/15 [?1585], /187/48.2 (March 14, 1586), /48.3 (March 10, 1586), /189/54 (May 1586), /200/61 [?1587].

[115] S.P.12/118/73 (November 1577), /187/48.2 (March 14, 1586), /48.11 (March 18, 1586), /189/54 (May 1586).

against his estate lay a very heavy load of debts, and he had already paid £140 in recusancy fines. His offer of composition, £80, reflects a limited affluence.¹¹⁶ Thomas Gawen of Wiltshire, ranked both as a gentleman and an esquire, had lands annually worth £333. 6s. 8d. in 1577. He was assessed £40 or one light horse in 1585; in 1587 he was unable to meet a levy of £25. His income in 1586 was certified to be £333. 6s. 8d. The reason for the discrepancy between his income in 1586 and his inability to meet the charge of 1587 is that his estate was in a state of confusion. The certified income of 1586 was only nominal, representing the amount credited to him as accruing from lands to which he held title. Actually, he had lost the usufruct of a part of his lands, which had been distrained for nonpayment of recusancy fines and rented out of £39 per annum, and all his goods had been sequestrated. From what was left to him he had to meet such heavy expenses as the care of seven dependents. He offered in composition £13. 6s. 8d. annually, which he could pay only if the lease of his distrained lands were cancelled and they were returned to him.¹¹⁷

Sir Thomas Gerrard, currently under suspicion of disloyalty, belabored his loyalty to the Queen and his desire to serve her in reporting his financial worth in 1586. He had been valued at £666. 13s. 4d. annually in lands and £600 in goods in Derbyshire in 1577 and 1580; he was not charged in the levies of 1580 and 1585; in that of 1587 he was unable to pay anything. His income in 1586 was £120. He explained his financial deterioration as the result of a very heavy burden of debt, including recusancy fines, dowries for daughters, and the expenses of other children, which necessitated the selling off of his lands; part of the remainder he had already devised upon his sons. He petitioned in lieu of composition to serve the Queen any place in the world; if this were rejected, he offered £30, one-fourth of his current income.¹¹⁸ John Gifford, esquire, of Staffordshire, was subjected to three appraisals of his estate in 1577: the first assessed his lands (annual rental value) and goods jointly at £333. 6s. 8d.; the second rated his lands at £40 annual rental

---

¹¹⁶ S.P.12/117/15 (October 26, 1577), /142/33 [?1580], /187/48.2 (March 14, 1586), /48.5 (March 10, 1586), /189/54 (May 1586), /200/61 [?1587].
¹¹⁷ S.P.12/117/26.1 (October 28, 1577), /183/15 [?1585], /187/48.2, 6 (March 14, 1586), /189/54 (May 1586), /200/61 [?1587].
¹¹⁸ S.P.12/122/28.1 [?1577], /142/33 [?1580], /187/48.2, 8 (March 14, 1586), /189/54 (May 1586), /200/61 [?1587].

value; the third, compiled by the Bishop of Coventry and Lichfield, appraised him and his wife jointly to be worth annually in lands £200 and in goods £400. The figures reported by the bishop were used in the levy of 1580, when Gifford was charged three lances. In 1587 he paid £50. The certified income from his lands in 1586 was £133. 6s. 8d.; his personal estimate was £180 gross and £100 net (after he had paid his debts). Against his income were the charges of six children and £80 per annum devised on sons; he had paid £40 in recusancy fines. His offer, £30, very likely was a fair proposal.[119] Robert Hare, gentleman, of a landed Suffolk family prominent in the law, had recently been released from prison; apparently over the years he had not fared well, because in the census of the Inner Temple of 1577 he was recorded both as not conforming in religion and as being long absent from the Inn. His income in 1586 was £40 annually. Possibly he was charged in 1585; in 1587 he was assessed and paid £25. His offer of composition, £6. 13s. 4d., was in line with his poor income.[120] John Hocknell of Cheshire, ranked both as a gentleman and as an esquire, had been confined in seven separate prisons within five years because of recusancy and had only recently been released on bond. His lands had been appraised at £20 annually in 1577; there was no income reported in 1586; he paid £25 in 1587. He was unable to offer any composition because of the heavy recusancy fines which he had paid and the distraint of his property for £220 in unpaid fines, which had been rented out at £10 per annum for twenty-two years to recover this sum. He was currently living, he declared, upon the charity of friends.[121] Nicholas Longford (or Langford), esquire, of Derbyshire, had until recently been imprisoned in the Marshalsea. A man of standing in his county, he was listed but his property was not appraised in the census of 1577; in a subsequent census he and his wife, Martha, were declared to be worth £400 annually in lands and £1000 in goods. This latter set of values was also recorded in 1580, when he was assessed two lances and two light horses;

---

[119] S.P.12/118/17.1 (November 14, 1577), /122/28.1 [?1577], /142/33 [?1580], /187/48.2 (March 14, 1586), /48.5 (March 10, 1586), /189/54 (May 1586), /200/61 [?1587].

[120] S.P.12/118/69 (November 1577), /183/15 [?1585], /187/48.2, 6 (March 14, 1586), /189/54 (May 1586), /200/61 [?1587].

[121] S.P.12/118/48.1 (November 29, 1577), /118/49 (1577), /187/48.2 (March 14, 1586), /48/12 (March 18, 1586), /189/54 (May 1586), /200/61 [?1587].

in 1585 he was charged £100 or two lances; in 1587 he paid £50 levied against him. His annual income in 1586, derived from lands, was £320; by that date he had already paid £80 in recusancy fines and was under suit for the remainder. His seeming inability to pay the £240 per annum in recusancy fines would make his offer of composition, £66. 13s. 4d., roughly one-fifth of his income, a reasonable proposal.[122] George Monox (no status determinable) had in 1586 a yearly income from lands of £40; he had, however, devised an annual living of £120 on his son. His offer of composition was £13. 6s. 8d.[123] Dame Elizabeth Paulet, of the family of the Marquis of Winchester, offered £100 in composition. Despite her rank it is difficult to appraise her wealth. In 1577 and 1580 her lands in Hampshire were worth £300 annually and her goods £300; in the latter year she was assessed two lances and one light horse; in 1587 she was charged the minimum, £25, which she paid. In 1586 she returned no statement of the value of her estate, but she indicated that her composition was limited by a heavy debt load which included the maintenance of one son serving with the Earl of Leicester, a second with Sir Thomas Cecil, and a third with Sir Francis Drake.[124] Erasmus Saunders, ranked both as a gentleman and as an esquire, had an annual income in 1586, with which he supported his wife and nine children, of £3. 6s. 8d., the remainder of his estate after property valued at £4 had been distrained. In 1587 he could not pay a charge of £25. His offer of £2 annually in composition indicated other sources of income or possibly help from relatives and friends.[125]

John Towneley, esquire, one of the more important of the Elizabethan Catholics, being steward of certain crown lands in Lancashire, was valued at £266. 13s. 4d. annually in lands and at £500 in goods in 1577 and 1580; in the latter year he was charged two lances and two light horses. In 1585 he was charged £66. 13s. 4d. or two lances in the archdiocese of York and £50 or two lances in the diocese of Chester; in 1587

[122] S.P.12/118/17.1 (November 14, 1577), /122/28.1 [?1577], /142/33 [?1580], /180/64 (July 1585), /183/15 [?1585], /187/48.2 (March 14, 1586), /48.10 (March 18, 1586), /189/54 (May 1586), /200/61 [?1587].
[123] S.P.12/187/48.2 (March 14, 1586), /48.11 (March 18, 1586), /189/54 (May 1586).
[124] S.P.12/117/10.1 (October 1577), /142/33 [?1580], /187/48.2 (March 14, 1586), /48.3 (March 10, 1586), /189/54 (May 1586), /200/61 [?1587].
[125] S.P.12/159/28 (March 22, 1583), /36 (March 23, 1584), /187/48.2, 6 (March 14, 1586), /189/54 (May 1586), /200/61 [?1587].

SOCIAL AND ECONOMIC STATUS OF CATHOLICS

he paid a levy of £50. His self-declared annual income in 1586, described by him as small, was £500; the official certification was much less, £200. The encumbrance of a large family, long imprisonment, and the payment of £620 in recusancy fines determined his offer of £66. 13s. 4d., more than he could afford, he asserted, but which he pleaded with the government to accept in order that he might no longer be plagued by indictments and informers.[126] Sir Thomas Tresham, the only acknowledged spokesman for the English Catholics, has disappointingly little record of his wealth in the 1580's. In 1587 he was charged and paid £50. He had been unable to pay all of his heavy recusancy fines, and a part of his lands and goods had been distrained to meet this delinquency; a suit to collect a part of the fines had also been instituted by the pursuivant, Hugh Cuffe, who was to receive a share if the decision were in his favor. Tresham had already paid £600 against these charges and was amortizing them by annual installments of £200, which, however, still left him with a total of debts of about £1000. From what we know of Tresham's subsequent career and his standard of living, we must conclude that he possessed sources of wealth invisible to us today; nevertheless his heavy debt structure and his offer of £100 in composition proved his inability to pay the required £240 in annual recusancy fines.[127] Tresham's brother-in-law, Lord Vaux of Harrowden, notoriously impecunious, reported a small income and heavy expenses. Besides the costs of his family, he had been charged £50 in 1587 and was officially recorded as paying half (he, however, asserted that he had paid the full sum). His offer of £80, for one with what was evidently a small estate and who evidently had no capacity to manage his finances, was undoubtedly a true statement of his ability to pay; further proof that this was so is the fact that at least temporarily, undoubtedly to save his estate, he and also his sons conformed in 1592, three years before his death.[128] Thomas Wyllford, esquire, of Kent, was worth £133. 6s. 8d. annually in income from lands in 1586; he paid

[126] S.P.12/118/45.1 (November 28, 1577), /142/33 [?1580], /159/31 (March 1584), /36 (March 23, 1584), /183/15 [?1585], /187/48.2 (March 14, 1586), /48.4 (March 10, 1586), /189/54 (May 1586), /200/61 [?1587].
[127] S.P.12/159/28 (March 22, 1583), /36 (March 23, 1584), /187/48.2, 7 (March 14, 1586), /189/54 (May 1586), /200/61 [?1587].
[128] S.P.12/159/28 (March 22, 1583), /36 (March 23, 1584), /187/48.2 (March 14, 1586), /48.3 (March 10, 1586), /189/54 (May 1586), /200/61 [?1587]; A.P.C., XXIII, 192 (September 14, 1592).

a levy of £50 in 1587. His ten children, recusancy fines of £250 which he had paid, and his current debt load of £200, determined his offer of composition of £50, the equivalent of his unpaid recusancy fines due before Michaelmas.[129] Francis Yate, gentleman, of Berkshire, in whose house the Jesuit, Edmund Campion, had been captured in the summer of 1581, was currently free, after being released on bond from Wisbeach Castle, where he had been imprisoned for over a year, and previously elsewhere. In 1577 and 1580 his lands had been assigned an annual value of £666. 13s. 4d., and in the latter year he had been charged four lances and two light horses; in 1585 the levy was £40 or one light horse; in 1587 he had paid the minimum charge, £25. In 1586 there were three estimates of his income: one valued it at £20; another, the official certification, was £100; the third, Yate's self-declaration, put it at £133. 6s. 8d., derived from rents. He had rented out his lands at £133. 6s. 8d. two years before, probably in the hope that the government would hesitate to distrain his lands because of legal complications which possibly might ensue. His offer of £40, one-sixth of the required amount recusants had to pay each year, was determined by his heavy debt load, the £420 he had paid in recusancy fines, and a suit pending against him for £200 in unpaid recusancy fines. We must assume that the offer of £40 was a truthful statement of his ability, both because the government knew so much about him and because it had treated him magnanimously in view of his involvement in Campion's case, legally a case of treason.[130]

Obviously London had very few Catholics, permanent residents, who were of standing and affluence. The leading Catholics reported from the capital were mostly confined there out of other counties. Cities, we must not forget, had generally been the first areas to turn to Protestantism both in England and on the Continent; even before Henry VIII's break with Rome anticlericalism had been noticeable in London. The constant presence there of the chief organs of government insured that a very active or widescale Catholic spiritual life could not exist.

Norfolk, although considered a stronghold of Protestantism, had a residue of quite ardent Catholic families. In 1586 twenty-seven persons

---

[129] S.P.12/187/48.2 (March 14, 1586), /48.5 (March 10, 1586), /189/54 (May 1586), /200/61 [?1587].

[130] S.P.12/117/17.1 (October 26, 1577), /140/36 (July 30, 1580), /142/33 [?1580], /183/15 [?1585], /187/48.2 (March 14, 1586), /48.11 (March 18, 1586), /189/54 (May 1586), /200/61 [?1587].

were listed, nine being esquires and twelve gentlemen. The values of six were given, the maximum yearly income being £400, the minimum, £133. 6s. 8d.; the total was £1250. A majority of those listed, twenty-one, offered composition; six were delinquent. The maximum offer of composition was £50, the minimum, 10s.; the total was not large in terms of the prominence of some of the Catholics, £181. 3s. 8d.[131] We have studied fourteen recusants. What is so interesting about them and makes them so representative of the Elizabethan Catholic gentry was that they were tied by blood, marriage, and long friendship; that their hopes had risen with Mary Tudor's rule and had been dashed to pieces with her death. The Bedingfield family, which had been associated with that monarch's life in East Anglia, is represented by five members. Edmund Bedingfield, ranked both as a gentleman and an esquire, apparently died after accepting summons to appear and make offer of composition before the commission appointed for that purpose. He was a recusant of very moderate affluence. In 1580 the annual rental value of his lands was £300 and he was assessed three lances; in 1585 the assessment was £50 or the option of one lance or one light horse; in 1587 the statement that he was deceased was entered against the levy of £25.[132] Elizabeth Bedingfield, a widow, was listed officially, along with various other Norfolk Catholics, as one of the principal recusants of Norfolk. Her annual income was only £10, but probably she had already devised her property on her children. Due to age and ill health she could not appear before the magistrates charged with making compositions, but she sent an offer of £3. 6s. 8d.[133] Henry Bedingfield, esquire, also listed as a principal recusant of his county, was charged £50 in 1587; the master sheet does not record that he paid, nor is there any other record of his financial status. His offer of composition, £6. 13s. 4d., probably reflected a deteriorated estate.[134] Humphrey Bedingfield, esquire, also listed as one of the principal rescusants of Norfolk, was worth in 1577 and 1580 £50 annually in lands and £200 in goods; in the latter year he was charged one lance. His certified income from lands in 1586 was £200. Either the earlier figures were grossly inac-

[131] S.P.12/189/54, 55 (May 1586).
[132] S.P.12/142/33 [?1580], /183/15 [?1585], /188/9.2 (April 10, 1586), /189/54 (May 1586), /200/61 [?1587].
[133] S.P.12/188/9.2 (April 10, 1586), /9.22 (April 6, 1586), /189/54 (May 1586).
[134] S.P.12/188/9.2 (April 10, 1586), /189/54 (May 1586), /200/61 [?1587].

curate or Bedingfield had acquired property over the years which would explain the increase in the value of his estate; nevertheless, his offer of composition, £10, was small, which probably indicated encumbrances which were not recorded.[135] Laurence Bedingfield, ranked both as a gentleman and an esquire and recorded a principal recusant of Norfolk, possessed in 1586 only an annuity of £13. 6s. 8d., to last during his mother's lifetime; his offer of composition was nearly one-fourth of this, £3. 6s. 8d.[136] John Downes, gentleman and a principal recusant of Norfolk, was a younger member of his family and possessed only a small estate. In 1577 he was listed in the census, but no property was recorded; in 1585 he was assessed £40 or one lance. In 1586 he reported that he possessed one farm, exploited to its maximum value, but the value was not given; his goods were worth £100. His chief encumbrance, his debts, amounted to over £100. He offered to pay £1 in composition as long as his farm was not distrained for nonpayment of recusancy fines.[137] Robert Downes, esquire and a leading recusant of Norfolk, declared his living to be poor. He possessed lands worth £160 annually and goods worth £100 in 1577; in 1580 the same value was assigned to his lands and he was assessed one lance and one light horse. In 1587 he was assessed £50, of which he paid half, £25. His certified income in 1586 was £400, against which lay a heavy indebtedness, including the payment of various annuities, which perhaps justified his offer of £20 in composition.[138] John Drury, ranked both as a gentleman and an esquire, and his son, Robert, were both listed as principal recusants of Norfolk. The elder Drury's annual value in lands in 1577, held jointly with his wife, was £50 and in goods £100; in 1580 the lands had the same recorded annual value and he was assessed one light horse. An assessment of £40 or one lance was placed against him in 1585; in 1587 he was charged but did not pay £25. His certified income in 1586 was £133. 6s. 8d., against which lay a heavy load of debts. The

---

[135] S.P.12/117/27.1 (October 29, 1577), /142/33 [?1580], /188/9.2 (April 10, 1586), /9.11 (April 6, 1586), /189/54 (May 1586).
[136] S.P.12/188/9.2 (April 10, 1586), /9.15 (April 6, 1586), /189/54 (May 1586).
[137] S.P.12/117/27.1 (October 29, 1577), /183/15 [?1585], /188/9.2 (April 10, 1586), /9.17 (April 6, 1586), /189/54 (May 1586).
[138] S.P.12/117/27.1 (October 29, 1577), /142/33 [?1580], /188/9.2 (April 10, 1586), /9.3 (April [?6] 1586), /189/54 (May 1586), /200/61 [?1587]. A Robert Downes was convicted of breaking the religious laws in 1561 (S.P.12/17/18, June 3, 1561, /18/1, 1561).

senior and the junior Drury jointly offered £10, which indicated an intention to prevent the dissipation of their estate, since obviously the increase in value between 1577 and 1586 was being eaten away by various charges.[139] Robert de Grey, esquire and a principal recusant of his county, was valued at £200 annually in lands and at £200 in goods in 1577 and 1580; in 1580 he was charged with two lances; in 1585 he was assessed £50 or one lance; in 1587 he did not pay the £25 levied against him. His certified income in 1586 was £250; his long difficulties with the government about his recusancy, reaching back for many years, insures that his offer of £13. 6s. 8d. was made honestly.[140] Henry Kervylle, esquire and a principal recusant, offered composition of £50. There is no other evidence of the value of his estate, but he, too, had long been under official surveillance, which would indicate that his offer was reasonable.[141] Henry Lovell, gentleman and a principal recusant, offered only £2; we have no other data about him to judge his financial worth.[142] Robert Lovell, esquire and a principal recusant, was suffering grave financial distress, caused by his imprisonment of eight years, by his heavy debts, by the care of a wife and six children, and by a distraint levied on his property at Michaelmas term, 1584; that part which had been distrained had been leased out at £33. 6s. 8d. annually. In 1577 and 1580 the annual rental value of his lands was £40, and he had been charged for one light horse in the levy of the latter year; in 1585 he was charged £40 or an option of one lance or one light horse. By 1586 his income had increased to £133. 6s. 8d., possibly because of property devised on Lovell by his mother. The encumbrances weighing upon his estate obviously reflect his assertion that his financial condition had deteriorated badly and justified his offer of £8 in composition.[143] Ferdinando Paris, esquire, a landholder both in Norfolk (where he was listed a principal recusant) and in Cambridgeshire, was assessed in both

---

[139] S.P.12/117/27.1 (October 29, 1577), /142/33 [?1580], /183/15 [?1585], /188/9.2 (April 10, 1586), /9.8 (April 6, 1586), /189/54 (May 1586), /200/61 [?1587].
[140] S.P.12/117/27.1 (October 29, 1577), /142/33 [?1580], /183/15 [?1585], /188/9.2 (April 10, 1586), /9.19 (April 6, 1586), /189/54 (May 1586), /200/61 [?1587].
[141] S.P.12/188/9.2 (April 10, 1586), /9.21 (April 6, 1586), /189/54 (May 1586).
[142] S.P.12/188/9.2 (April 10, 1586), /9.5 (April 6, 1586), /189/54 (May 1586).
[143] S.P.12/117/27.1 (October 29, 1577), /142/33 [?1580], /183/15 [?1585], /188/9.2 (April 10, 1586), /9.4 (April 6, 1586), /189/54 (May 1586).

counties in 1577 and 1580. In Norfolk his lands were valued annually at £200 and his goods at £200, and he was charged two lances in the levy of 1580; in Cambridgeshire his lands were rated at the annual value of £333. 6s. 8d. and he was termed "welthye" in goods in 1577; three years later his lands were assigned the same value and his goods were rated at £333. 6s. 8d., and he was charged with providing 3 lances. In the next few years either he lost property through financial reverses or he sold it or devised it on his children or the figures of 1577 and 1580 were an overvaluation, because in 1585 the charge was £40 or one lance and in 1587 he was named but no charge was placed against him. His income in 1586 was £133. 6s. 8d., which reflects a financial deterioration; his offer of composition, £30, less than one-fourth of his income, bears this out because he long lived under close government scrutiny.[144] John Yaxley, gentleman and a principal recusant, was of small value; his income in 1586 was £30, against which lay a heavy load of debt. There is no record that he was charged in the levies of 1580 and 1585 and it is unclear if he were the Yaxley listed but not charged any sum in 1587. He offered £5, one-sixth of his income, in composition.[145]

Northampton listed only two recusants, Thomas Lawe, whose status was not given, and Edward Royden, a physician; the former offered £6. 13s. 4d., the latter, £2, making a total of £8. 13s. 4d. Because the more representative recusants, Lord Vaux, Sir Thomas Tresham, and Sir William Catesbie, were confined outside of the county, we have not investigated these two persons further. It is evident, however, that Northamptonshire, an area of large estates and subject to the Protestant influence of Cambridge University, had no sizable residue of Catholics.[146]

Oxfordshire listed seventy-nine recusants (although we have not been able to recognize all the names as those of Catholics, but assume that they were): three were esquires; seventeen were gentlemen. The incomes of eight were given; the maximum amount was £160, the minimum, £10; the total was £730. However, all seventy-nine were included in the offers of composition; the total number of offers was fifty-three, but

[144] S.P.12/117/27.1 (October 29, 1577), /28.1 (October 30, 1577), /142/33 [?1580], /183/15 [?1585], /188/9.2 (April 10, 1586), /9.18 (April 6, 1586), /189/54 (May 1586), /200/61 [?1587].
[145] S.P.12/188/9.2 (April 10, 1586), /9.6 (April 6, 1586), /189/54 (May 1586), /200/61 [?1587].
[146] S.P.12/189/54, 55 (May 1586).

SOCIAL AND ECONOMIC STATUS OF CATHOLICS

twenty-six additional persons were included in sixteen joint offers. The maximum offer was £20; the minimum was 5s.; the total was £202. 15s. 0d.[147] We have selected six persons for further study. Lady Babington had a certified income of £150 in 1586; she was charged, but did not pay, £50, in 1587. Her offer of composition, £20, considering the unhappy notoriety of her family at this time, was undoubtedly reasonable.[148] Richard Owen, esquire, was valued yearly in lands at £100 and at £100 in goods in 1577; in 1580 his lands were assigned the same value and he was charged one lance; in 1587 he paid a levy of £25. His certified income in 1586 was £160, out of which he offered £20. Considering that he was long under close surveillance, this sum evidently represented a true picture of his resources.[149] Margaret Pitts, a widow who belonged to a family well-known for its unyielding Catholicism, was worth £300 in goods in 1577 and in 1580 and she was charged one light horse in the latter year; in 1587 only £12 was levied against her. Obviously such a small estate could bear little more than the £3. 6s. 8d. which she offered in annual composition, although possibly she had devised her lands on her children.[150] Edmund and Francis Plowden, sons of the eminent lawyer, offered a joint composition of £20. There is no other evidence of their wealth nor of charges against their estates; it seems most likely that their father had provided comfortably for them.[151] Lady Stonor, who was well-known to the central authorities as a militant Catholic, was worth £300 annually in lands and £200 in goods in 1577 and 1580, and was charged two lances and one light horse in the latter year. In 1587 she paid a levy of £25. Most probably she had devised her lands on her children, because in 1586 she was worth only £100 in annual income and her offer of composition was £15.[152]

Shropshire listed four recusants, three of them ranking as gentlemen.

---

[147] *Ibid.*
[148] S.P.12/189/54 (May 1586), /200/61 [?1587].
[149] S.P.12/119/5.1 (December 7, 1577), /140/36 (July 30, 1580), /38 (July 31, 1580), /142/33 [?1580], /159/28 (March 22, 1583), /189/54 (May 1586), /200/61 [?1587].
[150] S.P.12/119/5.1 (December 7, 1577), /142/33 [?1580], /189/54 (May 1586), /200/61 [?1587].
[151] S.P.12/189/54 (May 1586).
[152] S.P.12/119/5.1 (December 7, 1577), /142/33 [?1580], /189/54 (May 1586), /200/61 [?1587].

All four reported their incomes, the maximum being £66. 13s. 4d., the minimum, £6. 13s. 4d.; the total was £113. 6s. 8d. The four also made offers of composition: the maximum was £6. 13s. 4d.; the minimum was £1. 6s. 8d.; the total was £17. In a county so lacking in recusant affluence we have selected only one, Richard Lloyd, who ranked both as a gentleman and as an esquire, for further investigation. Although he was well-known for his intransigence, the only evidence of his estate was his certified income in 1586 of £66. 13s. 4d. His offer of composition was one-tenth of this, £6. 13s. 4d., which the official scrutiny under which he long lived verifies as a fair proposal.[153]

Southhampton, because of its location on the southern seacoast, occasionally caused alarm to Elizabeth's government for fear of a strong Catholic sentiment prevalent there. The census of 1586, however, does not bear out either evidence of great wealth or of great numbers adhering to Rome. Eleven persons were listed, including one esquire and five gentlemen. The worth of only one was given, £200 annual income. All eleven offered composition, the maximum being £40 and the minimum, £2, the total amounting to £89. 13s. 4d. In the original returns seven recusants, all in prison, were reported but not included in the master sheet of May 1586, probably because they made no offer, at least from that county. Two of these were women — the Lady Paulet, who was confined to the Fleet in London; and Elizabeth Beconshawe, currently incarcerated in Winchester gaol, who was reported to be worth nothing. The other five, all men of some distinction — William Hoorde (or Hurde), Thomas Owen, Nicholas Scroope, Richard Warmeford and Gilbert Welles — were confined at Wisbeach Castle, which contained only the most notorious Catholics.[154] We have investigated six of the recusants. William Beconshawe, gentleman, could offer only £2 in composition; there is no other evidence of his worth.[155] George Cotton, esquire, who had for years lived in prison and under surveillance, was valued annually at £300 in lands and at £300 in goods in 1577 and 1580; he was charged three lances in the first levy. In 1585 he was assessed £100 or one lance and one light horse; in 1587 he was required to pay much less, £25. His certified income in 1586 was £200. It is difficult to arrive at an estimate of his

---

[153] S.P.12/189/54, 55 (May 1586).
[154] S.P.12/188/16.1 (April 1586), /189/54, 55 (May 1586).
[155] S.P.12/188/16.1 (April 1586), /189/54 (May 1586).

worth: his property had been distrained for nonpayment of recusancy fines, but he described his estate as being small even before distraint; he had a heavy burden of debts, the care of ten dependents and the payment of three dowries; still another heavy charge weighing against him arose from lawsuits. He offered £40 in composition, which he could pay apparently only if his distrained lands were returned and he could use them as security for a loan.[156] George Lewkner, a lawyer ranking also as a gentleman, offered £6. 13s. 4d. in 1586, but in 1587 apparently he escaped paying £25 by conforming.[157] Elizabeth Titcheborne, a widow, aged and ill, held most of her property in trust. The annual rental value of her lands was £40 and the value of her goods was £600 in 1577 and 1580; she was charged one lance in the first levy. What she was worth in 1586 was not recorded, except that her estate was small, being what remained to her after heavy losses; out of it she had to pay heavy debts and support twelve dependents. Since she seems never to have been a person of much wealth, her offer of £13. 6s. 8d. was probably all that she could afford.[158] Nicholas Titcheborne, gentleman, possessed little, possibly because he had devised his property on his children. In 1577 and 1580 his goods were worth £200, and he was charged for one light horse in the latter year; in 1585 he was assessed £40 or one light horse; in 1587 he was charged but could not pay £25. He had no other living in 1586 but an annuity worth £3, which he offered to the government in composition.[159] Stephen Vachell, gentleman, was worth £50 annually in lands and £100 in goods in 1577 and the same amount in lands in 1580, when he was charged a light horse. The levy in 1585 was £50 or one lance; no value was given of him in 1586, but he offered £5 in composition. This small sum perhaps manifested a gradual change in religious sentiment; in 1587 he apparently evaded an assessment of £25 by conforming.[160]

---

[156] S.P.12/117/10.1 (October 1577), /142/33 [?1580], /159/28 (March 22, 1583), /36 (March 23, 1584), /183/15 [?1585], /188/16.5 (March 31, 1586), /189/54 (May 1586), /200/61 [?1587].
[157] S.P.12/188/16.1, 3 (April 1586), /189/54 (May 1586), /200/61 [?1587].
[158] S.P.12/117/10.1 (October 1577), /142/33 [?1580], /188/16.1 (April 1586), /16.6 (April 9, 1586), /189/54 (May 1586).
[159] S.P.12/117/10.1 (October 1577), /142/33 [?1580], /183/15 [?1585], /188/16.1 (April 1586), /16.12 (April 13, 1586), /189/54 (May 1586), /200/61 [?1587].
[160] S.P.12/117/10.1 (October 1577), /142/33 [?1580], /183/15 [?1585], /188/16.1 (April 1586), /189/54 (May 1586), /200/61 [?1587].

Staffordshire was for many years the stronghold of Catholicism in the Midlands, due to the recalcitrancy of a section of the gentry. Nevertheless, the picture of them presented in the master sheet of 1586 is not that of a group of any considerable prominence or of any considerable wealth. Of the twenty-seven recusants listed only two ranked as high as gentleman. The financial worth of only three was recorded; the maximum income was £100, the minimum, £30; the total was low, £170. All twenty-seven were included in twenty-three offers of composition, four being embraced in three joint proposals. The maximum composition offered was £20; the minimum was 10s. The total was low, £65. 16s. 8d.[161] We have selected six persons for further investigation. Richard Fitzherbert, ranked both as a gentleman and as an esquire, was worth only £3. 6s. 8d. annually in lands and £100 in goods in 1577; but in 1580 his lands were assessed at £100 and he was charged one lance. The government, apparently using this figure as a basis, placed a levy against him in 1585 of £40 or one light horse. He described his living as poor in 1586, when he reported his income to be £13. 6s. 8d.; in proposing composition he offered one-fourth of this sum, £3. 6s. 8d.[162] Dorothy Heveningham, a widow well-known for her unyielding Catholicism, included her servant, Katherine Comberford, whom she wholly supported, in her offer of composition of £10. Three separate appraisals of her wealth were made in 1577: one recorded her as worth £40 annually in lands; a second recorded her as worth £133. 6s. 8d. in lands and goods together annually; a third recorded her as worth £133. 6s. 8d. annually in lands and as worth £300 in goods. The third appraisal of her lands was that used in 1580, when she was charged one lance and one light horse; in 1587 she was charged only the minimum, £25. Her certified income in 1586 was £100, but her estimate was £30.[163] Ellen Maxfield (or Macclesfield) was the widow of a prominent Staffordshire recusant, Ralph Maxfield, whose death had left her with the care of their younger children and a considerable burden of debt. She and her husband had had their wealth jointly valued three times in 1577: one appraisal recorded the annual rental value of their lands at £20; a second placed both lands and goods

---

[161] S.P.12/189/54, 55 (May 1586).
[162] S.P.12/118/17.1 (November 14, 1577), /142/33 [?1580], /183/15 [?1585], /188/29.10 (April 1586), /189/54 (May 1586).
[163] S.P.12/118/17.1 (November 14, 1577), /122/28.1 [?1577], /142/33 [?1580], /188/29.2 (April 1586), /189/54 (May 1586), /200/61 [?1587].

at £100 annually; a third listed the annual worth of their lands at £40 and the total worth of their goods at £200. This third set of figures was recorded of the husband in 1580, when he was charged one lance; in 1585 he was required to pay £40 or to furnish one light horse; in 1587 against an assessment of £25 was the notation that he was deceased. In 1586 Ellen Maxfield and her son, William, held their living jointly; their certified income was £30. The offer of composition, £10, was made jointly to include not only Ellen and William Maxfield, but also the latter's wife, Ursula. William, after many years, was still a prisoner for recusancy; he was also burdened with the support both of his wife and of his seven children. His estate had been small while his father was alive. In 1577 one appraisal placed it at £5 annually in lands; a second recorded him as worth £40 annually in both lands and goods; a third stated that he and his wife jointly were worth £10 annual rental value in lands and the value of their goods was rated at £66. 13s. 4d. He was not included in the first levy; in that of 1585 he was charged £40 or one light horse; in 1587 he was unable to pay the £25 levied against him. Despite the government's longstanding supervision of the Maxfields, jointly and singly they were of little affluence.[164] Erasmus Wolvesley, esquire, had only a small estate, although we may surmise that he had devised some part of his property to his children. His wealth was subjected to three ratings in 1577: one assessed the annual value of his lands at £26. 13s. 4d.; a second appraised the annual worth of his lands and goods jointly at £200; a third valued Wolvesley and his wife, Cassander, at £100 annually in lands and at £300 in goods. This third set of figures was recorded as his assessment in 1580, when he was charged two lances. His certified income in 1586 was £40, half of which, £20, he offered in composition.[165]

Suffolk especially arouses interest, because the total sum of its Catholic wealth was far greater than in any other county, but a sum which was about equal to the total worth individually of some merchants, some gentry families, and some peers. The recusants listed numbered sixteen, of whom eight were esquires and seven were gentlemen. Thirteen re-

---

[164] S.P.12/118/17.1 (November 14, 1577), /122/28.1 [?1577], /142/33 [?1580], /183/15 [?1585], /188/29.3 (April 1586), /189/54 (May 1586), /200/61 [?1587].
[165] S.P.12/118/17.1 (November 14, 1577), /122/28.1 [?1577], /142/33 [?1580], /188/29.1 (April 1586), /189/54 (May 1586).

ported their annual incomes: the maximum was £1000; the minimum was £20; the total was £4420. All sixteen made offers of composition, the maximum being £50 and the minimum being £6. In view of the fact that each of the sixteen was legally required to pay £240 per annum, the total of the offers of composition is surprisingly low, £339. 6s. 8d.[166] We have studied the financial status of all of the sixteen recusants. John Bedingfield, gentleman, whose family, although prominent, was contemporarily of only moderate affluence in East Anglia, lived on an income generally amounting to about £40 per annum, derived solely from a lease for life of a part of the property of the late Sir Henry Bedingfield. He had heavy encumbrances: he had paid £10 in recusancy fines; his debts amounted to £600; he had not only his wife and six children but some others dependent on him. Obviously his offer of £10 was in line with his ability to pay.[167] John Daniell, rated both a gentleman and an esquire, stated that his living was small: in 1586 his certified income was £300, but the next year he did not pay a levy of £25. His composition, £20, in view of many years of trouble because of recusancy, was probably a fair figure.[168] Margaret Daniell, a widow burdened with debts and the care of her children, had an income in 1586 which was the same as that of John Daniell, £300. She, too, termed her living as small. In 1580 she had been appraised at £40 annual rental value in lands; her charge in the levy was one light horse; in 1587 she paid the charge of £25. Her offer of composition, like John Daniell's, was £20; it would seem a reasonable offer.[169] Henry Drury, rated both a gentleman and an esquire, was worth £40 annually in lands in 1580 and he was charged one light horse; in 1585 the assessment was £50 or one lance; in 1587 he paid a levy of £25. His certified income was £200 in 1586; his offer of composition was one-tenth of this, £20.[170] Henry Everard, esquire, sent in his return from prison, where he had long been confined. His encumbrances were many and heavy. His debt load was large; he had twelve dependents; his recusancy fines amounted

[166] S.P.12/189/54, 55 (May 1586).
[167] S.P.12/188/38.6 (1586), /189/54 (May 1586).
[168] S.P.12/188/38.9 (1586), /189/54 (May 1586), /200/61 [?1587].
[169] S.P.12/142/33 [?1580], /188/38.8 (1586), /189/54 (May 1586), /200/61 [?1587].
[170] S.P.12/142/33 [?1580], /183/15 [?1585], /188/38.16 (March 28, 1586), /189/54 (May 1586), /200/61 [?1587].

to £79, which, however, indicated that the authorities had not pressed him for the full sum. In 1577 he had been recorded as a member of the Inner Temple, but his estate was then unknown as he was no longer resident. The levy of 1580 recorded the annual rental value of his lands at £200 and he was charged two lances; in 1585 he was assessed £50 or one lance; in 1587 he was required to pay the minimum, £25, an obligation which he fulfilled. His certified income in 1586 was £133. 6s. 8d., but he personally reported it to be only £66. 13s. 4d. In offering £10 he begged that his composition would effect his release from prison.[171] Michael Hare, esquire, long familiar to the government as a most intransigent recusant, was currently imprisoned, a continuation of many years of deprivation of liberty during which he had paid heavily in recusancy fines and had accumulated a heavy structure of debt. In 1577 in the census of the Inner Temple, London, it was reported that his living was unknown and that he had long been absent from that center of legal studies. He was appraised at £200 annual rental value in lands in 1580 and he was charged two lances; he was assessed £100 or two lances and one light horse in 1585; he did not pay a levy of £50 in 1587. In 1586 he characterized his living as small; nevertheless his certified income, £800, was very large compared to that of most other Elizabethan Catholics. Obviously he considered his offer of composition, £50, to be adequate, since he added the earnest request that the government consider it to be acceptable in view of "the sharp and chargeable imprisonment that I have long sustained for this cause [recusancy]."[172] Ambrose Jermine (or Jarmyn), gentleman, had inherited from his father lands which were entailed; by his own evaluation in 1586 they brought him an income of £80; however, the official certification of his income was £100. In the levy of the next year he failed to pay a charge of £25, which probably can be explained by the care of his wife and three children and longstanding debts amounting to £133. 6s. 8d., part of which must have been unpaid recusancy fines, since his offer of composition, £13. 6s. 8d., was one-tenth of his total debt structure.[173] Robert Jetter, gentleman, who had

---

[171] S.P.12/118/69 (November 1577), /142/33 [?1580], /183/15 [?1585], /188/38.3 [?April ?1586], /189/54 (May 1586), /200/61 [? 1587].

[172] S.P.12/118/69 (November 1577), /142/33 [?1580], /183/15 [?1585], /188/38.10 (1586), /189/54 (May 1586), /200/61 [?1587].

[173] S.P.12/188/38.11 (1586), /189/54 (May 1586), /200/61 [?1587].

been in the official records as a recusant since almost the beginning of Elizabeth's reign, complained that over the years he had been greatly impoverished through imprisonment, debts, the care of his family, lawsuits and a fine. Some of his lands, the only evidence which we have of his financial worth, had been distrained and rented out at £36. 10s. 0d. per annum. In 1587 he could not pay the £25 assessed against him. His offer of composition, £6. 13s. 4d., indicates that he possessed other sources of income besides the distrained lands, unless it were from loans or charity.[174] Richard Martin, gentleman, had recently inherited an estate from his father which brought him the certified income in 1586 of £400 and which he described as poor. Perhaps his judgment, although self-appraised, and the care of his family, explains his very small offer of composition, £6.[175] Roger Martin, gentleman, whose certified income in 1586 was also £400, offered £26. 13s. 4d. in composition. He was valued at £133. 6s. 8d. annually in lands and charged one lance and one light horse in 1580; in 1585 he was assessed £40 or one lance; in 1587 he refused to pay a charge of £50. Perhaps this blunt opposition to the third levy stemmed from the heavy recusancy fines which he had already paid, his current debts and the expenses of his children, but in so critical a year as 1587 it was indeed daring and calculated to bring the wrath of the government down upon him.[176] Walter Norton, ranked both as a gentleman and as an esquire, personally valued his income from his lands at £100 in 1586, which was officially certified as correct. In 1585 he was charged £50 or one lance; in 1587 he was again charged £50, of which he paid half, £25. He pleaded a heavy load of debts and the expenses of a wife and four children to justify an offer of £20.[177] Edward Rookwood, esquire, had conformed in the 1570's; but later, at an unknown date, he had been reconciled to the Church of Rome. It was before the levy of 1580, in which he was included: he was valued at £200 annual rental value in lands with the accompanying assessment of two lances. His certified income in 1586

---

[174] S.P.12/188/38.7 (1586), /189/54 (May 1586), /200/61 [?1587].

[175] S.P.12/188/38.4 [?April ?1586], /189/54 (May 1586).

[176] S.P.12/142/33 [?1580], /183/15 [?1585], /188/38.13 (1586), /189/54 (May 1586), /200/61 [?1587].

[177] S.P.12/183/15 [?1585], /188/38.2 [?April ?1586], /189/54 (May 1586), /200/61 [?1587].

was £500, which ranked him as very moderately affluent among the contemporary gentry; in 1587 he was charged only the minimum, £25, which he paid. His small offer of composition, £30, can only be explained by the supposition that fines and imprisonment had taken a heavy toll of his resources.[178] Robert Rookwood, esquire, is more obscure. The only evidences of his worth are that he made an offer of £20 in 1586, and that he paid a levy of £25 in 1587.[179] What is so very interesting about the Rookwoods is that, despite a lack of great wealth, they were traditionally of sufficient prominence to merit a visit from Queen Elizabeth in the 1570's. The Sulliard family, too, was of consequence in East Anglia; like so many of their contemporaries there was considerable disparity of wealth between the senior and junior branches. Edward Sulliard, esquire, declared that his income in 1586 was £440; it was officially certified to be £300. He was charged £25 in 1587, but it is not clear if he paid this or if it were cancelled. His burden of debts was crushing, £1046. 13s. 4d.; he had already paid £440 in recusancy fines; and he took care of a number of dependents. Undoubtedly his offer of £40 was the utmost that he could pay.[180] Thomas Sulliard, gentleman, described himself as poor when he reported his income, £30, in 1586; the official certification was less, £20. In the levy of the next year he was named but not charged anything, which testified to the honesty of his offer of £6. 13s. 4d.[181] William Yaxley, esquire, appears to have been the wealthiest Catholic in East Anglia, at least of those recorded as convicted recusants in 1586. The official certification of his income in that year was £1000, but Yaxley asserted that outrents, annuities, reparations and other charges against his estate reduced his income to £220 per annum. It is not clear if his property were appraised in 1580; in 1587 he paid a levy of £50. Since he was long under official surveillance, his offer of £40, considering the debts which he listed, his numerous dependents, and the payment of £280 in recusancy fines, represented a fair proposal.[182]

[178] S.P.12/142/33 [?1580], /188/38.14 (March 28, 1586), /189/54 (May 1586), /200/61 [?1587].
[179] S.P.12/188/38.15 (March 28, 1586), /189/54 (May 1586), /200/61 [?1587].
[180] S.P.12/188/38.5 [?1586], /189/54 (May 1586), /200/61 [?1587].
[181] S.P.12/188/38.12 (1586), /189/54 (May 1586), /200/61 [?1587].
[182] S.P.12/142/33 [?1580], /188/38.1 (April 1586), /189/54 (May 1586), /200/61 [?1587].

Surrey, where recusants from other counties were at times confined, listed eleven recusants, including one knight and two esquires. A note appended to S.P.12/189/54 added that there were thirty-seven yeomen and handicraftsmen in various prisons in the county, who reportedly had neither lands nor goods, but whose religious persuasion is also not given. From the context we might conclude that they were Catholics, but it is only a surmise. The maximum income of the nine whose values were reported was £500, the minimum, £2; the total was £1313. All eleven offered composition, the maximum being £66. 13s. 4d., the minimum, £1; the total was £243. 6s. 8d.[183] We have examined eight of the eleven Surrey recusants. Edward Banyster of Hampshire, ranked both as a gentleman and an esquire, was worth £200 annually in lands and £200 in goods jointly with his wife in both 1577 and 1580; in the latter year he was charged two lances. In 1586 both his self-declared annual income and the official certification were £200; in 1587 he was charged only the minimum, £25 — it was made in Surrey, where he was still detained. The offer of composition, £30, considering his prominence as a recusant, was probably reasonable, but we have no data concerning his debts and other charges with which to make a judgment.[184] Robert Becket of Cornwall, ranked both as a gentleman and an esquire, was worth £66. 13s. 4d. annually in lands and £300 in goods in 1577 and 1580; in the first levy he was assessed one lance. In 1585 he was charged £40, but not for an alternative lance or light horse; in 1587 he paid the sum required of him, £25. In 1586 his certified income was £40; he offered one-fourth of this, £10, in composition. All the data concerning Becket's estate shows that it was small; but the keeper of the Marshalsea, where he had been confined since 1580, suggested that Becket had an income of £200 per annum; no evidence was offered in support of this and it was probably only a surmise.[185] John Beconsawe of Hampshire, gentleman, had been imprisoned since 1580 at the White Lion at Southwark. He was worth £800 in goods in 1577

[183] S.P.12/189/54, 55 (May 1586).
[184] S.P.12/117/10.1 (October 1577), /142/33 [?1580], /189/48 (May 31, 1586), /54 (May 1586), /200/61 [?1587].
[185] S.P.12/117/25.1 (October 28, 1577), /140/40 (July 1580), /142/33 [?1580], /159/36 (March 23, 1584), /169/26 (March 22, 1584), /170/11 (April 8, 1584), /180/64 (July 1585), /183/15 [?1585], /189/48 (May 31, 1586), /54 (May 1586), /200/61 [?1587].

SOCIAL AND ECONOMIC STATUS OF CATHOLICS

and 1580; in the latter year he was assessed one lance; in 1585 he was charged £40 or one light horse. In 1586 his certified value was "nil." Although he complained of his poverty, having no living amounting to 20s., he made two offers of composition, one of £6. 13s. 4d., the other, in the master sheet, of £10. Most likely friends were willing to help him out, since a petition filed in his behalf at this time sought his release from prison because of ill health and he was characterized as obedient in all things except religion.[186] Francis Browne, esquire, had an annual income from lands of £133. 6s. 8d. in 1577 and 1580 and in the levy of the latter year he was charged both one lance and one light horse. It is not clear if he were assessed in 1585; two years later, however, he was charged and paid £25. His certified income in 1586, which agreed with his self-estimate, was £91; we have no evidence of debts, fines, or distraint of property with which to appraise the reasonableness of his offer of composition, £20, except that it was a sizable part of his income when taken in conjunction with the normal debts of one of his rank.[187] Sir William Catesbie, one of the few Catholics of more than local prominence, declared his income to be £500 in 1586 and this was officially certified to be accurate. His offer of composition, £66. 13s. 4d., seems small in terms of his income; and the levy placed against him in 1587, £75, was below the maximum. We know nothing about his debt structure or payment of recusancy fines; but as he was long under close government supervision, the data which we possess undoubtedly reflects his wealth correctly.[188] Lady Catherine Copley apparently had lost or did not possess requisite data concerning her estate. She offered £30 in composition.[189] Thomas Pownde, gentleman, was worth £100 in goods in 1577; he was assessed £40 or one light horse in 1585; he received an annual income, it was recorded in 1586, of £12 from his mother, to whose care he had been paroled after years of imprisonment. He may possibly have been assessed in the wrong county in 1587 and therefore did not make any payment. His offer of £3 very evidently was all that

---

[186] S.P.12/117/10.1 (October 1577), /140/39 (July 31, 1580), /142/33 [?1580], /169/30 (March 23, 1584), /170/13 (April 8, 1584), /183/15 [?1585], /188/16.1 (April 1586), /189/21 (May 15, 1586), /48 (May 31, 1586), /54 (May 1586).
[187] S.P.12/117/14.1 (October 1577), /142/33 [?1580], /183/15 [?1585], /189/48 (May 31, 1586), /54 (May 1586), /200/61 [?1587].
[188] S.P.12/189/48 (May 31, 1586), /54 (May 1586), /200/61 [?1587].
[189] S.P.12/189/48 (May 31, 1586), /54 (May 1586).

he could afford to pay.¹⁹⁰ John Talbot of Grafton in Worcestershire, esquire, who was confined by conciliar order to Surrey, was valued at £1000 annually in lands and £3000 in goods in 1577 and 1580. In the levy of 1580 he was charged four lances and four light horses; seven years later he was required to pay £100, which he did. His self-declared income in 1586, which was officially certified as accurate, was £440, a rather low figure for one very close to a great earldom. The normal expenses of one of his station and the financial hardships consequent to the long period of restraint under which he had lived, besides pressing debts, made reasonable his offer of composition, £66. 13s. 4d.¹⁹¹

Sussex listed thirty-seven recusants, including four esquires and seven gentlemen. The income of only eight was given, the maximum being £92, the minimum, £4; the total was £219. 6s. 8d. Obviously this did not reflect the true wealth of the Sussex Catholics because eleven offered compositions, with a maximum of £50, although the minimum was very small, 10s. The total offered also was small, £123. However, twenty-six made no offer: five could not be found; two were "beyond seas"; ten were out of the county, two of them being in the Tower of London; five were dead; and four were conformists.¹⁹² If the figures for Sussex are accurate, most likely the more influential and wealthier recusants were among those out of the county. We have selected six of those listed for further investigation. George Britten, gentleman, had a certified income in 1586 of £40 and paid a charge of £25 in 1587. Depending upon difficulties of identification he may have been included in the census of 1577 and the levy of 1580 and he may have been imprisoned earlier in the 1580's. We have no evidence of debts or losses or distraint of property as criteria to measure his offer of £5, one-eighth of his income.¹⁹³ Edward Gage, esquire, had been living generally in London since his release from the Marshalsea about two years previously. In 1577 and 1580 he was appraised at £200 annual rental value in lands and at £200 in goods; he was required to furnish two lances

---

¹⁹⁰ S.P.12/117/10.1 (October 1577), /140/40 (July 1580), /159/36 (March 23, 1584), /178/74 (May 27, 1585), /183/15 [?1585], /189/48 (May 31, 1586), /54 (May 1586), /193/2 (September 1, 1586), /200/61 [?1587].
¹⁹¹ S.P.12/118/11.5 (November 5, 1577), /142/33 [?1580], /189/48 (May 31, 1586), /54 (May 1586), /190/11 (June 9, 1586), /200/61 [?1587].
¹⁹² S.P.12/189/54, 55 (May 1586).
¹⁹³ S.P.12/117/26.1 (October 28, 1577), /142/33 [?1580], /169/26 (March 22, 1584), /170/11 (April 8, 1584), /189/54 (May 1586), /200/61 [?1587].

SOCIAL AND ECONOMIC STATUS OF CATHOLICS

in the latter year. His income was not recorded in 1586, but the next year he paid a levy of £25. Since this was the minimum charge, his offer of £50 in composition would seem to be reasonable.[194] Thomas Gage, esquire, lived on an annuity in 1577 derived from a trust set up by his father from lands worth £40 annual rental value; he had no goods. For unexplained reasons, perhaps due to a partial loss of rents, his income in 1586, officially certified, was £20. He offered £5 in composition, which evidently was all that he could afford, although we have no knowledge of his financial encumbrances.[195] John Leedes, esquire, had a certified income in 1586 of £92, out of which he offered £20 in composition. We have no other data about his economic worth, except that he was charged £50 in 1587 but apparently died before he could pay it.[196] John Shelley, esquire, offered £20 in composition in 1586, and paid a levy of £25 in 1587. We have no other data of his financial value.[197] John Temple, gentleman, offered £6. 13s. 4d. We possess no other data concerning his estate.[198]

Wiltshire listed six recusants, of whom one was an esquire. The incomes of three were listed: the maximum was £500; the minimum was £20; the total was £550. All six made offers of composition, the largest being £20, the smallest, £1. 6s. 8d.; the total was small, £35. 6s. 8d.[199] John Codrington, gentleman, was worth £100, the profit derived from rents, in 1577 and 1580; and he was charged one lance in the first levy. His income in 1586, derived from two tenements, was £12, but would increase ultimately to £13. 6s. 8d. (20 marks). He offered £5 in composition, part to be paid at Michaelmas, the rest at Easter.[200] William Faulconer, esquire, declared his income in 1586 to be £300; the official certification, however, placed it at £500. His expenses were very considerable, especially as he had no ready money. He had already paid £500 in recusancy fines; he maintained three dependents; he had two annuities charged against his estate; in 1587 he paid a levy of £25 and

---

[194] S.P.12/117/15 (October 26, 1577), /142/33 [?1580], /159/36 (March 23, 1584), /189/48 (May 31, 1586), /54 (May 1586), /200/61 [?1587].
[195] S.P.12/117/15 (October 26, 1577), /189/54 (May 1586).
[196] S.P.12/189/54 (May 1586), /200/61 [?1587]. Leedes's death is not certain. A John Leedes appears in subsequent recusant records.
[197] S.P.12/189/54 (May 1586), /200/61 [?1587].
[198] S.P.12/189/54 (May 1586).   [199] S.P.12/189/54, 55 (May 1586).
[200] S.P.12/117/26.1 (October 28, 1577), /142/33 [?1580], /188/15, 15.1 (April 12, 1586), /189/54 (May 1586).

he may have been assessed in 1585, although it is not clear. The deteriorated condition of his estate is evident in his request that his offer of composition, £20, could be paid in two installments annually.[201] Robert Goldsborough lived on an annuity inherited from his father, which subsequently would be worth £10 for ten years. He offered £2 in composition, which he could pay only in two semiannual installments.[202] Henry Mayhew, gentleman, long an invalid, had disposed of his estate some years before, probably devising it on a son, except what was needed for supporting himself and his immediate family. He had been fined £66. 13s. 4d. in the Star Chamber for various causes, including hearing mass at the Spanish embassy some years before. He was paying this off at the rate of £4 a year for the next six years and 53s. 4d. for the seventh year; he had also deposited a bond of 100 marks (£66. 13s. 4d.) to appear before the High Commission. In 1577 and 1580 his lands had been appraised at £45 annual rental value and he was charged one light horse in the latter year. In 1587 he did not pay a levy of £25. His income in 1586 was certified to be £30, derived partly from twenty-nine arable acres, partly wooded. He offered £5 in annual composition, to include the Star Chamber fine.[203]

Worcestershire listed sixteen recusants, including one esquire, five gentlemen and one peeress. The total of the incomes, £217. 10s. 0d., represented the worth of only two persons, the larger sum being £200, the smaller, £17. 10s. 0d. All of the sixteen recusants made offers of composition: the maximum was £30; the minimum was 10s.; the total was very small, £86. 16s. 8d.[204] We have selected five recusants for further investigation. Dorothy Heath, a widow, was worth £1000 in goods in 1577 and 1580; she was charged one lance in the latter year. There is no record of her financial worth in 1586, but she offered £6. 13s. 4d., which was to include her son, William. In justification of this sum she pleaded a small living, the care of two children at home, an unpaid dowry of a daughter, and heavy debts left her by her husband.[205]

[201] S.P.12/183/15 [?1585], /188/15, 15.1 (April 12, 1586), /189/54 (May 1586), /200/61 [?1587].
[202] S.P.12/188/15, 15.1 (April 12, 1586), /189/54 (May 1586).
[203] S.P.12/117/26.1 (October 28, 1577), /142/33 [?1580], /188/15, 15.2 (April 12, 1586), /189/54 (May 1586), /200/61 [?1587].
[204] S.P.12/189/54, 55 (May 1586).
[205] S.P.12/118/11.5 (November 5, 1577), /142/33 [?1580], /189/54 (May 1586), /190/11.1 (June 9, 1586), /11.7 [?June ?1586].

SOCIAL AND ECONOMIC STATUS OF CATHOLICS

Hugh Lygon, gentleman, defended his small offer of composition of £2 as being the most which he could afford due to his continual illness. His living of £17. 10s. 0d. was certified to be income from annuities, out of which he supported his family. In 1587 he was unable to make payment of £25.[206] John Middlemore, esquire, pleaded that he was constantly in debt and unable to become solvent because of continuing expenses. No appraisal of his estate was given; obviously he had devised most of his property on his children, since his eldest son had an annuity of £40 per annum and additional sums, probably the income from a trust set up out of lands, and one married daughter had a dowry, part unpaid. He still had four children dependent on him. In 1587 he failed to pay a levy of £25. Judging from Middlemore's circumstances, his composition, £6, probably reflects accurately his financial worth.[207] Lady Mary Throckmorton had a certified income of £200, over and above all her heavy debts, including the care of three children. She offered £13. 6s. 8d., which in view of the prominence of her family must have been made honestly, although it seems small.[208] Lady Catherine Windsor was one of the very few among the 128 recusants who was of highly distinguished lineage. She was the daughter of the sixteenth Earl of Oxford and widow of the third Lord Windsor of Stanwell. Her financial resources, however, seemed to have declined over the years, partly due to an unfortunate subsequent marriage and divorce. In 1577 and 1580 she possessed only a moderate estate, obviously her widow's jointure, of £200 annual rental value in lands and £666. 13s. 4d. in goods; she was assessed two lances and one light horse in the latter year. In 1587 she paid a levy of £50. Her income was not recorded in 1586, but in offering £30 in composition she asserted that this would render impossible the payment of her debts and the maintenance of her necessary charges. She proposed this amount, nevertheless, to secure liberty of conscience and to prove her allegiance to the Queen. Very obviously, now advanced in age, she was confused about the circumstances of her life.[209]

[206] S.P.12/189/54 (May 1586), /190/11.1 (June 9, 1586), /11.11 [?June ?1586], /200/61 [?1587].
[207] S.P.12/189/54 (May 1586), /190/11.1 (June 9, 1586), /11.6 [?June ?1586], /200/61 [?1587].
[208] S.P.12/189/54 (May 1586), /190/11.1 (June 9, 1586), /11.3 [?June ?1586].
[209] S.P.12/118/11.5 (November 5, 1577), /142/33 [?1580], /189/54 (May 1586), /190/11.1 (June 9, 1586), /11.2 (April 2, 1586), /200/61 [?1587].

The 128 recusants whom we have investigated constitute in our judgment a representative sampling of the Elizabethan Catholics — the Catholics who in 1586, the year which we have taken as our criterion, were uncompromised; the Catholics who preferred conviction for recusancy to conformity to the Establishment. Conviction excludes from our consideration part-time conformists (as of the records of 1586) and persons, such as members of the Cornwallis family, who enjoyed immunity from prosecution. Although we have studied recusants in only twenty-two counties and S.P.12/189/54, 55 included the records of recusancy in only twenty-five, we feel certain from the data which we have used in the other chapters of this book that the records of recusancy of the counties omitted from the master sheet would not materially alter the judgments which we express in this chapter.

One hundred and ten of the recusants were men. Only one was a peer, the impecunious Lord Vaux of Harrowden, whose family had been ennobled only fairly recently; the two Talbots were related, one closely, the other distantly, to a great peer; some others were related by blood or marriage to the nobility, but did not stand in the line of inheritance. Seven of the 128 were knights, none of them persons of more than most minor importance in the Elizabethan world, except possibly Sir Thomas Tresham, who was the only recognized spokesman for his fellow Catholics. Forty-three ranked as esquires and thirty-seven as gentlemen; fourteen were variously listed as esquires and gentlemen. Three were lawyers, but a number of others had practiced law in the past; only one of the lawyers, James Braybrooke, was considered of some distinction in his profession. Two were physicians, but of so little importance as to be almost obscure. Three of the men bore no designated status. None of the 110 held official positions of any importance, except John Towneley of Towneley in Lancashire, who was steward of certain royal properties; some, however, may have been justices of the peace.

Of the eighteen women, one, Lady Catherine Windsor, by birth and marriage belonged to the peerage; another belonged to a recently ennobled family, Dame Elizabeth Paulet, of the family of the Marquess of Winchester. The other five listed as "lady" were apparently wives or widows of knights or perhaps for courtesy reasons bore the title. Except for one servant, the remaining eleven women were probably of gentry families or of wealthy urban families; it is not clear.

SOCIAL AND ECONOMIC STATUS OF CATHOLICS

The economic status of the Elizabethan Catholics can be pictured only most tentatively. They did not form a segregated group; they were an integral part of a locality, on terms of friendship with their Protestant neighbors, to whom they were frequently related by blood and marriage. Adherence to the traditional church did not raise bars of distinction socially or economically; this was especially true of the Catholic rural gentry, the most influential and affluent of those still belonging to the Church of Rome and who of necessity form the element by which we judge Catholic economic worth. The wealth of a Catholic family represented its inherited property and the competence of the head of a family to maintain or increase the size of his estate. Catholics, like their Protestant neighbors, reflected the standards of living of their area of residence; both groups struggled hard to manifest the standards of their class, even if it meant expensive ostentation, so characteristic of upper-class Elizabethan landowners. The distribution of wealth, prices, and living expenses varied in the different parts of England, which renders impossible any very exact picture of the economic worth of the Elizabethan Catholics as a group. But it was much more economic conditions and the expenses connected with one's status in society than recusancy fines which shaped the financial worth of the Elizabethan Catholic.

The importance of the recusancy fine imposed in 1581, £240 a year, is that it threatened bankruptcy to a good many families otherwise solvent and able to maintain their standard of living by adding an extra obligation, crushingly heavy. Elizabeth wisely recognized this situation when she opened to the Catholics the possibility of compounding for their recusancy fines; we today can judge this situation in the light of the plea of the Catholics of Berkshire contained in the well-attested county report of their offers of composition that "following the privatt zeale of our Consciences we are deprivable of our Liberties, and subiect to the continuall paymentes of farr greater somes of Money then eyther our goodes or ye yearly profittes of our Landes and Livinges can discharge or satisfye . . ."[210]

An unnumbered minority, we must conclude, of a certain economic, social and cultural grouping, the lesser gentry, tended to remain Catholic because of conscience or early education or environment or sentiment. They were not a cohesive bloc, but rather were scattered throughout

[210] S.P.12/187/45.1 ([?March 18] 1586). We have altered some of the spelling.

various counties. Since they did not form an economic unit, but instead reflected the conditions of their environment, we can only make a rough approximation of their economic worth.

Certain of the recusants, in filing reports of their wealth in 1586, reported their estates as "small" or "poor." Seven of these had yearly incomes of £200 or above:

(1) Michael Hare, Suffolk: income, £800; composition, £50; heavy recusancy fines and debts.
(2) John Towneley, Lancashire and London: income, £500 (official certification, £200); composition, £66. 13s. 4d.; heavy recusancy fines and other expenses.
(3) Robert Downes, Norfolk: income, £400; composition, £20; heavy debts.
(4) Richard Martin, Suffolk: income, £400; composition, £6; expenses of dependents.
(5) John Daniell, Suffolk: income, £300; composition, £20.
(6) Margaret Daniell, Suffolk: income, £300; composition, £20; heavy expenses.
(7) George Cotton, Hampshire: income, £200; composition, £40; heavy expenses.

The characterization of six of these estates as "small" and that of Robert Downes as "poor" was undoubtedly according to a generally accepted public estimate, which took into consideration social status and the holdings in land, income and the manner of living equated with that status. "Small" and "poor," however, were relative terms. They meant that the owners of the estates bearing such labels possessed lands of such extent that the income derived from them was insufficient to warrant heavy expenditures — expenditures for the acquisition of more land or any large-scale plan of enlarging and beautifying buildings or the buying of luxuries, all of which were evidences of class status. The heavy debt structure which six of these seven reported, as did so many others of the 128, further reduced their income and limited still further the possibility of increasing the manifestations of class. But if Hare's and Towneley's estates were small, then this is even more true of the majority of the 128 recusants since their estates per annum were worth even less, and in many of their cases the debt structure also was heavy. On the other hand, from all that we can infer, both Hare and Towneley lived fairly comfortably, if not ostentatiously, which, judging from evidence spread out over a goodly part of Elizabeth's reign, must also have been true of a certain proportion of those even less affluent. Very few were valued above these two recusants, but some of equivalent or slightly larger incomes would seem to us to have enjoyed the same or possibly a higher standard of living. These would be Thomas Throckmorton, John Gage, William Yaxley, Edward Rookwood, William Faulconer, and Edward Sulliard; we feel that certain others possessed invisible sources of income which also warrant their inclusion — Nicholas Longford, Sir Alexander Culpepper, Sir William Catesbie, John Talbot of Grafton, Sir John Arundell, Dame Elizabeth Paulet and Sir Thomas Tresham.

When we analyze the expenditures reported by the 128 recusants, other than the levies of horses, we find that forty-five gave some description of their structure of debts; forty-three listed dependents; six had settled dowries on daughters (one unpaid) and six had made provisions for sons, such as devising property on them; thirteen had had their property distrained for nonpayment of recusancy fines; and twenty-five had paid recusancy fines, wholly or partly. Thirty-five were currently imprisoned for recusancy or had been sometime during Elizabeth's reign. This was a serious cause of financial loss, since it disrupted the economy of a household, removing the legal head of the family, whose decisions were necessary in managing land, making sales of property, paying taxes and conducting the upbringing and education of children. Imprisonment, too, was the cause of ill health and expensive medical treatment.

If persons of the income and estates of Thomas Throckmorton, John Gage, Michael Hare, John Towneley, Edward Rookwood, Edward Sulliard, William Yaxley, Sir William Catesbie, John Talbot of Grafton, William Faulconer, and possibly also Sir Alexander Culpepper, Sir John Arundell, and Sir Thomas Tresham could not pay the required £240 per annum required by the statute of 1581, what was the income required to be able to pay it and yet maintain one's status in society? We cannot establish this without a complicated economic analysis beyond the scope of this study. But it seems to us that a recusant with £300 per year income, by practicing extreme frugality, by periodic borrowing, by alienating no lands in order to provide for younger sons and to endow daughters, could for a time have paid the fine of £240. But in the long run such an estate would have deteriorated. Interest rates, high in the sixteenth century, always cut deeply into income. Dowries for daughters and provisions for younger sons were fixed charges paid usually by annuities, which had to be met even in times of economic distress — family pride, if nothing else, forced the payment of them. And family pride forced the maintenance of some outward manifestation of status, even at the cost of increased debt. Obviously Elizabeth thought it justifiable to maintain the standards of status when she offered the recusants the possibility of making composition; obviously the Catholics intended to maintain the signs of class, even though it brought about the risk of distraints being levied on their lands and goods to recover unpaid recusancy fines.

But only very few received annually £300 or more — and the £300, we must remember, was not usually clear income, but also included services which could be measured by or turned into money and securities against which one could borrow (lands and chattels), which admittedly introduces a confusing concept of capital into the concept of income: Thomas Throckmorton, Buckinghamshire, £666. 13s. 4d.; John Gage, London, £800; Thomas Gawen, London, £333. 6s. 8d.; Nicholas Longford, London, £320; John Towneley, London, £500; Robert Downes, Norfolk, £400; John Daniell, Suffolk, £300; Margaret Daniell, Suffolk, £300; Michael Hare, Suffolk, £800; Richard Martin, Suffolk, £400; Roger Martin, Suffolk, £400; Edward Rookwood, Suffolk, £500; Edward Sulliard, Suffolk, £440; William Yaxley, Suffolk, £1000; Sir William Catesbie, Surrey, £500; John Talbot (of Grafton, Worcestershire), Surrey, £440; William Faulconer, Wiltshire, £500. Of these seventeen recusants, only Throckmorton offered as much as £100 composition; Yaxley, obviously the wealthiest, offered only £40 because of his expenses.

Probably only Thomas Throckmorton and William Yaxley with certainty and possibly also John Gage would economically rank above the lesser gentry; we might include Sir William Catesbie and Sir Thomas Tresham, judging from general appearances but no exact knowledge. Socially John Talbot of Grafton and possibly Sir Alexander Culpepper, Sir John Arundell and Edward Rookwood would also rank above the lesser gentry, despite their lesser means; Arundell, of course, presents us with a question, since we do not know his worth in 1586, but all evidence, including his composition, proves that he had a considerable income, limited by heavy expenses.

The question arises why the government considered these 128 persons to be of prominence, although of varying degrees of prominence, and why did it spend the time and money in keeping certain of them under almost constant scrutiny? The answer lies in the fact that in the hierarchical society of Elizabeth's day, the upper classes, including the lesser gentry, commanded a respect from and wielded an influence over the lower classes. Even a person lacking wealth, who belonged to a family of local or greater consequence, received this respect and exercised this influence. This explains the longstanding attention which the Council paid to the relatively nonaffluent Catholic gentry of Lancashire and Herefordshire. In Norfolk the thirteen recusants who paid compositions were all recorded as influential, although not one ranks as a person of sizable estate. To a government intent upon achieving at least exterior conformity to its religious policy, since conformity was considered basic to social and political stability, any dissenter who might influence others could not hope for long to escape official watchfulness.

Our conclusion, which is a repetition of the substance of this chapter, is that the largest group within Elizabethan society which remained Catholic was a network of families related by blood, marriage, and close friendship who socially and economically ranked for the most part among the lesser gentry of certain counties. Only a few of these families had roots deep in the past; most of them had risen to affluence and had become members of the gentility through success in law or in trade, which enabled them to become landholders and to become established as landed families. Some had been yeomen who by hard work and expansion of landholdings had in time been accepted as part of the gentility of their counties. But by Elizabeth's day the social rank of this network of families was well established and recognized by their neighbors of all classes, and in Mary Tudor's reign some of them had held influential positions and probably would have again if England had returned to Catholicism. During Elizabeth's rule their interest was chiefly in land; only a few of them seem to have been persons of any considerable education or of very cultivated tastes. Possibly only two, Edmund and Francis Plowden, sons of the great lawyer, had attended either of the great universities, although it seems probable that some of the others had, whether or not they had received degrees. Three were recorded as lawyers, James Braybrooke, George Lewkner and Francis Bastard, but some others had had legal training and at least some of them had practiced their profession in the past. Besides Braybrooke, Henry Everard and Michael and Robert Hare had belonged to the Inner Temple in the past; the census of 1577 listed three others without identifying them by their Christian names — Gawen, Ticheburne, and Yate — who may have been the persons of those surnames included among the 128 recusants; and a Bekinsall of Hampshire may have been either John Beconsawe or William Becanshawe.[211] Henry Mayhew (listed as Henry May) and Richard Tremaine had formerly been affiliated with Lincoln's Inn.[212] Richard Culpepper and Walter Norton had been members of Gray's Inn at one time, and certain others were listed as members in 1577 who were probably among the 128 — J. Bedingfield, J. Yaxley, and W. Yaxley.[213] Two physicians were listed among the 128 recusants, Thomas Fryer (or Freer) and William Woode, but we know nothing of their training since they were of little standing in their profession. Sir Thomas Tresham, who may have had legal training, was the only Catholic among the 128 who had any kind of national standing; a few, such as Sir John Arundell, Sir William Catesbie, and Lord Vaux were great magnates on the local level. No one of the 128 was an artist or scholar or writer of repute in an age of dynamic cultural development. Most of them seem to have been in middle age or beyond in 1586: they had been young at the time of Elizabeth's accession and by the 1580's they had shaped their lives and their interests around their families, their professions and their lands.

In the critical years of 1587 and 1588 and during the subsequent fifteen years of Elizabeth's reign the official policy toward the general body of the laity of imprisonment, fine, and distraint of property continued unrelaxed. But it did not grow harsher. The explanation, it seems to us, is that the Queen still wanted primarily the conformity of the Catholics; that penalization was a secondary aim. The levies of horses and the dealings for compositions of 1586–1587 showed that, by and

[211] S.P.12/118/69 (November 1577). [212] S.P.12/118/70 (November 1577).
[213] S.P.12/118/71 (November 1577).

large, the Catholics were an entity of limited influence and of moderate and less-than-moderate wealth. Obviously they could not be an internal threat; the negotiations for compounding between commissioners and recusants evinced no unity among them other than the sharing of a common religious belief. The general sentiments which they manifested exhibited no trace of treason and many signs of loyalty; the undertone of resentment to be found in some of the offers of composition was not sufficiently evidenced to negate the sincerity of the general Catholic loyalty. Given these circumstances it was, indeed, needless for the government to adopt a severer policy toward the Catholics; it was a measure of its statesmanship that it did not do so.

The government was by no means satisfied with the offers of composition. It could not but be angered by the bitter tone of some of the answers and the evasive tone of others. Despite the detailed returns the officials at Westminster still lacked a complete picture of the wealth, the social status, and the degree of influence of the recusants in the various counties, and it was clear to these authorities that at least some of the commissioners authorized to make compositions wanted the interest or did not exert sufficient energy to fulfill their obligations properly, either out of favoritism of certain recusants or awe at their social status. Part of the difficulty lay, too, in the fact that some recusants were assessed on the basis of their holdings in only one county, whereas they possessed much wealth in other counties. Some used an antiquated method of rating their livings, thereby reducing their compositions. In certain localities the magistrates made no effort to find and compound with any other recusants than those contained in the Council's schedule or they avoided getting in touch with persons through chicanery, or they listed as "non-inventi" landowners out of the county at the time.[214]

Progress was slow. The master sheet of May 1586, S.P.12/189/54, 55, showed that the offers of composition were very inadequate; the total was only £3,198. 5s. 4d. out of wealth certified officially at £11,924. 3s. 4d. (which, correctly, should have been £13,049. 3s. 4d.). Another return, that of October (?) 1586, reported concerning the answers from twenty-four of the counties; nine others remained uncertified.[215] When a year later

[214] S.P.12/194/73 (October 1586).   [215] S.P.12/194/74 (October 1586).

there were still deficiencies in the returns, Lord Burghley ordered an inquisition into recusants who had not compounded.[216]

The summaries of May and October 1586 and the wealth of detail upon which they were based amassed in the government's files a veritable mountain of information concerning the Catholics. The Queen and her Council found that the body of Catholics lacked the wealth to pay the yearly recusancy fines in full; that not all were willing to pay; that some attempted to escape the recusancy fines and other impositions by devising property on children and through fraudulent means, of which there was undoubtedly more than mere suspicion considering the total volume of data which the government accumulated; that the existing common law procedure, distraint of property, needed amending since it yielded an insufficient amount in compensation for unpaid recusancy fines. In the face of a crisis caused by Catholics on the Continent, Queen Elizabeth brought about the enactment of legislation by the Parliament which met October 29, 1586, which at one and the same time defined the procedure of distraint more clearly, regulated conveyances of property more carefully, forced the Catholics to pay a share of the expenses of the crisis, and provided a control over them through financial limitations. Chapter VI of the acts of that Parliament, dealing with distraints, will be discussed subsequently in this chapter. What concerns us here is that this carefully thought out legislation was designed fully to effect the government's purposes while not reducing the recusants to such penury that they might become public charges.

2. THE ADMINISTRATION OF DISTRAINT OF PROPERTY

The two principal statutes affecting the economic status of the Elizabethan Catholics were 23 Eliz. c. 1, enacted by the Queen's fourth Parliament in 1581 and 28 and 29 Eliz. c. 6., enacted by her sixth Parliament in 1586.[217] The former imposed a fine of £20 per month or £240 per year upon persons above the age of sixteen who were absent from the liturgy of the Establishment; the latter, the statute of 1586, provided that a distraint was to be levied upon two-thirds of the lands possessed

[216] S.P.12/205/10 (November 4, 1587).
[217] The most competent treatment of the financial penalties levied upon recusants is in C.R.S., LIII, *Misc.*, 291–307. It is treated less extensively in C.R.S., XVIII, *Rec. Roll*, xi–xxiv.

by a recusant who defaulted in paying his fines and upon all of his goods. Distraint involved the sequestration of property and its disposal by a court of law or the Exchequer; the defaulter also might be imprisoned for nonpayment of debt. Both distraint and imprisonment were longstanding legal practices going far back into the Middle Ages; Elizabeth, in fact, simply followed out the Common Law practices and various statutes dealing with property in her treatment of the property of the Catholics. Between 1581 and 1586 the government found that the Common Law procedure of distraint was not only slow and inefficient, but if carried out completely threatened a landowner with bankruptcy. To avoid this, the officials at times permitted recusants to pay part of the yearly fine of £240 and remitted the remainder. But there was no uniformity in this regard, and the law of 1586 was based upon a policy which would simultaneously penalize recusants for their nonconformity and yet not impoverish them — or, as an alternative, induce them to conform. An analogy, it seems to us, was worked out between the act of 1586 and the Statute of Wills of 1540 (32 Hen. VIII., c. 1.), which provided that a landowner could devise two-thirds of his lands held by the medieval tenure of knight service and all of his lands which he possessed in socage: the owner retained the title; the beneficial enjoyment (usufruct) went to another, but under terms which if not carried out entailed return of the lands to the devisor.

The procedure of distraint now came to be that a defaulter's lands were seized by the government and leased out, usually for a period of years (generally twenty-one, the most common period of time for which farmlands were then leased), to secure the unpaid balance. The defaulting recusant retained the title to his lands, since the Crown, again by analogy, was only the trustee for his property. The recusant owner might, at the discretion of the Exchequer, compound for a certain sum and save his estate. Such an agreement was precarious, especially if the value of the lands increased; the government might then annul the composition, distrain the property and rent it out. In the complicated case of Francis Parkins, which was probably typical, the government reopened a prosecution for distraint because the value of the property had increased after Parkins had already worked out a composition.[218] However, the Exchequer did not necessarily (at least for some years)

[218] C.P.59/91 (February 21, 1599).

demand an increase in rent from lands which had appreciated in value after the legal process of distraint and leasing out at a fixed rent had been completed.

As one goes deeper into the problems connected with the leasing-out of distrained lands, the picture becomes ever more involved. Complexities, the meat of lawyers, arose, if the distrained lands were subleased or if the Crown for some reason decided to terminate the distraint. The government might be almost overwhelmed with protests from recusants who retained title to lands which the usufructuary was ruining through neglect or deliberate injury; for if the officials did not intervene, the owners could obtain redress only through complex legal proceedings. And special assessments, such as the levies of horses, were rated upon the theoretical wealth of a man based on his title to land, not upon his actual income from a reduced portion of his holdings.

The administration of the law of 1586 was still not altogether satisfactory from the government's viewpoint. The Recusant Roll of 1592–1593, although quite ample, consisted in good part of the repetition of the names of persons convicted in various counties where they possessed property. Lord Burghley, in a memorandum of 1594, stated that the government had made a catalogue of those who paid the fine of £20 per month and had listed 161 recusants who had forfeited the rent of two-thirds of their lands.[219] This was, at best, a small number of distraints, considering the number of recusants obviously unable to pay the full annual recusancy fine. We do not know how many more paid their recusancy fines in full by 1600 or how many in that year were suffering the distraint of their property, but it was estimated at the turn of the century that the recusants collectively owed £7000 yearly to the Exchequer.[220] Not until Thomas Felton in 1597 was put in charge of searching out recusants delinquent in paying their fines in order to initiate such action as was necessary to compel them to meet their arrears was the procedure of distraint put on an efficient basis. Manifold opportunities, however, for abuses remained. Although the purpose of the law of 1586, to prevent the recusant from being so impoverished that he would become a public charge, was not negated, Felton's ruthlessness caused a good number of the Catholics to feel a growing financial distress.

[219] S.P.12/248/9 (March 6, 1594).   [220] S.P.12/276/62 [?1600].

Various examples, both before and after Felton's appointment, illustrate the working of the distraint of lands. In 1589 Robert Worsley, custodian of recusants in Lancashire, was granted the leases of lands of recusants convicted through his instrumentality (turning over to the Queen certain rents), a concession evidently made to repay him for losses involved in his custodianship.[221] In 1590 part of the rent from the lands of Sir Thomas Tresham, sequestrated for recusancy, was granted to a John Vacham (? Vachall).[222] And in the same year Queen Elizabeth gave to Elizabeth Hill, apparently a relative on the Boleyn side, £200 from the forfeitures of six recusants.[223] When Walter Norton, a long-time recusant standing convicted in Norfolk and in Suffolk, died in 1594, he was heavily indebted for his recusancy, for which his lands had been extended and rented out.[224] Two manors of Edward Banyster (or Bannester) situated in Sussex, with an annual rent of £82, were leased out for twenty-one years;[225] lands with an annual rent of £18 of three deceased recusants in Yorkshire, because of defaults in the payment of recusancy fines, were leased for the same period;[226] and two-thirds of the manorial lands of Thomas Blunt of Worcestershire were distrained and leased out, also for twenty-one years, at an annual rent of £13. 6s. 8d.[227] When Rooke Greene, an oldtime recusant many times convicted in Essex, died in 1602, he was deeply in debt for his intransigent recusancy, for which two-thirds of his lands had been distrained and leased out.[228]

In more ample detail the experiences of two very well-known recusants will make even clearer the serious losses, inconveniences, and harassments attendant upon the execution of judgments against property.

Thomas Gawen was first indicted for recusancy in 1581, and his lands and goods had been distrained and rented out to pay his recusancy fines. In 1591 this lease was revoked; and these lands and others more recently inherited from his mother were leased to another, who in turn subleased them to Gawen's children. Thomas Felton, the chief financial

---

[221] S.P.12/229/68 [?1589]; *A.P.C.*, XVIII, 278–279 (December 27, 1589).
[222] S.P.12/233/91 (Docquet: S.P.38/1; October [10], 1590).
[223] C.P.1596 (petition; 1590). [224] S.P.14/5/23 (December 29, 1603).
[225] S.P.12/273/48 (Docquet: S.P.38/6; December 18, 1599).
[226] S.P.12/273/50 (Docquet: S.P.38/6; December 23, 1599).
[227] S.P.12/274/22 (Docquet: S.P.38/6; January 22, 1600).
[228] S.P.14/5/23 (December 29, 1603).

agent for prosecuting recusancy, later sued out a new inquisition, bringing about a revaluation and a new rating of the lands; he then ejected Gawen from his holdings of 1700 acres, allotting to him 300 acres. Gawen, with a large family dependent on him, in the meantime had suffered almost continuous imprisonment. Feeling that no one could have satisfied the demands of the religious laws more fully, he asked that he be allowed to pay the Queen £20 a month in place of the rent reserved to her from his property, and that indictments pending against him be quashed.[229]

Robert de Grey had sustained great losses over many years because of his recusancy; perhaps the most ruinous was the loss of his woods, the best of which, worth £500, had been felled by Felton and his assigns and taken away. Besides this the yearly rental value of his land had been raised from £41 to £160, the maximum, de Grey claimed, for which all his lands were ever rented. Other property worth £160 had been seized, and his cattle and corn on the third part remaining to him were taken and sold for £25, the money being deposited with the sheriff. Felton and his assigns, it was asserted, had paid nothing in rent to the Crown, but had received £500 in rent for themselves. When some years before de Grey's losses were substantiated by the depositions of witnesses, the late Lord Burghley took pity on him and revoked the leases on the forfeited two parts, and a *supersedeas* had been granted to prevent further inquisitions into his property. Felton, however, had received a privy seal, granting to him any arrearages of de Grey's rent due the Crown. Because the regular rent to the Queen had been paid ever since the revocation of the leases (for the property was still legally sequestered, although de Grey had received back the use of it), to make this concession of profit to the grantee, Felton was also authorized to receive the surplus of de Grey's rents, after subtracting what the latter needed for his living. That recusant had indeed suffered heavily, paying in ten years £2,800 in recusancy fines. Now old, he begged for a measure of relief.[230]

Thomas Felton was now the key to the prosecutions for nonpayment

[229] C.P.370 (petition [?1599]); S.P.12/271/108 (July 22, 1599). The contents of this petition of Thomas Gawen to Sir Robert Cecil are difficult to verify from other sources.

[230] C.P.1305 (petition [?1600]). It is difficult to verify the contents of de Grey's petition from other sources.

SOCIAL AND ECONOMIC STATUS OF CATHOLICS

of recusancy fines. He began his duties in August 1597,[231] being empowered to conduct inquisitions into sequestrations of land, where some defect existed, such as non-execution, and into sums of money or other arrearages due to the Crown and unpaid, and to prosecute where there was nonpayment, evasion, or misevaluation.[232] The work was tedious and dangerous. Felton, in order to be compensated adequately, petitioned to receive one-sixth of the income from the sequestrated lands of each recusant whose conviction he secured, in lieu of his original annual payment of £200 to which rewards were also added. After much hesitation the Queen granted him the equivalent of this one-sixth from other sources, retroactive to the date of his appointment (August 24, 1597), less what he had already received.[233] Eventually, it would appear, his petition for one-sixth of the revenues from the lands of convicted recusants was granted to him.[234]

Felton and his associates, Sir Edward Greville and Sir Henry Bromley, worked with vigor. It is difficult for the historian today to determine their honesty and their competency, especially in regard to Felton; much of the data which we must use concerning him comes from obviously unfriendly sources. Cases in which the three were interested were very frequently referred to Chief Justice Popham; to secure more certain results, many recusants were reindicted.[235] These pursuivants then sequestered the lands and goods, including even those things most necessary to persons living off the land.[236] Under a ruling of the lord treasurer made after the enactment of the Parliament of 1586–1587 concerning distraint of recusants' property, anyone who brought about the indictment and conviction of a recusant would have the right to lease two-thirds of the land at the rent determined in the official evaluation, always saving the rights of the Queen being the understood premise. Many of these particular leases were indefinite in tenure, causing the recusant who had already paid heavy fines and otherwise had suffered

[231] S.P.12/283A/88 (May 7, 1602).
[232] S.P.12/270/118 (Docquet: S.P.38/6; May 24, 1599), /271/108 (August 1, 1599), /283A/88 (May 7, 1602), /286/56 [?1602], S.P.14/28/144 [?1607].
[233] S.P.12/283A/69 (March 31, 1602), /87 (April 28, 1602), /88 (May 7, 1602), /286/56 [?1602].
[234] S.P.14/28/144 [?1607].
[235] S.P.12/271/33 (July 9, 1599), /106 (July 31, 1599), /108 (August 1, 1599), /274/103 (Flanders Correspondence [extract]: S.P.77/6, April 26, 1600).
[236] S.P.12/271/106 (July 31, 1599), /107 (July 21, 1599).

substantial losses to endure much for his religion. Any subsequent increase in his wealth, whether through his labors or by inheritance, was now subject to distraint.[237] To insure that no one escaped, Felton had his agents travel up and down the realm on the lookout for recusants to be prosecuted.[238]

Felton by no means acted without suspicion or opposition. The Queen apparently had her doubts, and some opposition within the ranks of government officials developed against him.[239] A contemporary report, charging him with dishonesty, stated that while enriching himself he had increased the Queen's revenues only £1,000 a year, and much of what he had accomplished was actually the work of other agents.[240] In Durham, for instance, Henry Sanderson was responsible, at least in part, for raising the Queen's rental from recusants' lands in a very difficult area in which to labor.[241]

The commissioning of Thomas Felton to be the chief pursuivant made the prosecution of the Catholic recusants a lucrative profession. Technically his position was that of a law-enforcing officer; his purpose was to render efficient the hitherto more-or-less haphazard enforcement of the law dealing with those defaulting in paying their recusancy fines. But the vigor with which he carried out his work rendered him notorious, and his greed, whether supposed or real, brought him criticism. By the end of the reign the Catholics hated him perhaps more than any other of Elizabeth's officials.

3. THE LEVY OF HORSES OF 1598

Elizabeth in 1598 imposed a levy of horses for service in Ireland, which, due to administrative difficulties, ran on for some years to come. The Council, with precedents of the 1580's to guide it, sent out letters to the principal recusants of means, Catholic and Protestant, throughout the realm directing each of them to contribute £30 within ten days, the sum being the amount considered necessary for equipping and maintaining a horse and its rider. The first group assessed obviously were

---

[237] S.P.12/271/108 (August 1, 1599). Document has been injured and is slightly defective.
[238] S.P.12/271/33 (July 9, 1599), /106 (July 31, 1599), /108 (August 1, 1599), /283A/87 (April 28, 1602).
[239] S.P.12/283A/87 (April 28, 1602), /88 (May 7, 1602), /286/56 [?1602].
[240] S.P.12/286/56 [?1602].   [241] C.P.180/128-129 (June 27, 1600).

men of substance and among them we find William Faulconer, John Gage, Thomas Gawen, Michael Hare, Roger Martin, Edward Sulliard, John Talbot of Grafton, Thomas Throckmorton and Sir Thomas Tresham.[242]

By no means were all recusants willing to pay. Two gentlemen in Oxfordshire, apparently Catholics, declared that they preferred to answer in person to the Council rather than make a contribution.[243] After a period of some weeks had elapsed, five others, one of them being Thomas Gawen, still continued to neglect sending their money, drawing down upon themselves the threat of being cited before the Council.[244] Toward the end of August that body ordered five hitherto unsolicited recusants to pay £30, including William Roper of Kent and Rooke Greene of Essex.[245] Shortly afterwards the Council wrote to the Archbishop of York that the assessments for horses must be levied against both gentlemen and yeomen recusants, since recusancy was so very general throughout the north, and many in that category were known to be of good economic condition. It further directed the Archbishop to make the levy, as he, rather than the Council, would know better who should be assessed in the counties of Cumberland, Lancaster, Northumberland, York, and the diocese of Durham. The wealthier were to pay £30, the less wealthy £15, within ten days; anyone who refused was to appear before the Privy Council to explain his reasons.[246]

On August 31 the Council ordered forty-six recusants in various counties to pay £15, including some prominent persons previously overlooked, among them Humphrey Bedingfield, Robert Downes, Henry Everard and John Yaxley of Norfolk, and Sir Alexander Culpepper of Kent.[247] Similar orders were sent out on September 3 to seventeen recusants, two being women, although one of the men in this group was discharged by the Council because of insolvency.[248] Fifteen letters were sent the same day to the Bishop of Chester, who was to select fifteen recusants of means to whom they were to be delivered. That

---

[242] *A.P.C.*, XXVIII, 582–583, 588–589 (July 16, 1598); XXIX, 72–73 (August 21, 1598).
[243] *A.P.C.*, XXIX, 28–29 (August 1598).
[244] *A.P.C.*, XXIX, 72–73 (August 21, 1598).
[245] *A.P.C.*, XXIX, 79 (August 23, 1598).
[246] *A.P.C.*, XXIX, 111–112 (August 30, 1598).
[247] *A.P.C.*, XXIX, 116–118 (August 31, 1598).
[248] *A.P.C.*, XXIX, 131 (September 3, 1598), 231–232 (October 23, 1598).

prelate ordered four men and one woman in Lancashire to contribute £15 apiece, and sixteen men and four women were paired off in groups of two and ordered to furnish £15 between them.[249] On the first of October nine Dorset, Devonian, and Cornish recusants of substantial means, seven men and two women, were each assessed £15.[250]

The government intended to obtain full payment, but the force of its power was still weak in the north and success in making collections was balanced by outright refusals to contribute and by evasion. When a number of recusants in Lancashire in November 1598 refused to pay, the Council decided to make an example of them. Those most recalcitrant were commanded to appear before that governing body, and the Bishop of Chester was directed to order the rest to make payment or suffer penalty.[251]

In February 1599, the agent appointed to collect the levy in Yorkshire and the neighboring counties reported a serious deficit in the total amount he was required to gather, having obtained only £434 from twenty-five recusants. Nine recusants in Yorkshire, eight in Durham, and eight in Northumberland and Westmorland, owing an aggregate of £465, refused to make any payment.[252] In Lancashire most nonpaying recusants evaded apprehension by absenting themselves from their residences. The sheriff, perhaps intentionally, had had almost no success in tracking down those of the upper classes, but had little difficulty in finding persons of the lower classes or of more or less incapacitated condition.[253] By the next month twenty-eight were discovered and had paid in an aggregate of £280, having been assessed from £5 to £20 apiece; eight of these were conformists paying assessments against their wives.[254]

Due probably both to the continued need for armed horses in the Irish campaign and the slowness of some recusants to make payment, the levy had to be collected over a period of years. On February 4, 1600, twenty-three persons, including Robert de Grey, Richard Martin,

[249] *A.P.C.*, XXIX, 132 (September 3, 1598), 219–220 (October 6, 1598).
[250] *A.P.C.*, XXIX, 203 (October 1, 1598).
[251] *A.P.C.*, XXIX, 300–301 (November 22, 1598).
[252] S.P.12/270/36 (February 8, 1599).
[253] S.P.12/266/18.1 (January 12, 1599), /18.2 (January 6, 1599), /18.3 (January 1599).
[254] S.P.12/266/80 (February 1599), /270/41 (February 18, 1599).

and Francis Plowden, were ordered to make payment, nineteen of them being assessed £15 and four of them £30.[255] During the previous two years the collection of this tax had run into difficulties, as some had pleaded inability to pay due to the extending of their lands for recusancy. By another order of February 4 the Council directed an investigation into nonpayment.[256] On May 11 thirteen counties were certified as being delinquent wholly or partly in meeting the required sums and thirty persons who had not satisfied their assessments were ordered either to pay or to explain their noncompliance. Immediately this was modified, because four had paid (two of the four had paid half of the charge and were discharged); five had been discharged of their assessment; one was not a recusant; one was dead; and the levy against one was reduced by half, from £15 to £7. 10s. 0d. Of the remainder four were assessed £30 and fourteen were assessed £15.[257] In 1601 levies were placed on fourteen recusants in Berkshire, nine in Bedfordshire, seventeen in Buckinghamshire, and eleven in Cambridgeshire.[258]

Certain additional facts help to make clearer the economic condition of the Catholics at the end of Elizabeth's reign. Individuals in Hampshire, Kent, London, Wiltshire and Worcestershire had to pay in full whatever sum was levied upon them, a testimony of their ability either to meet the required £15 or £30. Others, however, received remission of part or of all of the levy against them because of their depressed financial condition. The Council permitted a Hampshire recusant, (? Gilbert) Welles, to pay only half of his assessment of £30; and the London counsellor-at-law, (? Arden) Waferer, received the same concession from the Lord Chief Justice. Robert Lovell of Norfolk and William Faulconer and Thomas Gawen of Wiltshire received discharges from their assessments, adequately proving the serious deterioration of their estates. In early May 1600 Samuel Love of Kent and William Wiseman of Essex were reassessed (possibly having failed to meet the first charge levied against them), and some others, including Lady Catesbie of London and Richard Lloyd of Shropshire, were assessed for the first time. Francis Gatacre of Shropshire, who once long before had conformed, was certi-

---

[255] *A.P.C.*, XXX, 53 (February 4, 1600). [256] *A.P.C.*, XXX, 43 (February 4, 1600).
[257] *A.P.C.*, XXX, 305–306 (May 11, 1600), 309–311 (May 11, 1600).
[258] S.P.12/283/65 [?1601]. We have been able to identify some, but not all, of the names to be those of known Catholics.

fied as deceased. The only recusant in Lancashire upon whom a levy was placed in May had already conformed and was relieved of his obligation.[259] Robert de Grey, who had been assessed the previous February, begged for relief, pleading his losses due to the legal disposition of his property by the pursuivant, Felton.[260]

Although the government collected a fairly voluminous body of information concerning the Catholics in the responses to the levy of 1598, it failed to make out a master sheet, sifted and checked as in 1587, which would give us well-authenticated data. Perhaps we should not be surprised at the hostile reaction of some to the levy and the unwilling or lackadaisical attitude of others: in the 1580's Elizabeth's life expectancy, since she was middle-aged, could be a factor inducing even recalcitrants to accommodate themselves to her rule; by 1598 and after, members of a disfranchised minority probably saw little reason to curry favor with her, if it worked to their financial disadvantage. But we must not overlook the fact that a sufficient number of Catholics paid willingly not to arouse the suspicion or the ill will of the Queen and her government toward them as a body.

[259] *A.P.C.*, XXX, 310–311 (May 11, 1600).
[260] C.P.1305 (petition [?1600]).

CHAPTER V

THE END OF THE REIGN

Throughout the reign of Elizabeth it has been very evident that the English Catholics lacked any effective leadership, spiritually or politically. Except for the brief flurry of the short-lived mission of Campion and Parsons in 1580 and 1581 and the literary output of so talented a person as Robert Southwell, the Catholics within the realm were almost devoid of writers, at least of writers who contributed substantially to a great age of culture or added significantly to the works about the spiritual life or to the religious polemics characteristic of the times. The exiles who went from England to the Continent, both priests and laymen, were, however, more vocal and more ambitious. Some of them engaged in intrigues against the Elizabethan regime; others, such as Thomas Harding at Louvain in the 1560's, wrote apologetical books. By the 1580's and more so by the 1590's the emphasis in the printed works had shifted largely to the field of political propaganda; the defeat of the Armada intensified this.

In the early years of the 1590's a priest, Wright (alias Dobson), wrote a short, closely reasoned book, *An licitum sit Catholicis in Anglia arma sumere, et aliis modis, Reginam et Regnum defendere contra Hispanos?*,[1] to justify to certain Catholic questioners — unknown and unnumbered — the rightfulness of defending Queen Elizabeth and their country against the Spanish king. The gist of this brief treatise was a rejection of the papal-Spanish program of recatholicizing England through con-

[1] We have used the translation from the original Latin in John Strype, *Annals of the Reformation and Establishment of Religion,* etc., III (London, 1728), 251–258, and also another edition, vol. III, pt. ii (Oxford, 1824), 583–597. The date and place of publication of Wright's little work is not known.

quest and the deposition of Queen Elizabeth I; the writing of such a work by a Catholic for Catholics indicated that a current of disillusionment was surely overcoming at least some members of the traditional church.

Another evidence of this disillusionment is a letter which Sir Thomas Tresham wrote to the Archbishop of Canterbury and the other privy councillors in March 1590, again defending the loyalty of the Catholics within England. He pointed out that he and his coreligionists were different from the Huguenots in France, being faithful and submissive to their ruler, not engaging in civil war against the lawful authorities nor bringing in foreign forces to fight their cause. Despairingly, because he and others must always suffer imprisonment whenever there was a threat of a Spanish invasion that placed a question mark over their loyalty, Tresham stressed that peace between England and Spain seemed impossible. Spanish aggression expressed itself in seizing English ships, putting the sailors to the galleys, and attempting attacks upon the realm. England, in turn, had harassed the Spanish treasure ships, entered into Spanish ports with hostile intent, and had assisted the Portuguese pretender, Don Antonio, against Philip II with armed aid.[2] But the vocal Tresham, pleading so frankly the cause of his coreligionists, stood apart from a body that, disfranchised, had become almost mute.

The strongest sentiment among the exiles on the Continent during the 1590's, a sentiment we find among the Catholics within the realm at the end of Elizabeth's reign, was the hope for a successor who would be a Catholic or at least kindly disposed toward the ancient faith. The first landmark expressing this, written toward mid-decade, was *A Conference abovt the next Svccession to the Crowne of Ingland,* generally but not of certainty attributed to the Jesuit, Robert Parsons. Typical of the dialogue form of that era, it treated of a civil lawyer expounding the legal and ethical aspects of monarchy and of a temporal lawyer analyzing the genealogy of the Tudors and related families and their rights to the English crown. The suggestion was put forward for a general agreement after Elizabeth's death by all the states of Europe to the enthronement of the Infanta Isabella, daughter of Philip II of Spain, as the most suitable candidate for England's throne.[3]

[2] H.M.C., *Var. Coll.,* III, 51-59 (March 25, 1590).
[3] We have used the first edition of this book, at the Houghton Library of Har-

The bitter reaction to this book on the part of some of the Catholics lasted until the end of the reign;[4] they felt that it threatened to involve them even more in the resentment of Elizabeth, who could not but consider such a writing to be an unwarranted intrusion into a crown prerogative. Already, within England, the ranks of the clergy were beginning to split over a number of questions — loyalty to the Queen, the constitution of an ecclesiastical authority for the clergy in England, and the relations between the Jesuits and the secular priests. Although each of these problems had its separate importance, judgments about them were coalesced into a single viewpoint by each set of disputants in the heated quarrels marking the closing years of Elizabeth's reign.

After the deposition of the Catholic hierarchy in 1559, Rome made no plans for episcopal supervision of Catholic needs in England until the abortive attempt to send the long-exiled Bishop Goldwell, onetime ordinary of St. Asaph in Wales, to England with Campion and Parsons in 1580. Undoubtedly, throughout this period approaching a generation, the papal authorities had considered that once England was recatholicized through conquest or diplomatic means, a hierarchy would be appointed; and Cardinal Allen, expecting the success of the Armada, composed a list of nominees for the various sees.[5] In the succeeding ten years there were still hopes of a conquest; and distance and administrative slowness in the curia and the existing control by Cardinal Allen explain such continued negligence. No doubt the peculiar position of that prelate, frequently styled "patriarchal," seemed feasible while he lived, although it comprised a system of ecclesiastical government that was extracanonical, haphazard, and, considering time and distance, very makeshift. In the uncertainty that followed his death in 1594, it was thought that another English cardinal ought to be appointed; but this never materialized, and the question of jurisdiction remained open for settlement.[6]

---

vard University, published in 1594 at N. (?) under the pseudonym of R. Doleman. It went through a number of subsequent editions. We wish to thank the Reverend Leo Hicks, S.J., of the Jesuit Farm Street residence in London for the use of a copy in his personal library.

[4] C.P.33/85 (June 21, 1595), 43/41 (August 1, 1596); S.P.12/274/111, 112 (April 23, 1600), /283A/70 (March 1602).

[5] Oratorians, *Card. Allen,* cvi–cvii, 303–304 (December 11, 1587).

[6] John Hungerford Pollen, *The Institution of the Archpriest Blackwell* (London, 1916), 1–4; Thomas Graves Law, *A Historical Sketch of the Conflicts between Jesuits and Seculars in the Reign of Queen Elizabeth* (London, 1889), xxvii.

Since by this time the position of Catholics and Protestants in England had become well-defined, any ecclesiastical organization of the former would tend to solidify them as a group and make more precise their attitude, hitherto amorphous, vis-à-vis the government. It could, as a consequence, bring in its train the possibility of a new, more hostile, much harsher policy on the part of the Elizabethan regime toward the Catholics. The choice of the religious superior, whoever he might be, whatever his outlook and rank, obviously would be the key to the new situation. In the spring of 1598, not a bishopric but an archpresbyterate, to be filled by George Blackwell as archpriest, was erected. Over him, vested with appellate powers, was the papal nuncio in Flanders. Since the Jesuit, Parsons, had been instrumental in determining this affair at Rome, the archpresbyterate possessed, however unwarrantably, a pro-Spanish tinge in the eyes of those secular priests who had come to the conclusion that the Catholics — all of them — should avoid irritating the government and instead seek for some measure of toleration. To these seculars, filled with an ever-deepening suspicion that the Jesuits were engaged in intrigues which embittered the Queen and increased the severity of the laws against the Catholics, the papal requirement that the archpriest follow the advice of the Jesuit superior in England rendered the new ecclesiastical organization still more odious. This resulted in two appeals to Rome by the dissentient priests, the second of which brought about some modifications in the constitution of the archpresbyterate, eliminating Jesuit influence, but not resulting in any rapprochement between Rome and England that might alter the condition of the English Catholics.

The significant fact for this study is that there is little evidence that the lay Catholics became involved in this quarrel between the seculars and the regulars.[7] A petition for toleration presented to James VI by the Scottish Catholics claimed that Queen Elizabeth's permission to the dissident seculars to make an appeal to Rome and her request that the French government extend diplomatic protection to four envoys of that group in the Eternal City had reacted in favor of the Queen, influencing

---

[7] The Jesuits in England at this time were few in number and the secular priests involved in the Archpriest Controversy were a minority of the whole. We are convinced, after considerable sifting of the evidence, that it is very hard to substantiate the claim that the Jesuits within England inculcated any pro-Spanish sympathy among the Catholic laity.

various English Catholics to turn away from foreign loyalties to fealty to Elizabeth.[8] Considering the disfranchised condition of the Catholics it was but normal that some of the laity would be anti-Elizabeth, whether or not they were pro-Spanish or were influenced by the current clerical controversy; two sources, admittedly biased, bear this out. The secular priest, Christopher Bagshaw, asserted in 1598 that the wisest among the lay Catholics wanted the priests to confine their efforts solely to the spiritual sphere;[9] and another secular, John Cecil, stated that a considerable number of English of both sexes within England and in exile came to the aid of the Jesuits during the adjudication of the Archpriest Controversy at Rome by declaring in their favor and against their opponents.[10] Some pro-Spanish sentiment was reported among the Catholics in the Midlands at the death of Elizabeth, but the proof is very meager.[11] An old-time recusant, Gervase Pierpoint of Nottinghamshire, and two Lincolnshire Catholics, Richard Thimelby and Edward Forset, were arrested in April 1600 for having in their possession a letter from Parsons to the Earl of Angus dealing with the question of succession and the claim of the King of the Scots. Since any communication from that Jesuit was a highly incriminating piece of evidence against any Catholic, they were imprisoned in London.[12] In the Gunpowder Plot it was asserted (but the evidence is conflicting so that we cannot be certain exactly what was the truth), that in the year before Elizabeth died, certain highborn English Catholics with Jesuit aid sent a layman and a member of that order to Spain to find out what help they could receive in case of rebellion. Whatever contacts these two messengers made in the southern monarchy, their mission resulted in nothing.[13] It must be noted, too, that in the State Papers is an anonymous pamphlet, "Discourse of the

---

[8] C.P.205/122 [?1602, ?1603].
[9] *Archpriest Controversy,* I, 205 (October 19, 1598).
[10] *Archpriest Controversy,* II, 61.   [11] C.P.99/124 (April 17, 1603).
[12] *A.P.C.,* XXXI, 85 (January 7, 1601); S.P.12/274/110, 111, 112 (April 23, 1600), /124 (May 2, 1600), /135, 136 (May 10, 1600). Gervase Pierpoint had personally assisted the Jesuit Campion in his travels. Richard Thimelby was thirty-five years of age and had not attended the Establishment for twenty years. Edward Forset was an openly admitted recusant.
[13] C.P.112/91 (November 26, 1605), 115/19 (March 15, 1606). Both documents state that a second attempt to secure an invasion was made by the same parties at the death of Elizabeth and accession of James I. The contemporary confession of the Jesuit superior, Henry Garnet, casts some doubt on the first plot, that of a year before Elizabeth's death (C.P.115/13, April 13, 1606).

providence necessary to be had for the settinge upp the catholick faith when god shall call the Queene out of this life," [14] which is similar at least in part to the ideas for the recatholicization of England contained in the *Memorial for the Intended Reformation of England*,[15] generally attributed to Parsons. Whether or not the "Discourse" was written in the realm and to what degree it circulated there or had any influence cannot be determined; certainly its proposals for a violent seizure of England were never attempted. Nor do we have evidence that any of the laity in the last years of Elizabeth's reign advocated such a course of action.

The immediate ecclesiastical superior above the archpriest, the papal nuncio to Flanders, Octavio Mirto Frangipani, Bishop of Tricarico, distressed at the war-torn conditions of northern Europe, hoped to obtain an amelioration of the treatment of the Catholics in England. On November 13, 1601, he wrote to John Skinner, an upper-class English Catholic living at Calais, begging that layman to use his influence with leading members of the Queen's Council with whom he was on friendly terms and at court both for the welfare of the Catholic Church and for peace. Skinner complied immediately with the nuncio's request, but could gain no hearing from any person of importance.[16] Bishop Frangipani made a second attempt to establish relations with the English government, sending a message to Sir Robert Cecil through the dissentient secular priest, Francis Barnaby, asking to make the acquaintance of that minister, if it might be to the mutual good of each.[17] This request also came to nothing. Well-intentioned as were the efforts of the nuncio, they were obviously doomed to failure because they coincided with the adjudication of the complaints of the appellant secular priests against the archpresbyterate then pending at Rome. The Elizabethan government could hardly entertain proposals from a subordinate diplomat at a time when papal policy was in the process of restatement, which might involve a repudiation of Frangipani's intent. And nothing was done after

---

[14] S.P.12/286/60 [?1598, ?1599]. This document is in an Elizabethan hand. S.P.12/275/56 is identical, but the hand is possibly of a later date.

[15] *The Jesuit's Memorial for the Intended Reformation of England*, etc., Edward Gee, ed. (London, 1690). We have seen no certain proof that Parsons was the author of this book; it was claimed to have been discovered among the abandoned effects of James II.

[16] C.P.183/79 (November 13, 1601), /90 (December 22, 1601).

[17] C.P.90/4 (December 15, 1601).

the decision in the adjudication had been given. Instead, Elizabeth's government, incensed at the terms decreed at Rome, ordered the exiling of all the priests[18] — but before this could be effected, the Queen died.

Clement VIII, as early as 1600, laid down plans for a future policy to be followed out at the time of Elizabeth's death. In July of that year he drew up three briefs, which he apparently sent to the papal nuncio in Flanders, Bishop Frangipani, to be kept for future use — one for the guidance of the nuncio, one for the Archpriest, George Blackwell, and one for the English Catholics.[19] The latter two, and possibly also the brief to the nuncio, were superseded by new directives about a year before Elizabeth's death.[20] The second communication to the laity commanded them in very uncompromising terms not to accept any new ruler, no matter how valid his claim by descent, unless he was willing not merely to grant toleration, but actively to promote Catholicism.[21] Separate copies of these second briefs to the clergy and to the laity were sent to the resident superior of the Jesuits within England, Henry Garnet, who briefly showed them to the Archpriest Blackwell. However, at the accession of James I, because the hope of a Catholic prince was so obviously futile, Garnet burned them.[22] The brief history of Pope Clement's attempt to bring about a Catholic succession shows, as did the litigation in the Archpriest Controversy, how little correct knowledge and how little understanding the authorities in Rome had of English affairs and explains the long and haphazard handling of the English question by the papal officials.

The persons most concerned, the Catholics within England, were too scattered and too lacking in cohesiveness to formulate a policy or to carry through a plan in regard to a successor. As early as 1599 it was reported that the Catholics — or some of them — were promising James VI of Scotland their support for the English throne in return for concessions and that the monarch had given them a favorable answer.[23] Others, too,

---

[18] S.P.12/285/52 (November 5, 1602).
[19] M. A. Tierney, *Dodd's Church History of England,* III (London, 1840), lxx–lxxi; IV (London, 1841), cvi–cviii. We have not found these three briefs of July 1600 in either the State Papers or the Cecil Papers.
[20] S.P.14/19/42 (March 13, [?1606]), /87 (March 26, 1606); C.P.115/19 (March 15, 1606).
[21] S.P.14/19/42 (March 13 [?1606]), /87 (March 26, 1606).
[22] S.P.14/19/42 (March 13 [?1606]); C.P.115/13 (April 13, 1606).
[23] S.P.12/271/105 (July 21, 1599), /106 (July 31, 1599).

believed that James had made the same promises to them and spread this news abroad, no one more ardently than the secular priest, William Watson, who possibly was mentally unbalanced.[24] Although Watson in his dealings with the northern monarch had probably spoken the feeling and the wish of the majority of English Catholics, he certainly bore no authorization to do so. In the existing conditions in England under Elizabeth I it would have been next to impossible to solicit Catholic sentiment or support for James of Scotland beyond that offered by small groups and individuals. Most probably the majority sentiment of the Catholics was that the decision concerning succession rested in other hands than theirs, as it did, and that they could only accept whatever happened.

When Queen Elizabeth died toward the end of March 1603, one current of opinion among priests and laymen expressed bitterness against her, and complained that the new monarch, James I, might have granted the Catholics toleration if they had possessed strength through unity under the leadership of an able peer. Alone, the amiable Lord Montague was a possible, but unlikely, leader.[25] Sentiment for a Spanish succession was reported to be found among Catholics in the Midlands, and opposition to the accession of James I,[26] but the general history of 1603 gives little evidence that this was widespread. Obviously, since the Catholics formed no bloc, they lacked the power at this vital moment to better their condition. Instead, when James arrived in England in April of 1603, the Catholics assured him of their loyalty and urged him to remember that they had suffered both because of him and because of his mother. Their request of him was very simple — private, if not public, freedom of cult.[27]

This paucity of evidence brings us up against the fact that only Sir Thomas Tresham expressed anything more conclusive than the vague and scattered opinions which we have just observed, and his viewpoint is important because he was the recognized spokesman for a responsible (although unnumbered and possibly small) group of Catholics. Shortly

---

[24] Samuel R. Gardiner, *History of England,* 1603–1642, I (London, 1887), 99–100, 108–109; D. Harris Willson, *King James VI and I* (London, 1956), 148–149; Tierney, *Dodd's Church History,* IV, xix–xx.
[25] S.P.14/1/7 [?1603].　　　　　　　　　　[26] C.P.99/124 (April 17, 1603).
[27] S.P.14/1/56 ([?April] 1603).

after James became king, Tresham explained his attitude in a paper setting forth why Elizabeth had had a better right to enact laws against the Catholics than James I had to continue enforcing them. Much of the content was probably the result of years of reflection concerning the doctrines of Catholicism and the reasons for England's dissent, lending a special significance to his words. Necessity, he asserted, for a firm support of the Queen's rule — a support which Catholics, not recognizing the legitimacy of her birth, would have had difficulty in manifesting — had forced Elizabeth to repress them as inimical to her rights. Her claim to the throne had come, not from legitimate birth, which neither Catholics nor Protestants recognized, but only from Henry VIII's will and an act of Parliament. If bastardy or other causes had disabled her from ascending the throne, the rightful heir after Mary Tudor was Mary Stuart. If this question had been raised and Elizabeth was still a practicing Catholic, the pope, presuming that he had acted as judge, most likely would have favored the Scottish queen in order to conform with previous papal decisions concerning Anne Boleyn and the Princess Elizabeth. Suspicion of Protestant leanings during her half-sister's reign and the influence which the French king possessed at Rome would further have militated against a favorable judgment. Prejudice, deep and lasting, would also have affected the decision because her mother had caused the abolition of Catholicism, the persecution of Catholics opposed to her marriage with Henry VIII, and the introduction of Protestantism. If the pope had thus ruled in favor of Mary Stuart when Mary Tudor died, the people would have adhered to the decision, since the majority of them, besides the clergy and the magistracy, were Catholic. Even if this had led to war, it would have made no difference, because Englishmen would have deserted Queen Elizabeth's cause completely, having no ties in religion or law binding them to her. Her opponent, Mary Stuart, possessed the further advantage of certain positive reasons which would attract support, because

Lastly, the Queen of Scots, ever firmly settled in the Catholic religion, a most virtuous and worthy prince, and so adorned with gifts of nature and fortune as none comparable to her, and withal the undoubted, righteous heir to Henry VII, and consequently to the crown of this realm if Queen Elizabeth was born in unlawful matrimony; and on the other hand the Lady

Elizabeth, if she should declare herself Catholic, yet no comparison to be had between them, but that the Catholics of this realm would much sooner make election of the Queen of Scots than of the Lady Elizabeth in manifold very principal respects, principally in the thereby happy uniting of these two realms.[28]

Tresham, it is thus evident, doubted the validity of Elizabeth's title as founded on birth, recognizing its legality only because Henry VIII and Parliament had sanctioned it. He conceded to Mary Stuart a strong claim through descent and on the grounds of religion, and viewed her accession as preferable to Elizabeth's. Why, then, did he profess so ardent a loyalty to Queen Elizabeth in the past? The answer would seem to lie, if we discard the fulsome flattery which he often used and credit Sir Thomas with sincerity, in the great respect for the established order characteristic of the time, in a dread of public disorder (so inimical to the welfare of the landed classes), and in a fear of foreign domination of England. Since by a valid law enacted by legitimate authority Elizabeth I possessed her sovereignty, it was understandable in Tresham's mind that she would take steps to preserve her position, even if it meant suppressing the church which he believed to be true. As a consequence a war of religion which would overthrow the legal sovereign and attack the good order of the Commonwealth was unjustifiable and inimical to England's best interests.

This opinion possesses further value in what it fails to consider. Tresham made no mention of Pius V's bull; he apparently did not view it as having any binding force. He also considered the legal enactments of England's governing institutions as the determinative factor in deciding the person of the monarch. Such a conviction bears the stamp of thinking that is secular and nationalistic; it is the product of a mind perhaps affected by Gallicanism, but certainly not formed by the currents of opinion exhibited in contemporary Continental Tridentine thought.

More than likely Tresham's ideas had been maturing over the years, and the patriotism of yesteryear had lost its meaning in the happy toleration which marked James I's first twelve months of rule. By 1603 he was undoubtedly embittered by the memories of harsh treatment under the preceding monarch in comparison with the more favorable condi-

[28] H.M.C., *Var. Coll.*, III, 128–132 [?1603].

tions which he was now enjoying. His previous acceptance of Elizabeth as the legal monarch and the person best fitted to promote the realm's well-being was becoming obscured in assessing an unhappy past, a repetition of which he hoped to prevent in the future.

CONCLUSION

In retrospect certain facts explain the pattern of Elizabethan Catholicism: (1) the Catholics were too few and too powerless either to prevent disestablishment at the beginning of the Queen's reign or to have a voice in the selection of her successor at the end of her reign; (2) the survey of the justices of the peace in 1564 showed that the majority of the local magistrates, drawn from the gentry, the most influential local class, adhered to the Establishment; (3) the one armed protest, the Northern Rebellion, failed because its sectional composition rendered it feeble; (4) the records of taxation and of censuses of recusants of the 1570's and the 1580's prove that the Catholics were of the minor gentry in wealth, status, and influence for the most part and formed sizable aggregations only in certain counties.

Elizabeth's policy did not reduce the Catholics to this minority status. Under her no persecution took place which duplicated that of Mary Tudor in England or that of Henry II in France; nor was there fratricidal strife, such as marked Germany in the late 1540's and early 1550's and France in the second half of the sixteenth century. The Catholic laity, reared since birth in a traditional belief, were judged to be civilly disobedient because of their nonconformity, but no more. The change of religion, in the eyes of the Queen and her Council, was a sovereign prerogative of the ruler of a state, who was responsible for all aspects of the welfare of a realm. Like governing officials of all ages, the Queen and the Council did not and could not overlook violations of the laws. Some injustices occurred and on the local level the authorities were occasionally very harsh, but executions of any of the Catholic laity were few and resulted from a confusing and subtle alignment of certain

CONCLUSION

Catholic activities with an attenuated concept of treason. All our evidence demonstrates that the Catholic layman did not live in fear of forfeiting his life but in dread of ruinous fines and repeated and expensive imprisonment. The best proof of this was the refusal of Elizabeth to do other than imprison the leading Catholics in the most critical of years, 1588.

Nor did adherence to the Church of Rome entail social ostracism. Marriages took place between Catholics and Protestants; they were friendly neighbors and equals in business relations; and Protestants unhesitatingly vouched to all levels of authorities that their Catholic neighbors, friends and relatives were loyal and obedient to all the laws except those defining religious belief.

The perplexing question, looking back over the forty-four years of Elizabethan Catholicism, is why the legally established church of November 1558, the Church of Rome, shrank to a small minority of Englishmen by March 1603? No great and sudden catastrophe had occurred in the interim; the Church of Rome simply diminished in adherents silently and rapidly, with little outward regret on the part of persons who had been born into it and now had willingly seceded from it.

When John Wyclif in the reign of Richard II attacked certain orthodox Catholic doctrines, the friars and monks hurried to the defense of the traditional beliefs; but Wyclif, like the sixteenth-century Huguenots, maintained his influence so long as he had powerful support. Under Edward VI there was a determined number of bishops and others who, in the face of a hostile government, defended much of the substance of traditional Catholic orthodoxy; lacking official support they were silenced. But in Elizabeth's day disestablished Catholicism had almost no bold apologists, other than some exiles of minor competency, belonging to the generation of 1559; and the later Continental-trained priests, however heroic their lives, were not the equals of the great Tridentine theologians who were their contemporaries on the Continent. And what surprises us is that the Catholic laity, unlike many of the Puritans, were so silent, so quiescent, so very anxious only to live out their lives in peace.

The great medieval church in England had had eminent scholars, great preachers and learned bishops, all of whom had helped to foster a deep spiritual life among clergy and laity alike. By the fifteenth century the church had sunk into inertness: the secular priest in the rural parish was a poorly trained apprentice with defective knowledge and no adequate spiritual formation for his high calling; the urban priest was somewhat better trained, though still defectively, in what today we would call secondary schools; only a minority of the regular and of the secular clergy received a university training, grounding them solidly in theology and in canon law, and only the members of the religious orders received something of a religious formation. Bishops were all too often chosen because of their ability to serve the civil power, not because they possessed the requisite spiritual and intellectual qualities necessary for their high ecclesiastical state. In the century and a half before the final settlement of religion in 1559 the secular and regular clergy had so declined in competency that the administration of a parish or of a diocese and the observance of the rules of the religious orders had become largely a matter of routine, emphasizing externals and legalisms at the expense of the interior spiritual life.

The failure of the medieval church, however, does not explain the quick success of the Elizabethan Establishment. Until well into the Queen's reign it was nondynamic; it, too, long needed a highly competent clergy, other than some of the bishops and some of the lower clerics. The most influential factor inducing widespread conformity undoubtedly was both the dominance of the royal power and the deeply ingrained, indeed almost sacrosanct, reverence, which all classes felt for the Crown. The upper classes by training and intellectual formation and self-interest obeyed the royal will, and the lower classes by long conditioning followed the leadership and the example of those above them. That small minority which retained its adherence to the Church of Rome did so because its roots went very deeply into Catholicism and it had been closely connected with the reign of the Catholic Queen Mary Tudor. In the spring of 1603, when James VI of Scotland came south to the realm of his inheritance, the Catholics of England realized only too clearly that their lot was one of frustration; that they constituted a disfranchised, leaderless, amorphous group dependent for their welfare upon the will and the whim of the governing authorities.

APPENDICES

APPENDIX A: SUMMARY OF S.P.12/189/54, 55 (May 1586)

County	Persons listed	Individual values					Compositions				
		Number	Maximum (£. s. d.)	Minimum (£. s. d.)	Total (£. s. d.)		Number	Maximum (£. s. d.)	Minimum (£. s. d.)	Total (£. s. d.)	
Berks	53						41 (53)	13 6 8	2 0 0	138 6 8	
Buckingham	18	4	666 13 4	66 13 4	300 0 0 (900 0 0)		12 (17)	100 0 0	10 0 0	171 10 0	
Chester	8	3	240 0 0	13 6 8	273 6 8		6	30 0 0	2 0 0	72 0 0	
Cornwall	2	1					1 (2)			10 0 0	
Devon	2				30 0 0		1			10 0 0	
Dorset	5						2	6 13 4	2 0 0	8 13 4	
Essex	4	3	236 13 4	40 0 0	419 6 8		4	40 0 0	2 0 0	78 13 4	
Gloucester	3						1 (3)			20 0 0	
Hereford	22						19	50 0 0	1 0 0	129 16 8	
Kent	12						5	80 0 0	10 0 0	190 0 0	
Lancaster	9	6	133 6 8	26 13 4	933 6 6 (453 6 8)		6	40 0 0	3 6 8	96 13 4	
Leicester	7						2			10 0 0	
Lincoln	1						1			20 0 0	
London-Middlesex	24	7	800 0 0	100 0 0	1910 0 0		22	100 0 0	1 0 0	849 13 4	

APPENDIX A: SUMMARY OF S.P.12/189/54, 55 (May 1586)

County	Persons listed	Individual values								Compositions								
		Number	Maximum			Minimum			Total			Number	Maximum			Minimum			Total		
			£	s.	d.	£	s.	d.	£	s.	d.		£	s.	d.	£	s.	d.	£	s.	d.
Norfolk	27	6	400	0	0	133	6	8	1250	0	0	21	50	0	0	10	0	0	181	3	8
Northampton	2											2	6	13	4	2	0	0	8	13	4
Oxford	79	8	160	0	0	10	0	0	730	0	0	53 (79)	20	0	0	5	0	0	202	15	0
Salop (Shropshire)	4	4	66	13	4	6	13	4	113	6	8	4	6	13	4	1	6	8	17	0	0
Southampton	11	1							200	0	0	11	40	0	0	2	0	0	89	13	4
Stafford	27	3	100	0	0	30	0	0	170	0	0	23 (27)	20	0	0	10	0	0	65	16	8
Suffolk	16	13	1000	0	0	20	0	0	4420	0	0	16	50	0	0	6	0	0	339	6	8
Surrey	11	9	500	0	0	2	0	0	1313	0	0	11	66	13	4	1	0	0	243	6	8
Sussex	37	8	92	0	0	4	0	0	219	6	8	11	50	0	0	10	0	0	123	0	0
Wilts	6	3	500	0	0	20	0	0	550	0	0	6	20	0	0	1	6	8	35	6	8
Worcester	16	2	200	0	0	17	10	0	217	10	0	16	30	0	0	10	0	0	86	16	8
Total: 25	406	81							11924 (13049)	3 3	4 4)[a]	297 (347)[b]							3198	5	4

[a] Our corrected calculation of the total.
[b] The 297 compositions included 50 additional persons contained in joint offers.

APPENDIX B: 128 Recusants in 22 Counties

Berkshire
James Braybrooke, esquire, lawyer
Martha Braybrooke
Buckinghamshire
Augustine Belson, gentleman
Edward East, gentleman
Henry Mansfield, esquire
Thomas Throckmorton, esquire
Cheshire
Lady Edgerton, gentlewoman
William Hesketh, gentleman
Henry Latham, gentleman
Richard Massey, gentleman
John Talbot of Salesbury (Lancashire), esquire
John Whitmore, esquire
Cornwall
Richard Tremaine, gentleman
Devonshire
James Courtney, esquire
Essex
Thomas Crawley, esquire
Rooke Greene, esquire
Thomas Hale, gentleman
Herefordshire
Richard Davis
John Gomond, gentleman
Edmond Jones, gentleman
John Scudamore, esquire
Thomas Scudamore, gentleman
William Woode, physician
Kent
Sir Alexander Culpepper, knight
Richard Culpepper, esquire
William Tyrwhitt (or Tirwhitt, of Lincolnshire), esquire
Lancashire
Richard Blundell, esquire
William Haydock, gentleman
Elizabeth Kigheley, widow

John Rigmaiden, esquire
Sir John Southworth, knight
John Westbye, esquire
Leicestershire
Walter Whitehall, gentleman
Lincolnshire
John Thimelby, esquire
London-Middlesex
Sir John Arundell, knight
Rowland Barker, gentleman, esquire
Francis Bastard, lawyer, gentleman
Katherine Bellamy, widow
Humfrey Cumberforde, gentleman
Sir Thomas Fitzherbert, knight
Thomas Fryer (or Freer), physician
John Gage, esquire
Thomas Gawen, gentleman, esquire
Sir Thomas Gerrard, knight
John Gifford, esquire
Robert Hare, gentleman
John Hocknell, gentleman, esquire
Nicholas Longford, esquire
George Monox
Dame Elizabeth Paulet, widow, gentlewoman
Erasmus Saunders, gentleman, esquire
John Towneley, esquire
Sir Thomas Tresham, knight
Lord Vaux of Harrowden, peer
Thomas Wyllford, esquire
Francis Yate, gentleman
Norfolk
Edmund Bedingfield, gentleman, esquire
Elizabeth Bedingfield, widow, gentlewoman
Henry Bedingfield, esquire
Humphrey Bedingfield, esquire
Laurence Bedingfield, gentleman, esquire
John Downes, gentleman
Robert Downes, esquire

APPENDIX B

John Drury, gentleman, esquire
Robert de Grey, esquire
Henry Kervylle, esquire
Henry Lovell, gentleman
Robert Lovell, esquire
Ferdinando Paris, esquire
John Yaxley, gentleman
   Oxford
Lady Babington, gentlewoman
Richard Owen, esquire
Margaret Pitts, widow
Edmond Plowden, gentleman
Francis Plowden, gentleman
Lady Stonor, gentlewoman
   Shropshire
Richard Lloyd, gentleman, esquire
   Southampton
William Becanshawe, gentleman
George Cotton, esquire
George Lewkner, lawyer, gentleman
Elizabeth Titcheborne, widow
Nicholas Titcheborne, gentleman
Stephen Vachell, gentleman
   Staffordshire
Katherine Comberford, servant
Richard Fitzherbert, gentleman, esquire
Dorothy Heveningham, widow, gentlewoman
Ellen Maxfield (Macclesfield), widow, gentlewoman
William Maxfield (Macclesfield), gentleman
Erasmus Wolvesley, esquire
   Suffolk
John Bedingfield, gentleman
John Daniell, gentleman, esquire
Margaret Daniell, widow
Henry Drury, gentleman, esquire
Henry Everard, esquire
Michael Hare, esquire

Ambrose Jermine, gentleman
Robert Jetter, gentleman
Richard Martin, gentleman
Roger Martin, gentleman
Walter Norton, gentleman, esquire
Edward Rookwood, esquire
Robert Rookwood, esquire
Edward Sulliard, esquire
Thomas Sulliard, gentleman
William Yaxley, esquire
   Surrey
Edward Banyster, gentleman, esquire
Robert Becket, gentleman, esquire
John Beconsawe, gentleman
Francis Browne, esquire
Sir William Catesbie, knight
Lady Catherine Copley, widow, gentlewoman
Thomas Pownde, gentleman
John Talbot of Grafton (Worcestershire), esquire
   Sussex
George Britten, gentleman
Edward Gage, esquire
Thomas Gage, esquire
John Leedes, esquire
John Shelley, esquire
John Temple, gentleman
   Wiltshire
John Codrington, gentleman
William Faulconer, esquire
Robert Goldsborough
Henry Mayhew (or May), gentleman
   Worcestershire
Dorothy Heath, widow
Hugh Lygon, gentleman
John Middlemore, esquire
Lady Mary Throckmorton, widow, gentlewoman
Lady Catherine Windsor, peeress, widow

BIBLIOGRAPHY

BIBLIOGRAPHY

The bulk of this study has been based on three manuscript sources, the State Papers, Domestic, of Elizabeth I and of James I, the State Papers, Domestic, Additional, of Elizabeth I and James I, both at the Public Record Office, London, and the Cecil Papers at Hatfield House, Herts., and the published *Acts of the Privy Council of England*. Considerable references to the Catholic laity are also to be found in the Spanish Calendars. Although there seems to be an abundance of manuscript materials in other archives we found that the State Papers and the Cecil Papers provided sufficient data to determine the cultural, economic, political and social pattern of Elizabethan Catholicism; further evidence would simply have added details.

PRIMARY SOURCES

Manuscripts

Public Record Office, London:

State Papers, Domestic, Elizabeth I: Vols. 4, 7, 11, 12, 16–21, 23, 24, 36, 39, 41, 43–48, 59, 60, 66–69, 71, 73, 74, 81, 88–91, 97–99, 105, 108, 112, 114, 115, 117–120, 122, 123, 126, 127, 129–131, 133, 136, 138, 140–144, 146–157, 159–163, 165, 167–170, 172, 173, 175, 178–181, 183–195, 197–202, 204–206, 208, 209, 211, 213–215, 219, 224–227, 229, 231, 233–235, 239–244, 247–251, 253, 255, 256, 259, 260, 262, 263, 266, 268, 270–276, 278, 279, 281–287.
State Papers, Domestic, James I: Vols. 1, 5, 17, 19, 28.
State Papers, Additional, Elizabeth I and James I: Vols. 9, 11–15, 17–21, 23, 25, 27–29, 32.

The State Papers, Domestic, Elizabeth (289 volumes), the State Papers, Domestic, James I (216 volumes) and the State Papers, Domestic, Additional, Elizabeth I and James I (35 volumes) contain both official and unofficial reports concerning Catholics sent in by civil and ecclesiastical authorities, letters and other data from private citizens and spies, some data from abroad, census reports and tax records. The contents are varied; they cover both national policy and local conditions. Although some of the documents have been published wholly or partly in various books, it is necessary to refer to the originals. The indispensable guides to the State Papers are:

Calendar of State Papers, Domestic . . . of Edward VI., Mary, and Elizabeth, 1547–1580, Robert Lemon, ed. (London, 1856).

BIBLIOGRAPHY

Calendar of State Papers, Domestic . . . of Elizabeth, 1581–1590, Robert Lemon, ed. (London, 1865).
Calendar of State Papers, Domestic . . . of Elizabeth, 1591–1594, M. A. E. Green, ed. (London, 1867).
Calendar of State Papers, Domestic . . . of Elizabeth, 1595–1597, M. A. E. Green, ed. (London, 1869).
Calendar of State Papers, Domestic . . . of Elizabeth, 1598–1601, M. A. E. Green, ed. (London, 1869).
Calendar of State Papers, Domestic . . . of Elizabeth, 1601–1603; with Addenda, 1547–1565, M. A. E. Green, ed. (London, 1870).
Calendar of State Papers, Domestic . . . of Elizabeth, Addenda, 1566–1579, M. A. E. Green, ed. (London, 1871).
Calendar of State Papers, Domestic . . . of Elizabeth and James I, Addenda, 1580–1625, M. A. E. Green, ed. (London, 1872).
Calendar of State Papers, Domestic . . . of James I, 1603–1610, M. A. E. Green, ed. (London, 1857).

Hatfield House, Herts.:

Cecil Papers: Vols. 2, 6, 10, 29, 30, 42, 43, 45, 53, 55, 58, 59, 61, 63, 65, 68–70, 72, 73, 77, 78, 80, 83, 85, 89–94, 96, 97, 99, 100, 103, 109, 110, 112, 113, 115, 118, 138, 141, 154, 157, 159–162, 168, 172, 176, 179–185, 187, 188, 190–192, 203, 205, 250. Petitions: 370, 1116, 1305, 1596.

The Cecil Papers, like the State Papers, Domestic, cover a variety of fields, and are indispensable to any study of Elizabethan religious history. They include both national policy and local conditions; much of our most valuable data about the latter years of Elizabeth I's reign come from them. The documents are not arranged in strictly chronological order, but are spread through various volumes. (We used as a principal guide to the documents at Hatfield House a set of volumes of the Calendars annotated by the late Richard Gunton, librarian to the third and the fourth Marquesses of Salisbury). The indispensable guides are:

Calendar of the Manuscripts of . . . the Marquis of Salisbury . . . at Hatfield House, 18 vols., Historical Manuscripts Commission (London: H.M. Stationery Office, 1883–1940).
A Collection of State Papers . . . 1542–1570 . . . [of] William Cecill Lord Burghley, Samuel Haynes, ed. (London, 1740).
A Collection of State Papers . . . 1571–1596 . . . [of] William Cecill Lord Burghley, William Murdin, ed. (London, 1759).

Printed Documents

Besides the printed sources mentioned above, various collections of documents are valuable and, in some cases, necessary guides to Elizabethan religious history.

Acts of the Privy Council of England, 32 vols., n.s., J. R. Dasent, ed. (London: H.M. Stationery Office, 1890–1907).
"A Collection of Original Letters from the Bishops to the Privy Council, 1564," etc., Mary Bateson, ed., *The Camden Miscellany*, IX, Camden Society, n.s., LIII (Westminster, 1895).

BIBLIOGRAPHY

Annals of the Reformation and Establishment of Religion, etc., John Strype, ed., vol. III (London, 1728); vol. III, part II (Oxford, 1824).

The Archpriest Controversy: Documents Relating to the Dissensions of the Roman Catholic Clergy, 1597–1602, 2 vols., T. G. Law, ed., Camden Society, n.s., LVI (London, 1896), LVIII (London, 1898).

Calendar of Letters and State Papers Relating to English Affairs . . . Simancas, 4 vols., M. A. S. Hume, ed. (London, 1892–1899).

The First and Second Diaries of the English College, Douay, Fathers of the Congregation of the London Oratory, eds. (London, 1878).

The Harleian Miscellany, William Oldys, ed., vol. III (London, 1745).

The Letters and Memorials of William Cardinal Allen (1532–1594), Fathers of the Congregation of the London Oratory, eds. (London, 1882).

Miscellanea, I, Catholic Record Society, I (London, 1905).

Miscellanea, II, Catholic Record Society, II (London, 1906).

Miscellanea, IV, Catholic Record Society, IV (London, 1907).

Miscellanea, VIII, Catholic Record Society, XIII (London, 1913).

Miscellanea, XII, Catholic Record Society, XXII (London, 1921).

Miscellanea: Recusant Records, Clare Talbot, ed., Catholic Record Society, LIII (n.p., 1961).

Recusant Roll. No. I., 1592–3., M. M. C. Calthrop, ed., Catholic Record Society, XVIII (London, 1916).

Report on Manuscripts in Various Collections, Historical Manuscripts Commission, vol. III: *The Papers of Sir Thomas Tresham* (London: H.M. Stationery Office, 1904).

Select Statutes and Other Constitutional Documents Illustrative of the Reigns of Elizabeth and James I, G. W. Prothero, ed. (2 ed., Oxford, 1898).

Three Fifteenth-Century Chronicles, James Gairdner, ed., Camden Society, n.s., XXVIII (Westminster, 1880).

Tudor Constitutional Documents. A.D. 1485–1603, etc., J. R. Tanner, ed. (Cambridge: The University Press, 1922).

Unpublished Documents Relating to the English Martyrs. Vol. I: *1584–1603,* J. H. Pollen, ed., Catholic Record Society, V (London, 1908).

Printed Books

We have examined various printed books of the Elizabethan era, written principally by exiled priests, to establish trends of thought. The principal guides are:

Bibliography of British History. Tudor Period, 1485–1603, Conyers Read, ed. (2 ed., Oxford: at the Clarendon Press, 1959).

Pollard, A. W., and G. R. Redgrave, *A Short-Title Catalogue of Books Printed in England, Scotland, and Ireland and of English Books Printed Abroad, 1475–1640* (London: The Bibliographical Society, 1926).

The Works consulted most extensively were:

Allen, William, *A True, Sincere and Modest Defence of English Catholics That Suffer for their Faith,* etc., 2 vols. ([new edition] London and St. Louis: B. Herder Book Co., 1914).

BIBLIOGRAPHY

A Declaration of the Trve Cavses of the Great Trovbles, Presvpposed to be Intended against the realme of England, etc. (n.p., 1592).

[Cecil, William (Lord Burghley)], *The Execution of Iustice in England for maintenance of publique and Christian peace,* etc. (London, 1583).

Gee, Edward, ed., *The Jesuit's Memorial for the Intended Reformation of England,* etc. (London, 1690).

Harding, Thomas, *A Confutation of a Booke Intituled An Apologie of the Church of England* (Antwerp, 1565).

Parsons, Robert, *A Brief Censvre vppon two bookes Written in Answere to M. Edmonde Campions offer of disputation* (Douai, 1581 [fictitious imprint; the book was published at East Ham, Essex]).

—— [John Howlet, pseudonym]. *A Brief Discours contayning certayne Reasons Why Catholiques Refuse to Goe to Church,* etc. (Douai, 1580 [fictitious imprint; the book was published at East Ham, Essex]).

—— [R. Doleman, pseudonym]. *A Conference abovt the next Svccession to the Crowne of Ingland,* etc. (n.p., 1594).

—— *De Persecutione Anglicana Libellus,* etc. (Rome, 1582).

—— [Andrea Philopater, pseudonym]. *Elizabethae Angliae Reginae Haeresim Calvinianam Propugnantis, saevissimum in Catholicos sui Regni edictum,* etc. (n.p., 1592).

—— [Andrea Philopater, pseudonym]. *Elizabethae Reginae Angliae Edictum* (n.p., 1593).

—— *An Epistle of the Persecution of Catholickes in Englande,* etc. G. T., tr. (Douai, [1582]).

—— *A Temperate Ward-Word, to the Tvrbvlent and Seditiovs Wach-Word of Sir Francis Hastinges knight,* etc. (n.p., 1599).

SECONDARY SOURCES

The books concerning the Elizabethan Catholics are numerous but vary greatly in quality and quantity of original research and in objectivity. The following list of books proved helpful in determining the economic, social, political and cultural pattern of the Catholics within Elizabethan society:

Birt, H. N., *The Elizabethan Religious Settlement* (London: George Bell and Sons, 1907).

Black, J. B., *The Reign of Elizabeth, 1558–1603,* 2 ed. (Oxford: at the Clarendon Press, 1959).

Bridgett, T. E. and T. F. Knox, *The True Story of the Catholic Hierarchy* (London, 1889).

Cristiani, L., *L'Église à l'époque du concile de Trente,* vol. XVII: *Histoire de L'Église,* Augustin Fliche and Victor Martin, eds. (n.p.: Bloud and Gay, 1948).

Dietz, F. C., *English Public Finance, 1558–1641* (New York: The Century Co., 1932).

Elizabethan Government and Society: Essays Presented to Sir John Neale, S. T. Bindoff, J. Hurstfield and C. H. Williams, eds. (London: The Athlone Press, 1961).

Frere, W. H., *The English Church in the Reigns of Elizabeth and James I* (London: MacMillan and Co. Ltd., 1904).

BIBLIOGRAPHY

Gardiner, S. R., *History of England, 1603–1642*, vol. I (1603–1607) (London, 1887).

Gee, Henry, *The Elizabethan Clergy and the Settlement of Religion, 1558–1564* (Oxford, 1898).

Gibson, T. E., *Lydiate Hall and its Associations*, (n.p., 1876).

Gillow, Joseph, *A Literary and Biographical History, or Bibliographical Dictionary of the English Catholics*, 5 vols. (London: Burns and Oates, 1885–1902).

Hughes, Philip, *The Reformation in England*, vol. III (London: Hollis and Carter, 1954).

Jessopp, Augustus, *One Generation of a Norfolk House* (London, 1879).

Jordan, W. K., *The Development of Religious Toleration in England*, vol. I (London: George Allen and Unwin Ltd., 1932).

────── *Philanthropy in England, 1480–1660: A Study of the Changing Pattern of English Social Aspirations* (London: George Allen and Unwin Ltd., 1959).

Knowles, David, *The English Mystical Tradition* (New York: Harper and Brothers, 1961).

────── *The Religious Orders in England*, 3 vols. (Cambridge: at the University Press, 1948–1959).

Law, T. G., *A Historical Sketch of the Conflicts between Jesuits and Seculars in the Reign of Queen Elizabeth* (London, 1889).

LeCler, Joseph, *Histoire de la tolérance au siècle de la réforme*, 2 vols. (Paris: Éditions Montaigne, 1955).

Mackie, J. D., *The Earlier Tudors, 1485–1558* (Oxford: at the Clarendon Press, 1957).

McKisack, May, *The Fourteenth Century, 1307–1399* (Oxford: at the Clarendon Press, 1959).

Magee, Brian, *The English Recusants* (London: Burns, Oates and Washburn Ltd., 1938).

Mathew, David, *The Celtic Peoples and Renaissance Europe* (London: Sheed and Ward, 1933).

Meyer, A. O., *England and the Catholic Church under Queen Elizabeth*, J. R. McKee, tr. (London: Kegan, Paul, Trench, Trübner and Co., Ltd., 1916).

Neale, J. E., *Elizabeth I and Her Parliaments, 1584–1601* (London: Jonathan Cape, 1957).

Pastor, Ludwig von, *The History of the Popes*, R. F. Kerr, ed., XXIV (St. Louis: B. Herder Book Co., 1933).

The Political Works of James I, C. H. McIlwain, ed. (Cambridge: Harvard University Press, 1918).

Pollard, A. F., *The History of England from the Accession of Edward VI to the Death of Elizabeth* (London: Longmans, Green and Co., 1910).

Pollen, J. H., *The English Catholics in the Reign of Queen Elizabeth* (London: Longmans, Green and Co., 1920).

Read, Conyers, *Lord Burghley and Queen Elizabeth* (London: Jonathan Cape, 1960).

────── *Mr. Secretary Cecil and Queen Elizabeth* (London: Jonathan Cape, 1955).

────── *Mr. Secretary Walsingham and the Policy of Queen Elizabeth*, 3 vols. (Oxford: at the Clarendon Press, 1925).

Simpson, A. W. B., *An Introduction to the History of the Land Law* (Oxford University Press, 1961).

BIBLIOGRAPHY

Simpson, Alan, *The Wealth of the Gentry, 1540–1660* (Chicago: The University of Chicago Press, 1961).

Tierney, M. A., *Dodd's Church History of England,* vol. III (London, 1840); vol. IV (London, 1841).

Usher, R. G., *The Reconstruction of the English Church,* vol. I (New York: D. Appleton and Company, 1910).

Willaert, Léopold, *Après le concile de Trente: La Restauration catholique, 1563–1648,* vol. XVIII: *Histoire de L'Église,* J. B. Duroselle and Eugène Jarry, eds. (n.p.: Bloud and Gay, 1960).

Willson, D. H., *King James VI and I* (London: Jonathan Cape, 1956).

INDEX

INDEX

INDEX

Allen, William, Cardinal, 45, 46, 47, 108, 255
An licitum sit Catholicis in Anglia arma sumere, et aliis modis, Reginam et Regnum defendere, 253–254
Anglesey, 41, 143
Archpresbyterate, 256, 258
Archpriest Controversy, 257, 259
Arden, —, 15, 33
Arden, John, 10
Armada (1588), 7, 134, 255
Armor, sequestration of, 134, 191
Arundell, Sir John, 32, 54, 139, 207–208, 237, 238–239, 240
Arundell, Thomas, 171
Atkinson, Robert, 58, 86
Atslow (or Atlowe), Dr. (?Edward), 65
Atslow, Luke, 81
Attorney-General, 73, 153
Awdley, Philip, 93
Aylmer, John, Bishop of London, 72, 86, 90

Babington, Dr., 38
Babington, Lady, 219
Babthorpe, Sir William, 43
Bagshaw, Christopher, 257
Baker, John, 65
Banbury, 143
Bancroft, Richard, Bishop of London, 165, 172
Banester, Dan (?Van), 46
Banester, Nicholas, 46
Bangor, diocese, 25, 41, 140
Banyster (or Bannester), Edward, 228, 245
Barker, Rowland, 208
Barlow, William, Bishop of Chichester, 13, 32, 42

Barnes, Richard, Bishop of Carlisle, 56–57, 63
Bassett, Gregory. *See* Gregory, Friar
Bastard, Francis, 208, 240
Bateman, Thomas, 93
Bates (or Battie), Anthony, 167
Bath and Wells, Bishop of, 83
Bath and Wells, diocese, 25, 28
Battle (Sussex), 42
Bawde, Thomas, 58, 86
Becket, Robert, 79, 228
Becanshawe, William, 220, 240
Beconsawe, John, 228–229, 240
Bedford, county, 30, 116, 146, 251
Bedford, Earl of, 31
Bedingfield, Edmund, 93, 95, 104, 215
Bedingfield, Elizabeth, 215
Bedingfield, Henry, 215
Bedingfield, Sir Henry, 15, 53, 93, 95
Bedingfield, Humphrey, 92, 93, 138, 142, 170, 215–216, 249
Bedingfield (?John), 87
Bedingfield, John, 224
Bedingfield, Lady, 14
Bedingfield, Laurence, 216
Bellamy, Katherine, 208–209
Bellamy, Thomas, 208
Belson, Augustine, 199
Belson, Robert, 199
Bentham, Thomas, Bishop of Coventry and Lichfield, 31, 33, 34, 41
Berkshire, 30–31, 98, 191, 195, 198, 235, 251
Best, John, Bishop of Carlisle, 16, 34
Biddolphe, Richard, 138
Bishop, Mistress, 42
Blackwell, George, 256, 259
Blaxton, —, 15, 33

INDEX

Blaxton, John, 10
Blundell, Richard, 205
Blunt, Thomas, 245
Bonner, Edmund, Bishop of London, 38
Book of Common Prayer, The, 27, 81, 100
Books, 34–35, 37, 42, 62–63, 71, 103; importation of, 40–41, 166, 172
Bown, John, 59, 87
Boxall, John, 61
Braybrooke, Dorothy, 199
Braybrooke, James, 86, 110, 198–199, 234, 240
Braybrooke, Martha, 199
Bristol, 148
Bristol, diocese, 25
Britten, George, 230
Broughton, 142, 143
Brown, Lady, 40
Browne, Francis, 229
Browne, William, 144-145
Brydge, Richard, 203
Buckingham, county, 30, 116, 186, 189, 195, 199, 251
Burghley, Thomas Cecil, second Baron of, 160–161, 163, 167, 168, 173, 212
Burghley, William Cecil, first Baron of, 11, 15, 127–128, 147, 153, 156, 160, 164–165, 170, 186, 241–242, 244, 246
Bury, 93, 94
Bush (or Busshe), Nicholas, 20

Caernarvon, 41
Cambridge, county, 29, 116, 156, 251
Cambridge, University of, 29, 91, 218
Campbell, —, 165
Campion, Edmund, 103, 117, 119, 120, 121, 214, 253, 255
Canterbury, archdiocese, 25, 28, 43
Carew (or Carewe), Richard, 87, 170
Carlisle, diocese, 16, 28, 34, 66, 161, 163, 168, 170
Carter, Dr., 44
Cary (Carey or Carewe), Lady, 20, 40
Cassey, Henry, 202
Catesbie, Lady, 251
Catesbie, Sir Thomas, 111, 139, 142, 218, 229, 237, 238, 240
Cecil, Robert, 153, 170, 258
Cecil, Thomas. *See* Burghley, Thomas Cecil, second Baron of
Cecil, William. *See* Burghley, William Cecil, first Baron of

Census of Catholics, recusants, 10–11, 69, 127; (1577), 81–87; (1592), 147–148
Chaderton, William, Bishop of Chester, 99, 100
Channel Islands, 12–13, 159
Chester, Bishop of, 99, 140–141, 249, 250
Chester, city, 105
Chester, county, 11, 29, 125, 147, 148, 200
Chester, diocese, 16, 28, 29, 31, 34, 98–100, 114–115, 149, 162, 190
Cheyney, Richard, Bishop of Gloucester, 32
Chichester, diocese, 13, 29, 32, 41–42, 72
Church of England. *See* Establishment
Church, Roman Catholic, 3–5, 28, 62–63, 123, 139–141, 159, 162–163, 166, 175–176, 235, 255, 256–259, 265–266
Clement VIII, pope, 259
Clerke, Henry, 117
Cliborne, Richard, 129, 130
Clithero, William, 102–103
Codrington, John, 231
Comberforde, Henry, 10, 81
Comberforde, Katherine, 222
Commission, Ecclesiastical, 9, 10, 173
Commission, High, 232
Composition of fines, 178, 193–195, 196, 234, 241–242
Conference abovt the next Svccession to the Crowne of Ingland, A, 254–255
Cope, Anthony, 53
Copley, Lady Catherine, 229
Copley, Sir Henry, 39–40
Copley, Thomas, 86
Corham, Roger, 59, 87
Cornwall, county, 29, 91, 147, 157, 195, 201
Cornwallis, family, 170, 179
Cornwallis, Sir Thomas, 15, 39, 128, 139
Cotton, George, 80, 139, 171, 220–221, 236
Council of the Marches of Wales. *See* Wales
Council of The North, 16, 31, 43, 66, 70, 146, 160–161
Courtney, James, 53–54, 201
Coventry and Lichfield, Bishop of, 77, 78, 79, 180, 211
Coventry and Lichfield, diocese, 28, 29, 31, 33–34, 41, 114
Coxe, John (or Devon), 18
Crane, Henry, 46, 47
Crawley, Thomas, 94, 159, 202
Culpepper, Sir Alexander, 139, 154, 205, 237, 238, 249
Culpepper, Richard, 87, 205, 240

—284—

INDEX

Cumberforde, Humfrey, 209
Cumberland, county, 28, 125, 147, 249
Cumberland, Earl of, 11, 16
Curle, Mark, 87, 128

Dacre of the North, Lord, 16, 34, 50
Dacre, Sir Thomas, 34
Daniel, John, 93, 96, 131, 224, 236, 238
Daniell, Margaret, 224, 236, 238
Darrell, Henry, 87
Davis (or Davies), Richard, 203
Dawtrey, William, 53
Denbigh, county, 91
Derby, county, 29, 141, 147, 191
Derby, Earl of, 45, 46, 99, 112, 128, 129, 131, 143, 146
Derham, —, 81
Devon, county, 29, 91, 147, 148, 190, 201
Discourse of the providence necessary to be had for the settinge upp the catholick faith when god shall call the Queene out of this life, 257–258
Distraint of property, 221, 226, 243–244, 245
Dorrell, Mistress, 157
Dorset, county, 148, 191, 195, 201
Douai, seminary at, 49, 64
Downes, Edward, 138
Downes, John, 92, 216
Downes, Robert, 92, 94, 142, 216, 236, 238, 249
Downman, William, Bishop of Chester, 34, 45, 46, 48, 49, 56, 84
Downs, George, 15
Dracot (or Draycot), John, 11, 76–77, 80, 139, 144, 159, 172
Dracot, Philip, 172
Drury, Henry, 15, 93, 96, 224
Drury, John, 92, 94, 216–217
Drury, Robert, 216
Durham, Bishop of, 31
Durham, county, 29, 148
Durham, diocese, 15–16, 29, 34–35, 66, 149, 161, 163, 167–168, 250
Dymocke, Robert, 35

East Anglia, 55, 81, 162, 180, 227
East, Edward, 199
Eccleston, Edward, 155
Edgerton, Lady, 200
Egerton, Thomas, 59
Elton, Anthony, 202–203

Ely, —, 10, 15, 33
Ely, diocese, 28, 29
Ely, Isle of, 29
Ely, palace of, 135, 137, 138, 141–142, 143, 154
Embassy, French, 17; Spanish, 17, 232
Erdswicke, Hugh, 77–80, 112
Erdswicke, Sampson, 77–79, 87, 112
Essex, county, 30, 72, 148, 191, 201–202
Establishment, 3, 7, 11–12, 27, 28, 44, 93, 99, 100, 103, 108, 116, 125, 140, 141, 159, 162, 163, 165, 166, 167, 168, 172, 173, 234, 264, 266; conformity to, 6, 26, 75–76, 131, 151–153, 169
Estates, evaluation of, 236–237
Etheridge, George, 38–39
Everard, Henry, 15, 87, 93, 96, 224–225, 240, 249
Exchequer, 146, 192, 243, 244
Exeter, diocese, 29, 166
Eyreman, Francis, 79, 87, 110–111

Faulconer, William, 231–232, 237, 238, 249, 251
Felton, John, 63
Felton, Thomas, 170, 244, 245–248
Feria, Count de, 21
Fiennes, Richard, 142, 143
Fitzherbert, Richard, 222
Fitzherbert, Sir Thomas, 11, 54, 111, 139, 142, 209
Flint, county, 91
Fludd, Evans, 15, 93–94, 104
Forset, Edward, 257
Fowler, Brian, 31, 33, 77–79, 109
Frangipani, Octavio, Mirto, Bishop of Tricarico, 258–259
Freake, Robert, 178, 192
French, Thomas, 46
Fryer (or Freer), Thomas, 209, 240
Fuljambe, Godfrey, 31

Gage, Edward, 105, 110, 154, 230–231
Gage, John (Hereford), 203
Gage, John (London), 105, 110, 139, 144, 154, 209–210, 237, 238, 249
Gage, Thomas, 231
Gatacre, Francis, 77–79, 251–252
Gawen, Thomas, 142, 144, 159, 192, 210, 238, 245–246, 249, 251
Gentry, 76, 88, 108, 120, 222, 227, 239, 264

INDEX

Gerrard, Miles, 163
Gerrard, Sir Thomas, 65, 75, 163, 192, 210
Gibbon, William, 93
Gifford, John, 77, 78, 104, 110–111, 129–130, 191–192, 210–211
Glamorgan, county, 30
Gloucester, county, 67, 91, 127, 148, 190, 195, 202
Gloucester, diocese, 25, 28, 29, 32
Godolphin, Sir William, 54
Godfrey, Richard, 59–60
Goldsborough, Robert, 232
Goldwell, Thomas, Bishop of St. Asaph, 96, 255
Gomond, John, 203
Greene, Rooke, 94, 95, 144, 154, 202, 245, 249
Greenwood, Thomas, 58
Gregory, Friar (Gregory Bassett), 10, 15, 33
Grey, Andrew, 58
Grey, John, 59
Grey, Robert, 11
Grey, Robert de, 92, 104, 138, 142, 217, 246, 252
Grindal, Edmund, Bishop of London, Archbishop of York, Archbishop of Canterbury, 11, 37, 52, 66, 72, 82
Gunter, Arthur, 42
Guzman de Silva, Don, 37, 38, 50

Hale, Thomas, 138, 202
Hampshire. *See* Southampton
Harding, Thomas, 40, 48, 60, 63, 253
Hare, Michael, 14, 86–87, 93, 95–96, 138–139, 155, 158, 225, 236, 237, 238, 240, 249
Hare, Robert, 86–87, 211, 240
Hare, William, 14, 86–87, 93
Hargrave (Hargraves), —, 45–46
Harper, Henry, 59
Hart, Richard, 10
Hartford, 135
Hastings of Loughborough, Lord, 19
Havard (Haverden), —, 10, 15, 20
Havard, Thomas, 33, 54
Haydock, William, 205–206
Heath, Dorothy, 232
Heath, Nicholas, Archbishop of York, 22, 39, 70–71
Heath, William, 232
Henry VIII, king, 8, 52, 261, 262
Hereford, Bishop of, 77
Hereford, city, 81

Hereford, county, 29, 115, 127, 131, 148, 149, 162, 163, 166–167, 173, 180, 190–191, 195, 202–203, 239
Hereford, diocese, 15, 28, 29, 31, 33
Hertford, county, 30
Hesketh, William, 200
Heveningham, Dorothy, 222
Hill, Elizabeth, 245
Hobblethorne, Lady, 20
Hocknell, John, 211
Hoord, William, 97
Hopkins, Stephen, 42
Horn (or Horne), Robert, Bishop of Winchester, 12, 13, 32
Hoxton, 121
Hubbard, James, 93
Hull, 101
Huntingdon, county, 30, 116, 188
Huntingdon, Earl of, 66, 72, 99, 115, 125, 128, 131, 167
Hussey, Gilbert, 104
Hussey, William, 43
Hutton, Matthew, Bishop of Durham, Archbishop of York, 160, 163, 167

Imprisonment for debt, 243
Income, 196
Inns of Court, 58–60, 70
Ipswich, 93, 94, 95
Ireland, 96, 187, 248
Ithell, Dr., 93, 94

Jackson, Edward, 81
James VI of Scotland (James I of England), king, 166, 174, 256, 257, 259–260, 261, 262, 266
Jermine (or Jarmyn), Ambrose, 225
Jerningham, Henry, 14
Jerningham, Lady, 14
Jetter, Robert, 15, 192, 225–226
Jewel, John, Bishop of Salisbury, 32, 40
Jolly, —, 18
Jones, Edmund, 203
Justices of the peace, 24, 27, 31, 52–55, 90, 151

Kent, county, 148, 190, 195, 204–205, 251
Kervylle, Henry, 217
Kigheley, Elizabeth, 206

Lambeth, 79
Lancaster, county, 11, 29, 45–48, 63, 70, 72, 98–100, 106, 112, 124, 125, 140–141,

INDEX

162, 163, 168–169, 173, 174, 180, 205, 239, 249, 250, 252
Langdale, Alban, 10
Latham, Henry, 200
Lawe, Thomas, 218
Lee, —, 44
Leedes Castle, 135
Leedes, John, 231
Leedes, Mr., 42
Leicester, county, 30, 127, 149, 186, 189, 195, 207
Leicester, Earl of, 99, 105, 120, 126, 192, 212
Levy of Horses, 177, 178–180, 186, 244; (1580), 181–182, 186, 197; (1584), 180, 186, 187–188; (1585), 180–184, 186–187, 188, 192–193, 197; (1587), 181, 184–186, 187, 197; (1598), 248–252
Lewkner, —, 42
Lewkner, George, 221, 240
Lewys, 42
Lincoln, Bishop of, 107, 137
Lincoln, county, 30, 101, 148, 149, 186, 191, 195, 207
Lincoln, diocese, 28, 30, 31
Llandaff, Bishop of, 83, 91
Lloyd, Richard, 220, 251
London, Bishop of, 41, 80, 97, 98
London, city, 25, 30, 116, 124, 165–166, 180, 192, 214, 251; Catholic prisoners at, 97, 111, 150
London, diocese, 28, 30
London-Middlesex, 30, 116, 135, 148, 186, 188–189, 195, 207
Longford, Martha, 211
Longford, Nicholas, 163, 211–212, 237, 238
Lord Chief Justice, 86, 251
Lord Keeper, 41, 86
Lord Treasurer, 247
Lother, Gerard, 59
Love, Samuel, 251
Lovell, Henry, 217
Lovell, Lady, 129
Lovell, Robert, 93, 129, 138, 142, 217, 251
Lovell, Thomas, 93, 94
Luson, William, 10, 33
Lygon, Hugh, 233
Lyngen, Richard, 192

Maidstone, 135
Mallerie, Sir William, 43
Manchester, 101, 124
Mansfield, Henry, 199

Marshall, Dr., 11, 45–46
Marten, Christopher, 101
Martin, Richard, 226, 236, 238, 250–251
Martin, Roger, 93, 96, 142, 226, 238, 249
Mary Stuart, Queen of Scotland, 49, 50, 51, 261, 262
Massey, Richard, 200
Matthew, Tobie, Bishop of Durham, 167–168
Maxfield (or Macclesfield), Ellen, 222–223
Maxfield, Ralph, 222–223
Maxfield, Ursula, 223
Maxfield, William, 77–79, 223
Mayhew (or May), Henry, 232, 240
Mayne, Cuthbert, 81, 89
Memorial for the Intended Reformation of England, 258
Metham, Sir Thomas, 43–44
Middlemore, John, 233
Middlemore, Robert, 54
Midlands, 180
Mollineux, John, 47
Molyneux, Sir Richard, 49
Monckton, Christopher, 101
Monmouth, city, 29
Monmouth, county, 30, 127, 149, 160, 163, 166–167
Monox, George, 212
Montague, Viscount, 10, 22, 102, 154, 260
More (?Thomas), 131
Morgan, Philip, 10
Morley, Lord, 55, 65
Morris, George, 91
Morton, Nicholas, 62
Moryson, Thomas, 178
Moses, Friar, 42
Mugge, —, 15, 33
Mugge, Walter, 10
Murren, John, 11, 45, 46

Nevill, Sir John, 43
Norfolk, county, 25–26, 30, 71, 116, 124, 142, 148, 150, 163, 191, 195, 214–215, 239
Norris, Edward, 174
Northampton, county, 30, 127, 149–150, 153, 163, 190, 195, 218
Northern Rebellion. *See* Rebellion, Northern
Northumberland, county, 29, 116, 149, 168, 173, 250
Northumberland, Earl of, 38, 50, 63
Norton, Walter, 59–60, 87, 138, 142, 145, 226, 240, 245

INDEX

Norwich, Bishop of, 92, 93, 94, 104, 110, 170
Norwich, diocese, 28
Nottingham, county, 31, 146, 149
Nowell, Alexander, 48, 75, 76, 169

Oglethorpe, Mark, 59–60
Osbaldeston, Edward, 46–47
Owen, Richard, 139, 219
Oxenbridge, Andrew, 117–118
Oxford, county, 30, 67, 101, 148, 189, 195, 218–219, 249
Oxford, diocese, 26
Oxford, University of, 12, 20, 91, 101, 115

Page, James, 53
Paget, Lord, 22, 105
Palmer, Richard, 59
Paris, Ferdinando, 93, 138, 154, 159, 217–218
Parker, Matthew, Archbishop of Canterbury, 25, 27, 42, 48, 61
Parkins, Francis, 243,
Parsons, Robert, 103, 119, 253, 254, 255, 256, 257, 258
Paulet, Lord Chidiock, 32, 53
Paulet, Dame Elizabeth, 213, 234, 237
Paulet, William, 32
Peckham, Sir George, 106, 171
Pesshall, Thomas, 77
Peterborough, diocese, 28, 30, 35
Philip II, King of Spain, 38, 155, 254
Pickering, Thomas, 170
Pierpoint, Gervase, 112, 139, 257
Pilkington, James, Bishop of Durham, 17, 34, 66
Pitts, Margaret, 219
Pius V, pope, 6, 48, 49, 61, 262
Plowden, Edmund (junior), 219, 239–240
Plowden, Edmund (senior), 32, 53, 55, 86, 102, 119, 198
Plowden, Francis, 219, 239–240, 250–251
Pollard, —, 58–59
Poole, David, Bishop of Peterborough, 23, 31, 33–34
Poole, Lady, 42
Poole, Thomas, 42
Pownde, Thomas, 229–230
Prescott (Lancs.), 169
Priests: Jesuits, 96, 107, 118, 120, 257; seculars, 107, 118, 258, 259
Privy Council, 9, 21, 37, 41, 71, 72, 75ff., 91, 92, 95, 97, 98, 99, 101, 105, 107, 110, 114ff., 120, 126ff., 135ff., 143, 144, 146, 148, 149, 151ff., 168, 174, 177, 242, 249, 251, 258, 264
Property, assessment of, for taxation, 241

Quadra, Alvaro de, Bishop of Aquila, 17, 21–22

Racton Parish (Sussex), 42
Ratclyffe, Charles, 124
Rebellion, Northern, 49, 50, 55–58, 99, 179, 264
Recusancy and recusants, 12, 21, 27, 40, 56, 69–74, 92–96, 107, 108–111, 113–114ff., 128–129, 140ff., 174–175, 177, 187, 192, 193–194, 197, 198, 237–238, 244, 245, 247–248
Recusant Roll (1592–1593), 178, 179, 197, 244
Regnans in Excelsis, 50, 61, 63, 262
Richmond, Archdeaconry of, 29, 99–100, 160
Rigmaiden, John, 46, 206
Ripon, 101, 160
Robinson, Dr., 11
Robinson, Henry, Bishop of Carlisle, 161, 163, 168
Robinson, Nicholas, Bishop of Bangor, 41, 58
Rochester, Bishop of, 77, 117
Rochester, diocese, 25
Rollestone, Francis, 54
Rookwood, Edward, 92, 94, 156, 158–159, 169–170, 226–227, 237, 238
Rookwood, Mr., 14–15
Rookwood, Robert, 227
Roper, Thomas, 87, 117
Roper, William, 39–40, 53, 87, 249
Royden, Edward, 218
Rutland, county, 30, 127, 149–150, 163

Sacheverell, John, 11
Salisbury, Bishop of, 90, 115, 117
Salisbury, diocese, 30–31, 115, 166
Sander, Elizabeth, 97
Sander, Nicholas, 42, 63, 97
Sanderson, Henry, 168, 248
Sandford, Thomas, 174
Sandys, Thomas, Bishop of Worcester, Archbishop of York, 32–33, 84, 125
Saunders, Erasmus, 192, 212
Scrope (or Scroope), Nicholas, 139, 220

—288—

INDEX

Scudamore, John, 10, 15, 33, 54, 190–191, 203–204
Scudamore, Thomas, 204
Seborne, Richard, 33
Sedgewick, Lady, 99
Shelley, Henry, 87, 112
Shelley, John, 163, 231
Shelley, Richard, 105
Shelley, Thomas, 163
Shelley, William, 53, 105, 110
Shropshire (county of Salop), 29, 30, 148, 166–167, 219–220
Siggeswike, Dr., 44
Solicitor-General, 153
Somerset, county, 148, 191
Somerset, Thomas, 20
Southampton, county (Hampshire), 31, 32, 42, 97, 116, 126, 127, 148, 190, 220, 251
Southwark, 103, 112
Southwell, Robert, 123, 253
Southworth, Sir John, 48, 112, 129, 130, 206
Stafford, county, 11, 29, 76–80, 104, 115, 131, 141, 148, 166, 172, 186, 189, 222
Stapleton, Thomas, 13, 42, 63
Statutes of Parliament: (1540), 243; (1559), 5, 6, 41, 73, 152; (1563), 23–24; (1571), 49, 64; (1581), 107–108, 126, 235, 237, 242; (1585), 125–126; (1586), 126, 178, 197, 242–243, 247; (1593), 146–147, 153
Stonor, Lady, 219
Stourton, Lady Anne, 170–171
Stradling, Sir Thomas, 20, 55
Suffolk, county, 13–15, 26, 30, 71, 116, 142, 148, 190, 195, 223–224
Sulliard, Edward, 93, 95, 139, 144, 154, 158–159, 227, 237, 238, 249
Sulliard, Thomas, 93, 96, 227
Surrey, county, 31, 116, 126, 148, 150, 186, 189–190, 195, 228
Sussex, county, 81, 148, 190, 195, 230

Talbot, John (of Grafton), 105, 130, 138, 142, 144, 154, 157, 158, 230, 237, 238, 249
Talbot, John (of Salesbury), 46, 200–201
Temple, John, 231
Thimelby, John, 144, 159, 207
Thimelby, Richard, 257
Thirlby, Thomas, Bishop of Ely, 22, 61
Throckmorton, Lady Mary, 233
Throckmorton, Thomas, 54, 144, 155, 157–158, 199–200, 237, 238, 249

Titcheborne, Elizabeth, 221
Titcheborne, Nicholas, 221
Towneley, John, 75–76, 106, 128, 169, 212–213, 234, 236, 237, 238
Tregian, Francis, 32, 81
Tremaine, Richard, 79, 87, 157, 171–172, 192, 201, 240
Tresham, Sir Thomas, 108, 119, 121, 131–134, 137, 138, 142–143, 144, 154–155, 157, 158–159, 213, 218, 234, 237, 238, 240, 245, 249, 254, 260–262
Treves (or Travis), Matthew, 47
Tudor, Mary, queen, 4, 8, 52, 53, 239, 264
Tunstall, Francis, 46
Tyrwhitt, John, 106
Tyrwhitt, Robert, 106–107, 207
Tyrwhitt, Sir Robert, 35, 106, 109
Tyrwhitt, William, 106–107, 109, 111, 130, 138, 139, 144, 205

Usufruct, 243, 244

Vachell, Stephen, 221
Vaux (or Vause), Lawrence, 10, 45, 46, 48, 49
Vaux of Harrowden, Lord, 54, 136–137, 144, 154, 192, 207, 213, 218, 234, 240
Vavasour, Peter, 43
Vavasour, Thomas, 117
Vavasour, Sir William, 164

Waferer, Arden (or Ardell), 58, 86, 192, 251
Waldegrave, Sir Edward, 18–19
Waldegrave, Lady, 39
Wales, 20, 29–30, 84, 91, 116–117, 148, 162, 166–167, 173; Llandaff, diocese, 26, 30, 58; St. Asaph, diocese, 25, 57–58; St. David's, diocese, 25, 57
Wales, Council of the Marches of, 67, 70, 91, 127
Walsingham, Sir Francis, 91, 117, 125, 127, 128, 180, 197
Warwick, county, 29, 31, 150, 166, 189
Westbye, John, 46, 47, 206
Westmorland, county, 28, 116, 125, 148, 170, 250
Westmorland, Earl of, 16, 50
Wharton, Sir Thomas, 18, 19
Whitehall (or Whythall), Walter, 207
Whitgift, John, Bishop of Worcester, Archbishop of Canterbury, 83, 138, 143, 156, 158, 164, 169, 172, 173, 254

INDEX

Whitmore, John, 201
Wiltshire, 30–31, 98, 149–150, 153, 163, 190, 195, 231, 251
Winchester, Bishop of, 80, 97, 117, 143
Winchester, diocese, 12, 28, 31, 32, 116, 159–160, 166
Windham, Edmund, 40, 93, 94, 118
Windsor, Lady Catherine, 233, 234
Wisbeach Castle, 117, 138, 155–156, 173, 214, 251
Wolvesley, Erasmus, 76–79, 80, 128, 223
Woode, William, 204, 240
Worcester, county, 30, 31, 131, 148, 186, 190, 232, 251

Worcester, diocese, 28, 31, 32–33, 160
Wyllford, Thomas, 213–214

Yate, Francis, 86, 214
Yate, John, 32, 53
Yaxley, John, 87, 218, 249
Yaxley, William, 15, 87, 227, 237, 238
York, archdiocese, 17, 28, 31, 100–101, 115, 141, 249
York, city, 100
York, county, 31, 43–44, 51–52, 66, 125, 148, 162, 167, 189, 250